STOP BINGEING!

STAY IN CONTROL
OF YOUR EATING

STOP BINGEING!

STAY IN CONTROL OF YOUR EATING

Lee Janogly

RIGHT WAY

Set in 11 ½/13pt Times by County Typesetters, Margate, Kent.
Printed and bound in Great Britain by Cox & Wyman Ltd., Reading, Berkshire.

The *Right Way* series is published by Elliot Right Way Books, Brighton Road, Lower Kingswood, Tadworth, Surrey, KT20 6TD, U.K. For information about our company and the other books we publish, visit our web site at *www.right-way.co.uk*

For Maurice, my love, my life.

ACKNOWLEDGEMENTS

I would like to give a big "thank you" hug to my journalist daughter Sharon for her invaluable help and comments during the writing of this book – such as "Didn't they teach grammar at your school then?!" – and, indeed, to all of my children, Sharon, Gary, Warren, Carolyn and Laura who managed to stop saying "Mummy, will you –" long enough for me to finish this book.

Thank you Jean Ashley for the great illustrations.

CONTENTS

CHAPTER	PAGE
Foreword	9
1. YOU are a Binger	11
2. Trigger Situations	30
3. "I'll Just Have a Little Bit"	51
4. Let's Start	70
5. What you Eat	98
6. Let's Go Shopping	119
7. Weight Off Your Mind	128
8. Going, Going, Stuck	154
9. Staying on the Straight and Narrow	181

FOREWORD

This book addresses a very special audience – the BINGER.

If, when suffering from stress or boredom, or even at other times, you find yourself eating vast amounts of food and are unable to stop, then YOU are a binger. Diet books don't work for bingers because, when that craving starts, the diet goes out the window. If this compulsive cycle of *craving – resisting – giving in – bingeing – guilt – anger* seems to be ruining your life and making you fat and miserable, I might just have the answer!

Have you noticed that when you binge, you usually go for the same foods every time? These are your "trigger" foods. Most people seem to have one or two trigger foods that "start them off" on a more general binge – foods that are usually high in fat and sugar. They are also likely to be the ones that make you fat, miserable and out of control.

I used to be a binger just like you. I discovered that **the way to stop bingeing is by not eating the foods that make you binge. The way to stay slim is by cutting out the foods that make you fat.** That's all there is to it. I don't binge any more.

You think you will feel deprived? Wrong! Deprivation is

not about whether you can eat chocolate or not. Deprivation is about feeling fat and miserable, not being able to wear the clothes you want, and feeling that your whole life is dominated by food. By eliminating one or two trigger foods from your life, you can be liberated, slim, in control of your eating, and free to eat EVERYTHING ELSE.

The reality is: you cannot eat everything you want and still be slim. Most diets encourage you to "have a little treat every day": i.e. eat some of your trigger foods. This works for some people. It won't work for you. If you are a binger, one taste of your trigger food evokes such a strong psychological response that you feel COMPELLED to go on eating. Fat people say, "I'll just have a tiny bit please"; slim people say, "No thanks, not for me".

Are YOU still saying, "I'll start again tomorrow"? How many times are you going to repeat the same patterns and expect different results? Get real! You DO have a choice: you can either eat your trigger foods or be slim and binge-free.

During my many years as a diet counsellor, I have kept a close watch on the science of nutrition; nonetheless, my method is based not on the latest scientific fad but on plain (but knowledgeable) common sense and long experience of how to achieve a real end to bingeing. I will take you through simple steps that will ultimately enable you to be in control of food instead of being controlled by food. There are no unbalanced diets or recipes in this book. I do not preach about "supplements", "enzymes", "detox" or any other nutribabble – just a method that *works*. YOU decide what you are going to eat, when, and how much. I simply act as your guide.

This book will set you free – from the bingeing, the bulging, the guilt and the misery. Let's do it.

1

<u>YOU</u> ARE A BINGER

Excuse me! Yes you – with the thighs – I'm talking to you. YOU are a binger. How do I know? Well, for a start, you picked up this book, so FOOD must play a pretty big part in your life. I bet even now you are thinking about the food you shouldn't have eaten yesterday but did; the food you have eaten today but wished you hadn't; and the food you shouldn't eat tomorrow but probably will.

Secondly, well, I don't wish to be rude but aren't those your "fat" jeans you are wearing? That means your weight is up at the moment or you would be wearing your "middle-sized" jeans. Your "thin" jeans are languishing in the wardrobe along with all those other – now sadly unfashionable – clothes you bought the week you were a size 10.

I bet you even think like a binger. Check these out:

- You've been invited to a friend's house for a meal. A non-binger would think "Great, I don't have to cook tonight; I won't bother much with food during the day because she always lays on a good spread". A binger thinks, "I've got to eat tonight anyway so I might as well pig out all day and start my diet again tomorrow".

- A piece of crust falls off the edge of the apple pie and you pop it into your mouth. A non-binger thinks "Mm that's nice, I'll have a piece of that for dessert tonight". A binger cuts off a large slice and says "Oh well, I've blown it now. I'll eat it all today and have a really strict diet day to-morrow".

- It's Christmas and you've had several days of heavy meals, boozy parties and fattening snacks. A non-binger thinks, "My clothes feel a bit tight. I'll be extra careful for the next few days". A binger thinks "It's nearly New Year's Eve so I'll carry on eating until 1st January and then have only fruit for three days to start my diet".

- Your mother phones. She disapproves. Of what? Everything. A non-binger will reason that she doesn't need anyone's approval to live her life in her own way. A binger will head for the butter, put some bread underneath it and eat her way through the loaf, as a way of stuffing down all the angry retorts she didn't say.

- A non-binger goes on a diet two weeks before her holiday so she will look nice in her bikini. A binger goes on a diet two weeks before her holiday so she can GET INTO her bikini.

Need I go on? No, I thought not. You ARE a binger. You are not anorexic; you couldn't not eat. You are not bulimic; you just could not bring yourself to do whatever is necessary to make yourself vomit. You, and thousands of others like you, are controlled by food, in a constant battle over what you should and shouldn't eat. One lapse and you go on picking at junk food for the rest of the day.

It wouldn't be so bad if you enjoyed the experience but, even as you are eating, you are getting more and more miserable, angry and frustrated. Yet you cannot stop. Food becomes a comforter when you feel down, a tranquilliser when you feel jittery and "something to do" when you are bored.

You are not necessarily fat. Not all bingers are fat. Some stay slim by not allowing a binge to last longer than one or two days before reverting to normal eating. Conversely, not all fat people are bingers. Some get fat simply by overeating at mealtimes or eating too much of the wrong foods. Fat or slim, a binger's weight is rarely stable, often fluctuating by as much as a stone over a four month period. This tends to coincide with the binger's mood swings, from elation after eating less to abject misery after a prolonged session of bingeing.

To a binger, the most frightening thing is that helpless feeling of being out of control and unable to stop shovelling food into your mouth, whether you are 5 stone or 5 pounds overweight.

Slimmers tend to starve themselves, eat diet products and think about food constantly. This could be described as having a "fat" mentality. Other people eat what they like and food is just another part of their lives, like work, friends and shopping. Theirs would be a "slim" mentality. Although not necessarily obese, bingers are invariably fatter than they want to be. Therefore, in order to be slim, and stay slim, they need to change their "fat" mentality to a "slim" mentality.

To achieve this you have to go through various stages. While you are constantly on a "diet" and striving to reach some mythical goal weight, you are locked into an endless daily struggle that takes up a lot of your time and saps your energy. Being off a diet does not mean stuffing your face with the entire contents of your nearest deli. It means that for a short period of time – between six and twelve weeks – you follow this programme and learn to be in control of your eating. If you can manage this, it becomes a habit which, ultimately, will help you achieve that "slim" mentality.

I am sure you have lost weight many times before, so you will know that the most difficult part isn't usually losing the weight but keeping it off afterwards. In the past there have always been certain triggers – foods, situations, feelings – that have stopped you keeping that weight off successfully. By learning to identify these triggers you can prevent those situations recurring, and you can get off the binge/diet see-saw. The secret of losing weight isn't so much what you eat as being IN CONTROL of what you eat.

This is the direct opposite of bingeing, which is stuffing food mindlessly into your mouth without really tasting or enjoying it – a condition in which all you can think about is what to eat next. Bingeing is eating a lot of something today because you are not going to eat it tomorrow – or ever again!

Only recently has binge eating become recognised as a widespread eating disorder. There has been little real help available other than conventional diet books, which are useless to bingers because, once you are overcome by the urge to eat, the diet goes out of the window.

This book then is not primarily concerned with weight loss but is aimed at you – the binger – who wants to give up this destructive habit. However, changing your focus will help you lose weight and stabilise it at a lower level. If YOU are a binger, then this book is for you: it will tell you why you do it, how it affects your life, and how you can stop.

I have been an exercise teacher and diet counsellor for thirty years. No, don't worry, this is not a hip, thigh (or any other part of your anatomy) diet book! The majority of my clients are female and range from teenagers to women in their seventies. Typical behaviour involves eating far too little to satisfy normal bodily requirements, followed by huge quantities of food at one sitting; eating normally most of the time but then gorging on fatty, sugary food when under stress; blaming events like parties, or other people – "She put this gigantic plate of chips in front of me. What was I supposed to do?!" – for their weight gain. These people admit that they "should" do more exercise; however, they make the effort when they feel "slim" but not when they feel "fat". They all wish for a fairy godmother to come along and wave a magic wand so that they can eat as much as they like and not put on weight.

You may easily feel you are the only one who has this obsession with food. This is simply not so. A revealing survey carried out by *Cosmopolitan* magazine in 1993 found that roughly 80-85% of women had some sort of food problem; i.e. they were on a diet or locked into a rigidly controlled eating plan. Most of the people surveyed felt that they ate too much and thought of themselves as "greedy" or "disgusting". Half the respondents didn't know why they over-ate but couldn't stop. Many of the women confessed that stringent diets left them feeling tired, cold and suffering from overwhelming guilt if they succumbed to normal hunger pangs.

Whatever their sizes, this 80-85% of women professed to be unhappy with their weights but felt trapped in this lifestyle. Eighty per cent is an incredibly high percentage of the female population, although it could be argued that only people who had a problem with food would bother to complete this kind of questionnaire in the first place.

However, these results do confirm my own experiences as a diet counsellor. Over the years I have advised a wide range of people who are all unable to stop stuffing food into their mouths once their minds click into "binge mode".

So I do know what you are going through. I know that

you want to be slim, you are happier when you are slim, and you do get fed up with what you perceive as an endless battle with food. You would like to live "normally", to be able to eat what you like and not put on weight. Like most of my clients, I am sure your shelves are full of all the latest diet books. Admit it, you've tried them all, haven't you? You probably got diarrhoea with the Beverley Hills diet, or wind with the F-Plan, or giddy with the Rotation diet. You tried not mixing protein and carbohydrate, milk and meat, gloss and emulsion – and it still didn't work. However apparently outlandish – Limmits, Trimmets, Vomits, Grommets and the Cambridge formula – you've been there, done that. Your choice of diet has always been governed by the two magic phrases: "Lose weight quickly" and "Eat as much as you like". You've counted calories, fat units, sin-points and the numbers game on Countdown. You know the calorie content of every food you've ever eaten from "apple" to "zucchini" and can recite little slogans like: "A moment on your lips, forever on your hips" (Oh, please!) but you are still not happy. Why? Because the diets didn't work? No – they did work, while you stuck to them. Diets always work the first time you try them. You start off very enthusiastic and follow the instructions to the letter. You love it when the pounds start to drop off, and you can carry on until you reach goal weight. And then what happens?

Well, being a binger, you eat for various reasons other than hunger, as we know. You might think the occasional binge doesn't matter but, if it goes on for several days, your mentality changes, from happy and confident (slim) to slight panic ("I still look slim, don't I?") to self-anger ("Come ON now!") to fatalism ("I can't stop eating") to despair ("Oh, sod it; back to the cabbage soup").

Because your attitude is so half-hearted, you find it very difficult each time to stick to the powdered drinks, or whatever, for days on end, and every fourth day or so turns into a dieting disaster. Eat, drink and be heavy! It happens every time. You then cast around for a new diet – no problem there as loads of new diet books are published every year, usually by an "I was once fat and now I'm thin and gorgeous and, if I can do it, so can you" type of author. And they work. All diets, however bizarre, cause weight loss, but nobody can *stay* on a regimented "diet" devised by someone else if it is vastly different from the way that individual normally eats. You can try. You *have* tried. It's boring and time-consuming. So, as soon as you go back to your normal eating (well, normal for you), the weight piles on again. The same old pattern prevails, over and over again. It just doesn't seem to sink in: if you keep on repeating the same actions, you will keep on getting the same results.

Organised diets do not work *in the long term* – generally speaking. One current estimate is that four women out of every hundred manage to keep their weight at the lower level once they have lost it. Probably many of them have a vested interest in staying slim, being those people who end up on breakfast-time TV or as leaders of the local slimming club.

Basically, people do not like being told what to do. Initially, you may be thankful to hand over the responsibility for your food intake and let someone else decide what you will eat at each meal. However, doing this is like putting yourself in prison, handing the key to someone and saying "Here, live my life for me". With so many different personalities, tastes and lifestyles, there cannot be one diet that suits everyone. You also have to live in the real world, which means eating out and going to parties, holidays and family get-togethers. So it's more than a bit difficult to fit in the "165g chicken breast (without skin), 55g rice and free veg" demanded by your set "diet" for that day.

The strategies you are usually told to stick to on your diet are not the ones that will help you keep weight off permanently. That is why so many people regain the weight eventually. As a binger, you need new strategies which will enable you to stay in control of your eating; ones that leave you free, not struggling.

It took me years to discover the correct strategies. Like other diet counsellors, I would initially advise my clients to stick to a low-fat diet and include lots of fresh fruit and vegetables. They all lost weight and were delighted. Then, after a few months, the weight seemed to creep on again, slowly and insidiously, and they appeared to be powerless to stop it. I would sympathise, reassure and we would start again. They would again lose weight, feel much better and go off triumphantly to live slim, sure that they had beaten the enemy this time. And so often they had, temporarily. Weeks, months, sometimes a couple of years would go by, but then I would get a phone call: "Er, do you remember me? Can I come and see you?", and off we would go again.

This used to puzzle me. These clients were so delighted to be slim. They all professed to feel better, look younger, have more energy. So why would they allow the weight to creep back on again? They obviously didn't do it on purpose.

The answer came to me out of the blue. I was watching an interview on television with the singer, Cher. She was asked how she managed to keep her fabulous figure, and she replied "I would rather be slim than eat chocolate brownies". Then I realised; that's it! You can't be slim AND eat chocolate brownies all the time. If you want to be slim, you can't eat everything you like whenever you like. That is reality.

After some initial difficulty in getting the message across, I found that it worked – *permanently*. My clients stopped bingeing, lost weight and stabilised at the lower level, just by adhering to the simple truth: that the only way to stop being fat is to stop eating the foods that make you fat, and the only way to stop bingeing is to stop eating the foods that make you binge. End of story. Like Cher, you have to decide what you want – whether to be slim, or to eat the sort of food that made you fat in the first place – you can't have it both ways.

For bingers, this means giving up one or two "trigger" foods that start them off on a binge. Most clients react with horror when I suggest this because it is contrary to everything they have been taught by the conventional diets they have always followed. Here is a typical reaction: "But I would feel deprived; I deserve a little treat; I crave a sweet taste; I can't give up chocolate altogether".

You think you'll be deprived if you can't put a piece of

chocolate into your mouth. THAT is deprivation? I'll tell you what deprivation really is for a binger:

It's being controlled by food.
It's being unable to stop eating.
It's a feeling of despair.
It's being dismayed by the sight of yourself in the mirror.
It's not being able to wear the clothes you want.
It's chafed skin where your inner thighs rub together.
It's being embarrassed on the beach in a bathing suit.
It's getting puffed walking up a hill.
It's putting on large-size tights and discovering the crotch won't even come up to – where it should come up to.
It's going into a store and finding the only thing that fits you is the make-up.

You want more?

Deprivation is feeling panicky around food; as though not only your food choices but your whole life is out of control. It's feeling shaky and unsure; that you don't measure up in some way – although to what, you don't quite know. Deprivation is hating yourself and the way you look.

Wake up and smell the (no calorie) coffee, binger! This is your LIFE. Is this what you are prepared to live like just for a piece of chocolate? Is it OK to be held to ransom by a biscuit? Are you willing to sacrifice being slim, attractive, full of energy, happy and self-confident for the sake of a momentary taste of something sweet?

Giving up what, for most people, is just one trigger food does not make you deprived. It sets you free; from the bingeing, from the guilt and anger, from the daily struggle with food – and leaves you free to EAT EVERYTHING ELSE.

Your previous diets have probably failed because they have allowed you (or you have allowed yourself) to indulge in some trigger food every day. Whatever they/you called it, a "sin", an extra 500 calories for a "treat", a "reward" – this was meant to help you stick to your diet.

For some people this works. For you, a binger, it doesn't. It may for a while but your trigger food is endowed with so much emotional and psychological baggage stored in your brain, that one bite releases feelings and memories that overwhelm you and make you go on eating. Initially the weight may go but the bingeing problem is still there and, sooner or later, you will put back that weight.

So, this book is definitely not going to tell you what to eat. How do I know what you like to eat? Do you really need to follow someone else's format or go to some place to be weighed and applauded for getting it right? You are not an idiot. You don't need a group leader or a diet sheet to control your food intake. You have the intelligence to do that for yourself. You just need to know the strategies to put it into practice.

This advice also applies to men, although the familiar male "beer-gut" is usually acquired by overeating – and drinking – at mealtimes, rather than mindless bingeing. There are fewer male bingers as women tend to binge because they internalise negative feelings and assume that everything is their fault, whereas men tend to direct their guilt outwards and blame other people. Hence, "I only eat what my wife puts in front of me". Yeah, *right*!

"The last thing I want to be is fat – so why do I binge?"
Since more and more bingers are coming out of the fridge – so to speak – psychologists are working overtime to discover why you need to use food in this way. Many people look for a release from the stresses of everyday living. For some this will be alcohol, for others a prescription drug like Prozac. Or they may smoke heavily. With you, it's eating!

Fortunately you have probably chosen the least harmful as far as your health is concerned, unless you smoke or drink heavily as well, but your chronic bingeing is doing immeasurable harm to the way you see yourself, and the way you imagine other people see you.

The other problem with using food as a calming agent is that it is the one vice that is totally visible. Smokers, and even alcoholics, can still be slim and appear in control most of the time. You, however, with your fluctuating weight and "fat" and "thin" clothes, cannot hide your obsession from the outside world.

I have learned from my clients that the worst aspect of dieting/bingeing is putting back the weight you lost before. You dread seeing family and friends if you have gained weight since you last met, especially after all the congratulations. It's as if the additional pounds are visible evidence of you being somewhat of a failure.

A woman's size is also something that everyone, including herself, feels free to discuss openly. "I've put on so much weight" you will greet your friend apologetically.

"Nonsense" she lies, eyeing your bulges with inward satisfaction. Other vices are never discussed in the same way. You are unlikely to hear someone saying, "I must have a drink because I am a raging alcoholic" or "Excuse me, I must go and smoke a joint" (!)

Yet preoccupation with food and weight seems to be a bond that unites women – like being members of the same club. They discuss their problems with food and the difficulties they face in controlling their weight, feeling comforted when other women confess the same things. Nowadays, eating any fattening food in front of other people is always accompanied by an explanation or an apology.

Some women feel they need to be slim in order to succeed and, once they get to their "correct" weight, they can become obsessively preoccupied with staying there. ("Does this lipstick make my face look fat?") For them their weight becomes the benchmark against which they measure their appearance and achievements – which is rather sad. Obviously people look, and usually feel, better when they are slim and shapely and they enjoy the compliments that go with losing weight. This is why slimming clubs are so popular.

But why has this preoccupation with body shape, leading to erratic eating as it does, become so widespread over the years? It's easy to blame the idea that we live in a culture which discriminates against women and makes them feel that, whatever their shape, it is the wrong one. "Culture", however, does not force you to stock your fridge with your trigger foods for the sole purpose of stuffing your face at the first sign of stress. Something is still causing you to abuse food in this way. You tell yourself you are eating for comfort but what happens when you finish the food? You will feel better initially but what about the problem that caused you to require comforting in the first place? Presumably that is still there, so how soon will you need more "comfort" – and then more? You are confusing immediate pleasure with long-term happiness but, if the short-term comfort comes from alcohol, drugs or food, the pleasure will be outweighed by disaster soon afterwards – in your case, when you try and get into your jeans.

Firstly, therefore, you need to acknowledge that you do have a food problem. You may think it is normal behaviour to have an argument with your mother and then go home and eat a whole packet of chocolate digestives. It's not.

Some problems, though, may be long-term – for examples, having a rotten job, a bad relationship, family rivalry and so on. Where this is happening the associated food problems can go on year after year as if they were your "chosen" way to resolve the difficulties. You, however, are only able to view the bingeing as some form of weakness in

your character – of being out of control. All you can think
about is whether you are having a "good" day or a "bad"
day. In these cases your actual weight isn't necessarily the
problem; neither is your bingeing. They are more likely to
be symptoms of what is going on in your life.

When you feel trapped like this there may appear to be no
solution. Maybe you can't change the basic problems in
your life. However, you will certainly be able to cope better
with everything if you are in control of your eating. With
this book, therefore, you are not going on a diet. You are
making changes. Diets come to an end. Changes are permanent.

In the chapters that follow, I will take you through strategies for binge control and healthy eating, invariably
leading to bringing your weight down. Some of the examples demonstrating various attitudes and behaviours arise
from experiences portrayed by previous clients. Obviously,
here, I am not using their real names.

A common experience is the presence of two "voices" in
your head; one urging you to eat something fattening and
the other telling you not to break your diet. This state of
mind has come up so often in my circles that these voices
have become known as Fat-U and Slim-U. Fat-U will say
something like "Come on, you know you want it; one little
bit won't hurt", while Slim-U counters with "No, don't eat
it; you know it always starts you off on a binge". The two
voices rage backwards and forwards in your mind with the
ultimate winner usually being Fat-U. Whichever voice you
are controlled by depends on how you perceive yourself at
the time.

When Fat-U takes over and you feel that compulsion to
eat, you can find any number of reasons to justify it at that
particular moment:

"I am absolutely starving."

"I've got a splitting headache."

"I can still get into my black trousers."

"I've been so good all week, I'm entitled to a bit of a treat, surely!"

"I didn't have time for lunch so –."

"I'll be really good tomorrow."

The rationalisations go on and on, appearing to give you perfectly credible permission to indulge in behaviour that just a few days ago you would have considered entirely unacceptable.

However, if you can become aware of the words that Fat-U uses to tempt you, you can learn to arm Slim-U with a more convincing argument to counteract them. Being aware is half the battle.

The key to winning the battle is to identify, and give up, your trigger food (or foods): the foods that, once you start eating them, you can't stop, and which lead to the bingeing misery you know so well. If there is a food that you can't control, then that food is controlling you. Get rid of it. You can eat everything else – whatever you like – just not that food. There are no diets in this book; instead I will give you some guidelines as to the sorts of food that will keep you healthy and give you the most energy. The basic responsibility is yours – you are the only one who puts food into your mouth – so you make the choices.

You also need effective strategies to deal with cravings. A binge, in my view, is always precipitated by three thoughts: what I call the 'think-thought' – "Oooh, that looks nice"; the 'crave-thought' – "I would really like to eat that"; and the 'binge-thought' – "To hell with it, I am GOING to eat that!" I will show you how to break the link between the 'think-thought' and the 'crave-thought' before the 'binge-thought' can take hold.

Eating is a habit. We eat the foods we are used to eating,

at the times that we are used to eating them. If you have always binged on certain foods in certain situations in the past, you will binge on the same foods in the same situations in the future. That is why those foods have got to go.

Habits form "grooves" in the subconscious mind. Every time you repeat the same action, the groove gets a bit deeper until you repeat this behaviour without thinking. You can't really change deep grooves in your subconscious. The only way to alter a bad eating habit is to start a *new* habit and continue with it until it gets so deeply ingrained that it becomes a way of life for you and overlays the old groove.

Suppose I told you that, in future, every time you clean your teeth you will have to hold your toothbrush in the opposite hand to the one you normally use. How do you think that would feel? Yes; very strange. In fact, sometimes you would forget, start to use your normal hand and then change over when you remembered. It would feel very awkward and uncomfortable for the first few weeks but, as you continued doing it, you would probably get used to it. In the end it would become second nature to you and would feel perfectly natural. In fact, if then you were to change back to the old hand, *that* would probably feel uncomfortable!

In this book we will examine your personal food habits and how to change those behaviours and attitudes about food and eating that keep causing you to binge. All eating habits are learned and can therefore be "unlearned", or at least replaced with more appropriate behaviour. New babies don't come out of the womb thinking "Oooh, I really fancy a Ben & Jerry's Chunky Monkey ice cream".

Forget willpower. When it fails you this just makes you feel guilty. I prefer to think of success as being in control. The very idea of willpower conjures up a state of continuous denial; whereas being in control means being aware of what your body needs and making conscious decisions to deal with that. (Besides – a binger's definition of willpower is the ability to resist temptation only until she is sure no one is looking!)

On some diets you may feel that you are too much in control as it is – with the rigid guidelines you lay down for yourself, the meticulous weighing of every morsel and the noting of the number of calories. But that is not the sort of control I mean here. Being in control does not have to be restrictive. You are in control in lots of areas of your life. You use "appropriate" behaviour in different situations: work, social, personal life. What is so different about being in conscious control of your eating behaviour?

Once you have been through all the reasons and excuses why you can't – "I would feel deprived", "I get so hungry", "I've got no willpower", "I can't resist crusty bread and butter" – you come to a point where you realise that no one else can live your life for you. No one else cares whether you are fat or thin – or what you eat. Only you can decide what you put into your mouth. You make your choice and live with the consequences. It is just a matter of deciding what is important to YOU. Most people go through life not really knowing what they want yet certain that what they have isn't it!

The decision, however, starts in your mind, not in your mouth. How you think is more important than what you eat because the right thoughts will guide you towards food that is nourishing and healthy. If you start the day thinking "I mustn't eat very much today because I want to lose weight" you will suddenly find that you are starving hungry. Have you noticed that? If you think "I am going to eat sensibly today, starting with a good breakfast", your body will respond by giving you the energy you need to carry you through the day.

This is being in control of your life rather than letting your life be controlled by food. Eating an apple for lunch, a banana for dinner and nothing else is not being in control.

It's being stupid because you are starving yourself. Bingeing is a symptom of starvation. It's your body's way of making sure you stay alive. It is, therefore, your continual focus on the "diet" that, paradoxically, stops you losing weight. When you think of yourself as a slim, healthy person, your body will strive to accommodate you in this wish.

Let's be realistic. You are living in the real world where there will always be stress. If you can learn to deal with that stress, you won't need to anaesthetise yourself with food. Food can't resolve stressful situations. It won't settle arguments. It won't repair relationships. On the contrary – your bingeing is probably masquerading as a substitute for dealing with them.

A binge rarely appears out of the blue, even if it might seem that way. There is always some past trigger that nudges your mind towards thoughts of food; an uncomfortable feeling, a conversation or event, even the aroma of a certain food can awaken past memories and set up a craving. To prevent that craving turning into a binge you have to break the link between the initial "think-thought", the "crave-thought" and the "binge-thought". That link is YOUR TRIGGER FOOD. If that particular food is not available and you have programmed yourself not to eat it, then the binge doesn't happen. If you want to stop bingeing, you have to stop eating the food, or foods, that make you binge. It's as simple as that. You will find it just as easy to eat healthily as it is to eat junk. After that – once you realise there is no fairy godmother – everything falls into place.

In olden days food meant survival. In modern times it's equated with celebration and enjoyment of life. And why not? You worked for it, you deserve it, so why shouldn't you eat it? Unfortunately for bingers the fact that some foods might ruin your health, appearance and even self-esteem, doesn't always seem to be a good enough reason to offset the immediate need for gratification through whatever food takes your fancy.

Mothers all over the world have rewarded with chocolate, comforted with biscuits and hot milk, and said "Here, eat this; everything will be all right." You believed it – and it was all right. That's why you believe it now – when it isn't!

Our parents and grandparents didn't necessarily know about nutrition and the dangers to health of high fat and sugary foods. We do; and with this knowledge comes responsibility to choose food not just by taste, appearance and texture, but also by how it affects our health.

Food is for life, not just for Christmas. Your body needs a wide variety of foods to be strong and healthy and the more you increase your knowledge of nutrition the easier it will become to make informed choices.

For a binger, having your weight under control is one of the greatest freedoms you can accomplish. It may sound like a paradox but, CHOOSING to act responsibly in the knowledge that you can eat whatever you want, is most definitely the "secret" that allows you to live slim and binge-free.

Each day you succeed makes the next day easier. Nonetheless, as you examine and attempt to change any destructive patterns in your life, it may indeed sometimes feel as if you are attempting to brush your teeth with the wrong hand; however, in time, the new way of thinking will become second nature.

By the end of this book you will know what to eat to suit your personal lifestyle. You will also be equipped with the strategies and the mental armour to prevent yourself bingeing. You don't have to enrol anywhere or pay any money. You just have to read on. OK? Good. Let's do it.

2

TRIGGER SITUATIONS

"I hate myself!"   (Right.)
"I'm a complete failure."   (If you say so.)
"I can't stop eating."   (Mm hm.)
"All my friends are skinny."   (Lucky them.)
"I feel totally out of control."   (And?)
"I wouldn't blame him if he went off
with someone else."   (Good one that!)
"I bet everyone is talking about me."   (No; you're not that
                                                important, Ducky.)
"No one understands what it's like."   (Oh, I do, I do.)
"I can be good for days then something happens and I'm
like a madwoman!"
"My daughter told me not to collect her
from school."   (That's a relief!)
"I look at these slim girls walking
around in tight jeans and I want to die."   (Yawn.)
"My husband never says anything but
'I *know*'."   (Know what?)

"Sometimes I get so ratty with him and
the kids but it's not their fault."   (It probably is.)
"I never eat in front of other people."   (Why not?)
"I hide food all over the house."   (From whom?)
"It's much worse in the winter when
it's cold."   (What is?)
"I can't stop eating."   (Oh shut up!)

Yes, dieting can make you tired, grumpy, crave high-fat foods and take away the enjoyment of socialising with friends. **It can also turn you into a binger.** Yet, books and magazines continue to publish "revolutionary" diets and theories about why people store fat. New drugs like orlistat (brand name Xenical), which prevent the body absorbing the fat in food, are now being prescribed for those who are 30% overweight. But like Fenfluramine, which works directly on the brain to stifle hunger and which has now been withdrawn because of the possible risk of pulmonary hypertension in users, there are often adverse side-effects from trying to control hunger with drugs.

And so, when you finally accept that there is no magic formula which will dissolve your flab overnight and allow you to eat anything you want and stay slim, it is time to try something that works. Read on.

When a new client registers with me, I start a file, jotting down her history and eating habits. I also note any insights which may help me understand the binge mentality. There are many reasons why a client is driven to consult me in the first place. For those who wish to break their habit of binge-ing, there is usually a moment – generally in the middle of a binge – when they become aware of "watching" them-selves from another part of the room. Upon "seeing" their hand repeatedly reaching into the cupboard or fridge, going from bowl to mouth, breaking open another packet or spooning up ice cream, a feeling of the utmost irritation and futility comes over them. It is at this moment that they realise they need help.

For those needing to lose weight, the most popular reasons for making a start seem to be remarks overheard: for example "When is your baby due, dear?" when you thought you were just beginning to look normal again after the birth three months ago; or "That lady will need two seats, won't she Mummy?" (on the bus); "Why is she looking at the dresses – the only thing that would fit her is a scarf" (in Selfridges); "I always wondered who bought those giant-sized knickers!" (in Marks & Spencer); "Mummy, has that lady got a baby growing in her bottom?"

Holiday photos, a zip which won't do up, an unexpected glimpse of some frumpy, dumpy female in a plate-glass window which, horror of horrors, turns out to be you: all these can contribute to the jolting realisation "I must go on a diet. I'll only eat grapefruit till the fat has gone". And so begins the starve/binge see-saw.

Compulsion

As a chronic binger you are *compelled* to turn to food whenever your ordered way of life is disturbed. Rather like a computer programmed to "self-destruct", you feel as though you are controlled by some external force against which you are helpless. When a compulsion strikes, you can be amazed by its intensity. Even if you have to get into your car at midnight and search for an all-night deli or a garage, you're off.

Binge eating is like an addiction. This means you have lost the control that allows you to say "This isn't good for me; I am not going to do this". You may think you are "addicted" to food. Wrong. You are "addicted" to EATING. Binge eating is the transference, for hour after hour, of

edible substances from plate/packet/carton/tin straight into your mouth. This continues regardless of taste or texture, veering from sweet to savoury and back again, using a spoon, fork, knife, fingers, and often standing up with one eye on the door in case anyone should come in and see you. Eventually, the lateness of the hour or the very real need to throw up causes you to stagger upstairs to your bedroom. You drop off to sleep – only to wake again at 2.30 a.m. in a bath of perspiration and with a feeling in your throat of impending nausea. The following morning you look at your bloated face in the mirror and vow "never again".

In the days following an enormous binge you seem to feel the cold a lot more and experience waves of fatigue at odd times. This causes you to sleep more than normal, which is simply your body's way of dealing with the misery pulling you down. The trouble is that when you feel this bad you crave the comfort of your favourite foods but then get angry with yourself if you succumb to eating them. So on the one hand you are comforting yourself with food and on the other you are berating yourself for doing so.

Why would any intelligent woman put herself through such an uncomfortable way to live? Let's look at the main reasons:

Too Stringent Dieting

You want to lose weight – quickly. Never mind how long it took to acquire those extra pounds, you want them gone – NOW. You decide to eat only fruit, yoghurt and cottage cheese for a week to "give yourself a start". The first day is fine because you feel strong and virtuous and you mentally tick off "day one" when you go to bed. The next morning you have lost 3 lb. Yesss! You are terribly tired by the evening and wake up on the third day with a raging headache and what feels like a black hole inside you clamouring to be filled. It just takes one small incident, like someone driving into the parking space you were about to reverse into, when you snap – dive into the nearest shop and buy loads of biscuits, cakes, chocolate and ice cream – go home, and eat the lot. You probably eat four Mars bars in the car on the way! Later you feel sick – both physically and mentally.

You can't cure yourself of eating too much by eating too little. It doesn't work. All you are doing is depriving your body of the fuel it needs to get you through the day. No one can tolerate such rigorous, self-imposed restraint for long. You haven't been eating enough, so your body needs to "catch up" regardless of whether you are hungry or not. So – when you eat four Mars Bars in one go – your motivation has more to do with how much you can stuff in whilst you are on a temporary relapse binge than a genuine craving for Mars Bars. All because you are not going to eat them when you "start again tomorrow". Er, haven't I heard that before?

Wanting To Be Too Thin
We all know the media continues to publish pictures of skinny models and promotes extreme thinness as the "norm". That topic has been well documented but knowing it doesn't seem to make any difference. It remains a fact that too many women are dissatisfied with their bodies because they think these images represent an ideal shape to which they should aspire. Deep down you *know* you could never sashay down a catwalk in clothes designed for a stick insect. Just as you *know* that very few women resemble the firm, toned bodies that slink along American beaches in television programmes.

It is fairly easy to lose weight once you put your mind to it. However, one of the reasons many people fail to keep their weight off, and end up bingeing, is that they are aiming too low. They are so obsessed with being thin that they can't enjoy just *being*, and therefore continuously strive for the unattainable. It is just not possible to starve yourself into a skinny shape when you are not genetically programmed to BE that thin. Your body will fight you all the way and, when there is a Slim-U/Fat-U conflict between mind and body, your body invariably wins.

You need to be slim, not thin. Models are thin. American soap opera stars are thin. They are paid to be. You are not. No one is rushing up to you with a contract to host a TV talk show. You want to be *slim*, which means being a nice shape and within a 5 – 7 lb range of what you consider to be your goal weight. Forget about a rigid target. Most women's weight fluctuates from time to time depending on what they eat or drink, fluid retention and pre-menstrual whatever; therefore the number on the scale should be an *indicator* – not the holy gospel. If you want to weigh 9 stone, then 8.12

to 9.3 is fine. The objective is to be healthy and well, with enough energy to get through the day and to be in control of your eating. You want to feel confident that you look good in clothes and can wear anything in your size straight off the rack in a clothes shop. Too thin just looks scrawny. It doesn't look attractive or healthy.

Stress

As more and more women become high achievers, some seem to suffer from the same levels of stress that were previously attributed mainly to men. The type of woman who wants to reach the top of her profession can, as a result, become impatient and dismissive of the mundane activities in life such as eating. She will rush her food and will often conduct conversations with the telephone in one hand and a hamburger in the other, unaware of what she is eating, or how much. She also finds it difficult to stick to a weight loss programme because she gets impatient with any apparent lack of progress – she wants to be slim NOW, and is more likely to go the starvation route than to opt for safe and steady weight loss.

Even if you are not at management level, you can still experience a lot of stress at work. As more industries "downsize", you may be expected to do more work than you can comfortably handle; this may entail working longer hours, or feeling obliged to take on work that other people don't want to do. Maybe you feel that you are being unfairly treated? That is stressful in itself.

Stress at work and arriving home exhausted can often make you reach for the nearest item of food rather than a nutritionally planned meal.

Even staying at home in the company of fretful babies or home-wrecking toddlers, day after day, can send a woman diving into the fridge to relieve the monotony.

How about social occasions? How do you feel when you have to walk into a room full of strangers at a party or social gathering? Can you go up to a group of people and introduce yourself, or is it easier to grab a drink and some peanuts? Most people feel uneasy in situations like these, especially if they haven't got a partner with them for support. It's not surprising that they end up eating whatever is on offer rather than face the embarrassment of appearing awkward.

Perfectionist Attitude

Everything has to be just so: your hair, your clothes, your makeup. You hate anything sloppy or untidy. You are critical and judgmental, both of yourself and other people. You tend to do everything yourself because no one else does it the way you like it. If you can't get something exactly right, that translates into "Why can't I get ANYTHING right?" Wanting the perfect body, you probably apply equally strict criteria to your dieting decisions as well, and therefore try and lose weight by missing breakfast or lunch or limiting your food intake drastically. The perfectionist is adept at internal mental shouting sessions: "I am so fed up with myself; I am such a pig; what is *wrong* with me?" – leading to self-pity: "I can't do anything; I'm just useless; what's the point in even trying?" – and even on to projecting your negative thoughts unjustifiably into the future: "I'll never be able to lose weight; I will just get fatter and fatter and never be able to wear nice clothes".

You perfectionists are so hard on yourselves, so critical. For some reason, being a binger conspires to exclude even admitting to the positive aspects of your lives. You rarely give yourselves credit for the plus points: holding down a difficult job, juggling home and work, managing people, finance, or being a good mother. You even manage to avoid giving yourselves credit for the days when you don't binge:

"So I stuck to my diet for three weeks – so what? I must have put on at least a stone over the weekend!"

This attitude is so common amongst my clients that we tried to figure out where it came from. I am sure that in a lot of cases you had a mother or father who was very critical of you. Nothing was ever right or good enough. Sometimes overprotective or domineering parents put too much pressure on their children to modify their behaviour so that it is acceptable to others. They correct every word and action to the extent that the children lose the capacity to make their own decisions. These children can grow into adults who find it difficult to be discerning: to choose the things and people in life that are best for them. They tend to rely on other people's opinions but will believe the disparaging remarks rather than the complimentary ones. This just reinforces what they believe about themselves.

When you criticise yourself it means you don't like something that you are doing. You are, in effect, becoming your own parent, telling yourself off for not being good enough. As you nearly always criticise yourself for the same things over and over again, this constant nagging clearly isn't working. Maybe it's time to try a new tactic. You are an adult now. It doesn't really matter what anyone else thinks. You are not living in the past. You can exercise complete control now over what you do, how you think and what you eat. You don't have to be perfect. Nobody is; so whose criteria from the past are you trying to meet? You can't go on blaming your mother, or anything else from your childhood for your bingeing; that way you just get stuck in this groove and remain a victim by repeating the same patterns over and over. The forces ruling your life twenty years ago probably no longer exist or, if they do, surely it's time to do something about them. You are not a victim of circumstance. You are a person who can choose exactly what to do with her life. Please stop being so hard on yourself. The past is over.

It is time to move on and let go of behaviour patterns that keep you living in the past. Do you really consider yourself a failure because you couldn't stick to some diet that didn't even suit your lifestyle?

Childhood Experiences

For some women the habit of bingeing for comfort begins in childhood. Here's Stella, a former client, aged 46:

"I used to dread mealtimes when I was a child. My parents are now divorced but I wish they had done it years ago instead of the constant sniping. For some reason my father always used mealtimes to have a go at my mother, whether it was about her cooking or her appearance – she was quite plump – or to blame her for something I, or my sister, had done wrong. She would be cold and sarcastic in response, and I used to sit between them, so utterly miserable that I just could not push the food down past the lump in my throat. Then they would turn on me for wasting food, saying how come I was so fat when I didn't eat anything? Now, many years later, I realise that their anger was really directed at each other, not at me, but I used to get so upset and would often leave the table and run up to my room and cry. I would dive into my secret hoard of chocolate and biscuits and stuff my face till I felt sick. Sometimes my sister would be on the receiving end of their wrath but this didn't seem to affect her nearly as much. The result is that I am extra careful with my own children's sensitivity to whatever problems my husband and I might have. I always try and make mealtimes as pleasant as possible."

When someone treated this way as a child grows up, these feelings of being "on trial", which make it difficult for her to eat, can still sweep over her on occasions when she sits at a table with other people. She may well tend to eat sparsely in similar company and then make up for it when she gets home.

Sweets and chocolates are still regarded as a treat in some homes, to be given as a reward or withheld as a punishment. This may assign undue importance to them so the child often becomes sneaky in order to get them, pinching them out of the cupboard when no-one is looking or buying them with pocket money and hiding them.

This reaction appears to return in adulthood as a habit many women have of secreting food around the house on the pretext of stopping themselves eating it – a bit pointless really as they know exactly where to look for it when the need arises!

Let's look at some more scenarios that trigger a binge. One or two of these may be familiar to you.

"Something Is Bothering Me"

Susie: "I had been eating quite sensibly but on this particular evening I felt a bit niggly. I can't really describe it. I knew I couldn't be hungry because I had finished my evening meal less than an hour earlier, but the feeling persisted. I said to myself 'What about some fruit? That can't do any harm!' So I ate an apple, but that wasn't right. I needed something stodgy. I made a slice of toast and, ever mindful of calories, spread it with Marmite. Then I toasted another slice and put jam on it this time. Then I thought 'This is ridiculous – get out of the kitchen', so I went back into the living room but just couldn't settle. I returned to the kitchen and made another piece of toast, this time spread with butter and cream cheese. Then I made a sandwich and suddenly I was into a full-scale binge that went on all evening. I behaved as if there were a flashing neon sign on my stomach saying 'Insert food here'."

This sort of "niggly" binge is often a result of a problem

causing conflict in your mind, one which may be nothing to do with food. It could be connected with work, an emotional problem, or a behavioural one – "I wonder if I should have done/said that?". Almost any difficulty that causes you self-doubt or concern can manifest itself as a feeling of anxiety in your mind, which you then attempt to alleviate with food. While you are actually eating you feel a sense of relief, and you grow calmer as the food begins to fill you up.

We all know that eating is a pleasurable activity but, in this case, the pleasure is short-lived. All it does is distract you, temporarily, from thinking about the real problem.

You are unlikely to think clearly about anything while you're stuffing food into your mouth but, unfortunately, as you continue eating, a new problem arises: you begin to feel bloated and uncomfortable. After that you may start getting panicky and irritated with yourself because you feel fat. You certainly do not eat in order to get fat – you hate being fat – but because you feel panicky and out of control, "fat" now becomes the problem instead of the original conflict which triggered the binge.

You are left with the usual negative thoughts about yourself – your "obvious" lack of willpower, your fat thighs, how much you hate yourself and so on. You probably then see yourself as weak and useless and get angry, which rapidly turns inwards into misery, making you long for some comforting chocolate. The trouble is that the original cause of the niggly feeling is still there, unresolved; just temporarily buried under an avalanche of food. This is how bingers use food to try and solve their problems; and then believe their problems are either connected to "food" or "being fat".

Of course what you need to do is identify what is really bothering you and resolve it – instead of looking for food – but life isn't that easy. You can't always link your feelings immediately with what is causing them. All you know is that something is there, giving you a trembly sensation inside, which you interpret as hunger.

Emotional hunger and physical hunger do feel similar. A sensation of emptiness perhaps best describes both. So you eat to fill the void. No one has ever been able to define exactly what hunger is or what it feels like. A binger only knows that she wants to eat – NOW.

Logically, you know that you should only eat in response to genuine physiological hunger rather than as an antidote to anxiety or boredom but, even when you know what the problem is, you may still decide to give in to the urge to eat.

That is why, after a binge – however long it lasts – and especially if it wasn't caused by obvious reasons like the sight or smell of a favourite food – you need to try and figure out what actually made you reach for food in the first instance. Could you have prevented it? Is the same situation likely to recur? Is there a defined series of events or a train of thought that makes Fat-U take over your brain, or was there one particular problem you needed to fix?

If someone upsets you, do you hold back from answering sharply to avoid starting a row? To suppress angry words with food rather than say them and perhaps suffer guilt afterwards is often the cause of compulsive eating. The illogical mind-set that does this figures that you can always get rid of fat but that a rift with family or friends will be harder to handle and could drag on for years. By recognising the triggers that cause a particular binge, you can be prepared if a similar situation arises.

"I'll Start on Monday"

Kathy: "I always start my diets on a Monday. I also persuade myself that to avoid future temptation I have to finish up all the fattening food in the house over the weekend because I am not going to eat any of that stuff any more – from Monday onwards. I conveniently overlook the fact that this will make me 2 lb heavier before I even start!

"Anyway, the last time I did this, I started off OK. I had fruit for breakfast, fruit and yoghurt for lunch, grilled whatever and veg for dinner. That was fine until I took my little girl to a party a few days later. I offered to help with the clearing up. There was just one sandwich left on a plate which I absent-mindedly popped into my mouth. I realised with a jolt that I had now broken my diet and called myself a few names. I decided to start again the next Monday and made that my excuse to have some birthday cake and, on the way home, I stopped off and bought four chocolate éclairs and ate them in the car. Then I just went on eating as if food was going out of style, until the Monday, when I started again."

This way of thinking "I must get rid of all the bad food before Monday" typifies a rigidity of behaviour displayed by most bingers. Then, when it all goes wrong, they usually feel useless and demoralised. You know the pattern by now. "I'll start again on Monday" conjures up such an image of deprivation that they easily rationalise eating frantically until then.

Kathy, and others like her, will have to learn that living slim is a lifestyle, not a defined period of deprivation that starts on a certain day and ends when you reach a particular number on a scale. Otherwise – then what do you do? Get fat again?!

"I Can't Cope"

This often seems to be triggered by one small incident, though it may well be the culmination of a whole series of events. You have a row with your man/mother/ teenager/builder; you get a parking ticket; a burst pipe is dripping through the ceiling and, as a final straw, you cut your finger on a piece of kitchen foil.

You summon up Slim-U who tells you to keep calm and deal with each incident as it arises, reminding you that everyone goes through phases like this from time to time. Unfortunately, Fat-U then takes over and says "Sod that! Eat something; you'll feel better".

Which little voice do you listen to? Yes, I thought so!

"It Wasn't My Fault"

Well, Joan? "It wasn't my fault! I mean it! I was at this dinner party. Some bloke took me and I hadn't met the hostess before. A succession of plates loaded with food arrived in front of me. What was I supposed to do? I didn't want to be rude so I ate it – all of it. I had a second helping of this fabulous white chocolate mousse and demolished the bowl of After Eights with my coffee. It really was not my fault!"

All right, I know. At buffet parties you can pile your plate up with salad and nibble happily all evening and, even in restaurants, you can say a firm NO to dessert knowing that you can't sneak into the kitchen two hours later and polish off anything that's left. At a small dinner party, however, it can be difficult to stick to non-fattening food. You don't want anyone to ask whether you're on a diet, especially if the hostess has obviously gone to a lot of trouble to prepare tasty and unusual food. So you tuck into everything and justify it on the grounds that you can't upset the hostess, you will definitely cut down the next day, and surely one meal won't make any difference. One meal won't but the fact that, when you get home and even though it's 3 a.m., you go into the kitchen and have a cup of tea and a packet of chocolate biscuits because, well, you've "done it now", *does* make a difference! (What do you mean "How do I know you do this?"?)

Paradoxically, a binge can be triggered by just thinking that you have eaten too much. It sounds strange because surely when you are full you shouldn't need to eat any more food. Ah, that's what non-bingers feel. When a binger is extra full, she *feels* fat – even though at that time she might not necessarily *be* fat. Her perception is that feeling empty and hollow equals thin, whilst feeling full and bloated equals fat. So, if she leaves the table feeling even slightly over-full, she can start to think "I've eaten all that; I might as well keep going". That thought is instantly followed by "I'll eat only fruit tomorrow to make up for it". It's as though you are *punishing* yourself for being out of control. Eating is not a criminal offence but you behave as if it were.

"Tomorrow" always starts when you wake up, even if you don't get to bed until 4 a.m.

Was it the taste?

Sometimes just the sight, smell or taste of something can start you off. Maybe you see someone eating something you fancy and suddenly feel ravenous.

One cause of this sort of binge may be a diet that limits you to bland foods like cottage cheese, yoghurt, carrots, salad and apples. This fodder may well satisfy your hunger but your taste buds will rebel. Food with a lot of flavour doesn't have to be fattening. Herbs, for example, can transform a taste while adding almost no calories to a recipe. Everybody needs different flavours – sweet, salty, sour – as well as textures – soft, chewy, crunchy – in order to be fully satisfied by their meals. Taste is important. If you fancy a spicy taste, then even eating something really filling like a whole loaf of bread is unlikely to satisfy you until you get the taste you want. Be aware that depriving yourself of flavour too much can induce a binge when you are faced with food that makes your mouth water.

The other extreme, mixing too many flavours/textures in one meal, can also be detrimental because the taste of the food you are eating is strongly influenced by what you have eaten before it. Your taste buds go into "taste adaptation" when you eat a lot of the same thing. For example, the first bite of cheesecake is amazing but if you had to eat the whole cake you would be pushing it away by the end, pleading that you were full up. This is "sensory specific satiety", meaning that, normally, you will only want to eat so much of one thing in one meal.

However, if you are then offered a different taste and texture from cheesecake – salty cashew nuts? – you could begin eating again as if you were still hungry. That is why on a binge you switch from sweet to savoury and back again. The range of tastes and flavours seems to override your taste adaptation and encourages you to overeat. Bingers, therefore, must not deny themselves all tasty food but, at the same time, need to beware of being led on the rampage with so much choice that they can't resist switching flavours.

The "Association Binge"

Benita: "I was driving along and stopped at some traffic lights. There was a dress shop on the corner and I looked in, remembering I needed a dress for my niece's wedding in a couple of weeks' time. Then I thought 'Oh no, I hope I won't be sitting at the same table as my brother-in-law because the last time we met I had a terrible row with him which left me really shaken up.' As I recalled that incident I suddenly had this vague awareness that I needed something to eat. I don't know why because I wasn't really hungry. I thought 'OK what do you want, a Danish pastry? No, something spicy. A sausage roll, I desperately want a sausage roll'. Isn't that ridiculous? I tried to put it out of my mind but the thought of that soft, flaky pastry and spicy sausage-meat filling was too much – I now felt as if I were starving. I told myself to forget it, especially as I was sticking to my diet really well at the time. Yet, just ten minutes later, I stopped outside a bakery and bought, not one, but six sausage rolls and ate them then and there. Why? Why on earth would I do that? I wasn't even hungry but the craving was so intense, I just HAD to have them."

Once at home, Benita had a drink to wash it all down and chastised herself for being so stupid. Berating yourself like

this feels as compulsory as the initial urge to binge. The next stage, as you know, is the decision "not to eat anything else for the rest of the day", which Benita duly made.

Half an hour later, however, she was opening a packet of crisps and the binge was in full swing. The ritual ended when she woke up the next morning feeling terrible and vowing it would never happen again. She forgot entirely that it was the memory of that row with her brother-in-law that started the whole thing off.

Because that angry incident ended so unsatisfactorily and went unresolved, now, possibly years later, the recollection of the upset had translated itself into a fearsome hunger. It was what we call an "association binge" trigger.

I asked Benita to think back to where she was when this row with her brother-in-law took place, and was not surprised to hear it was at a family Christmas lunch. When I then asked if there were any sausage rolls there at the time, Benita, intrigued, confirmed that there were.

This response becomes more predictable once you understand that almost everything that happens to you is recorded somewhere in your subconscious mind. Your memory often retains not just the words spoken but the whole environment including what you were wearing, who else was there and so on – much like a colourful scene in a play – especially if it's a time or event which really interests and excites you. These become your happy memories. Regrettably, unhappy, painful memories also stick. So when something makes you recall a deeply unpleasant incident, you not only re-experience the original emotional feedback, you probably replay at a subconscious level everything that went with it as well. You are likely to react to it in much the same way you reacted at the time which, in Benita's case, had been to stuff her face with the Christmas sausage rolls!

If Benita couldn't understand her own behaviour, then Jenny was even more puzzled.

Bingeing Out Of Habit

Jenny is a talented actress and supplements her income by after-dinner speaking. Intelligent, witty and amusing, Jenny is much in demand for charity balls or formal company dinners. Jenny, however, is also a self-confessed binger and, whenever she is agitated, will grab at the nearest edible substance to calm her nerves. Unfortunately, her "nerves" as the years progress seem to take longer and longer to calm down and so Jenny's weight soars and dips accordingly.

By cutting out chocolate and biscuits, Jenny has learned to control her weight for much of the time. However, as she confided when she first came to me, "I still fall apart whenever I am due to give another talk".

"I was terrified the first few times I had to stand up in a room full of people", she told me. "It's entirely different from acting on the stage – when you have a script and can immerse yourself in the character. Instead, when you see all those eyes looking at you, expecting to be entertained, it's terrifying. After my first talk, I invited questions from the audience. One of them really threw me. I then found myself contradicting something I had said earlier and bumbling on, talking rubbish, for the rest of the evening. As soon as I left the hall, I made a bee-line for the nearest sweet shop and stuffed my face all the way home.

"My talks regularly dissolved into chaos in the first year but, after that, I got much more confident. My trouble is that, even now, when people have applauded and congratulated me and I know I've done well, I *still* find myself diving into a sweet shop and buying loads of goodies to eat on the way home. Why?"

We worked out that it was little more than a habit. Jenny had programmed her mind over and over again that, after a talk, she should go into a food shop and buy sweet, comforting food. Your "mind" is completely impersonal, as we will discuss in Chapter 7.

This particular corner of Jenny's mind didn't care – despite her improving professionalism – whether a speech went well or not. Her mind only knew that when she left the hall she would go on autopilot into the nearest sweet shop.

To overcome this habitual behaviour, I encouraged Jenny to make herself a little picnic to take on these assignments – for example, a sandwich with a yoghurt, banana, apple and a drink – and leave it in the car. (She had explained how she was always too terrified to eat before she spoke which she believed was probably why she felt so ravenous afterwards.) Having food already prepared in the car meant that Jenny could still indulge her habit but with nourishing food rather than sugary rubbish.

Now Jenny never leaves home for a talk without some sort of snack in her bag and her weight has been stable for over a year.

Think back to your own last binge. What were the "trigger situations" that invited Fat-U into your life at that particular time? What was the first food you stuffed into your mouth? Suppose that food – or, for that matter, any of your personal "trigger" foods – hadn't been there at the time. Would you have binged? Think about it.

3

"I'LL JUST HAVE A LITTLE BIT"

Yes, some people can eat whatever they like and stay slim. You can't. It's not fair. That's right – so what are you going to do about it? You can't change the fact that, if you want to be slim, you will have to say no to the food that makes you fat. No one who endures that struggle to lose weight sets out to put it all back on purpose. However, something always seems to go wrong. You see something you fancy and say to yourself "I'll just have a little bit".

The danger of "just have a little bit" is that the next day you remember the taste and think "well, a little bit won't hurt every now and again". Every now and again becomes every day and, before you know it, you are back into the bingeing pattern that made you fat in the first place.

Past diets have almost certainly instructed you to reduce the number of calories you consumed each day. Does "reducing" your food intake promote a sense of deprivation, even subconsciously? Possibly it does. You were also probably told you should allow yourself a little treat of your favourite food each day. Although this may have worked on some days, on others I expect you found it just made you want to go on eating. Some dieters do not have a binge habit. They can eat a small amount of their favourite food and then stop. This is not the case if you are a binger. You are a compulsive eater and, if you even taste a trigger food, all the old cravings and feelings associated with that food will come back and you will want more. If you haven't been able to control a particular, fattening food in all the years of dieting, you are deluding yourself if you think that you can have "just a little bit". (When, by the way, did you ever have "just a little bit" of *anything*?) That is why you are still struggling.

Trigger foods, trigger behaviours and trigger situations never change. Unless you learn to control them you will not be able to stay slim, whatever your diet. As economist Milton Friedman said in another context: "There is no such thing as a free lunch".

For some bingers, the idea of giving up a certain food is completely alien. They immediately regress to toddler stage: "I want my choccy! Why can't I eat cake?!" The fact that your favourite foods make you fat, listless and prone to bingeing doesn't seem to register. You still believe, like a child, that you can stay slim and yet continue to eat whatever you want. You are so entranced with this stupid food that even LIFE is passing you by.

I repeat, you cannot eat everything and still be slim. Everything you have tried and succeeded in – career, relationships – has taken hard work and compromises in order to achieve your goals. You win some; you lose some. The reality of food is no different. In order to win here, you need to stop resenting adjustments you will have to make if you are to beat your bingeing. Until you take this *first step* you won't achieve permanent weight loss. The mind-set that has for so long fed you the "big lie" that giving up one or two foods means you will be deprived is the real control-freak keeping you fat and in the grip of binge eating. Once you stop being controlled by your trigger foods, you will be free.

You are not deprived. People living on the streets and sleeping in doorways may be deprived. Many children in third world countries are deprived. No one living in any economically sound country is truly deprived – certainly where food is concerned. No one is forcing you to give up anything. Living slim does not mean living without food; it means living without the *one or two* foods that trigger *your* bingeing. You know what they taste like. You have eaten more than enough of them! You also know that they have not been beneficial to your life. You knew when you indulged that they would make you put on weight again. Why else would you have hung on to your "fat" clothes?

Once you can say to yourself "I know I can eat whatever I like but I *choose* not to" you are on the winning track. Rather than wistfully thinking "I'd like to eat this but I can't because I'm on a diet", think positively – "I choose not to eat this because I know it is bad for me". (Fat people say "Cut me a thin slice"; slim people say "No thanks, not for me".)

Eating good food is a pleasurable experience. It is immensely satisfying to sit down for a good meal with your family and friends around you. Food should enhance your life but should never be allowed to *become* your whole life.

Being controlled by food is much the same as being controlled by drugs or alcohol; whereby you may even get shaky and fearful if you can't have it when you "need" it. If you really want to **stop bingeing** and be in control of your life, you have to choose which is the more important to you – slimness or your trigger food – and stick with it.

Taking this *first step* is better than willpower – it's control power. For there will be no more fighting between Fat-U and Slim-U in your head about whether or not to eat one of your trigger foods. The decision is already made – you don't eat it. That's it.

This self-choice is the very opposite of deprivation; it's freedom and, every time you make it, you get stronger and gain more self-control. At the moment you may actually believe, mistakenly, that you can't live without chocolate or whatever but, in a month's time, you will be amazed to see how much better you feel.

As Tara, one of my clients, put it: "I'd tried every other method of losing weight and nothing worked. I hated the thought of giving up my biscuits – that was my teatime treat. The fact that I picked at food from teatime onwards didn't seem to register in my mind – still less that it was the biscuits that started me off. I put off the decision for ages. I kept thinking 'What would I eat at teatime? What would I put out if friends came?' But I was still fat. Finally I thought 'Oh well, I'll try it'. From that moment, I felt lighter and happier, even though I hadn't started yet! I had spent my life worrying about food. Now I was clear about what I could and what I could not eat. There was no longer a struggle every day to try not to eat biscuits because I can eat whatever I want – *except biscuits* – and that's that".

Tara makes the point well. As with many problems, you mull over all the possible solutions and finally choose the most sensible. Having made the choice, the feeling of a weight lifting off your shoulders can be almost palpable because, rightly or wrongly, that is the direction you have chosen and there is no turning back.

Changing a deprivation mind-set is the hardest bit to accept in this programme. I can understand if you are still feeling dubious about what I am saying, but once you put it into practice, I promise you it will all fall into place.

Some people have to abstain from particular foods for

medical reasons; for example because those foods would cause them to go into a coma or die. Some people don't eat certain foods for religious reasons. They don't consider themselves deprived. Just as reformed alcoholics recognise that they can't have one drink, you have to accept that you can't have even a little bit of any of your trigger foods – the ones you can't control.

When you get past the barrier of deprivation-think, you will discover that there is a vast selection of delicious food just waiting for you to try and enjoy. Think of what you CAN eat rather than dwelling on the yucky food that clogs up your life.

Once you eliminate the yuck, the world is your menu. There are no recipes in this book and no calorie-counted portions to measure. On this programme, YOU choose what you are going to eat. All you will lose is weight and your habit of bingeing.

Identifying Your Trigger Foods
I never cease to marvel at the inventiveness of bingers as far as trigger foods are concerned. Benita, whom we met in the last chapter, always starts her binges with a slice of toast on which she spreads mushy banana. She covers this with a thick slice of cheese and tops the lot with butter, before melting the cheese to a gold brown under the grill. After about six of these, interspersed with ice-cold diet(!) fizzy drinks she feels suitably nauseous and is able to stop. Stella, however, prefers a carton of ready-made custard into which she tips a packet of peanuts and raisins before shovelling in the whole lot with a spoon.

Everyone has different food triggers. Some people can avoid nuts at home but will polish off a whole bowl at a party with an alcoholic drink. Sometimes a woman will only eat chocolate before her period but during that time she's unable to stop bingeing on it. Others can eat one slice of toast with marmalade quite happily but, if instead they put cheese or peanut butter on it, they will then eat their way through the whole loaf.

It may be just a type of food, like creamy desserts or "picky" foods that you eat with your fingers, that starts you off. Sweet biscuits, salty crisps or ice cream are other typical culprits. Some clients say to me "With me every food is a trigger food" but you will find that this isn't so. Most bingers can isolate one or two, usually unhealthy, foods, that almost always start them off. If you are overweight, you certainly didn't get that way by eating grilled chicken and broccoli, or fruit and yoghurt. No – you, and nearly everyone else who is struggling with excess pounds, got that way by eating high fat, high sugar, stodgy or creamy foods that are easily available and slip down without you even noticing. You haven't made time for lunch so you grab a couple of Kit Kats and a bag of crisps – which you can eat on the run – without thinking of the consequences. Does that ring a bell with you?

Let's take a look at some of the main trigger foods:

Chocolate

Ah, chocolate! What is in this mysterious, dark, smooth substance that is the cause of so much accumulated flab and the downfall of so many good intentions? Can someone really become a "chocoholic" – unable to get through the day without that magic fix of caffeine, theobromine and phenylethylamine?

Answer: Yes, people can actually become addicted to chocolate. This affliction is more prevalent than you may think, affecting mainly women who, according to psychologists, find the smooth rich texture deeply sensual.

Sensual? Well personally, I don't really get turned on by

a large Curly Wurly but other women I've talked to concur with the psychologists' diagnosis.

The true chocoholic often has an intolerance to either the cocoa, the sugar or the vanilla contained in chocolate. When she digests the chocolate, her body finds that particular substance a threat, so it reacts by producing antibodies to fight against the substance. This sets up the craving cycle: eating chocolate produces antibodies, antibodies circulating in the bloodstream "need" chocolate to work on, so causing a craving; eating more chocolate stimulates more antibodies to be produced; these add to the craving; and so on. As a result, the more chocolate you eat, the more you may crave. This cycle can only be broken by completely cutting out the one substance you crave – chocolate.

This is very difficult for the genuine chocoholic because, as with any addictive substance, there are withdrawal symptoms. The main one in this case is a feeling of lassitude caused by the withdrawal of the stimulants which promote a temporary lift in her mood – temporary, that is, until she notices the physical effect on her thighs.

Phenylethylamine is a chemical similar to the hormone released when you're especially happy or in love. This helps to explain why, when you break off a relationship or have a row with your partner, you may well rush to eat chocolate to compensate. This is also linked with causing migraine headaches in some people – the phenylethylamine, that is, not your partner!

If chocolate is your trigger food you obviously go for a sweet taste. You could substitute dried fruit or those large dates that you can buy loose in most grocers/supermarkets (stored and eaten straight from the freezer, they taste like toffee!) – not as a binge food but as a satisfying alternative when the chocolate craving strikes.

Biscuits

If your hand reaches automatically for the biscuit tin, this
means you tend to go for "picky" foods – anything that can
be picked up with your fingers and transferred straight into
your mouth. Do you find yourself following the waiter
around at wedding receptions pinching all the canapés, or
always "trying" a couple of grapes in Tesco before buying
the bunch? I bet when you take your kids to McDonalds,
you just order a coffee for yourself and then pick at their
fries while they are eating!

If you *must* pick, at least empty out that biscuit tin and
refill it with mini-rice cakes or plain popcorn.

Cakes and Pastries

You might not only have a sweet tooth, you may like your
comfort food to be stodgy as well. With a mouth full of this
sort of food not only do you not have to think, you can't
even talk and, as the food fills you up, you begin to
feel calmer and less frazzled – for a while. Then what? You
need a drink! This makes you feel bloated but strangely
unsatisfied. You are left hungry for more food – but of a different taste. How about – ?

Crisps and Nuts

Some people can ignore sweet food but, once bingers start
picking at nuts, they don't stop until the packet/bowl/house
is empty. Their problem doesn't always stop there. Salty,
crunchy foods like nuts and crisps are high in fat and, like
sugar, tend to hold water in your tissues making you feel full
and bloated. This in turn induces the feeling that you "might
as well go on eating".

Ice Cream

"Why can't I just have a portion?" whinged Joan, a former client; "Why do I always finish the whole blinking pot?" Because, Joan dear, you are a binger and, like most bingers, you eat it straight out of the carton instead of putting a modest portion into a bowl and the rest straight back into the freezer. So, whatever size the carton, you will invariably finish the lot before moving on to something else.

In "bingeitis extremis" ice-cream lovers tend to stock up on such treats as creamy desserts, trifles, sundaes, and ready-made banoffi pie which, again, you eat out of the carton. If ice cream is one of your trigger foods, it should have no place in your freezer. This applies especially to those commercial varieties which are high in sugar and cream.

Instead you should try frozen yoghurt or making your own ice cream. There are several reasonably-priced ice-cream makers on the market and, for example, it doesn't take long to chop up and liquidise a mango, add some plain, low-fat yoghurt and artificial sweetener, and churn them into a delicious ice-cream ready and waiting in the freezer for when that craving strikes. Quicker still – and cheaper – buy some ice-lolly moulds, fill them with your favourite low-fat flavoured yoghurt and bung them in the freezer. An instant binge-saver!

Bread

Bread can be an "anger" food. If you are bursting with rage at someone, it can be deeply satisfying to break off chunks from a crusty French loaf and stuff them into your mouth. "I'll show him!" you think, chewing furiously; "Just wait till I've finished this loaf – then see how he feels". (!) Bread is usually accompanied by butter – which goes nicely with cheese – which needs some crisps to go with it, and so on. If bread is a problem for you, take a look at how much you eat during the day. Is it toast for breakfast, a sandwich for lunch and a roll with your evening meal? If so, you probably believe there is no way to eliminate this trigger food from your life. One practical answer is to switch to cereal for breakfast and increase your intake of protein at other meals. Most bread bingers are amazed at the change in their shape and energy levels once they have eliminated this allegedly staple food.

Wheat Products

Many people now avoid all wheat products, including cereals and pasta, either as a way to lose weight or because they have decided they are suffering from an allergic reaction. This approach is heavily promoted by some alternative therapists and nutritionists as a way to overcome bloating, constipation or diarrhoea, aching joints and skin eruptions. If you lose a bit of weight as well, then they can claim the credit too, and that's fine.

There is little scientific evidence backing these theories. Nor is there much proof available for many of the other "fashionable" food intolerances, such as those to meat or milk – unlike the well-established dangers encountered by some people when eating shellfish or peanuts, which can cause immediate and dangerous allergic reactions. If you believe you may have an allergy caused by any particular food, talk to your doctor.

One good way to find out if you truly are allergic to wheat is to cut out starchy carbohydrates like bread, pasta and flour-based products for a couple of months. Just live on meat, fish, fruit and vegetables and see if you feel better. You will certainly lose weight!

Chips

"I just can't resist a plate of chips" sighed Bobbie. "They are so picky; you just pop one in your mouth and then you have to have another one." No you don't Bobbie! You sling out the chip-pan at home; you don't order them in restaurants; and it's "Goodbye Mr. Chips".

Chip bingers also tend to go for other high-fat foods like fried fish or chicken, roast potatoes, spare ribs and oily salad dressings. They seem to enjoy the greasy taste and texture in their mouths. Unfortunately, the fat you eat is the fat you wear. Believe it! Obvious substitutes are baked potatoes and grilled fish or chicken. Boring! Listen – don't shoot the messenger here!

Pizza

Perhaps even more than a fry-up, pizza is the one food that seems to "start people off". Most often it is quoted by the same people who opt for bread when the going gets tough. That doughy, cheesy taste is satisfying and filling but, soon afterwards – they say – you definitely "need" something sweet. Fortunately this one is easy to avoid by simply not ordering pizza as a takeaway and avoiding the places which serve it. If pizza triggers your binges then you can live with every other food – except pizza. It's your choice.

Alcohol

Uh-oh! It's strange how many slimmers "forget" to include alcoholic drinks when calculating their daily calorie totals. Maybe because plain tea, coffee and water don't have any calories, they naturally assume that all liquids just slip down accordingly and don't count. Wrong! Ounce for ounce, alcohol has more calories than either carbohydrates or protein and contains nearly as many as fat.

I'm sure you have read that small amounts of alcohol are good for you. Moderate drinkers have been found to have higher levels of protective proteins in their blood than non-drinkers. These proteins are believed to help prevent the accumulation of fatty deposits in the arteries, so heading off the risk of heart attacks. It is also possible that moderate doses of alcohol relieve stress and relax the muscles. However, as with all aspects of nutrition, just because a little of something may be good for you, it doesn't follow that more will be better.

Alcohol carries an added danger for bingers because when the "reasoning" part of your brain is also relaxed, you eye your trigger foods – nuts? – crisps? – and think "Oh, sod it! I'll start dieting again tomorrow." If that has happened to you before, it will happen again . . .

Dairy Products

Like some of the anti-wheat "propaganda", cutting out all dairy products has become fashionable as a method of weight loss under the guise of food intolerance. If butter, cheese or ice cream are your trigger foods, then indeed they should have no place in your life. However, skimmed milk, low-fat yoghurt and fat-free fromage frais are excellent sources of calcium and other minerals so, unless you are genuinely lactose-intolerant, it is not necessary to cut out dairy products.

Your Special Enemy – SUGAR

How do you produce an addictive substance? You take the juice of a poppy and refine it into opium; then you refine this, first to morphine and, finally, to a strange white powder called heroin.

How do you make another apparently addictive substance? You take the juice of a cane and refine it to molasses; then you refine it, first to brown crystals and, finally, to strange white crystals called sugar.

I have put sugar (i.e. refined sugar) under a separate heading because, for many people, sugary food is the prelude to a binge. In this sense, I liken sugar to a narcotic drug, one on which you can get hooked, and which has damaging side effects. Besides the obviously sweet, prepared/manufactured foods like biscuits, cakes, chocolates, sweets, jam, jelly and ice-cream, you will find that there is refined sugar in mayonnaise, tomato ketchup, cereals, drinks, tinned fruit, baked beans, and even stock cubes.

Sometimes, sugar is put on labels under different names, so watch out for all those words ending in "-ose": glucose, sucrose, fructose, lactose, maltose, Waitrose, Tescos – all full of sugar!

Also watch out for honey, maple syrup, raw sugar, muscovado sugar, molasses – the list is endless. However, the consumption of *natural* sugars, in moderate quantities, is a very different matter from eating large amounts of refined sugar. For example, fructose in a piece of fruit, or lactose in a portion of milk pudding, is not likely to be "addictive" or make you fat. Likewise, the small amounts of sugar in tomato ketchup or mayonnaise are unlikely to cause you to finish the whole bottle!

Refined sugar contains neither vitamins nor minerals. It is practically pure carbohydrate, good for immediate energy but easily consumed in excess and lacking the fibre and valuable nutrients contained in natural sugars.

Refined sugar quickly leads to putting weight on because you rarely eat the stuff by itself. It is usually eaten in the form of tempting cakes, chocolate bars or pastry which all already contain a lot of fat – a substance which, as you know, is another concentrated form of calories.

When you are hungry and eat, say, a bar of chocolate, the sugar is absorbed almost immediately into your bloodstream. This causes your blood sugar level to shoot up rapidly. In turn your pancreas produces the hormone insulin to clear the sugar from your blood and deliver it to the body cells. There it is used for energy; however, when the cells are full up, the excess is *converted into fat*.

Unfortunately, the large amount of refined sugar in the chocolate causes your blood sugar level to shoot up so quickly that your pancreas tends to secrete too much insulin. The result is that, later on, your blood sugar level plummets below where it was initially, causing a feeling of intense hunger and a craving for – you've guessed it – more sugar to mop up the unused insulin.

That is why insulin should be regarded both as a HUNGER HORMONE and a FAT STORING HORMONE. Look at it this way: if your diet is high in foods containing refined sugar and which therefore cause your body to over-secrete insulin, you may just be programming yourself to feel hungry most of the time. Does this ring a bell?

Although there is no scientific evidence that sugar is actually an addictive substance, many of my clients have confided that, after indulging in sugar, they often feel down in the dumps and ratty. Is it the realisation that they have "broken their diet" that is making them feel that way, or the refined sugar that is causing their brain chemistry to produce a lethargic, grumpy state?

Your body is not designed to handle large amounts of sugar in concentrated form. Natural carbohydrates like those found in oats, wholemeal bread, fruit and vegetables take ages to be absorbed into your blood-stream, giving your pancreas a chance to secrete just the right amount of insulin to maintain your correct blood sugar level, without the violent swings caused by refined sugar.

Incidentally, the only one of the "-ose" ending sweeteners that doesn't demand insulin is fructose, the natural sugar found in fruit; this is metabolised straight into the liver and body cells without the use of insulin.

By now I hope you can see why refined sugar is your enemy. In excess it makes you hungry and fat, causes dental decay and is possibly contributing to "pulling you down". As refined sugar is a number one trigger, either in the form of chocolate, cake, biscuits, desserts or alcohol, how do you give it up? Well, although it does mean giving up all foods that contain it to excess, like the aforementioned, it doesn't mean having to give up sweet food altogether. Bananas and small amounts of dried fruit like raisins and apricots can substitute for biscuits. Artificial sweeteners used in moderation are also acceptable and nowadays you can buy a wonderful selection of cakes and sweets made for diabetics which taste exactly the same as the "real" thing. Because these are sweetened with Sorbitol instead of sugar, they won't produce the over-secretion of insulin that makes you want more and more. Indeed, if you eat too much Sorbitol, you will get galloping diarrhoea – which is another deterrent to overeating!

Many of my clients who have succeeded in eliminating sugar from their lives have been amazed at the difference it has made. Beyond losing weight, those who had suffered from premenstrual tension, haemorrhoids, continually feeling off-colour and having permanently puffy eyes, reported a tremendous improvement in these other departments. Some menopausal women who felt wretched because of hot flushes and night-time sweats noticed a reduction, and sometimes a complete cessation, of these symptoms. I am not suggesting refined sugar necessarily directly causes these symptoms but, if you suffer from any of the above, it may not be a bad idea to try cutting out sugar.

I have found with former clients that it usually takes three weeks to get used to living without refined sugar – that is twenty-one consecutive days. When people express reservations about this, I suggest setting aside one month as an experiment to see how they get on. That is just long enough to see if it makes a difference. If you really don't feel measurably better after that time, then you can choose where you want to go from there, and maybe just narrow it down to eliminating one or two main, sugary culprits. Those of my clients who chose to go back to eating high refined sugar content foods, however, almost without exception found that they felt so bloated, lumpy and revolting that, eventually – after one or two false starts – they soon cut refined sugar completely from their lives.

If you do have a problem with sugary food and think you can't live without it, then listen to an old client of mine, Angie:

"I was the biggest sugar 'addict' of all time. I could quite happily put away three or four large bars of chocolate during one evening's tele-viewing – in fact, people thought I was being sponsored by Cadbury's! I would buy half a pound of those fancy, cream-filled Belgian chocolates and eat them in one go. I got fat – miserable – dieted – got less fat – happier – ate junk again – got fat – irritable – fed up – and so on. I listened to all the 'blah' about giving up your trigger foods and thought 'can you just imagine me living without sugar? – I'd die!' However, after one horrendous night when I woke up at 3 a.m. in the morning and was actually sick, I thought, 'This is ridiculous. I am going to stop eating this stuff. I am fed up with my whole life being ruled by sugar.' So I stopped. I slung out all the sweets and chocolates and started reading all my packaged food labels more carefully. I won't say it was easy. In fact, it's much the same as giving up smoking – and worse really – because you don't have to smoke but you do have to eat. I still had violent cravings for a sweet, comforting taste, especially before my period. However, I would eat a whole box of dates instead and this seemed to do the trick. I soon cut this down to half a box – and then to just a couple of dates if I felt peckish. I have lost over two stone and have a lot more energy, which is strange, because I used to believe that sugar gave you energy. I realise now that when you stuff down loads of refined sugar the effect is just the opposite – it makes you tired and lethargic. I don't say I will never eat sugar again but, now I know what it does to me, I will certainly do my utmost to avoid it".

In spite of the fashionable fad of cutting out a variety of foods as a method of weight loss (have you tried organising a dinner party lately?!), it is not necessary to eliminate all the foods you enjoy to live healthily – only the one or two that trigger your binges and send you spinning out of control.

So, have you identified your trigger foods yet? The best

way to do this is to write down all your favourite foods and then see if they fall into a specific category:

Sweet foods: chocolate, biscuits, sweets, cake.
Creamy foods: ice cream, butter, cream cakes, desserts.
"Picky" foods: anything that you eat with your fingers.
Salty foods: crisps, nuts, chips, bacon.
Fatty foods: *fried* chicken/fish, *roast* potatoes, spare ribs.
Stodgy foods: bread, pasta, pizza, steamed puddings.

Then check which one you turn to first when your brain clicks into binge-mode: "I must eat something". If you share a common binger's habit, that of categorising food into "fattening" and "slimming", you will recognise your trigger foods as ones you try to give up when you are on a diet – and ones you have definitely been scoffing when you gain back the weight. Bingers tend to have an "all or nothing" mentality. For example, once you start eating "junk food", you tend to pick at that all day and then don't have room or appetite for healthy food at proper mealtimes.

Have you decided? Good. Now think about this food. You like it but it does not like you. It makes you fat, sluggish, erodes your self-esteem and makes you binge. This food is your enemy. It is not a treat, your "afternoon snack", a reward, or a comfort; it – or they – are all your enemies. You do not need them in your life. If you can't moderate your intake, you must eliminate them. When you remove the trigger you remove the binge.

Banish today the thought, "Does this mean I can never have chocolate/crisps/cream cakes for the rest of my life?" Today is not the rest of your life. It's just today. You are not going to eat that stuff today. You can only live one day at a time. When tomorrow comes you will decide what you are going to eat then. Don't glamorise any of your trigger foods in your mind with – "I'll miss you, my choccy, my friend"

– sort of thing. Chocolate is not your friend; it is only a lump of fat. Either walk away from it or – if you really must – eat it with the full knowledge that you will be wearing it the following day. Whatever your decision, take responsibility for it and don't blame your diet, your recent parking ticket or mother-in-law. It is your choice every time. The only power food has over you is the power you give it.

4

LET'S START

Step One – When to Begin
The start point of your new programme needs to be chosen
very carefully. This does not mean having yet another "last
supper" on the premise that you "start tomorrow". You
usually feel so awful the day after a massive binge that, by
mid-morning, you will be convinced you "need" to put
something bulky into your stomach to quell that sick, empty
feeling – rather like an alcoholic believes he "needs" a drop
of whisky to relieve a hangover. You should not begin this
programme until you are really strongly motivated to do so
and, preferably, not until you have read this book all the way
through.

Monday, or the first of a month, may be a good chrono-
logical start point but, if you are in the middle of a divorce,
house move, or some other stressful situation, it won't work.
Doing three days and failing yet again is worse than putting
it off for another couple of weeks until you are absolutely
ready. Most women overeat when under stress, and it's hard

enough to change established habits. So, if you plan to give up smoking as well, do one or the other but not both at the same time!

Do not start if you have a lot of social engagements coming up in the near future, especially if they involve food and/or alcohol. You will learn how to deal with all that when you are well established in your new regime but, at the beginning, you are more likely to find such occasions become excuses to slip back and binge.

Similarly, don't plan a dieting regime for a specific event such as a wedding or a holiday. You are unlikely to get a permanent result because, once that event has taken place, your commitment will falter and you are highly likely to go back to your old bingeing habits.

Ask yourself if you are really motivated NOW.

Think about bingeing and starving and the see-saw of misery this entails. Think about your three sets of clothes.

Then think about being at a weight that is right for you all the time. Imagine eating food that you enjoy and not having that daily mental tussle over any of your trigger foods. Imagine *being in control* of your eating and feeling good about yourself. Surely that is what you deserve!

However, this is a commitment that only you can make and, if you are not ready to make it right now, it doesn't matter – leave it for a while until you are. (Do be honest with yourself though, so that "waiting" doesn't turn into "never".)

Step Two – Pinning Down Your Trigger Foods
By now you should have a pretty good idea of your main trigger foods. Yes, that's one culprit: that tin, full of innocent-looking biscuits, colourful, foil-wrapped choc-bars, and shiny crisp packets – those reservoirs of fat that

have been messing up your life for years! All of these are out – from NOW.

Please go through your cupboards and sling out anything that has triggered a binge in the past. Be ruthless. If biscuits are your downfall and you keep a supply in case friends pop in, throw them out; then stock up on any brands you don't like. Explain to your children that, from now on, they must buy their own sweets and keep them safely out of your reach. (I've heard how you raid the sweetie-tin and then rush out and replace everything before they get home from school!)

If you think that giving up access to your favourite foods will force you back into binge mode you are mistaken. Bingeing depends absolutely on availability. Without that, cravings will subside. If you allow yourself to have trigger foods in the house you can almost guarantee that, one day, you will binge on them. Get rid of them.

Step Three – Decide Your Goal Weight

Women tend to put on weight in a predetermined manner. The usual pattern starts with fat settling around the tops of your thighs; then it quickly adds on your hips and tummy. Your face takes on that podgy look, your midriff swells into that elegant spare tyre, and finally the tops of your arms get flabby and you start to slop delightfully out of the top of your bra.

You lose weight in reverse order. People will remark how thin your face looks before registering that you still have a hefty layer of fat round your nether regions. This is because hips and thighs contain the most fat cells, so they are normally the first places to store extra fat as well as the last to give it up.

Do not think of yourself as over-weight – when, really, you are over-fat! You need to reduce the amount of fat in your body to acquire the slim look you desire. However, you must accept that women need a certain amount of fat in their bodies both to balance their sex hormones and to protect internal organs, especially those connected with child-bearing. So, if you want to have children, you must avoid becoming too thin – although one of my clients, struggling with three argumentative teenagers, once let slip that, had she known there was a choice, she would have settled for thin any day!

Some people presume they are overweight only because of their jeans – er, genes. Their parents are fat so they assume the condition is hereditary. While some families may be predisposed to gain weight more quickly than others, it is debatable whether this is genetic or environmental. Are you fat because your mother is fat or does the whole family exist on junk food and have an aversion to exercise? Although you may not be able to change your inheritance cards, you can almost certainly adjust your lifestyle to prevent yourself becoming permanently fat.

Genes, however, do play a major role in determining your shape and size, controlling, for example, how much fat you store easily and where on your body it's distributed. If you have a broad back and big boobs, you will always look fairly hefty above the waist. If your hip bones are wide, then have loads of children but don't expect slinky, narrow hips. You can also blame just being female for the "cellulite" on your thighs and bum.

Let's talk about cellulite. The word was actually invented by the French so they could sell their yucky creams which claim to get rid of it. Of course these don't work or every-one would be slim and smooth – even you – and most women's magazines would have to go back to writing about flower arranging and knit-your-own condoms.

You may have read claims that the fat round your thighs and bottom is different from ordinary fat, or a result of bad circulation whereby toxins get trapped in this area so that dieting alone does not have any affect.

These assertions are not entirely true. Some women do have an excess of fat that is notoriously hard to shift but the fat on your bottom is simply that – the fat on your bottom. It is the same fat which covers the rest of your body to one degree or another.

The British Nutrition Foundation analysed cells from the areas where women complained of dimpled skin, and cells from the arm where the skin was smooth. They found no difference at all in composition. The fat is simply denser in some areas so it *appears* different, feeling more lumpy and looking dimpled in what is popularly known as the "orange peel" effect.

This fat is not full of toxins – what a preposterous idea! As any doctor would tell you, poisons in such concentration would more likely prove fatal than encourage fat deposits.

"How can I get rid of cellulite?" is one of the most frequent questions I am asked. The answer is: you can't. You can massage it, pummel it, wrap it in tight bandages, and plaster it with mud, wax, seaweed and day-old rice pudding – none of this will make the slightest difference. Neither will muscle stimulation pads or horrid little machines grinding into your flesh. Lots of people, presumably with the requisite number of brain cells, lay out dollops of hard-earned cash for creams or gels that promise to disperse cellulite. Where these products part with reality is that, whereas they are suggesting ways of making the skin appear *less lumpy*, the consumer wants help in making the same area *slimmer*. I assure you, any cream that could dissolve cellulite would have to dissolve the skin first.

Just remember that news travels fast, so, if by the remotest chance any of these anti-cellulite treatments really worked, then *nobody would have any cellulite*. But they have. It's yours – learn to love it.

When you start your programme with this book, it is essential to aim at a realistic target. Consider how, as your weight has gone up and down over the years coinciding with your binges and diets, your shape has always swelled and retreated in the same places. I am sure you know your own body pattern very well in this regard! You must recognise that even if your body shape is never going to be as perfect as you'd like, there has to be a point in your fat/slim spectrum at which you can be reasonable happy.

This point hopefully should coincide with a certain number on the scales – your magical "goal weight" – which you are determined to reach come hell or high water. If you already have such a figure in mind, is it feasible? Do take into account that you may have to re-evaluate your target if you have tried for several years without actually reaching that number. An unachievable target can only be counter-productive. It is equally pointless trying to get your weight too low if you can't maintain it at that level. There just aren't enough magazines for us all to be on the covers!

Since how you look is the most important thing, why not dispense with the scales altogether and just go for a certain measurement? For example, if you are happy with your hips measuring 36-38 inches, which will ensure you can fit into a size 10 or 12, then aim for that, rather than getting frustrated if the scales won't drop below a certain number.

A perfect body doesn't guarantee a perfect life. If you have such an impossible goal you will always find something about your body to dislike. Be honest: if the scales habit is permanently ingrained, choose a realistic, desirable and appropriate weight and be prepared to fluctuate two or three pounds either side of that figure. Then forget about it. Once you are in control instead of being controlled by your food, you will reach your natural goal weight automatically.

All you have to do is relax and get on with your (binge-free) life.

Step Four – When You Eat

When you go for long periods of time without eating or on a very low calorie "fad" diet, your metabolism slows dramatically. Your metabolic rate is the rate at which your body processes food and converts it into the fuel that allows you to run up the stairs or push a trolley round the supermarket. Each person has a *basal* metabolic rate. This is the measure of how many calories your body needs in order to maintain its vital functions when you are doing nothing.

You use energy (calories) all the time, even when you are sleeping, to keep your body functioning, your lungs expanding and contracting when you breathe, your heart beating, your blood circulating and your body warm. Known as thermogenesis, the average woman uses about 1,500 calories a day just to exist.

Your whole being is programmed for survival. Thousands of years ago, long-term food shortages were the norm, so the body learned to conserve its fat stores to stop us humans all starving to death. It did this by slowing the metabolic rate to conserve energy. This "learned" reaction, stored in genes down the generations, resurfaces at once when you drastically reduce your calorie intake. Your body doesn't realise that you are doing this on purpose or that the local supermarket is just round the corner; it just assumes you might starve to death, so it acts to save you – by slowing your metabolism to conserve existing fat. After all, fat is just stored energy.

If your metabolic rate is working efficiently and you are eating enough of the right kinds of food, you will burn up that fuel fairly quickly. If you have a slow metabolic rate from reducing calories too much, you won't have much energy. What's more, if much of what you do eat contains too much fat and refined sugar, even this won't get burned up properly, and what is left over will find its way to be stored in your fat cells.

It makes sense then, to increase your metabolic rate so that everything you eat gets burned up as quickly as possible and preferably before it gets converted into fat.

One way to do this is by eating. This may sound ridiculous when you are trying to lose weight, but the very fact of eating raises your metabolism to deal with the digestion and processing of the food. Therefore *when* you eat is just as important as *what* you eat.

To keep your metabolic rate high you should eat lots of little meals throughout the day instead of ignoring food during the day and eating a whacking great meal in the evening.

This means eating by the clock and not letting more than two to three hours go by without putting some food in your mouth, whether you are hungry or not.

I get looks of disbelief from some clients at this statement.

"What's the point of eating when you are not hungry?" they demand. Some say "I'm far too busy to think about food during the day and, apart from a light breakfast, I don't eat anything until the evening". (Then as far as I can make out, they continue eating until bed time!)

For non-bingers there is less point in eating by the clock because they are in control. When non-bingers are hungry they have something to eat. When bingers feel hungry they don't always know whether it is genuine or not, because they tend to have lost the capacity to recognise what the physical sensation of real hunger feels like.

The part of your brain that detects hunger is called the hypothalamus. This "reports" hunger signals from your body when you need food. After eating, the hypothalamus soon withdraws these "reports" and you stop eating. Well,

most people do. You may have been abusing your hypothalamus for so long that it doesn't know what the hell it is
doing any more!

The hypothalamus works by determining the amount of
glucose (blood sugar) in your blood. If the level goes too
low, you feel tired and hungry. When you push the glucose
level too high, the excess gets converted into fat. Excessive
periods without food will make the level drop, and the
bingeing that so often follows will inevitably put on layers
of fat. Eating small amounts of food every couple of hours,
however, will enable you to balance your glucose level so
that you don't get excessively hungry and will also give you
enough energy to keep you going throughout the day.

You can still think along the lines of breakfast, lunch and
dinner; however, add at least two snacks in between and perhaps a slice of toast last thing at night. Going to bed hungry
does not encourage sleep and you are likely to be found in
the kitchen at 3.30 a.m. with the biscuit tin and the daily
crossword in front of you.

Going without food for long periods in order to lose
weight really is self-defeating. It used to be thought that the
metabolism only slowed down after stringent dieting over
several days but we now know that this happens after several hours without eating. Therefore, the common ploy of
cutting out lunch in the belief you will lose weight only
initiates your fat-storing mechanisms to go into overdrive
and to hang on to that fat for dear life.

When you do eventually get to that main meal in the
evening, you will store even more than if you had eaten
something at lunch-time, because your metabolism is still
working at the slower rate. You will also probably eat far
more than you "need".

To illustrate this, let's assume you are overweight with an
abundance of fat round your hips and tummy. We'll call it
your "bulge" for want of a better word. When you

"overeat", which means consuming more calories at one meal than your body needs to function for the time being, your body uses the amount of calories that it needs, and shunts the rest off towards your bulge. Once happily stored there as fat, this resource will stay, to be conserved for use later, very reluctantly, when needed. It makes sense therefore, to circumvent this reactive body mechanism by eating little and often. In this way the small amount of food that you eat gets utilised straightaway by your body and there should be nothing left over to add to your bulge. In fact, your body should gradually begin to draw some energy from those reserves of fat you are going to lose.

By eating this way, you are training your body to burn food rather than to store it as fat. When you recognise that your stomach is about the size of your own clenched fist, you can see that it isn't designed to take in a large amount of food at one sitting. It much prefers smaller, well chosen "meals" at frequent intervals during the day.

Therefore, you must accept that, if you want to lose weight and stop bingeing, you have to EAT. This can be a daunting prospect for many women who have been struggling NOT to eat for most of their lives. You should eat every 2 – 3 hours all through the day. This means that, when you have finished a meal, you look at the clock and count forward two and a half hours; so that you know your next meal is scheduled for any time during the half hour following.

Eating *by the clock* will stop you feeling hungry, keep you calm and eliminate the need to binge. The discipline will also keep your metabolism high and prevent fat storage. Think of food as fuel, and your body as a very effective furnace burning up all that fuel during the day. If you let the furnace go cold, it takes ages to heat up again and burn at its top rate. Eating moderately at regular intervals will provide the energy for your body to function and stay healthy whilst gradually lowering the amount of fat kept in store.

This is why breakfast is so important. During the night your metabolism slows right down. If you don't give it a kick-start with some food in the morning, it will remain ticking over at the slower pace until you do eat.

If you feel you can't face food first thing in the morning, that's OK. A drink will suffice and, even if you have your first solid food at around 11 o'clock (as long as it isn't a large Danish pastry!), you can still call that breakfast and carry on every 2-3 hours after that. As long as you are eating regularly throughout the day, it doesn't matter what time you start, assuming it's not too late into the day.

The overall *amount* you choose to eat at each meal is important, more so than *what* you eat because, if your body needs the calories, it will use them, whether you eat lettuce or cake. Anything not needed will get stored in your bulge, so even so-called "healthy" food can become fattening if you eat too much of it. Obviously though, you could eat mountains more lettuce before experiencing weight gain than you could eat cake. Your metabolic rate is not directly influenced by the amount of food you eat so, even eating a little bit – two crispbreads or an apple – will show a measurable increase in energy expenditure.

Eating little and often is known in America as "grazing". For you, grazing *small* quantities of food is the best way to control your appetite and break the destructive bingeing habit. Knowing that you are going to eat again anyway in an hour's time also deflates the binge-urge to cram in as much as you can now.

Calories

I find a lot of slimmers permanently stuck in "calorie-mode". Whilst you do need to be aware of the calorie content of the food that you eat, this doesn't mean that you have to weigh your food and count calories for the rest of your life. If you know that a medium apple is about 50 calories and a mere ounce of butter is 210, you don't have to be a genius to realise that if you eat more apples and less butter, you will lose weight. Calories are always approximate anyway. You can never work out exactly, to the last calorie, how many you eat in a day; neither can they give you information on the percentages of fat, protein or carbohydrate. For example, a 500-calorie meal consisting of chicken, potatoes and broccoli provides you with a much better nutritional balance than a 500-calorie meal consisting of almost entirely protein, like a large steak. For this reason it is better not to rely solely on calorie-counting.

Nonetheless, having a calorie awareness in your head should be like knowing your multiplication tables. Once you know which are the most calorific foods you can apply sensible eating habits automatically.

For a binger, living slim is definitely not just about calories; it is about being in control. It doesn't matter how many calories are in one chip; what does count is how many chips you eat. If crisps are your trigger food, there is no point buying a packet of half-fat crisps just because they contain fewer calories than normal ones. Eating them will simply start you off on a binge of ten more packets.

Step Five – Food Diary
Another reason calorie-counting is ineffectual is because so many people are sabotaged by the hidden calories they forget to convert, such as those unconsciously swallowed when:

• Licking the lid of the yoghurt after opening it for your child

- Nibbling the rest of the lamb chop left by your husband

- Eating the bit of broken biscuit that fell on the floor

- Eating the bit of broken biscuit that didn't fall on the floor

- Popping into your mouth any crumbs of cheese stuck to the grater

- Licking the wooden spoon after pouring cheese sauce –

- Then scraping out the saucepan

- Picking off the crusty bits from round the edges of a pie-dish – and so on.

To promote awareness of these habits, the dietary special-ists who run obesity clinics use a technique called "behaviour modification". Their methods work on the premise that you often eat without realising it, and that becoming *aware* of your eating patterns can help you to change them and establish new and healthier habits.

They ask you to keep a specialised food diary. You must write down not only what you have eaten, but how much of it, in which room you ate it, with whom, how you felt at the time, how hungry you were on a scale from 1-10, what you were doing (e.g. watching television) and whether it was a planned mealtime or a snack. Whew! I happen to think that to accomplish this you would either have to give up your job or put your children on "hold" because you wouldn't have time to do anything else!

However, I do support keeping a modified food diary for a while – simply noting down what you eat and at what time. This gives you an insight into just how much more you put into your mouth daily than you may have been aware – information which can act as an important binge deterrent.

For example, if you were about to eat a Haagen Dazs double chocolate almond and toffee ripple ice-cream, you would possibly think twice about so doing because:

1. You couldn't be bothered to write it in your diary, and
2. You don't know how to spell Haagen Dazs.

On the other hand, I fear that, were you to be in "bingitis extremis" at the time, you might first eat the ice cream, then neglect to write it down, and finally abandon the whole idea of keeping the food diary. I have known this happen!

Usually though, a diary works very well, especially if you know that you only have to do it for a limited time.

The initial stages of a new eating regime are the most difficult. It is probably fair to say that it takes three weeks – twenty-one consecutive days – to get into any new pattern, be it giving up smoking, drinking or whatever. Your body seems to need that time to adjust. After that it gets progressively easier. By writing everything down you are focusing your mind on the project in hand, and from now on this has to be the priority in your life.

So next time you go out, please buy a notebook. In it you are going to record everything that you eat and drink for one week. Don't think of yourself as being on a diet during this time. Don't specially change the way that you eat. Just write it down and note the time beside each entry. To do this you will have to keep your notebook with you when you go to work and keep it in the kitchen when you are at home. Write down what you eat immediately or you will forget. If you try and do it at the end of the day, you are bound to leave out the grapes you nicked from that bunch on your colleague's desk while you waited for her to get off the phone, as well as the cheesy puff you found under the magazine on the coffee table . . .

After one week, review what you have written. Strangely

enough, most of my new clients find that they lose a couple of pounds just doing this, even though I tell them not to change their normal eating habits. What I want you to discover is your individual eating pattern – what you eat and when you eat it. This is food awareness.

For example, do you have breakfast? When are the "extra hungry" times when you need something, either to boost your energy or calm you down? Do you eat the same foods most days? Are you eating too much junk food like choc bars and takeaways? Is most of your food processed or do you cook from scratch? Do you eat any fresh vegetables or fruit at all?

Your diary of your "food week" will help you judge what you need to change to ensure you are eating in the best possible way. Please try and overcome any resistance to doing this – that "Oh I can't be bothered with this" feeling – because this is the start of changing your life for the better. Bingeing usually follows a pattern. If you can learn from your past behaviour, you can learn to overcome clear personal pitfalls and be in permanent control. Prevention is the cure for bingeing. The key to it lies not so much in the precise foods that you eat but in understanding the effect those foods have on you. You are trying to discover which foods work for you and which send you spinning out of control.

After the first week, decide whether you feel up to doing something similar to this for another six weeks. Yes! I am, now, asking you to consider treating this as a six-week project that you must complete as an essential element of your strategy of living slim and binge-free. Once you've done the first week you'll see it's not such a drag after all.

However, from week 2 onward, I suggest you keep your diary in a slightly different way. I would like you to decide what you are going to eat each day and write it all down *before* the day starts. Then you can tick off each item as you come to it. This means thinking much further ahead and planning your meals and snacks beforehand, rather than suddenly realising "I'm hungry" or "It's lunch-time, what shall I eat?"

Planning ahead and having the right food to hand stops you picking up whatever is easily available at the local fast food outlet and which may not be as healthy as you'd like.

All this planning might sound obsessive to anyone who is not a binger, but you are – and this is the next step to being in control of what you eat.

Write down everything you will eat/drink each day, always keeping at least one day ahead of yourself. If you are going to be eating out, you generally have a rough idea of the sort of restaurant you are going to and what you will order. You can pencil in a good guess and change it afterwards if necessary. If visiting friends this is more difficult but you can be careful what you eat there and jot it down later.

With most people, individual day-to-day food habits are roughly the same – give or take the odd sandwich filling. The writing down process also helps you plan for those difficult times during the day, for example between 4 and 5 o'clock when you may well be more likely to eat a trigger food, not least because it is perhaps the only type of food available. You can organise to take a healthy snack with you for that time, which can avert many a potential bingeing disaster.

Don't become too obsessed with sticking "to the letter" of your diary. Otherwise the slightest slippage could become an excuse to indulge in a classic binge. Your diary is merely a food list, not the holy gospel. If someone offers you a drink that is not on your agenda for that day, accept it if you want to, and write it down later. As long as you stayed in control, you can still put a huge tick through the whole page at the end of the day.

Step Six – Exercise

Being in control of your eating, reducing your fat intake and
eating small amounts of food at regular intervals will prevent your body from storing fat. To ensure that your existing
fat is effectively released from your fat cells and to encourage your body to get used to burning fat, you also need
regular aerobic exercise to help to tone your muscles so that
you have the correct ratio of fat to muscle. I don't mean you
should turn into one of those body builders you see on television, covered with Mazola; it's just that strong, toned
muscles, as opposed to weak, flabby muscles, give you a
much better shape. How you look is more important than
what you weigh. Slim and firm is in; waif-like – or podgy –
is out.

There, I've said it – the dreaded "E" word. Well?

"I haven't got time to exercise."	(You've got time to watch *Eastenders*.)
"I'm exhausted by the time I get home."	(Good Morniiiiing!!)
"I'm much too fat to get into a leotard."	(What's wrong with leggings and a T-shirt?)
"I tried a class once and I was so stiff the next day I couldn't even sit on the loo!"	(No one told you to overdo it.)
"I don't understand 'Aerobic-Speak'. What's a 'grapefruit'?"	(You mean a 'grapevine – it's a simple dance step.)
"I wouldn't want to get too thin."	(Dream on, Sweetheart!)
"I run around after the kids all day – that's enough."	(No it isn't.)
"Who wants to get all hot and sweaty?"	(Who said you had to?)
"My hair will go all frizzy."	(Oh, we can't have that now, can we?)

"Wouldn't it make me even
more hungry?" (No.)
"I haven't got the energy." (That's because you don't
exercise.)

"I don't want to build
bulgy muscles; I'm not Arnold
Schwarzen-whatsisname!" (Too right!)
"I've got a bad arm."
"I've got a bad back."
"I've got a bad leg." (Oh shut up! Anything
else . . . ???)

"Do I *have* to exercise?" is the most common whinge – er, question – I get from new clients. I can only answer that every woman I have counselled who has lost weight *and* kept it off has found a way to incorporate some sort of physical activity into her lifestyle. It doesn't have to be an intensely energetic regime done under sufferance. You're looking for something that fits in with your life and which becomes an enjoyable habit. If you feel that you have to exercise solely to lose weight, it won't work. You will never stick at doing something you hate – it merely serves as a constant reminder that you are too fat.

I know from my clients' experience that long-term success in taking sufficient and regular exercise is, for many women, the most difficult step. This may be because it requires the greatest time commitment, so is not altogether surprising.

Let's look again at some of your objections:

You have no time. Listen, if you can find time to have your highlights done, you have time to exercise, believe me. It's just a matter of organising your life.

You are exhausted. Are you exhausted when you go to a party after work and manage to dance all night? No.

However tired you might be, a different environment with cheerful people and music soon changes your mood. Physical activity actually wakes you up by supplying more oxygen to the brain and muscles so that you feel more alert. It also increases your supply of adrenaline so that you have more energy.

You say you run around all the time so you don't need extra exercise. Not true – believe me! Cleaning the house, chasing after the kids, shopping or going to work are not the same as a consistent, structured plan with periods of *sustained* movement, and this is what you really need.

Exercise will make you hungry. Continuous movement stimulates the liver to release stored glucose. When this high glucose level is perceived by the hypothalamus – the part of your brain that controls hunger – it correctly assumes that you do not need food right now, so the hunger signals are not activated.

A large proportion of my younger clients, those in their twenties and thirties, are already doing some sort of regular or spasmodic exercise – either aerobic classes or circuit training in the gym – when they come to me. They are the ones who find it easiest to eliminate their trigger foods and learn how to stop bingeing.

For many other people, however, the word "exercise" conjures up pictures of heaving, sweaty bodies, contorted limbs, inflated health club subscriptions and exorbitant osteopath bills.

It doesn't have to be like that. Tell me: what might you be prepared to tolerate in an exercise programme? I usually get answers along the following lines:

"Something I can do by myself/with my partner."
"Something I could fit in to my lunch hour at work."
"I don't want to have to buy special gear or equipment

like weights or gadgets."

"I can't follow complicated dance steps – I would feel a right berk."

"I don't want to get all sweaty."

"I'm hopeless with computerised equipment – I can't even work the microwave!" (Oh, for goodness sake!)

Well, bearing all that in mind and if no other form of exercise grabs you, I have the answer! May I suggest that you WALK? Yes, you are going to put one foot in front of the other lots of times, and this will tone up your muscles AND burn off that fat at the same time.

You do walk; you tell me. Uh-huh – from the hotel to the beach, from the house to the car, from the TV to the fridge. That is not exactly what I *mean*. As part of this new, healthy lifestyle that you are about to adopt, I suggest you get out that front door and walk, not going anywhere in particular, but as a form of exercise. If you have any concern about this, obviously you will check with your doctor who, I'm sure, will agree that (barring any medical problem) walking exercises all the muscles in your body, particularly those in your legs and bum.

When you work these, your largest sets of muscles, you draw fat from all over your body to burn up as energy. Walking is cheap, easy and effective. You don't have to join an expensive club; you don't need any fancy equipment; and you don't have to compete with some leggy bimbo with a bum like two peaches separated by a thong of lycra. You can do it any time you choose and there is hardly any risk of hurting yourself – unless you walk into a tree! Walking improves your circulation and, apart from low-impact aerobic classes, it is one of the few exercises that helps to sustain your bone mass which, incidentally, is vitally important in preventing osteoporosis.

As with all exercise, striding along in the sunshine will

encourage your brain to produce endorphins which lift your mood, relieve tension in your body and unclutter your mind, allowing you to think much more clearly (thoughts like "Why didn't I bring an umbrella?").

You are going to start off modestly and gradually build up until your body gets used to the stimulus to burn fat. By the end of week three you should be walking for a good forty-five minutes each session.

First you will need a good, solid pair of trainers. Go for a good make like Nike Air, Reebok or Avia. I know they're expensive – but you are worth it, aren't you?

You don't need fancy jogging outfits – anything comfy will do – and for additional inspiration, you may like to consider buying a Walkman. Walking just for its own sake can be dull but not for you. Having a personal stereo means you can go to the local library and take out a "talking book". There are hundreds of fabulous book tapes recorded by some of the world's finest actors. Each "book" can last from two to eight hours, so, when you go on your walk, not only will you be toning up your body and burning fat, you will be brilliantly entertained as well.

If you are more motivated to stride along in time to some music, make some special collections of your favourite songs. One of my clients has a real penchant for rock 'n roll and can't help singing along with her old favourites. Unfortunately, when you have headphones on, you don't always realise how loud you're singing; she collects many a strange look on Hampstead Heath by suddenly punching the air and screaming "Great balls of fire!"

The way to succeed is to set aside specific times for your walk on three or four days a week. This is important, as it is the frequency of the exercise as well as its duration that makes it work. Three or four times is much more effective than only twice a week.

Decide never to let two days go by without walking.

Choose the time carefully. This is your exercise time. You need to get into the habit of doing it as a set routine, not as part of anything else. If you are a "morning" person then setting your alarm earlier may be right for you – or you may

prefer to go in the evening. If you work in an office, a stride round the nearest park at lunch-time is infinitely preferable to sitting in Pret à Manger.

The point of setting aside definite times is to motivate yourself to get out of that door and, for the first three weeks, this may be very difficult. After that, you will, if you persevere, even begin to feel a bit edgy if you are forced to cancel one of your walks! Soon taking your walk will become a habit that you do without thinking, like locking your car.

When you walk quickly, you start burning up the carbohydrates in your muscles and you will feel warmer, however cold the day. After 20 minutes or so, once the carbohydrates, in the form of glycogen, are used up, you should start to burn fat. Though individuals vary on this, essentially, the more you walk, the quicker the weight will come off. This is why you need to build up to 45 minutes if possible – to get that fat mobilized!

Don't expect miracles overnight. You may not see any change in your body shape for at least six weeks but it will happen eventually. One day you will look down and see a curve of muscle definition in the front of your thighs instead of wobbly fat and you will know you are on your way.

The number of calories you burn each time while exercising is not the key factor; what counts is the cumulative effect produced in your body. Ignore those little charts in magazines listing the number of calories burned during various activities. So what if washing the kitchen floor only uses up 15 calories an hour. (Who washes the kitchen floor for an hour?!) When you raise your metabolic rate through exercise, it stays raised for the next few hours, so that everything you eat during that time will be utilized by your body faster and not stored as fat.

Don't let anyone or anything distract you. You don't need

anyone to walk with; this is *your* exercise time. Go on your own. You will soon come to treasure this time by yourself, listening to a story or your favourite music without someone saying "Would you mind doing this for me" or even "Mummy!" Do not feel guilty about taking this time for yourself. You both need and deserve it.

So far so good but are *you* ready to inject this commitment into your life?

What will you get out of each walk? You will lose more weight and raise your metabolism for the next few hours. You will suppress your appetite, look and feel healthier, firm up your body and get a great sense of achievement. You will also suppress your desire to binge.

What's the trade-off? Well, it is going to take time. You need to put aside about 45 minutes three or four times a week. This may take a certain amount of organisation. You might get slightly sweaty if the weather is hot and, at the beginning, your leg muscles might ache a bit.

Be warned! There will be some days when you won't feel like doing it. Days when you will have to summon every inner resource you possess in order to get yourself out there walking.

However, as with any decision, if what you think you'll ultimately get out of it outweighs the inconvenience of actually doing it, you are more likely to do it.

Assuming your answer is "Yes, I'll do it" ("I'll try it" isn't a commitment) check out the following guidelines:

Decide on the date you are going to start. Organise your exercise times for that week. Write them in your food diary.

Be realistic. If you have never been good at heaving yourself out of bed early, don't plan to walk in the mornings. If evenings are better, pick a time when you don't have other commitments like taking your daughter to her ballet class. Maybe there is a television programme you could tape and watch later. If you do plan to go in the evening, lay your clothes out ready on your bed before you leave for work so you see them when you come in. If you use your lunch hour, mark it in your diary so you don't subconsciously arrange a meeting for that time, giving you an excuse not to go.

Your target minimum exercise routine is three times a week. Remember, it is the cumulative effect of using your muscles in this way that conditions your body to burn fat on a regular basis.

Work up within 2 – 3 weeks to 45 minutes actual walking time. You need this amount of time to activate your enzymes to release fat. Think of every minute over 25-30 as a real fat-burning minute.

Developing an activity programme you can live with takes time, patience and a firm commitment. You have to be able to keep going through the tough as well as the easy days if you want to reap the rewards.

As final proof of the benefits of aerobic exercise I asked one of my clients, who is a very young-looking lady in her late sixties, how she managed to retain her youthful appearance. "I cycle regularly" she told me. I was just thinking that there must be hidden benefits in cycling that I don't know about, when she added, confidentially " – between my house in Kensington and my plastic surgeon in Harley Street!"

How Long Does It Take?

I'm always asked this. Whether someone has four stone to lose or only ten pounds, I always give the same answer: a year. When they look surprised, I tell them not to think of putting a time limit on what they are doing because there is no point. Bingers always seem to think of a diet like a prison sentence: "I've done 3 months, 3 weeks, and two and a half days . . ." What are you going to do when your "time" is up? Get fat again?

There is no time limit. It is establishing the process (of reaching and maintaining your proper weight) not some number on a scale or a dress size that is your real goal.

Being in control of your eating is a skill that will last a lifetime. Provided that your commitment remains steadfast it doesn't end when you reach goal weight. To achieve a healthy way of eating that you can live with comfortably will take a year to get firmly established.

So, what else must you do for the next twelve months while you are eliminating the binge and watching the scales go down? Everyone is different. As you have lost weight before, you will have a rough idea of your own personal pattern. Just concentrate on today – each day – and let the end result take care of itself.

The numbers on the scale will go down, sometimes slowly, sometimes fast, occasionally not at all for brief periods. At certain times, they might even go up a pound or two due to water retention. This is when you stay cool and don't allow Fat-U to go into the "See, I told you it wouldn't work" routine. The numbers on the scale do not always clearly reflect what is happening to your body at any given time. They reflect the *results* of what is happening and these results sometimes take time to register.

Don't worry. If you avoid your trigger foods, you don't binge, and so you automatically eat less. Carry on with this over a sustained period of time and your body HAS to metabolise calories from your fat stores to use as energy.

Diets, in their desperation to seize people's imagination, have to be increasingly bizarre: for example, the Cabbage Soup Diet consisting of unlimited vegetable soup; the Ice Cream Diet – a scoop of vanilla ice cream after every meal; the Mirror Diet, where you only eat naked in front of a

mirror (except at some smarter restaurants!). I am just waiting for someone to bring out the Tranquilliser Diet – on
which you take four Valium tablets before each meal. It
doesn't make you eat less but most of it falls on the floor!
(Well, *I* thought it was funny!)

Let's recap the first steps of your new programme:

- Decide when you want to start. Try and choose a three-
  week period with no anticipated stress or binge-triggering
  social arrangements.

- Identify your trigger foods. Go through all your cupboards and eliminate all traces of them. From now on you
  are free.

- Decide on a realistic goal weight, taking into account
  your age, inherited body shape and the weight you have
  got down to before and which seemed to be the "right"
  weight for you – even though you think you might look
  better slimmer.

- Buy a notebook that is going to be your food diary for the
  next six weeks.

- On your starting day, decide what you are going to eat for
  that day and at what time. Write your menu down in your
  diary.

- Check that the food you are going to eat is readily available.

- Decide on a form of exercise that you would be prepared
  to do regularly three times a week. If it is walking, pick
  the times that are most compatible with your lifestyle

and block them out in your diary so nothing else dare intrude.

- **START** on the allotted day.

You are on your way to living slim and binge free.

5

WHAT YOU EAT

I get some strange answers when I ask people what was going through their minds the last time they unintentionally popped something into their mouths:

"I was desperate for something sweet."
"It leapt into my mouth of its own accord." (Yeah, *right*!)
"It would get thrown away otherwise."   (What are you,
                                          a wheelie-bin?)
"She went to all that trouble to prepare it." (Tough!)
"I was bored/tired/fed-up."   (And now fat.)
"I was excited/happy."   (And now fat.)
"It was just sitting there on the plate (Looking at
   looking at me."   you?!)
"I spread Nutella all over my boy-friend (Thank you for
   and – "   sharing that.)

Know What You Are Eating
The food that you eat, and when you eat it, has got to reflect

your own personal taste and lifestyle. To live slim you have to eat, but eat "slim".

People get muddled about food regardless of their intelligence. A well-known public figure was very proud of the fact that he had lost two stone: "The secret is keeping protein and carbohydrate apart" he once declared firmly " . . . and never mixing the two at the same meal". He then went on to describe his breakfast: cereal (carb.) with a glass of skimmed milk (protein). Fine!

Another quote, this time from a former top model: "There are times I get so hungry. In Paris, I felt like fainting all the time. Now I try to follow a diet that is low in carbohydrates and sugar, eating lots of protein like fruit and vegetables. But because I've cut down on sugar, I don't have the energy I had".

Yes – you've spotted it: Fruit and vegetables are not protein foods. They are carbohydrates – and ALL foods, not just sugar, supply energy.

It is understandable that so many people get confused. First you hear so much that is anti protein and fat, and how you should eat more carbohydrates – then the next minute you are told not to eat biscuits and cakes *because* these are carbohydrates. You may have read that the amount of fat you eat should be 30% of your daily food intake but, how on earth are you expected to work that out when you don't know how much you are eating in the first place?

To make sensible choices you do need to know what you are eating. You don't actually eat carbohydrates, protein or fat; you eat foods which are made up of varying proportions of these elements. For easy reference there is a comprehensive list of major, common, food groups given at the end of this chapter, arranged so as to highlight quickly their relative protein, carbohydrate and fat contents.

Simply put, **protein** foods are used by your body mainly

to repair and maintain the cells; **carbohydrates** are mostly converted into glucose to be used by your muscles as energy; **fat** provides warmth and healthy bones, eyes and hair. As you know, it is healthier to get your calories from such lean foods as fish, chicken, beans, rice, fruit and vegetables than from high-fat foods like chocolate or crisps. However, the basic equations still apply: if you eat more calories than you use up in energy, whether from protein, carbohydrates or fat, you will put on weight and, if you eat fewer calories than you use in energy, you will lose weight.

Strangely, your first priority may be to stop being afraid of food! Slim people eat food all the time. So can you. Once you get past the deprivation mind-set and eliminate the one or two trigger foods that are controlling your life, you will discover that there is a vast, unlimited selection of food that you can eat heartily and enjoy without any risk of a return to binge mode.

I am not going to tell you precisely what to eat – you "KNOW" for the most part which foods to eat and which to avoid – but I will give you a "blueprint" to follow to keep you slim, control hunger and provide you with the energy you need to get you through the day.

Let's run through the various food groups in no particular order:

• Choose complex, starchy, carbohydrate foods such as wholemeal bread, potatoes, whole wheat pasta, brown rice and cereals such as porridge or Shredded Wheat. Try and avoid simple carbohydrate foods such as those containing white flour and refined sugar.

• Vegetables are one of your most reliable sources of vitamins and minerals. The stronger the colour, like deep orange carrots and dark green broccoli, the more vitamins they are likely to contain. You are also getting the greatest number of nutrients for the fewest number of calories. Three to five servings a day are recommended.

- Fruit. Two or three pieces a day should fill those gaps between meals. Again the brighter the colour like strawberries or oranges, the more vitamins they contain.

- Protein Foods. Your first choice should be fish, fish, fish: sole, salmon, plaice, trout, prawns, tinned tuna and sardines - there are so many varieties. This is one of the healthiest protein foods you can eat. Next go for chicken, turkey, lean meat, cottage cheese, egg whites and all types of beans.

- Dairy Foods. All your calcium needs will be met from one or two daily helpings of either skimmed milk, yoghurt, low-fat cheese like cottage cheese or fromage frais.

- Fat. Try and stick to very small servings of vegetable oil or low-fat spread. If you can keep a picture in your mind of one level tablespoon of fat – in any form – that is all you need each day to keep you healthy

Here are just a few more facts about "food awareness". Different foods react in your body to produce different effects. Protein foods are filling and will satisfy your hunger for a longer period of time than will any other food group. Protein contains the amino acid tryptophan which encourages your brain to produce the feel-good neurotransmitter, serotonin. (Neurotransmitters are chemicals that pass "messages" from one nerve to another.) An adequate supply of serotonin in your brain keeps you calm, cheerful, relaxed yet energized.

The main source of serotonin, however, comes from carbohydrate-rich foods, such as the starchy variety listed above, together with fruit and vegetables. That is why, when you are feeling ratty or stressed out, you may tend to crave sweet, stodgy and filling carbohydrate food. After a while, when the increased production of serotonin kicks in, you feel your mood lifting. (The anti-depressant drug, Prozac, works by increasing the amount of serotonin in the brain.)

If, though, at this time you do choose simple carbo-hydrates, containing white flour and refined sugar, hoping for the same immediate "lift", you may be disappointed. These foods tend to induce an over-production of insulin which will ensure that the energy-surge is short-lived and may well promote cravings and tiredness soon after.

The worst combination of food you can put into your body, as far as your health, well-being and weight are con-cerned, is fat combined with sugar. You know which foods these are! Obviously it is not possible to calculate fat levels to a precise percentage, but being aware of the foods that contain fat or are cooked in it will enable you to make healthier substitutes. Meats like lamb and pork, fried food and dairy products like cream and butter tend to be the prime sources of fat. Check the food lists at the end of this chapter to help you select healthier choices.

Planning Your Meals

You need to choose the foods that will best serve your needs throughout the day. Presumably, in the mornings, you will want to be especially awake and active; the afternoons are a time you expect to feel calm, yet still alert, ready to tackle or complete creative, mental or physical work; once the evening comes along you are ready to wind down and relax. Above all you do not want to experience any gnawing hunger or cravings during the day that threaten to send you spiralling off track.

To help you meet these energy requirements, it would be

beneficial to eat some kind of protein for breakfast and lunch; then, as the day wears on, to veer towards carbohydrates. One of the best "wake up calls" for an empty stomach is some light protein such as low-fat, unsweetened, live yoghurt. This will line your gut with healthy bacteria, nourish your body and your brain and wake you gently and completely. Wait for at least 15 minutes for the yoghurt – or a few sips of skimmed milk if you don't like yoghurt – to work its magic before having your breakfast. Then a combination of more protein such as eggs (for prolonged alertness) with a carbohydrate like toast (for sustained energy) will set you up for the morning. Cereal (carb.) with milk (protein) will be equally effective.

Make protein the major part of your midday meal as well. If you had cereal for breakfast, then a chicken or tuna sandwich and/or salad would take you through the afternoon without your feeling hungry.

One reason that protein foods are both satisfying and slimming is that your brain does not allow you to eat massive amounts of protein at once. After digesting a small amount of protein, your brain sends very clear signals that you are now full up. Think about this. When did you last eat 3 whole chickens or 5 steaks at one sitting? You couldn't!

Your brain also has a limited capacity for accepting carbohydrates; maybe you could eat half a French loaf without anything on it – but a whole one? I don't think so.

Unfortunately, your brain will accept excessive fat or alcohol intake with scarcely a "murmur". It fails to account effectively for what has already passed your lips, and the "full-up" signals are so weak that you can easily ignore them. You just keep on eating: crisps, chips, chocolate, cake . . . and slipping down that extra drink.

I am sure you get the picture. If you want to keep your hunger at bay quickly and safely and for a sustained period of time, go for protein. Your body has to work quite hard to convert both protein and carbohydrate into a form that can be stored in your cells. It would much rather use it straight-away for energy. Dietary fat, unfortunately, is already practically in its storage form and therefore slips all too easily into your fat cells.

If you usually feel a bit peckish around 4 p.m., by all means have a carbohydrate snack but try and stay off anything directly containing sugar or fat; these merely tend to set up a craving for more of the same.

For maximum weight loss, I suggest you make your evening meal either protein and vegetables, or wholly carbohydrate. This has nothing to do with so-called food combining. It is just a way of making sure your meal will be satisfying without causing that heavy, saturated feeling that sometimes encourages you to "pick" your way through the rest of the evening. A carbohydrate snack an hour before you go to bed – try nibbling on dry Raisin Wheats – should ensure you get a good night's sleep and wake up energised, clear-headed and ready to go.

The above needs to form the background to your own blueprint for healthy eating. The following examples should help point out the right way:

Good Breakfast: Orange juice, porridge with skimmed milk, sweetened with a little powdered artificial sweetener.

Good Breakfast: Whole grain cereal such as bran flakes, with skimmed milk, half a banana cut up into it, plus a few raisins for sweetness.

Good Breakfast: Omelette made with 3 egg-whites and 1 yolk, cooked in a pan wiped with a "smidge" of olive oil, grilled tomatoes and mushrooms, whole grain toast with low-fat spread.

Unwise Breakfast: Fried eggs, bacon, sausage, etc. (All that fat will set up a craving for more fat later.)

Unwise Breakfast: Sugary cereal (more than 5 grams per serving) with milk. (The high sugar content will be liable to leave you with hunger pangs quite soon after.)

Unwise Breakfast: White toast, butter, marmalade. (See above.)

Good Lunch: Cold, cooked chicken or salmon or tuna, chopped up in a mixed salad with low-fat dressing. Side serving of brown rice or grainy brown roll.

Good Lunch: Ham or prawn sandwich on whole grain bread, with raw veg.

Good Lunch: Baked beans on whole grain toast, mixed salad. Fruit yoghurt.

Unwise Lunch: Pasta or jacket potato. (Will make you sleepy during the afternoon.)

Unwise Lunch: Steak. (Too heavy in middle of day.)

Unwise Lunch: Hamburger with French fries, pizza made with white flour, or cheese baguette and crisps. (Too much fat/simple carbohydrate can easily set up a craving before teatime!)

Good Dinner: Chicken – roast, grilled with herbs or stir-fried with 3 or 4 different vegetables: carrots, broccoli, asparagus, Brussels sprouts. (Protein, no starch.)

Good Dinner: Grilled salmon or plaice, Hollandaise sauce made with skimmed milk, sweet potato, cauliflower, green beans. (Protein, no starch.)

Good Dinner: Brown rice risotto made with onion, carrots, courgettes, red pepper, mushrooms. Green salad. (Carbs, no protein.)

Good Dinner: Whole wheat pasta with tomato and mushroom sauce, mixed salad. (Carbs, no protein.)

Unwise Dinner: Soup, large steak, jacket potato, peas. Apple pie. (Too heavy, too much, inviting indigestion.)

Unwise Dinner: Fried fish or chicken, chips. (Too much fat with no vegetables to balance.)

Good Snacks: Mid-morning – Fruit, yoghurt or fruit-flavoured fromage frais.

Mid-afternoon – Fruit, pretzels, crisp breads with sugar-free jam or with Marmite and rice cheese (from health food shop), dried fruit.

Late evening – Organic sweetened cereal nibbled dry with a hot drink or slice of whole grain toast with sugar-free jam. If very hungry, a small bowl of porridge.

Unwise Snacks: Chocolate, cake, creamy desserts, biscuits, crisps, peanuts – oh, you know all this!

Have a "survival kit" handy of snacks that you like: fruit, packets of raw veg, like carrot sticks, cauliflower florets, baby corn – all available in supermarkets if you are short of time – yoghurt, raisins, popcorn, pretzels, low-fat "baked" crisps, rice cakes, Ryvita – whatever. A rice cake topped with a cheese slice is a filling snack with a cup of tea. Most offices have a little fridge for milk, where you can hopefully store your nibbles one day at a time.

No, you are not expected to turn up at work every day with a picnic basket! I am just suggesting that you plan your snacks rather than picking at your trigger foods because you haven't made alternatives available. If you wait until you are hungry, you end up "thinking" with your taste buds.

It only takes a few minutes to plan ahead properly so that you know what you are going to eat that day and when. If this sounds like a big deal and your initial reaction is "I haven't got time" – then you should reassess your commitment.

Keeping your food diary is essential for the first six weeks. You have to stay focused. After that point it gets easy; you get into the rhythm and can expect to scrap the diary in due course.

Once you have set your starting date, you may find it beneficial to plan for the first *seven* days in one go. In this way you can have all the food you need in the house or know that it is available at local shops. By planning ahead you directly challenge any subconscious resistance to what you are doing and establish your new, permanent way of eating – that is every 2 to 3 hours – which will pre-empt hunger and allow you to stay in control.

We discussed in a previous chapter that most eating is habit. I am sure you had much the same thing for breakfast this morning as yesterday – and the day before that. So as long as you eat *something*, it is not difficult to switch from a jam doughnut mid-morning to a banana. You are not changing the habit of eating; you are changing what and how frequently you eat, which will then become your new habit.

Make breakfast easy: you have enough on your mind first thing in the morning to bother about being creative so early on! Spread your food intake out more. If you have a sandwich for lunch, why not eat half at lunch-time with a big salad, and the other half at 4 o'clock when everyone else in your office is nibbling Kit Kats and crisps? Get into the habit of eating "half now and half later (or tomorrow)" – banana, yoghurt, whatever. Instead of eating dessert straight after dinner, save it for later in the evening when you normally fancy something but are not quite sure what. The objective is not to get hungry and trigger a binge at the sight of something tempting.

Eating in this way means that sometimes you will have to carry food around with you. I know this sounds like a real drag but it doesn't take a moment to wrap something in foil and shove it into your bag. You will get used to it.

The main reason for preparing your own food beforehand is to prevent your having to rely on canteens and restaurants where your choices may well be limited to fattening menus. Although many food outlets offer low-fat, calorie-counted items, you still can't be sure what is in them. It takes two minutes to make a sandwich and stick some lettuce, cucumber, tomatoes and carrots into a polythene bag to go with it. This little meal can be eaten anywhere – in the car – in the park – in the office – at the hairdresser.

If you are at home most of the day then obviously you will not need to get all your food ready at one time but, once you have planned what you are going to eat for the day, do stick to each day's plan meticulously, at least for the first six weeks. Don't plan to have sardines on toast for lunch and then open the fridge and polish off last night's lasagne instead.

If you are really too rushed in the morning to think about food, set aside time the night before so that you can get what you need out of the freezer. This soon becomes as natural as deciding what to wear each day.

You must *make the time* for this, whether it is part of your morning routine or is better done the evening before. If you don't allow yourself the planning time, you will fail.

Eating this way you are establishing Slim-U firmly in the driving seat. If you go on eating haphazardly, you will continue to allow food to control you. This doesn't stop you joining your family for regular meals, provided you stay off any of your trigger foods. If pasta is one of your trigger foods and you are making that for your family, prepare something else for yourself.

Have A Salad

Try to get into the habit of having a salad every day. I like the American idea of eating a salad as a starter before the main course and, to this end, I suggest that you keep in your fridge at all times:

- A packet of mixed lettuce leaves, available from all supermarkets.

• Carrots, scraped and kept in a bowl of cold water.

• Broccoli florets, best kept in a polythene bag.

• Celery – cut the root bit off, wash and stand upright in a
  mug of cold water.

• Tomatoes, cucumber, cauliflower, mushrooms, chicory,
  red (or yellow or green) peppers, white cabbage

Just chop up a handful of each of these raw ingredients
into a bowl, pour over some non-fattening dressing, and eat.
As the average calorie content of all these ingredients is
about 5 per ounce, you can have quite a large bowlful.

Rather than a creamy, mayonnaise type or an oil dressing,
try the following. You need: a large tub of 0% fat fromage
frais, a small bottle of oil-free vinaigrette (about 10 calories
in the whole bottle), some grainy mustard and some powdered sweetener. Put half the tub of fromage frais into a
bowl, add 1 level teaspoon of mustard, and a third of the
bottle of the oil-free dressing. Beat it all together until it's
nice and creamy, adding 2 or 3 teaspoonfuls of the sweetener (more or less to taste; none of these measurements
needs to be precise) and there you have it.

You can slosh this over your salad or use it as a dip, or
whatever. It's completely fat-free and will keep fresh for
several days in the fridge.

Perhaps you could eat this salad immediately you come
home from work as this seems to be a vulnerable hunger-
time. As it consists of fibrous raw food, it takes quite a bit
of chewing. The healthy properties of high-fibre food are
absorbed into the blood stream slowly, so it should tide you
over till dinner time, or stop you picking at the remains of
the children's tea. (Bingers put on more weight with their
fingers than they do with their mouths!) I know it seems a

strange concept to come home from work and eat a salad instead of your usual cup of tea and a bun or glass of wine and packet of cashews, but who says you have got to be conventional? Do what works to keep you on track. If your partner is late coming home and it's more than three hours since you last ate, have your salad and join him for the main course later.

If you come home cold and shivery in the winter, how about a small bowl of cooked vegetables instead of the cold salad? Use carrots, broccoli, Brussels sprouts, courgettes, cauliflower, beans etc. Choose three or four different vegetables, cut them up into a bowl and steam or microwave them for five minutes. I know what you're thinking now: "I can't just eat VEGETABLES, for goodness sake!" Why not? OK, vegetables are rather boring to eat on their own. So heat up half a tin of low-cal soup (probably no more than 30 calories) and pour this over the cooked veggies to make a tasty sauce.

Another tip from a client is to keep roasted root vegetables in the fridge. Choose from the following: aubergine, courgette, red onion, red and yellow peppers, parsnip, turnip or celeriac. Chop four of the above vegetables into chunky pieces and put them in a foil baking tin – easy to sling away afterwards to save washing up. Spritz them sparingly with olive oil and put them in the oven like you would do roast potatoes, for about an hour. Either eat them hot, or transfer to a Pyrex dish and keep in the fridge so that you can eat them cold. A couple of spoonfuls makes a delicious addition to your normal salad.

Vegetables are normal food for slim people. So don't be misled into thinking of them as diet food for a fat person. Get off the diet mentality. You are not on a diet. The very thought of being on a diet makes you feel deprived – and hungry.

Weighing Food
As a hangover from previous diets, some people seem to have a set of weighing scales attached to them by an invisible umbilical cord. Forget them. You KNOW what a serving of meat or fish looks like! Obviously a breast or leg portion of chicken is the norm, as is a small plaice, sole or trout. Make a modest sandwich. You don't need a triple-decker.

When you get bored with certain foods, switch to others. This is obvious, I know, but it may not naturally occur to you to have turkey instead of chicken, parsnips instead of potatoes. Keep individual portions of cooked chicken and salmon in the freezer to chop up into a salad for lunch. They are available in every supermarket.

Above all, stick to your planned and timed meals and snacks even if it means munching your apple on the bus going home from work.

Ready-Prepared Meals
It is difficult to work out the exact proportions of protein, carbohydrate or fat contained in ready-prepared dishes, so the best way to choose is by the number of calories; up to 300 per serving is fine. You need to be aware that they generally contain more salt, fat and preservatives than you would use if you were cooking fresh food, but these meals do come in handy if you're pushed for time.

Eating In Restaurants
The basic rules of eating out for bingers, are:

• Have a snack before you leave home – a slice of toast, or a banana or yoghurt. Eat it some time between your tights and your mascara. This is not enough to spoil your appetite but just enough to dull the hunger pangs and stop you diving mouth-first into the bread-basket when you get there.

- For the first six weeks, don't look at any menu. Decide beforehand what you are going to eat, preferably sticking with melon or salad to start, followed by fish or chicken with vegetables or salad. Then you shouldn't go wrong.

- Be the first to order so you won't be swayed by what your friends are having – their choices are their problem.

- Control must be the first priority when choosing food wherever you are. When you are fully in control you can be more adventurous.

- Avoid your trigger foods. If butter is one of them, either hide it behind the flowers or ask for it to be removed from the table, along with the bread, once everyone has taken what they want.

- If you find yourself at a pizza/pasta restaurant and pizza is your trigger food, go for the pasta. This may be more fattening at the time, especially if served in a creamy sauce, but it won't start a binge. Pizza will evoke all the old cravings and will be much more fattening in the long run. Eating something fattening once will not make you fat; eating something that is sure to trigger a binge will.

- If you do decide to have something higher in calories than you would normally have, because this is a speciality of that particular restaurant, eat and enjoy that one dish but *don't use it as an excuse to have everything else on the menu*. Once eaten, forget about it and, the following day, just go back to your normal blueprint of eating. Don't think of cutting down to make up for the damage you've done. This will only trigger the diet mentality again.

• For dessert: if there are no plain berries – strawberries or raspberries – or fruit salad, ask the waiter for some melon or sorbet or give this course a miss altogether.

• Don't worry about what other people think. You can eat what you like and, if you don't want to drink alcohol or eat dessert, that's your choice. Other people have the same choices though, so keep the lips zipped.

EAT!
Never let more than three hours go by without putting something in your mouth even if it's just an apple. I repeat that this means eating by the clock rather than by traditional scheduled mealtimes or when you are hungry. If you have breakfast at 7.30 a.m. before going to work, then get caught up in general office routine and don't get a lunch break until 1.30 or 2 p.m., that is too long without revving up your body furnace. This mistake often results in choosing hurriedly and unwisely, and then eating too much and too fast.

In practice you will find that most of your food breaks do coincide with natural meal times anyway – it's just the snacks in between you have to remember. What you eat at each meal naturally affects your mood and your energy levels. Eat wisely and you should feel great throughout the day from the minute you wake. Make an unwise food choice at some point and you risk spending the rest of the day bingeing to compensate for the way that choice made you feel. Eating fat will set up a craving for more fat. (When was the last time you ate one crisp?) Eating a large amount of refined sugar will flood your body with insulin which will set up an urgent demand for more – and then more.

When you start with your new commitment to planned eating, don't worry if you find that your mind is totally pre-occupied with food, what you are going to eat and when. This is quite normal and only lasts a short while until you get fully into it. Soon you will go through the day eating in the correct way without giving it a further thought.

Take it one day at a time. You know you could eat whatever you like but, for today you are choosing to eat small amounts of healthy food at regular intervals. You should not experience hunger because you always know you are going to eat again in a couple of hours.

The purpose of this chapter has been to make it easier for you to make informed choices – because that's what being in control is all about.

FOOD LISTS

STARCHY CARBOHYDRATE FOODS

Bread:	white bread, wholemeal or brown bread, rolls, croissants, pitta bread.
Crispbreads:	Ryvita, Melba toast, water biscuits, cream crackers, bread sticks.
Snacks:	Crisps, Twiglets, pretzels, popcorn, rice crackers, Ritz crackers, Rich tea biscuits.
Grains:	Rice (white or brown), rye, oats, barley, wheat germ, Bulgar wheat.
Pasta:	All shapes – spaghetti, macaroni, noodles.
Vegetables:	Potatoes, peas, corn, sugar snap peas.

BREAKFAST CEREALS

Low in Sugar	Medium Sugar	High in Sugar/Fat
All Bran	Alpen	Coco-Anything
Cornflakes	Bran Flakes	Frosted Shreddies
Porridge	Cheerios	Frosties
Puffed Wheat	Crunchy Nut	Harvest Crunch
Raisin Wheats	Cornflakes	Most Mueslis
Shredded Wheat	Crunchy Oat	Sugar Puffs
Shreddies	Bran	Sugar Ricicles
Special K	Fruit & Fibre	
Sultana Bran	Fruitibix	
Weetabix	Golden Grahams	
	Rice Krispies	

NATURAL CARBOHYDRATE FOODS

Vegetables: All other vegetables apart from the starchy variety mentioned above: broccoli, cabbage, carrots, sprouts, onions, etc.

Fruit: All fruit, apples, pears, bananas, strawberries, etc.
Freshly squeezed fruit juice.

COMBINED PROTEIN AND CARBOHYDRATE FOODS

All the different beans: butter beans, broad beans, soybeans (used in tinned baked beans), chick peas, lentils, kidney beans (make sure they are well cooked).
Quorn.
Tofu.

PROTEIN FOODS

BEEF

Low in Fat	Medium Fat	High in Fat
Beefburger (low fat)	Beefburger (regular)	Barbecue ribs
Braising steak (lean)	Fillet steak	Beef tongue
Filet mignon	Liver	Bologna
Forerib (lean), roast	Meatloaf	Brisket
Minced beef (lean)	Minced beef (regular)	Frankfurters
Rib (lean), boneless	Rib, roast	Luncheon meat
Stewing steak (lean)	Rump steak	Salami
Topside, roast	Surloin steak	Salt beef
	T-steak	Sausages

PORK

Low in Fat	Medium Fat	High in Fat
Gammon	Bacon rasher, grilled	Pork chop
Ham, boiled	Bacon steak, grilled	Pork sausages
Parma ham	Gammon rasher, grilled	Spare ribs
Pork fillet (lean)	Minced pork	Streaky bacon
Tenderloin (lean)	Shoulder of pork, roast	

LAMB AND VEAL

Low in Fat	Medium Fat	High in Fat
Veal chops	Lamb cubes (lean)	Chump steak
Veal fillet, roast	Leg of lamb (lean), roast	Loin chop
	Minced lamb (lean)	Neck cutlet
	Rack of lamb	Shoulder, roast
	Veal cutlet, grilled	Veal escallop, fried

PROTEIN FOODS

POULTRY

Low in Fat	Medium Fat	
Chicken without skin Turkey without skin	Chicken with skin Duck Goose Pheasant Turkey with skin	

FISH

Low in Fat	Medium Fat	High in Fat
All white fish Shellfish Smoked salmon Tinned salmon Tuna, tinned in brine	Anchovies, drained Kippers, grilled Sardines Smoked mackerel Tuna, tinned in oil	All fried fish Fish fingers

CHEESE AND DAIRY

Low in Fat	Medium Fat	High in Fat
Cottage cheese Cheese spread (light) Egg whites Fromage frais Quark (low fat) Parmesan, grated Skimmed milk Yoghurt (low fat)	Cheese slices Cheese spread (regular) Curd cheese Edam Half-fat cheese, e.g. ricotta Mozzarella Semi-skimmed milk Whole eggs	Brie Cheddar Cream Cream cheese Full cream milk Greek yoghurt Gruyère cheese Ice cream

FAT! FAT! FAT!

You may be surprised at some of the items listed below under FAT as cheese, nuts and seeds are officially protein foods, but they contain such a high proportion of fat that I am including them here so that you know to limit them in your eating plan if you choose to do so.

Unsaturated fat	Saturated fat
Avocado pear	Bacon
Flora and similar	Bacon fat
French dressing	Butter
Margarine	Cake
Mayonnaise (low fat)	Cheese, except cottage
Mayonnaise (regular)	cheese (see above)
Nuts: almonds	Chocolate (sorry!)
cashews	Chocolate biscuits
peanuts	Coffee whitener
pecans	Coconut
walnuts etc.	Cream
Oils: corn	Cream cheese
olive	Crisps
safflower	Ice cream (not sorbet)
soybean	Lard
sunflower	
Olives	
Salad dressing, mayonnaise type	
Seeds: pine nuts	
pumpkin seeds	
sunflower seeds etc.	

6

LET'S GO SHOPPING

Naturally, you are a very careful, competent shopper . . . you always:

1. Make a list of everything you need and stick to it.
2. Know exactly where everything is, including the manager, so you can avoid trailing up and down unnecessary aisles.
3. Avoid those high-cal, tinned foods that are marked down in price and displayed in baskets at the end of aisles because some klutz dropped a pile of tins and dented them.
4. Check the label to see how much fat, sugar, sodium and calories the product contains before you buy packaged items.
5. Throw away those coupons offering you a free Walnut Whip if you buy 400 tins of Whiskas.
6. Never just "pop in" for something when you are hungry. That will lead to decisions made with your taste buds,

instead of your brain.
7. Never buy chocolate to eat in the car, telling yourself it doesn't count because it's outside the house.
8. Never talk loudly and earnestly to your child so that all the other shoppers have to turn round and smile indulgently at you.

Who Me? NEVER!

Supermarkets may love you but rarely as much as they love your money! All products are cunningly laid out for people who can't resist impulse buying. Almost everyone makes some sort of list but 99 out of 100 shoppers buy plenty "additional somethings" that are not on that list. The supermarkets count on you to do this. That is why they hide your most frequent purchases in a different place each week so as to force you to reach the aisles you might otherwise never pass. The one exception, in most cases is at the check-out, where the sweets and chocolate (buy me! buy me!) are in permanent residence.

Fruit and Vegetables

Come on, try something different for a change instead of the usual cauliflower, cabbage, carrots, courgettes and corn; there are other letters in the alphabet. Mange-tout, asparagus, spinach – and get some of those pre-washed and pre-cut carrots and lettuce hearts for between-meals nibbles.

Meat

Be wary here as the fat content of meat varies enormously between different types and cuts. Although one package may weigh the same as another, it could have twice as many calories depending on its fat content. Up to 68% of the calories in processed meat, like salami and bologna, is from fat. Check the food lists at the end of Chapter 5.

Dairy Foods

Advice: you want to stay slim? Don't buy cheese. It's as simple as that. Apart from cottage cheese, anything solid and yellow is mostly pure fat – believe it!

Manufacturers are rushing out lower-fat versions of every edible substance, hence low-fat spreads which are achieved by adding water. As they cost roughly the same as butter, this is pretty expensive water. Do you need to buy these? A quick swipe with low fat mayo will moisten a slice of bread enough before you add a savoury sandwich filling, and be far more economical calorie-wise, as will merely wiping the base of a pan with olive oil before frying.

Cereals

The cereals your children nag you to buy depend on which toy comes in the packet or upon what you get if you send off 500 packet tops, rather than their nutritional value. Cereals you see on television with happy little people jumping around and singing usually contain the most sugar. Ads showing a miserable, stick-like girl spooning down some bran-based something and then posing with her body at its skinniest angle contain the least sugar. Guess which are the only ones your children will eat?

Recommended Cereals: Porridge oats, Shredded Wheat, Bran Flakes, muesli base to which you add your own fresh or dried fruit, or any cereal containing more than 5 grams of fibre per 100 grams.

Not Recommended: Anything with the words "sugar" or "frosted" in the title or containing more than 5 grams of sugar per 100 grams.

Once the words "low-fat", "sugar free" and "in natural

juice" are imprinted indelibly on your brain, you should be able to bypass the high-cal traps waiting for you on the shelves. However, although a lot of these products are lower in calories than their "normal" counterparts, some of the descriptions and brand names can be very misleading if you are trying to lose weight or stop bingeing. For instance, those chewy "health and vitality" granola bars and carob-coated cereal bars are mostly around the 160-180 calorie mark, much the same as a Cadbury's Cream Egg. They can go from mouth to hips in 30 seconds flat!

Muesli, correctly promoted as a "healthy" cereal, is nonetheless full of fruit and nuts thereby making it one of the highest calorie breakfast cereals you can eat, even without added sugar. Although wholemeal bread is made with brown flour instead of white, it is unlikely to be lower in calories. "Polyunsaturated" – often applied to margarine – essentially has the same number of calories per unit of weight as butter.

One of my clients, Rachel, was puzzled by her apparent inability to lose weight until I discovered she was liberally dousing her salads with "pure" olive oil. "But it's 'pure'" she protested when I pointed out how fattening this was; "It says 'virgin' on the label". I had to explain that, unviolated as it surely is, you nonetheless ingest 120 calories from a mere tablespoon.

Read the Label
So – how can you find food that is convenient, healthy and low in fat and calories? Why, by checking out the nutritional information on the label of course. Oh yes? Some labels provide so much detail that they are impossible to understand, whilst others are deliberately misleading.

For example, a packet of butter informs you that 100 grams will supply your entire recommended daily intake of vitamin A and a third of the vitamin D you should have. How wonderful – until you realise that 100 grams is half the packet. If you ate that much butter every day, you would have serious dietary problems. Just reading the label, however, could convince you that eating so much butter might contribute to a balanced diet.

On a pot of cream the cost is given "per ml" but the nutritional information is in grams. So – suppose you have 284ml of cream, how much fat does that contain if there are 23.5g of fat in 100g? Go figure - ?

At the moment there are no specific rules controlling the information food manufacturers print on their product labels, which is why many of the claims are confusing. You may be confronted by four similar products labelled respectively: "low in saturates", "low fat", "reduced fat", "lower in fat". Lower in fat than what? Which do you go for? Even a product labelled "fat free" can be fattening if you eat a lot of it.

Legally, all printed declarations should be honest with no intention to mislead the customer. But manufacturers can, and do, make small but insignificant changes to existing products just so they can stick the words "lower in fat" or "high in fibre" on the label.

Low-fat spread is not, strictly speaking, low fat. It has about 40% fat but can be described as low fat because it has less than butter or margarine. In order to preserve the pure image of butter, the marketing men succeeded in getting a law passed to ensure that anything described as "butter" has to be at least 80% fat.

Manufacturers are under no obligation to provide any nutritional information but they usually do, stating the number of calories, and the protein, fat and carbohydrate values of the food. Typical values are usually given for both 100 grams and what they consider to be an average serving. Calorie values are listed under "Energy" because a calorie is

a unit of heat and energy. You usually find two different figures here: calories, written in their proper form of
kilocalories (kcal) which is what you are probably used to,
and kilojoules (kj) – the word "joule" being an international
term for a measure of heat. I'm sure you couldn't care less,
but 1kcal is equivalent to 4.2kj. It doesn't matter which one
you get used to, provided you always look at the same one
when comparing the calorie content with a similar product.

Being aware that the population as a whole would benefit
from a reduction in its overall fat intake – especially of
saturated fats – food labels usually give a value for total fat
per serving and then an indication of how much of this is
saturated. Health guidelines recommend that we eat no more
than 10 grams of saturated fat per day but this is very difficult to work out in practical terms.

Although the above nutritional information is voluntary, a
list of ingredients is required by law on nearly all processed
food – i.e. foods composed of more than one ingredient.

These must be listed in order of decreasing weight so, if
sugar is the first item on the list, that product contains more
sugar than anything else. This can be deceptive as both
sweeteners and salt come in many different guises and can
be listed under several different names. As an example, take
a look at the list of ingredients in this crunchy bar purchased
from a "health food" shop: "Rolled oats, **raw cane sugar**,
vegetable oil, **honey**, almonds, hazelnuts, wheat germ,
wheat bran, sesame seeds, sunflower seeds, **molasses**,
flavouring (vanilla essence, almond essence)."

As you can see, sugar is the second ingredient after rolled
oats, so there must be quite a lot of it – but it is also ingredient no. 4 and ingredient no. 11 – so goodness knows
how much sugar you are ingesting here in your "healthy
snack".

There is also quite a bit of fat in this crunchy bar. The only
one mentioned by name is the third ingredient, vegetable oil

but what about the fat to be found in the almonds, hazelnuts, sesame seeds and sunflower seeds? It's the combination of all these that makes it so chewy. I'm not saying don't eat it – just check the label and be aware of what you are eating so you can make an informed decision.

Here's another example – an off-the-shelf low-calorie lunch offer. What exactly is it though? "Noodles, **salt**, corn starch, malto dextrin, **monosodium** glutamate, chicken fat, chicken meat, hydrolysed plant protein, **spices**, dehydrated parsley, turmeric, dehydrated carrots."

Yes, it's a nice bowl of chicken noodle soup. Note that the second, fifth and ninth ingredients are all salt or close relations thereto. In many packet soups most of the soup's flavour comes from these (no calorie) salts, and this allows manufacturers to stress the low calorie content legitimately. Besides various health hazards related to a high consumption of salt, it is not a binger's friend. If your trigger foods are items like crisps or peanuts, you may find, after a prolonged eating session, that the scales have risen by two or three pounds due to water retention. A non-binger would simply shrug this off and resolve to cut down on salty food; a binger, noting her puffy eyes and fingers, would get dispirited and probably carry on eating.

Interestingly, you may not see a full ingredients list on certain foods such as ice cream, mayonnaise, bread, milk, cheese, pasta products, flour or cocoa, because these foods must contain the same basic ingredients, and these are specified under government standards. If the manufacturers add any other ingredients, then only the extra ones must be listed.

Food Additives

Food additives such as colours, flavourings and preservatives also have to be listed. The actual name or 'E' number doesn't have to be stated, just the words "artificial flavouring" – so if you are allergic to anything, you may only find out by trial and, more often, a violent rash.

If you add vanilla essence to a cake, you are using a product that has been made by extracting liquid from a vanilla pod. If you use vanilla *flavouring*, the liquid in your little brown bottle may never have been near a vanilla pod and is probably artificially produced.

The same applies to strawberry yoghurt, which is a plain yoghurt containing bits of real strawberries (plus some colouring or the strawberries would look brown and you wouldn't buy it). Strawberry *flavoured* yoghurt, on the contrary, has never been near a strawberry and is simply enhanced by artificial flavouring. The same standard applies to crisps; there is no bacon in bacon-flavoured crisps; they just taste as though there is.

What's light about "lite" – and why can't they spell? This term, applied to food products, can mean just about anything. It could mean that it's lower in calories, paler in colour, lower in alcohol, sodium, fat or even finer in texture. The EU did try to set a standard by restricting the use of the word "light" to foods with less than 50 calories per 100g or with 25% fewer calories than an equivalent product. Unfortunately, no manufacturer took a blind bit of notice of this rule. At the moment, a tin of peaches in "light syrup" is really peach segments in a thick, gungy, sugary, calorie-laden syrup, which happens to be light in colour. Hardly a weight-watcher's interpretation of "light".

A product labelled "low calorie" is supposed to contain no more than 40 calories per serving. Unfortunately the serving size wouldn't satisfy a gerbil. The binger's reaction to a product labelled "low calorie" is to assume you can eat a lot of it. In real life, only your mind assumes it's a diet food; your body doesn't.

Don't be conned into thinking a product is necessarily

healthy because it is labelled "cholesterol free". This should mean two milligrams of cholesterol or less per serving. However, cholesterol is only found in products of animal origin, like eggs, meat, poultry and shellfish. Foods that come from plants don't contain any cholesterol. Therefore, if you see a bottle of vegetable oil with the label "cholesterol free", you may get the impression that this is healthier than other oils. This is not so. There is no cholesterol in any vegetable oil.

Some of the claims on the delicious, nutritious milk-shake or biscuit-type replacement meals will have to be amended when a new EU directive comes into force (notably the words "delicious" and "nutritious"). These claims include the number of pounds likely to be lost in a week, and phrases such as "rapid weight loss" and "the healthy way to lose weight".

The word "enriched" on the label means that some nutrients lost during the processing have been put back. "Fortified" means extra vitamins and minerals are added, such as vitamin D to milk, so ensuring that children get an adequate supply. A breakfast cereal may be fortified with iron, which is meant to enhance its nutritional value. Some manufacturers presumably hope this will detract from the amount of sugar they have added – or what may be missing, such as other essential micronutrients.

I hope this chapter will give you some idea of what to look for on product labels. Don't become too obsessive though or you will find yourself checking the number of calories on a packet of toilet tissue!

Remember only one thing when out shopping: **if you don't buy it, you won't eat it**. You don't binge back home because you can't have your trigger foods; you binge because they *are* there – in abundance. Leave them on the supermarket shelves. Move on.

7

WEIGHT OFF YOUR MIND

In 16-something, the philosopher, Rene Descartes declared: "I think; therefore I am". Had Mr. Descartes been a binger, he might have said "I think I am fat; therefore I am fat".

Your thoughts and beliefs influence everything you feel about yourself and everything you do. Research shows that the people most likely to succeed with any new programme, whether giving up smoking or losing weight, are those who truly believe that they will succeed. Those who say "I can", will. It really is "all in the mind". Let me speculate that, in the past, when you have decided to start one of your infamous diets, you would usually do three days, binge on the fourth, try another two days maybe but then delve into the biscuit tin on the flimsiest pretext. Yet, all the time, you must have known that, if you were even slightly less than committed, it was destined to fail.

Hopefully, however, on at least one occasion you made a firmer decision: "OK; this is it. No half measures this time; I want to shift this weight once and for all" – and a strong, positive feeling did come over you. Even if you didn't get down to your desired weight, you probably got within a few pounds of it.

If you didn't stay down there for long, that's another issue. What matters is that the initial achievement proved that if *you* really make up your mind to do something, you *can* do it.

Despite such successes many people remain convinced that they can never lose weight. After years of trying new diets, they have become used to castigating themselves for being so weak-willed. Each time another diet fails is furnished as "proof" that what they feel about themselves is true.

Is it true or is it the thoughts that they have fed into their minds that have caused them to have a "fat attitude"?

If you consider yourself too fat at the moment, how did you get that way? Was it just the food you ate? Or was it the thoughts that governed the regular impulses that made you overeat? Those thoughts didn't only encourage you to overeat, but to binge on the very type of foods that you knew would make you fat.

In this context, food has nothing to do with weight. Food is necessary for your well-being and will only make you fat if you eat too much of the wrong kind. What drives you to eat too much of it is much more likely to be founded in your attitude towards how you should look or how you should feel.

The way to get off this endless binge/diet treadmill has to be to change your thought patterns. You will never get slim until you are "slim" in your mind – then your body will automatically follow. If you try and do it the other way round, with sole emphasis on the food aspect, you will probably lose weight but, sooner or later, back it will all come; the weight goes – the problem stays.

I am pretty sure that whenever you "break your diet"

you ultimately blame your lack of willpower. Sometimes, though, it could be your deeper, subconscious thoughts that cause you to sabotage your own efforts to lose weight. What do we mean by that?

Well, what sort of person are you? We all have a "sense of self" which is based on past experiences, successes and failures, other people's opinions and our own reactions to all of these. We then proceed to act on that "self" as if it were true. From childhood, a casual remark made half in jest – "Oh, you're so clumsy!" or an overheard "She's useless at Maths" – can embed itself into your mind. The next time you accidentally drop something, that remark pops back into your head and you think, "I'm so clumsy". Well, haven't you just "proved" it? The problem is that, now, you have started to accept that perhaps you *are* clumsy. Anything you believe to be true, whether it *is* or not, can have a remarkably negative impact on your behaviour . . .

Past clients have told me all sorts of nonsense:

* Food eaten in the evening automatically turns to fat.
* If you eat fruit with a meal it will rot in your stomach.
* If the whole family is fat it must be in the genes.
* Doing exercise is dangerous if you are over 50.

Do your own beliefs have an unduly negative influence over the way you deal with food? If your mother was into the "Eat up - think of all the starving children" routine, you may find it difficult to throw food away. In that case, ask yourself who exactly will benefit if you don't leave half a lamb chop on your plate? Logically, the answer is no-one: sometimes food has to be slung out – get used to it!

Most cases of comfort eating have their roots in childhood. As a baby, your first experience of food was being held and cuddled at the same time as being fed, so you equated loving with a full tummy. It's understandable then that, when you feel misunderstood and deprived of love, you fill your tummy to compensate.

What else could you have absorbed from your home environment when you were growing up? In some homes, mealtimes are fraught with tensions and criticism: table manners, untidy hair, bad grades at school. If yours was like this it can hardly be surprising if still today, when under stress, you often stuff yourself with food then berate yourself as though you were your own parent. As a child, did you eat meals in front of the television? If so, this may be the reason why you feel the urge to snack during your evening's viewing even now. Maybe when you were young you frequently had to wait to go out and play with your friends until lunch or dinner was finished. This ensured that you gulped your food down as quickly as possible because you knew everyone was waiting for you outside. The fun started when you had finished eating so even today, in adulthood, you may be continuing to bolt your food out of sheer habit. As a youngster, your tea was probably ready when you got back from school. Is it any wonder now, that you feel hungry when you get inside the front door after work?

If you retain these childhood images, and we all do, it is very difficult to imagine that your life could be any other way. You may rationalise your behaviour by saying "Well, that's how I am" but, admit it, that is *not* how you *have to be*. By changing your thoughts you can change your life for the better.

Examples of a "Fat Attitude"

Sally is a prime example of how beliefs "programmed" into your mind can affect you. Sally, a divorcee, has been on every diet regime going and has lost and regained the same three stone over and over again. Sally's excuses for never losing weight permanently include:

"No diet can ever work for me; I've got no willpower".

"I've never been able to stick at anything – never mind a diet – for very long".

"The only way I can drop a few pounds is by practically starving myself!"

Sally has convinced herself for so long that she can't stick to a diet that it seems as though, each time she tries, she subconsciously has to "prove" that this is indeed the case – and so she fails again.

Why does Sally keep doing this? Why does she keep spending so much money on different diets which never work? Could she actually be getting some sort of satisfaction out of it? The very idea sounds ridiculous but, if you think about it, every time it happens Sally gets to reinforce her beliefs and can say to herself "See, I was right. I can't stick to a diet. I've just got no willpower."

As well as the satisfaction of being "right" she also gets to moan about her troubles to all her friends and, in return, receives sympathy and acknowledgement: "Yes, I tried that diet as well and I had to give up after three days, I felt so awful". This makes her feel better. She is not the only one then.

Understanding that these are in fact empty "satisfactions" has helped Sally a lot. More significantly, Sally has come to realise that she has been avoiding the pleasure of seeing herself as the slim person she claims she really wants to be.

We discussed her fears. I asked her "What would you miss about being fat?" After the first incredulous "Don't be daft!" Sally faced the fact that talking about diets has been making up a high percentage of conversation with her friends. Since her divorce, most of her friendships have been forged at slimming clubs. Sally has been afraid that, if she gets slim, she might have nothing to talk about. She enjoys seeing her friends at the meetings and going out for a mineral water afterwards. She even admits that trying these different diets gives her "something to do" - a goal to work towards. Her worry is that this motivation will disappear if she actually succeeds in losing weight.

I urged Sally to build new thought patterns establishing a positive image of herself as a slim and healthy person. She was to tell herself that she didn't have to follow the latest fad or starve to lose weight. She just has to plan and eat sensibly, give herself time and get on with the rest of her life. Sally decided to take up her old hobby of painting with water colours, to set aside regular exercise time and to stop discussing diets with her friends. Maybe this time she will do it – maybe. She is going about it the right way now.

Marie, so far, has never managed to get slim and, at 5 ft 3 ins, weighs nearly 17 stone. Although professing to "hate being so fat", she, like Sally, insists that she can't lose weight. Marie lives alone and works for a firm of solicitors as a personal assistant. Although highly intelligent, she has never felt compelled to further her extensive knowledge of law.

"Just look at me" was her response to my suggestions that she could easily better herself in this way. Marie seriously believed that clients would think "If she can't deal with her own obvious problems, how will she deal with mine?"

Lonely and with few unmarried friends, Marie admitted that being fat was a way of getting sympathy and attention from people even at the cost of occasional ridicule. She had such a low opinion of herself that it gave her a warm feeling that anyone would be interested in her even at that level. She had, however, come to realise that she was using her weight to stop herself trying to achieve anything purposeful with her life, and as an excuse for when she failed at anything else.

I persuaded Marie to end her love affair with family-sized cakes (she used to eat a whole fruit cake over the course of an evening). I also managed to talk her into enrolling on a course of evening classes studying law.

"At least when I am studying, I won't be eating!" she said, shyly showing me her big notebook with the following week's eating plan already pencilled in. I think Marie will succeed this time.

Tune in to Your "Auto-Pilot"

Your subconscious mind is an amazing gift. Automatically following any instruction you choose to give it, this powerful, indirect part of your mind can help you achieve any goal you want. I will refer to this brilliant mechanism as your auto-pilot.

When you first start any new diet, provided you fix your mind steadfastly on the end result, i.e. a slimmer, firmer shape, your auto-pilot will strive to help you achieve it.

The secret is to swamp it with positive commands only. If you allow yourself to get bogged down with thoughts such as "I can't do this", "I desperately need to eat that doughnut", your auto-pilot just switches to the new – and wrong – instruction and says "OK, eat the doughnut". If, however, you can quickly override such distractions and re-focus on the original slim image you have projected, your auto-pilot will cheerfully switch back again to boost your resolve to succeed.

So your auto-pilot doesn't care whether you are fat or slim; it just follows your instructions. The danger is that, if you allow negative thinking to get the upper hand at your conscious mind level, it will work just as willingly for you the other way! If you continuously tell yourself how awful you look and how you hate your body, your auto-pilot will assume that you *want* to hate your body. Accordingly, it will arrange for it to crave the more fattening varieties of food and ensure your wish comes true. Then you can hate yourself even more. Your auto-pilot doesn't decide, it just agrees and backs up your wishes. Many people involved with sport will recognise how programming success breeds that success. For example, if you play tennis and visualise yourself emulating Pete Sampras' serve often enough, it won't be long before you can! Conversely – and quoting a former client – "I just have to think the word 'Cadbury's' and, 'instantly', 3 lb of fat attaches itself to my thighs!"

You can't just re-program your auto-pilot to "think slim" all the time, as it works below the level of consciousness. But, if you can learn to trust it, you can practise giving it the right instructions and use it to your best advantage.

Food doesn't talk. Food itself has no power over you. It can't force you to pick it up and eat it. Any power that a particular food has is the power you have given it: for examples, when you think you have no choice; when you listen to Fat-U saying urgently "I must have that".

Fat-U doesn't care that eating ice cream makes you fat, or that you might have a high cholesterol count or get puffed when you climb the stairs. When Fat-U tells you to eat ice cream the implication is "eat it now". The ice cream makers don't care about you either. As long as there are people who are willing to buy their products they will continue making them. Every time you give in, you are reinforcing the power of that trigger food to control you. Your auto-pilot always agrees – remember.

Mechanistic diets, like counting every calorie or practising food combining, are no doubt excellent diversions to be followed. Where they fail bingers long-term is in programming your mind correctly for success and then allowing your weight to shed.

"Naturally" slim people each carry the thought in their heads that "It doesn't seem to matter what I eat; I never put on weight". Have you heard any of your skinny friends express this concept? Or even "I wish I *could* put on a couple of pounds". (Hate! Hate!) Somehow their bodies follow their thought patterns and they stay slim. They know that one piece of chocolate isn't fattening and couldn't conceive of anyone eating a half pound slab at one sitting. But for you, the binger, as we know, that one square of chocolate could spell disaster.

In order to knock out such disasters, you need to change your self-image. When you believe that you should measure up to some other person's "norm" but can't do so, you can feel inferior. You are not inferior; you are not superior: you are simply you. You don't have to fulfil anyone else's expectations. You just have to be who you are.

Why are bingers so loath to admit good things about themselves? In diet counselling sessions, I sometimes ask clients to write down all the negative things they believe about themselves on one side of a page and all the positive things on the other side. The negative thoughts seem to come thick and fast:

"I'm too lazy to do any exercise."

"I can't stay motivated long enough to finish anything – except a cheesecake!"

"I am completely untidy and disorganised; there are unpaid bills everywhere."

"I have no willpower at parties; I always eat everything in sight."

Positive traits? Somehow these always seem more difficult to recall:

"If I say I will do something, I always do it punctually."

"I'm always there when the kids come home from school."

"I can pre-set the video." (This one got a round of applause.)

Like those of most of my clients, I'm sure your list of negatives is longer than the positives. But are these negatives really true? OK – you think you are disorganised. Suppose you decide that from now, this instant, you are going to stop messing about, and get yourself together. First, you will make a list of things that must be done; then you will number them in priority order, and then set to deal with each and tick them off one by one. For example: (1) pay bills (2) organise school run, etc. What would happen then? Your life would run more smoothly and you wouldn't always be chasing your tail to get a cheque in the post before they cut off your phone.

You go from "I am so disorganised" to "I am getting myself together". Once you do that deep down inside, you will find that your behaviour really does change to make it true. However, to wipe away "I can't" and substitute "I can; I will" you have to mean business. Like everything else, the more you do it, the easier it gets.

If you have a destructive pattern that you can't break, ask yourself why? If you can't answer that, try asking another way. "If I no longer behaved like that, what would be different?" Often the answer comes back "My life would be much better".

Precisely.

You can't change anything that has happened in the past. You can only use any past mistakes as a way of learning how to cope in the same situation in the future. Then let them go. Life can only be understood backwards but it must be lived forwards. It's time to move on. If you have previously decided that you are a certain sort of person and behaved in ways to verify that, you can equally choose to change, simply by behaving differently. Visualise yourself acting, feeling and "being" as you want to be: a slim, healthy person with a body to match. Then, in time, you will be. Imagine the food that you eat being processed to nourish your body and make you fit and strong but not fat. Your autopilot will automatically guide you towards the sort of food that will do just that.

These exercises build positive new "memories" into your autopilot and will help to dissipate old, negative feelings.

The minute you decide to stop giving power to the past, it loses its power over you. Any sentence starting with "I can't" puts you in a position of weakness. Change it straightaway to "I can" – even if you feel anything but positive at that moment. You can always add " – maybe not right now but eventually" or "I am determined to get on top of this and not be beaten".

Everything you do implies choice, whether it seems that way or not. Thinking "I choose to eat carrots rather than biscuits" instead of "I ought to eat carrots rather than biscuits" makes it an act of free will rather than a drag. Yes! The words you use are important. If you say "I don't want to be fat any more" your auto-pilot will latch on to the words "fat" and "more". Say instead "I am going to be beautifully slim, and fit and healthy". Your subconscious mind has no hidden agendas. It simply obeys. The answer to "I can't stop eating" is "Then how can I help you? Let's go and see what's in the fridge". The answer to "I can lose weight" is "OK – let's go for a walk then".

Everybody "talks" to themselves all the time. You are constantly seeing, judging, evaluating in this way. Therefore, make this conscious dialogue with yourself to reverse all the negative things you usually say. When you look in the mirror, focus on positive things: "You look really nice; that flab will soon go; you are working on it. You're doing fine so far today; keep it up". Never underestimate yourself. Think of what you want to do as easy and it will become so.

By building yourself up instead of putting yourself down all the time, you will rise above feeling threatened or upset by every chance remark. Being a few pounds overweight does not make you a worthless person. See yourself as liked, wanted, accepted and able, and you will develop a feeling of oneness with other people and become less vulnerable. You can't please everyone and you don't have to.

When I make this point during counselling sessions someone invariably mutters: "You haven't met my mother-in-law/boss/social worker. She makes me binge every time". Not true. YOU make you binge every time. She may be the catalyst but your mother-in-law does not physically stuff food into your mouth. You do.

Destructive emotions such as self-pity, anger and resentment can flare up at any time. You may find that they are often linked to the same person or a similar situation recurring time and again. By hanging on to such feelings, you are possibly hanging on to your fat as well. Finding someone to blame for situations in which you find yourself is very common. It can build to the point where you feel wronged by the most innocent remark and dissolve into comfort eating.

You may feel, for example, that other people "owe" you gratitude or appreciation and you resent it if this is not forthcoming. Notice, however, that the resentment itself is not caused by them: it is simply your own emotional response. They are probably blissfully unaware of your expectations. Don't use food to punish yourself (or anyone else for that matter). That solves nothing. Instead, take responsibility and accept that the only person your gnawing anger can hurt is you. The solution is obvious. You stop.

When you can isolate the trigger, you can take steps to neutralise the effect. Once you know your enemy, you can remove the powerful hold over you.

Another cause of mindless eating is guilt. (Guilt is hereditary: you get it from your mother!) Rationalise this. Nobody's life has been affected because you ate a cream cake. You have nothing to feel guilty about. The only promise you have broken is the one you made to yourself. This doesn't mean you have to punish yourself by starving – or bingeing - for the rest of the day. Reaffirm your promise to yourself to live slim and move on.

Check if your thought and bingeing patterns match any of these:

All or Nothing: Everything is either black or white, good or bad. If something doesn't turn out exactly as planned, the whole day is sabotaged. The typical example: You were tired and absentmindedly picked at a small piece of your trigger food. "That's it; I've blown it now. I might as well carry on eating and" – you know the rest of the sentence . . .

It Will Never End: One or two niggling events herald a day of misery. It is raining. Your car won't start. The battery is flat. "Uh-Oh, I can see that this is going to be a bad day and this rain is going on forever". Bad day equals bingeing day.

Jumping to Conclusions: You think negatively even when there is no real reason. For example, you ask a colleague if she would like to go for a drink after work, and she says she can't because she is too busy. Your heart sinks: "I must have said something to upset her". You haven't – she simply doesn't have time today. Don't eat your heart out!

It Must Be My Fault: Your husband was overlooked for promotion at work. You blame yourself: "I knew I shouldn't have worn that low-cut dress at the Christmas party. I thought his boss looked at me a bit funny". (The truth is he was probably drunk!)

This sort of self-imposed stress can build up to the point where it becomes difficult to focus on anything positive. Stress is exacerbated by the way you think and feel.

Although you can't entirely eliminate stress, you can learn to manage it so that it doesn't become an overwhelming or destructive force in your life. Try and disperse feelings of frustration and anger as soon as possible. The faster you can act to change to positive thoughts, the sooner your stress levels decrease – and the less likely you are to commit "bingeicide".

Food Cravings

Because food addictions are so similar to those of alcohol and drugs, the "pleasure pathways" in your mind are activated in much the same way. When you crave a certain food, you are experiencing the same, but less intense, urge as you might for a drug. The feeling is so strong you want to act on it immediately and get that food into your mouth.

What you have to remind yourself, in the cold light of day, is that, no matter how intense the craving may be at that moment, a craving is all it is – a feeling, an emotion. It is not an order to be obeyed. By changing the words in your mind, you can zap that destructive, ongoing dialogue and move on. What dialogue? Well, surely you recognise: "Ooh, that looks delicious – I bet it has zillions of calories – shall I?" and "I've been good today so far – no; leave it – maybe one small bit? – if I don't have any dessert tonight?" and so on and on.

Here are a few more binge thoughts. Practise coming up with an effective challenge so you can win the internal argument each time.

Binge Thought: "It's only 50 calories a slice."
Zap: "It's not how many calories in each slice, but how many slices I'll eat."
Binge Thought: "The company is picking up the bill; I might as well eat it."

Zap: "It doesn't matter who's paying; if I eat it, it will end up on my thighs."

Binge Thought: "It says 'half fat' on the label, that means I can eat twice as much."

Zap: " 'Half fat' doesn't mean 'Half the number of calories'. Don't start."

Binge Thought: "That smells really yummy."

Zap: "FAT smells yummy; and that's all it is."

Binge Thought: "I had all those chips for lunch, so I might as well keep going."

Zap: "That's done and past; forget about it. Don't blow the whole day."

Binge Thought: "I've been really good, I deserve a reward."

Zap: "Being slim and in control is my best reward."

Binge Thought: "I've had a rotten day at work; I'm so stressed out."

Zap: "Being miserable because I'm fat won't help."

Binge Thought: "I really love the taste of that."

Zap: "Do I love it enough to wear it? No."

Binge Thought: "I'm premenstrual and really crave something sweet."

Zap: "Eating sugar will probably make me feel worse."

Binge Thought: "I'm meant to be on holiday. Surely I should be able to enjoy myself?"

Zap: "I'm not going to blow everything I've achieved for a plate of chips!"

Binge Thought: "It looks wonderful."

Zap: "Yes – on the plate – not round my waist! Nothing 'wonderful' there!"

I'm sure you get the idea. Practise, practise, all the time. You may need to have these sorts of internal conversations several times a day before your mind acknowledges that you are now in charge. This sort of conscious thinking is what will charge the batteries of a "remote control" for your autopilot. You are programming yourself to use it to good effect. Soon your autopilot will be "changing channels" before a binge-thought can get in the frame.

Key Phrase
Sometimes, especially during the first few weeks, Fat-U is so insidious that you don't actually "hear" any words. The urge to binge is simply a *feeling* that comes over you, like a shift of gears in your head – a feeling so strong that it rushes to overwhelm your voice of reason. The way to resist is to have a couple of key phrases sufficiently strong to zap that feeling before it can turn into a thought. One that seems to work for most clients is a firm "Don't start; don't get the taste". You know full well that, once you experience the taste of whatever is tempting you in your mouth, you will go on eating. So, instantly the first inkling of a binge-feeling, or thought, word or picture (or worse – a sighting or sniff) of one of your trigger foods starts to form, tell yourself firmly: "Don't start: don't get the taste". Then remove yourself, or the food, from any chance of physical temptation.

Other phrases suggested are "It's just a lump of fat, leave it" or "You do not eat that stuff any more – move on". Decide on a punchy key phrase that will suit *you*.

Accompanying your key phrase with a graphic image like slamming down the phone or putting a big mental cross through the "picture" lends added impact. Your key phrase or graphic is essential if you are to stop any binge thought dead in its tracks. If you let one take a grip, other physio-logical changes take place: you suddenly feel hungry, your mouth waters, you feel a bit weak and shaky and all this convinces you that you *need* that food. Beating the craving

gets harder by the second. You have to convince yourself fast that you *don't* need food that will sweep you away back into feeling fat, bloated and miserable. No taste is worth that.

Practise your key phrase every time you are tempted. You

will soon find that it will override the old "Ooh, I'd love some of that" and the craving will simply disappear.

Social eating cravings are usually triggered by the sight and smell of food. Cravings at home are more usually triggered by hormones or moods: frustration, boredom or grouchy children can all send you scurrying into the kitchen. Until you become a practised binge-thought zapper, you may well need a way to hold on to your non-binge countermand long enough to prevent the same binge thought resurfacing a few moments later. That's where you need a different strategy:

Displacement Activities

A "displacement activity" is one that will distract your mind off food for the next half hour or so. It should be something totally unconnected with food that you like doing or that you had planned to do at some point. Examples:

Dig out some old photo albums
Check your bank statement
Tidy out a cupboard
Make that phone call you've been putting off
Tidy your make-up drawer
Go and post the letter in your out-tray
Do a crossword puzzle
Give yourself a manicure – you can't eat with wet nail polish
Play computer games.

The best course of action if you are at home may be to get out of the house. Grab your Walkman and go for a walk. If the snack-attack is really fierce and you need to put something in your mouth, eat a melon – a whole one – then go for a walk. If your binge thought arose because you caught sight

of some tempting food and you can get rid of the offending food by stuffing it in the bin, then do so. It is permissible to throw food away that is bad for you, even if it isn't really "bad" food.

Since binge thoughts will inevitably present themselves sooner rather than later, you will find it easier to stick to your resolve if you decide in advance what your next few displacement activities are going to be and write them down in your food diary. This will ensure you are not standing in the kitchen thinking "Now, what was it I was going to do? I'll just eat this sardine and lemon curd sandwich while I decide". Somehow, writing down two or three displacement activities in advance turns them into a commitment and, when it comes to the crunch, you will keep to it – however grudgingly – rather than risk a wholesale binge. This is having a positive action ready to combat a negative thought.

A word of warning though: when you feel a binge-thought welling up, probably the last thing in the world you will want to do is stick to your chosen task. In fact you may have decided to ignore this bit just to leave yourself a loop-hole in case you screw up again. That's OK – it's up to you – but, if you keep your promise to yourself, you win; if you don't, you lose. If you are wishy-washy about this, you will stay on the binge-roundabout and reinforce your ability to make up convincing excuses to justify your behaviour exactly like you always have before.

A Blip

Occasionally – unless you are inhuman – you will give in to a craving. I am not talking about a binge here, just a momentary blip. A packet of biscuits is a blip. Sometimes too many elements will combine against you and your resolve will fly out the window. This is not a tragedy unless you consider it a green light to go on eating for the rest of the day. The important thing is what you do next. A blip only turns into a binge if you carry on eating. Say to yourself firmly "Stop eating, NOW!" Then say "It's done; forget it; move on". You can't "uneat" what you have just eaten. Therefore, put it firmly out of your mind and then carry on with what you are doing.

Do you think that slim people never overeat on occasions? Of course they do. They just don't dwell on it. They forget about it and move on. So should you. The only way to handle a small lapse is to acknowledge that it's happened and get back to normal eating.

Deal With It

If you do find yourself in an awkward trigger situation, learn to deal with it. Come and eavesdrop on a joint counselling conversation with three clients.

"Your aunt is at home recovering from an operation. When you phone to ask how she is, she invites you round for a cup of tea. You ask her not to prepare anything special as you are trying to lose weight. When you get there she has made a cake especially for you. What do you do?"

They thought about it for a while. Then Lynda said "I suppose I wouldn't really like to upset her after she had gone to all that trouble. I would eat a slice".

"So you would get fat just to please your aunt!" said Sarra incredulously. "Cake is my number one trigger food. I would just say 'No thanks, I don't want any'."

"But I made it specially for you" Lynda said in her best "hurt aunt" voice.

"I don't care" answered Sarra. "I just don't want any."

"Isn't there another way of dealing with this?" I asked.

"Well" Jill came in. "I would probably tell her that the cake looked absolutely delicious, but that I have just had an enormous lunch – not entirely untrue – and could I possibly take a slice home with me to eat later?"

Right! Jill managed to handle this without offence and, more to the point, without eating. She would accept the lovingly-wrapped package with gracious thanks and probably present it to the traffic warden about to book her car, so making everyone happy.

Dealing with trigger situations is never easy. Client, Kathy, asks:

"My daughter made some chocolate chip cookies at school and they were sitting there in the kitchen begging to be eaten. I wasn't particularly hungry but, wherever I was in the house, I could "see" those chunky biscuits in my mind, and so I kept thinking 'I must have one' even though I knew that, if I ate one, I would eat the lot. What do I do in that sort of situation?"

Think of a strategy to deal with it. This is your daughter's schoolwork, not just a snack for you. Who would appreciate them more? Suggest to your daughter that she wrap them up nicely and take them to Grandma next time you go. Repeat "Don't start; don't get the taste" or your own key phrase, and put them away out of sight. Having involved your daughter in your plan, you can't now go back on it and eat them yourself.

Think about the words that tempted you too: "I must have one". Who says? What do you mean "must"? Why do you have to obey a command which, logically, has no authority? If you quickly re-word the phrase "It would be nice to have one of Sophie's biscuits" then the compulsion is not really there. Then you can answer "Yes, it would be nice but I choose not to have one right now". In the moment that it takes to do this you have weakened your craving. You realise that this feeling is not some monstrous outside force you can't control. You don't have to take orders from a biscuit. Every time you succeed, winning gets easier.

Communication

People around you are not always helpful when you are trying to change your eating habits. Your children might eat fattening snacks in front of you; your husband might think he will cheer you up by buying your favourite chocolates. You don't want to upset them by screaming "You know I'm on a diet!" so you get more frustrated and, as these feelings build up, you are more likely to turn to food, the last thing you really want. However, you can make things easier for yourself.

Let people know what you want from them. Your family are not mind-readers. SAY to the kids "Look, I want to cut out crisps for a while. Please help me by not scrunching them in front of me because I'll only want some."

Beware the "you" word. Instead of starting a conversation with "You" – e.g. "You always buy those chocolates when you know I'm trying to lose weight" – use "I" instead. "I have a real problem seeing those chocolates sitting there. I would much prefer it if you didn't buy them for a while". A "you" statement can sound accusing. An "I" statement describes how you feel and is less likely to antagonise the person on the receiving end.

Many women find it very difficult to express what they really want. They feel selfish about putting their needs above others but, when you think about it, you don't have to do anything – especially eat – solely to please someone else. Your needs are just as important but they may have been submerged over the years by putting your children first or bowing to other people's opinions to keep the peace.

Mental Rehearsal
Here is another client, Geraldine:

"I started this new job in December as a PA in a very large firm and was told that everyone was expected to turn up at the Christmas party. I felt so nervous walking in by myself because I only knew the other two girls in my department and I couldn't see them straightaway. Everyone was talking and laughing and I felt so self-conscious about being alone. I gravitated towards this big table which was covered with snacks. I remember thinking 'Nobody knows me here so I can eat what I want and it will give me something to do'."

Poor Geraldine! How could she cope with all those negatives?

She could have had a mental rehearsal. This is a brilliant tactic before you go anywhere that involves food. She could have imagined herself arriving there, greeting people with a

smile and selecting appropriate sorts of food and drink. She could have visualised herself chatting with friendly people and watching the trays of hors d'oeuvres go by – only reaching out if there were raw vegetables on display. Always picture yourself succeeding and you will.

Geraldine would also have been wise, at a practical level, to have had a sandwich before leaving for the party so that she wouldn't be starving hungry when she got there, and to have arranged to meet her co-workers beforehand so that they could walk in together.

Stay Positive

A common cause of negative thoughts is a tendency to exaggerate the difficulty of what you are trying to achieve. A lot of bingeing takes place as a result. It happens especially when people feel they have too much to do and won't be able to fit it all in, which can make them feel edgy, panicky and – ravenous!

If you feel yourself getting shaky when everything turns chaotic around you – stop! Sit down calmly – one more minute out of the day won't make all that difference – and look at the tasks crowding in on you rationally. You can only do one thing at a time, and everything will get done in its turn – or not! Either way, there are plenty of hours in which to do them. Try not to create a mental picture of a mass of jobs to be completed by tomorrow or this afternoon. Even on the busiest day, the crowded hours come one at a time and the problems come in single file. You can cope, and you usually do, don't you? Stay calm and work out your priorities. You won't get anything done faster if you turn instead to food, and then feel bloated and sick or get smudges of cream cake over your clean print-out.

I often hear the lament: "If only I could lose this fat/stop bingeing, I would be so happy". Why can't you be happy now? This way of thinking means that you are putting your life on hold for some time in the future. You will still be living the same life – only a few pounds lighter! Happiness, or rather, contentment is, to some extent a mental habit that must be learned and practised in the present. It depends very much on being content with what you have – your home, your family, your job – and trying not to let circumstances or other people dictate to you how you should feel or react. This is not to say you can't be ambitious. It is only pointing out that maintaining pleasure in the stage you are at is equally important.

Sometimes it is very difficult to be upbeat and positive. Every family experiences sad and painful events occasionally. This is natural but you can make things easier for yourself if you do not add your own feelings of self-pity or resentment to the misfortune.

To achieve happiness you must accept yourself for what you are. By substituting positive thinking for the destructive kind, you are not changing your "self"; you will, however, creatively improve your own image of yourself. When you feel self-confident you will act that way.

Clients who have succeeded in gaining control over their eating are the ones who have made a conscious change in their thinking about food. Their internal dialogue is encouraging, self-supporting and positive. They don't make deals with food – "If I eat this now, I won't eat anything tonight". If you try and make deals the food always wins. You are intelligent – the food isn't. Think about *what you want to achieve* and imagine that it is already happening. Then your autopilot will say "OK, let's do it. You feel great".

8

GOING, GOING, STUCK!

Here we go. It's first thing in the morning. You've been to the loo and taken the clips out of your hair. You are completely naked and it's time to weigh yourself. You arrange the scales on the flattest part of the floor and check that the pointer is exactly on zero. You put one foot on, balancing against the wall with your hand. You ease the other foot on and gingerly let go of the wall. Your reaction to the result of this pantomime depends on whether the final number displayed is higher or lower than your expectations.

Get Your Balancing Act Right!
Let us assume that for some reason your weight has gone up one teensy weensy fraction of a pound. Oh no! It can't be! You have stuck faithfully to your diet for the last three weeks (apart from that one disaster with the lemon meringue pie, but we won't go into that!) and you should have lost at **least** 5 lb.

You step on the scales again, arranging your feet slightly differently this time and holding your breath. The result is the same. OK – the best of three. You go into the kitchen where the floor is flatter. You check that the pointer is actually on zero and not nudging over a bit. Right – now – you pull in your tummy and hold on to the fridge with both hands whilst you put one foot softly on to the scales. You leave the other foot in the air and gently let go of the fridge one hand at a time. Sh**! You get off in disgust.

Yet you felt so virtuously slim this morning. Before you got on the scales you looked in the mirror and registered that you did, indeed, look quite slim. The roll of fat around your midriff definitely had a sharp – well, slight – indentation, and you could plainly – well, almost – see your hipbones, if you stretched your arms up over your head. Pleased with this image you decided to weigh yourself even though you had weighed in only two days before.

The result was almost certainly caused by the body's natural fluctuations in water content, but it has the most disastrous effect on your mood even though your weight is only a fraction of a pound up. NOW, when you look in the mirror, you see bulges round your thighs which were definitely not there two minutes ago. Now you look *fat* – you look *very* fat.

With the simple action of standing on the scales your mood has changed from optimism to despair and this affects your whole day. Yesterday was a "good" diet day; you wore a straight skirt with a tailored shirt tucked in at the waist. Today, you choose something dark, long and baggy, and skulk off to work feeling fat and betrayed.

That is only the start: you can't concentrate on the papers on your desk because your mind is going over and over the same incredulous thoughts. You haven't eaten *anything* fattening – well, apart from four crisps which the new temp offered round yesterday but four lousy crisps – I mean to say! Maybe the scales are wrong? No; the evidence is staring you in the thighs. You have gained. Your mind, now miserably controlled by Fat-U, shifts to "What's the point?"

Whereas yesterday you felt slim and attractive, with Slim-U firmly in charge of your eating, today you allow the reading on the scales – this *number* – to affect your day, your mood and your life. You feel frumpy, unattractive and, what's more, *starving*. What's the point of dieting, of striving to improve yourself, of *anything* for that matter? Nothing works. You almost feel like crying.

By the time the tea trolley comes round, you are determined to grab the most fattening item you can find and shove it angrily into your mouth. Who cares? So you'll be fat! So what! Munch, munch, munch – tea lady, come back! Have you got any more of those Danish –?

Extreme? I'm not so sure. By jumping on the scales every couple of days, you are allowing a mechanical object not only to measure, but to judge you, and to dictate that above a certain number, you are somehow unacceptable as a person.

Do you see how pointless this is? What *difference* does it make what you weigh? You need to be slim, fit and healthy with enough energy to get through the day. Scales only tell you how many pounds you weigh. They do not tell you, for example, about your body's fat or muscle content – so you don't know how much fat you have lost or how much muscle you have gained. This is why I recommend that you hide those scales in the garage, or somewhere equally inaccessible, and only get them out to check your progress occasionally. There is nothing you can do to change your weight right now – this second – so acknowledge and accept that, whatever it is, that's fine. You will soon know when you have lost weight; it will show when you look in the mirror and when you can grab handfuls of material round your waistband. Meanwhile, why go in for self-inflicted grief, obsessively checking daily ups and downs against some guesswork target figure?

One of my clients is an actress and recently auditioned for

a leading role in a West End production. She had been losing weight successfully and steadily for some months. However, a "nervous nibbler", she picked at nuts, raisins, Smarties and bourbon biscuits as she studied the script. By the day of the audition she felt fat, lumpy, and petrified. On an impulse she got on the scales and found to her delight that she had lost 4 lb. Wow! She decided all that nervous energy must have burned up more calories. Her mood lifted as she scanned her wardrobe deciding what to wear. She picked a slim, blue skirt, got into it easily, and sailed off to the audition feeling light, cheerful and optimistic. She got the part – "no contest" – she was by far the best. When she got home she discovered her small son had been playing with the scales and they were, in fact, reading 6 lb lighter than they should have been.

So, instead of losing 4 lb, she had actually gained 2 lb. I wonder if she would have still got the part had she known?

So powerful are these numbers psychologically then, that even a deficit on the scales can cause problems. Suppose you find you have lost 5 lb. You are delighted with this result and then calculate that, at this present rate, you should have lost another 5 lb by next Thursday and then at least another 2 lb by the following Monday. Oh yes?

Fat-U seizes on this thought, because this reminds you that you would like to be even thinner. Fat-U then tries to tell you that, as you are obviously unhappy with yourself right now, you should do what you have always done in this situation: eat something. The mistake here is in trying to jump ahead of your experience. You are as you are *today* and that's fine.

The "Other People" Problem

The fatter you are, however, the more difficult it is to look in the mirror and simply say "Well, this is me" without experiencing a wave of desperation. Not only do you have to work against your own prejudices but you also have to get by in a world where well-meaning people hint that you would feel much better if you lost some weight – as if it were that easy!

However difficult it seems, you have to decide that, from now on, you are not going to be affected by what other people say. You are how you are. It's nothing to do with anyone else – the same as it won't be any of their business when you get slim.

The Way Forward

The way to stop bingeing is to take control of your eating. Being out of control – even some of the time – doesn't mean you are weak-willed, stupid or self-indulgent. It's just your way of dealing with the pressures of life and the proliferation of sweet, stodgy, comfort food that surrounds you. You can change this simply by changing *how, when* and *what* you eat.

To achieve anything worthwhile takes work, focus and endurance. It is no different with food. It may be hard, sometimes, but not as hard as continuing to binge and being miserable.

Everyone has their own pattern of weight loss. However, most people go through similar stages on their way to reaching the weight at which they eventually stabilise. When you, personally, will experience each stage, or to what degree, obviously I can't say, but let me give you some hints about each one. The first three weeks are the most important – the initial twenty-one consecutive days – because it is during this period that most people jack in any new diet plan. If you can get through that and continue with your food diary for a further three weeks, you will be well on the road to living slim.

The First Week

On your first day it is permissible to get on the scales. Weigh yourself without any clothes on so you can't kid yourself that your knickers weigh 5 lb. Check what the scales say and record it. Be detached and non-judgmental. This is what you weigh and it is neither good nor bad: it just is.

By now you have been through the kitchen cupboards and got rid of your main trigger foods (hopefully not down your throat). Don't try "giving yourself a start" by only having bananas or whatever on the first day. That's fat thinking. With this plan you give yourself permission to eat.

Try to overcome any resistance to writing your food choices in your diary. I *know* you know what you are going to eat. I *know* nobody is going to look at what you have written and say "Well done". However, "knowing" and "doing" are two different things. There is always a period of transition between starting something new and seeing results. Writing down your food intake is a way of helping you to focus on the project in hand and is very important. Just do it – it's not forever.

Don't forget to plan your walking – or other exercise – times. Try to get in three days this week.

You should feel fine during the first week, though you may find yourself running to the loo and peeing quite a lot. This is because you are likely to be eating more fruit and vegetables which contain large quantities of water and act as a mild diuretic. You are also cutting down considerably on salt or sugar (according to which category of trigger food you go for), both of which hold water in your body tissues.

By the third day you will feel lighter but only because of the water loss. It takes time before your body realises that what you really want to lose is FAT.

If you usually pick at food while watching television, plan your evening snack very carefully and what time you are going to eat it. Be especially careful during the weekend if that is the time you usually socialise, even when this is usually informal. You still need to decide what you are going to eat and drink, and stick to it – even if exactly *when* depends upon other people. If alcohol is not a trigger food for you, and you can stop after one or two drinks, then happily include it.

By the end of the first week you will notice a difference in your face. Even your eyes should seem clearer and less puffy.

You can tell yourself you did brilliantly well this week; you look great, you feel slimmer and more attractive, you can deal with everything in a calm and controlled way – *and you didn't binge*.

The Second Week

During your second week, there may be the odd day when you suddenly feel starving or crave your trigger food. There is no reason why you should suddenly feel hungry on a particular day if you are following your plan and eating at short, regular intervals. The reason may be stress, hormonal changes or whatever. If this happens, do your utmost to keep Fat-U at bay – that little voice telling you that this is all nonsense and pleading that you can have your usual Kit Kat with your mid-morning coffee. Fat-U detests change and will try hard to undermine your efforts.

Eat more vegetables on this day, either raw or cooked. If you are worried that it will annoy your co-workers if you sit at your desk crunching raw carrots, don't be. That's their problem.

When you feel a hunger pang, ask yourself if this is genuine hunger or just a niggle. These feelings usually happen in the evening. If you ate properly at your last meal, including some protein, it is probably a niggle. Tell yourself that you can eat something again in an hour. Then deliberately keep busy in the meantime. If the niggle gets worse and you find yourself prowling from room to room getting more edgy by the minute, eat something really stodgy like a bagel – slowly, with a cup of tea – then go and clean your teeth. This seems to signal the end of the day and the end of eating. But it's only 9 p.m. I can hear you exclaim! So? Would you rather spend the next two hours emptying the contents of the fridge into your mouth and THEN clean your teeth?

When attempting to change your eating habits you want to avoid the following: tiredness, constipation and hunger. More than any other factors, I am sure these are responsible for most people abandoning their diet plans early and choosing to stay fat.

Try not to get tired. It is not always physical movement that causes fatigue. Mental stress does it too, especially when you try to juggle work, children, parents, etc. Exhaustion comes on quite suddenly – an overwhelming surge of weakness sweeps over you – and you usually grab the nearest sugary snack to "give you energy". You then convince yourself that your body must "need" sugar. It doesn't.

Your body is going through tremendous changes as it adapts to the new regime. An occasional surge of tiredness is quite common at the beginning, usually because your body previously relied on false bursts of quick-fire energy supplied by trigger foods. This effect will pass. Each time you resist a particular craving, you are strengthening Slim-U's presence in your life and weakening Fat-U's hold over you.

Can you rest somewhere for half an hour around lunchtime or when you get in from work? I know this sounds impractical but, if you can find somewhere to lie down flat on a bed or on the floor and consciously relax your whole body, it makes a great difference to the way you cope with the rest of that day.

Previous diets may have left you constipated. It's really uncomfortable walking around feeling bloated and heavy and this could also be the cause of the diet-induced headache experienced by some people. The main causes are lack of fibre, too much protein, or the food intake being cut too low. If you have tried the "Eat as much protein as you like" type of diet, you will know what I mean. However, with your plan devised along the lines I have described in this book you should not suffer from constipation.

Are you being meticulous about your exercise? Check out **Step Six** in Chapter 4. Don't let anything or anyone put you off. Exercise is a vital component if your plan is to succeed. As you stride along for your walk, or engage in other exercise of your choice, imagine your legs getting slimmer and firmer and all the fat round your waist being burned up with every step, lunge or whatever. Keep going, you're doing fine.

If you *really* don't feel hungry for food a couple of hours after breakfast, then there's no necessity to eat mid-morning. A drink will suffice but do make sure you eat at your next scheduled mealtime. Don't just have coffee *then*, as well, even if you are in the middle of something important. EAT. If you are genuinely short of time open a small tin of Heinz Weight Watchers baked beans and eat them out of the tin with a teaspoon. WHAT? You would never dream of doing that! Why not? Do it! Get off the "conventional" mind-set. You are not on a diet here. You have been struggling not to eat for years. It's time for a change and you are simply choosing to eat a wide variety of food whilst excluding the trigger foods that screwed up your life before.

Some days you will eat more than on others – so what? Some days you will be hungrier than others – or colder, or busier. This is called life. The point is not what you eat, but how you live each day. Just concentrate on eating small – I repeat, small – healthy meals at regular intervals and, I promise you, the pounds will take care of themselves. When you get used to eating every couple of hours, you will discover that you are generally satisfied and rarely hungry.

The Third Week
If you do blow it during the initial three weeks then, possibly, you were not ready to make this commitment in the first place. Please do re-read the first few chapters. Take the time to evaluate your life carefully and constructively and, when you have a clear period ahead of you, start again.

Try not to weigh yourself for at least ten days after you start. When you do, you will find that you have lost quite a few pounds. Good. Don't get too excited by this. You already know that what has "evaporated" so far is mainly water. One or two salty or sugary meals could retain fluid and send the scales back up again. Your body has to go through a series of changes before it starts burning fat at a steady rate of 1-2 lb a week on its way towards a happy living weight. Never expect to lose weight faster than this: you don't want to lose muscle. If any diet promises an excessively quick weight loss, you can be sure that some of that weight will be lean muscle. You are only aiming to reduce your body fat by shrinking the size of your fat cells. You need your muscles to give you a smooth, rounded shape, and this will gradually happen as you keep to your new rules.

During the third week, if walking is your thing, it is time to go a bit faster. Not jogging – just walk at a slightly brisker pace, as though you are changing into a higher gear. Take longer strides, reaching out from the hip, and make your arms swing in a bigger arc to keep pace. These long strides will loosen up your hip joints and lower back – really good!

Sometimes you simply will not feel like it. You will wake up and it's cold and miserable out there and the easiest thing in the world would be to turn over and go back to sleep.

Don't. Exercise cannot work if you don't do it. All right! Tell yourself that you will just do your "minimum" walk round the block today, not the longer route. Maybe you will just walk to the fruit shop, buy an apple and eat it on the way home, and that's it for today.

Whatever it is that will encourage you to get out there, go for it. If it's raining, stick your hair in a hat, put on a rain-coat and take an umbrella; if it's sunny, put on Factor 15 and your sunglasses but GO! Just get out of that door. After that your legs will take over. You will be so glad you did because the feeling of health and well-being that envelops you after a bout of exercise really has to be experienced to be believed. It's a sort of mild euphoria which makes you happy, full of confidence and ready to take on the world. The phenomenon has been well recognised among the medical profession and has been confirmed over and over again by many of my clients.

The Plateau
When you eat sensibly and less, food doesn't get stored as fat. Eventually there will be a steady deficit, so that your body has to start burning fat from your thighs.

Before this miraculous event can take place, however, you are bound to hit "the plateau". This is when everything seems to come to a halt. You are following the eating and exercise plan but you are not losing any more weight and, sometimes, to your horror, you might even regain a pound or two.

The plateau hits every dieter at some point, usually around the fourth week or, if you were quite heavy to begin with, around the eighth or ninth week. It can last anywhere from one to three weeks and, unless you are unusually resilient, you will undoubtedly begin to despair of ever losing weight, let alone keeping it off.

The easiest way to explain what is happening during this time is as a sort of physiological stocktaking. Your body has been working quite hard at adjusting to your new regime, and has now called a temporary halt to reassess the situation.

Until now, your body has been used to receiving food high in fat and sugar, metabolising some as energy, and storing the rest as fat. Now that you have cut back drastically on those foods, your body is becoming more efficient at producing energy from the stored fat round your hips, thighs and elsewhere. Your metabolic rate has also had to adapt to your new style of eating, and may decide to slow down a bit temporarily, in spite of the exercise you are doing, until it is sure what you are up to.

During the first few weeks, as explained earlier, you will have lost quite a bit of water. You will also have cut down on the amount of salt you are taking in and your kidneys need to adjust to this decrease in sodium.

During this plateau period, your body is therefore in a state of adjustment, ready for the next drop in weight. You need this plateau for all sorts of reasons, some of them psychological. You could look on this as testing the strength of your commitment. You have tried many diets before and none of them has worked on a long-term basis. Now you know that living slim has to be a way of life in which you – not food – are in control, your resolve should be strengthened.

Understand what the plateau is and don't get disheartened when you hit it. This is the "barrier" you have to break through in order to get where you're going. Remind yourself that this is temporary and that, once your kidneys and your metabolism have sorted themselves out, your weight will start to go down again. Although nothing appears to be happening, a whole lot is going on inside your body which is very important for your future shape.

The "Click"

Suddenly the plateau will end and your weight may drop 3 lb in one week. Congratulate yourself that you have come through a difficult time. You will probably now feel a surge of energy, and may experience a genuine feeling of such happiness and well-being that it will surprise you. You will then realise how clapped out you were before. Somehow you are much more relaxed with other people and in a more contented frame of mind. It's a strange feeling which can only be experienced subjectively. I call it "the click" – meaning that it all clicks into place. It's a sudden realisation that the programme is working. Someone once described it as if a curtain had been drawn back and the window opened wide to let in the sun. You know what you are going to eat today, and you are looking forward to each meal. You don't have to write it down any more. You automatically mash up some tuna with a splodge of mayo and stick it in a sandwich to take with you. No problem. You don't feel hungry, because your body seems to sense that there will be food in a couple of hours' time. You haven't given your trigger foods a thought in days. Whereas your eating habits may have been totally erratic before, you now realise that it is just as easy to eat sensibly as it was to eat junk. It just needed a bit more planning ahead. You accept that if you want to be slim and stop bingeing, you simply can't have everything you want – but you can have everything you *need*. You are alert, have loads of energy and your reactions are quicker both mentally and physically.

Many clients have told me that when they begin this programme they feel dubious and unsure. Some find it difficult to remember to eat something every three hours whether they are hungry or not. Others struggle with giving up their trigger foods. Once the "click" takes place, however, they all say "Oh! Now I know what you mean". When the "click" will happen to you, I can't say, but just hang in there and wait: you will know.

When you work out your own eating plan it becomes the basis of your food lifestyle. It is YOUR plan, just for you, *with* the food that you enjoy eating but *without* your own trigger foods. This is your personal blueprint; your day-by-day eating plan. It is what works for you.

However, you should be constantly on your guard. Now happily settled into your new way of eating, you may feel that you couldn't imagine going back to bingeing like you used to. Don't be too hasty!

There is always the temptation to reward yourself for being "good" with a little bit of one of your trigger foods. You may even tell yourself you are in control now so it can't do any harm. You would be wrong. Trying to eat any of a food that triggers your compulsive eating behaviour would, believe me, be torture. Just as smokers and alcoholics must control their enemies, you must recognise that a mere taste will reactivate all the old cravings and the binge mentality that you have been struggling get away from. Food is meant to make your life better, not worse. Don't start. Please!

There will come a time when you decide to measure how many inches or centimetres you have lost. You have dropped about 9 lb and you feel good. You wrap the tape measure triumphantly round your hips and look – and look again. Your hips measure the same as the last time. No! This cannot be! The scales say you have lost weight. Why haven't you lost any girth?

Don't panic – the two events do not necessarily happen simultaneously. The fact that you have lost weight may have registered on the scales and in your mind, but your body hasn't cottoned on yet. It takes time for your body to realise that some fat has gone and to shrink itself down a little. It will catch up eventually.

Sometimes the reverse happens – especially as you gradually extend your walking or increase your favourite exercise and your muscles get nicely toned up. Your jeans feel loose but the numbers on the scale disagree. This is because muscle weighs more than fat and your newly-firm thighs are thinner because you have tight muscle there instead of flabby fat. Measure for measure fat takes up FIVE times as much space in your body as muscle. Think of a compact little muscle sitting there in your arm and of a great splodge of fat five times its volume – but weighing the same – surrounding it. Then decide which you would prefer to create the shape of your arm. When you make the right choices you are winning even if the scales dawdle quite a while before confirming the fact. I repeat; living slim is an ongoing process, not a result.

Now is the time to sling out all those old large clothes and buy some new ones. Take them to the charity shop NOW. Don't leave them hanging in the cupboard "in case". In case of what? I know what you're thinking: "If I put on weight, at least that ghastly skirt with the elasticated waist is still there". Not for much longer! Sling it.

If you really love those skinny trousers that won't quite do up at the moment, leave them in the spare room. At least you won't come face-to-crotch with them every time you open the wardrobe.

Some people would advise you deliberately to hang those trousers where you can see them every day to give you the incentive to stick to your programme. I don't agree. This is the same sort of thinking that advises you to stick a picture of a skinny model on your fridge to prevent you reaching inside to finish off last night's dessert. Well, you are never going to look like that skinny model (thank goodness!). You are going to look like you, which is much nicer. Looking at her all the time could just pull you down. By the same token, don't put a picture of a fat lady up there either. A large lady leering at you every day may suggest to your subconscious mind that you actually want to look like that and will summon up Fat-U to help you do just that. Those strategies don't work. If you must put something on the fridge, photocopy the last page of this chapter, fill in your name and stick that on instead.

When you buy your new clothes, take no notice of the size on the label. Don't stalk off muttering "I'm not buying a blinking size 16 *anything*!". Size tickets fall into the same category as your scales – they are there to provide a number, not a judgment. If it looks good on you, buy it.

When you have been losing weight steadily over a period of weeks you will probably start to get a reaction from other people. Some will tell you that you look fantastic. Others, especially your mother, may tell you how ill you look. I would say ignore them all – most of the time. This is for you – no one else. However, when friends and family are of one voice – that you should seek medical advice – you would be foolhardy not to check it out with your doctor. Bingeing can be obsessive and, if this was a key factor in your overweight problem, it makes sense to realise that you dare not allow yourself to become obsessive in the other direction. That could lead to an excessive loss of weight, beyond a normal level, and into anorexic or bulimic illness. You know how dangerous that could be. Therefore, if you tend to be obsessive, take care and keep yourself open to sound advice.

Mainly though, the less than kind comments are apt to come from people resenting change. They perhaps find it more comforting to see you as the chubby person they are used to, rather than this slim lady who looks so great.

Living slim means your family making adjustments too. Otherwise, usually without meaning to, they can subconsciously sabotage your plan. They might buy your trigger foods, or say things like "You looked better when you were a bit fatter" or "I can't get through to you any more. You seem different". Sit down and talk about it.

The "Special"

It usually takes six consecutive months before you can truly claim control over your trigger foods. During this time you will have expanded your food repertoire, discovered new tastes and flavours and reached the stage where the sight of a trigger food doesn't produce the old longings and cravings any more.

Now that you are securely attached to your eating blueprint, I would like to introduce you to **"The Special"**. (If you are not yet there, though, please wait awhile. You'll see why in a minute!)

I am well aware that no one lives in a vacuum and I realise that, knowing that your trigger foods are around somewhere, it is asking a great deal of anyone to give them up permanently. In fact, for some people the very thought of *absolute* permanence is enough to make them abandon the whole programme. Fortunately, once you are totally in control of your eating, it is still possible to sample your trigger food once in a while on a special controlled occasion: **The Special**. This is a simple, one-off deviation from your blueprint; a compromise to allow you to enjoy your main trigger food without letting it become a fat trap ever again. However, before you can even contemplate a Special, my advice is that you must have steadied at your goal weight for at least six months and you must be totally committed to maintaining your healthy eating plan directly after your Special exception. Even then, if you are not confident of your control, it would be best not to contemplate a Special until perhaps you have passed the 12-month mark.

A Special means enjoying a trigger food only in controlled circumstances – a "special occasion". For example, birthday cake *on a birthday*, Christmas pudding *at Christmas*, liqueur and a chocolate *after* a dinner party – in other words when the occasion is finite and thereby limited to one specified time. You do not buy that food to keep at home; neither do you look for other occasions to eat it; nor do you touch leftovers the next day.

Specials must be rare. If a Special happens every week, you will soon find it happening every day and you are back to square one. By making your special occasions few and far between, you can enjoy the taste of your trigger food without losing control. This will only work for you if your trigger food is controllable. For example, you might love some extremely fattening speciality of a certain restaurant, and stay in control only by limiting your visits to that restaurant to once or twice a year. On the other hand, a sweet dessert like tiramisu could start you off on a weeklong binge. Therefore you must be very careful which trigger food you choose as a Special – or it will choose you.

Uh-Oh, A Binge!

Sooner or later it will happen. You can't believe it! You were fine! You hadn't even thought about any of your trigger foods for weeks – then suddenly, here you are, standing in the kitchen stuffing food into your mouth. Why?

A binge is inevitable sooner or later. You are still living the same life as before and the same situations are likely to crop up. Before, you resolved many of them by bingeing. Now you are able to control this most of the time but there will come a "test" you just fail. This is not a tragedy. Do not make a crisis out of it.

The important thing is to limit the binge as soon as possible and get back on track. You may feel guilty and awful about your lapse but you must recognise it for what it was: on one day you ate more food than you had intended. OK – a lot more food you say – so? Look around you. The world hasn't come to a shuddering halt. Nobody died because you ate a cream cake (and the rest!). You did not replace all the weight you had lost in that one splurge of madness. Come on now; it "ain't over till the fat lady sings!" In any event, suffering guilt doesn't burn off calories – unfortunately.

Accepting a *temporary* loss of control is part of your blueprint learning curve. You *are* in control but the faint groove of a binge mentality is still imprinted on your subconscious. You may have lost the weight but you haven't entirely lost the problem. Try to discover whether it was anything unusual that made you binge so that you can deal with it better next time. Was it some person who always winds you up whenever you meet and with whom you find, after ten minutes in her company, that you are always in dire need of CRT (chocolate replacement therapy)? We all know people like that. If so, the next time, don't react. Practise saying "You're probably right" to whatever she says, whether she is or not, and leave it at that.

Did you entertain your friends and stock up with all YOUR favourite foods? That was just asking for trouble. Just because you like honey-roasted cashews, you don't have to buy them. Your friends will eat anything.

Let's deal with the following day. This is a very important day for lots of reasons. You ate a lot of fatty and sugary stuff yesterday, so you may feel a bit off-colour. Your body is not used to it any more. You have reactivated your taste for your trigger foods and your body will crave them. Do not let this become a battle of wills between Fat-U and Slim-U. Dig out your notebook, write down what you are going to eat today and stick to it. If you feel a bit nauseous, leave out protein for today. Go for plain rice or baked potato, vegetables and/or salad. Don't starve yourself to "make up for the damage" or, if you are that way inclined, do excessive exercise. You may feel tired, in which case make a point of having a rest if you are at home, or find somewhere to relax for a while at work if you can.

One lapse, one binge truly does no harm unless you carry it over to the next day. You will find absolutely no change in your body shape at all. Remember, you would have to eat an extra 7,000 calories to gain two pounds: and in one day – I don't think so!

There are bound to be times when you will find yourself in situations where making sensible food choices is almost impossible. When you can't escape eating something you hadn't intended, do it and forget about it. Provided you think of it as an isolated incident, then you won't lose control.

Knowing when you are triggered to eat is just as important as what triggers it. For most people the worst trigger times are: between 4 and 6 p.m. if at home with children; immediately you get home from work; watching television; family reunions; and weekends. The following tips may help:

- If you habitually pick at food whilst you are cooking, try not to cook when you are hungry. Stay out of the kitchen except when you are actually preparing meals. Don't linger at the kitchen table reading the paper.

- Keep food out of sight, out of mind and out of mouth! No biscuits in transparent containers, no bowls of sweets or nuts in the sitting room. What you see is what you eat.

- Sit down when eating. I am sure there is a statistic somewhere proving that more weight is gained when eating standing up. And use a plate and a FORK. Too many bingers eat with their fingers, straight out of packets, jars, tins and fridges. What is in your fingers today will be on your hips tomorrow. Soak cooking pans in water before you sit down. This stops you scraping the crusty bits round the edges afterwards, scoffing more as you clear away.

- No, you do not have to set an attractive place setting for yourself with flowers on the table as specified in some women's magazines. (Oh, please!) However, sitting down to a proper meal means you are concentrating on what is in front of you instead of letting your fingers go idly from food to mouth. By the same token, reading or watching television while you are eating means you are likely to finish everything on your plate without being aware of what, or how much, you have eaten.

• Shop alone. A companion will pop things into the trolley which YOU will end up eating. Don't kid yourself you are buying those multi-packets of choc-bars because the children like them. YOU like them.

• Do not eat on the phone. It's the height of bad manners and the epitome of uncontrolled eating.

• Never miss a meal. It's only fat people who say they never have time to eat. If you wait until you are hungry you end up eating compulsively, too quickly and too much.

• Don't pile up your plate. If it's not on your plate, you won't eat it.

• Make sure you have loads of healthy food in the house at all times. I know you are busy with your job or your kids – or both – but you can't eat healthily unless you have the right food available.

I am sure you will soon find your own strategies that help you stay on track, so I thought I would share a few that my clients have come up with over the years:

Rosie: "If you don't want to eat something, tell people

you are allergic to certain foods. I know I am – I break out in fat."

Susie: "When entertaining friends, beware. You are very vulnerable at 2 o'clock in the morning, surrounded by tempting leftovers and debris, and feeling more than a little drunk. Bung anything that will keep straight into the freezer as you remove it from the table – preferably even before your guests have left. This will prevent you knocking back three large spoonfuls of pudding in the kitchen and then walking back into the dining room with a tray of coffee and a large dollop of cream on your chin. Everything else, sling in the bin. Then go to bed. The dirty glasses can wait till the morning."

Gillian: "If you feel stressed about some incident and can't get it out of your mind, try the following: sit quietly and close your eyes. Picture yourself on a beach quite near the incoming tide. Conjure up in your mind the situation that is bugging you, and "build it" into the shape of a sandcastle. Relive every moment of it – what you said, what she said, how upset you felt, how angry – during and afterwards. Shovel into your sandcastle all the angry words; bash down the snide comments with your imaginary spade – hard. Slap in a few extra handfuls of sand for the things you would like to have said, but didn't. Make your fantasy stronghold into a solid pile of sand. When you have exhausted the whole scenario, lie back on your imaginary sun-bed and let the warmth of the sun sink into your body. Relax. Watch as the waves come nearer and nearer until they swirl around your sandcastle and it gradually – gradually – disintegrates. With each wave a little bit more of the anger and frustration dissolves into the sea – and away from you. Soon it's gone. You can forget it – and move on."

Paula: "The two-second pause works for me. When faced with a trigger food, I force myself to stop and ask myself three questions:

1. Do I really want this?
2. If I eat it, how will I feel later?
3. Will it be worth it?

This allows me just long enough to answer NO to 1 and 3. Sometimes the answers to 1 and 2 are "Yes" and "SICK" – but that's my problem!"

Myra: "I do jigsaw puzzles to keep my hands and my mind off food. There is a vast half-finished puzzle permanently on my dining room table. The only trouble is that any neighbour popping in for whatever reason can still be found there the following morning, muttering "I'm sure this piece goes here" or "I'll leave you to do the sky".

Lizzie: "I practise my own version of aversion therapy. I was at a board meeting at work and, as well as coffee, there was a plate of sponge cakes on the table. I thought 'I can't sit and look at that cake all afternoon', so I imagined the

slices were little yellow washing-up sponges. It was quite easy to resist them after that. I expanded on this theory and imagine ice cream is shaving foam, crisps are dead leaves, alcohol is petrol, and chocolate – well, that's something dogs leave on the pavement. Sorry! This works for me, but then I've got a pretty lurid imagination!"

Carol: "Whenever I get a craving, I immediately pick up the phone and get through to one of my friends and talk, talk, talk. Half an hour seems to do it. My phone bills are enormous. I am now slim – and divorced!" (Oh dear!)

I like Gillian's way of solving problems by her "sand-castle" visualisation. Here is something similar that can be used as a displacement activity to program your mind for success. Try it next time a craving strikes and threatens to undermine your success.

Remove yourself from the danger area, sit quietly and close your eyes. Breathe deeply and consciously relax. Clear your mind of all thought, as though you are looking at a screen of black velvet on the inside of your forehead. See yourself on that screen walking along a country lane which stretches to the horizon. This represents your future life. A little way ahead, there is a mirror and you see yourself reflected therein exactly how you want to appear – slim, attractive and smiling. Go on, have a good look. This will be you. Now turn around and look back the way you have just come. There is another mirror there, showing you at your fattest and frumpiest. You are dressed in that baggy outfit that you hate, stuffing food into your mouth. You are frowning and miserable. Now turn around again and look at the "you" in front of you. She moves away a bit and starts danc-ing along the road, looking firm and supple, and you follow. Now look back and see the fat you. No! Quickly turn to the slim you. Yes! Follow her. Turn again. The fat you is fading slightly. Turn again to look forward and the slim you is beckoning you to follow her. You move eagerly forward towards the image in the mirror then stop and glance back for a moment. The fat image in the other mirror has faded completely. You turn and go forward again towards your new slim self. When you reach the mirror, you jump through it, straight into your new, slim image, moving cheerfully along the road of your life.

Keep looking down the road at the slim, successful, attractive you and keep walking. You will soon catch up with her.

These suggestions will help you stay in control and avoid mindless eating – just choose which strategies you feel will work for you.

Soon people will say to you "You're so lucky to be slim". Lucky! If only they knew! Just smile and agree.

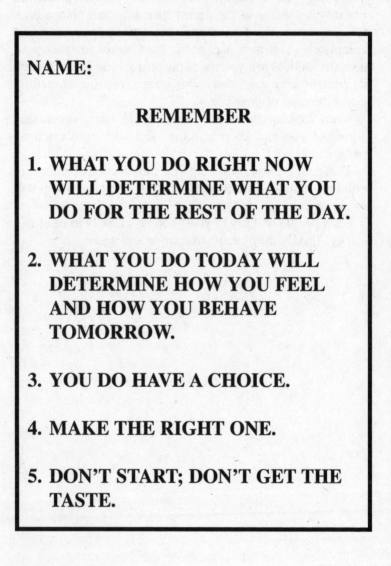

NAME:

REMEMBER

1. **WHAT YOU DO RIGHT NOW WILL DETERMINE WHAT YOU DO FOR THE REST OF THE DAY.**

2. **WHAT YOU DO TODAY WILL DETERMINE HOW YOU FEEL AND HOW YOU BEHAVE TOMORROW.**

3. **YOU DO HAVE A CHOICE.**

4. **MAKE THE RIGHT ONE.**

5. **DON'T START; DON'T GET THE TASTE.**

9

STAYING ON THE STRAIGHT AND NARROW

When you first set out to change your eating pattern, your motivation is high. Once you get used to writing down your daily menus, it becomes a satisfying exercise when you tick off each mini-meal as you come to it. At the end of each day, put a huge tick through the whole page and a little note of how it went: "Easy day", "hungry at tea-time", "pasta for lunch too heavy", etc. In this way you build up a written record that you can look back on and see if your "difficult days" coincide with your monthly cycle or any other recurring events.

The benefit of this process is that you can learn a lot about yourself. Some people find that they need to eat some sort of starchy carbohydrate at every meal if they are not to feel a lack of energy soon after. Others do better with a meal predominantly high in protein, like eggs, grilled fish or a ham salad at lunchtime. Test yourself with various foods at different times to discover what suits you best.

Get to know how you feel at certain times during the day. If you are a morning person and you do your best work early in the day, you may need more food then to keep your energy level high, and less as the day goes on. If you like a filling lunch, you probably don't need to eat a lot of food in the evening as well, just to keep your family company. Do what is best for you.

Discover the best time of day to fit in your exercise. Most clients like to jump into a tracksuit and get out the house first thing in the morning before their brain can register any objections. Once they start thinking "I'll go later", it doesn't seem to happen.

You are most vulnerable to giving up on exercise in the first three weeks. You may decide you are too busy, or too tired after a heavy day at work, or that you are not feeling very well. Be aware of these feelings and try to overcome them. Tell yourself to get your shoes on and get out that door!

Even if all is going well on the food front, sometimes, for one reason or another, you may find yourself feeling ratty and desperate to put something in your mouth. Old habits die hard and, in spite of your commitment, you just *know* that you are going to eat *something* in the next few minutes – so at least make it a premeditated choice. If you have a prepared list of non-binge options, you can save yourself a lot of anguish later on.

The wisest thing to eat, when you feel this bugged, is what your body actually needs: a combination of protein and starch to assuage your hunger and restore your energy. Some suggestions:

Pitta bread spread inside with cottage cheese and stuffed with as much salad as you can cram in.

A rice cake topped with Soya cheese.

A plain yoghurt tipped over a cut-up banana in a bowl.

A mug of chicken soup with a roll or a bagel.

These work better than just fruit because, eaten on its own, too much fruit can be watery and unsatisfying. This claim is fiercely contested by some clients who swear that having a watermelon in the house, during the months they are available, has prevented many a binge. Eaten freely, it makes you feel seriously bloated – which, of course, you simply pee away.

Store one or two of these permitted foods in your head and your cupboard for this sort of emergency – or write them at the back of your food diary as a reminder.

Another stumbling block can be if you hit a second (or third) **Plateau** of the sort explained in Chapter 8. You have lost weight but there's more to go, and now nothing is happening.

This is a danger time for bingers, especially if you allow indecision to take hold. On the one hand you want to be slim; on the other hand the old feelings and temptations keep coming back to haunt you. You are caught in the middle somewhere and the lack of progress isn't exactly strengthening your resolve.

Additional plateau phases may happen. Do your best not to let a plateau blow you off course into a full-scale binge. I know it's not easy, but get rid of offending food, remove yourself from temptation and verbally reinforce your commitment to live slim. Don't fall into the "I'll start again tomorrow" trap: it's dangerous because these few words can allow Fat-U back into your life armed with all the triggers you have now recognised and taken such trouble to avoid. Also "I'll only eat fruit tomorrow to make up for it" is another way of letting yourself be controlled by food. Hang in there. The phase will pass and you will find that you feel "normal" again. Re-read some of the earlier chapters of this book to remember all the reasons why you started the programme.

Whatever happens foodwise in these circumstances, don't give up on the exercise. However rotten you feel, a brisk walk or a body conditioning class will clear your mind, lift your spirits and get you back in touch with your body.

Since your walking or exercise regime got up to speed the scales may not yet have dropped dramatically but the flab is going, I'm sure, which is what you want. As one client observed "My bottom is now at the top of my legs instead of half way down the back of my thighs!"

Let's assume you have overcome every setback and now have only a few pounds to go to reach your goal weight. You may become a bit nervous of this stage because you know from past experience that keeping the weight off is the hardest part. Don't worry. You are now firmly established with your personal eating blueprint, and maintenance will mean no more than continuing just the same as you have been doing.

Keeping your weight stable simply means remembering all the strategies that worked for you and kept you going through the trigger temptations, and all the other times you staved off a major relapse.

Think of your personal blueprint as the norm: the eating plan you come back to after you have had a **"Special"** – or a holiday – or any other occasion where you temporarily deviate from your daily life.

A False Sense of Security

Because you are just concentrating on eating healthily and not bothering about the weight loss aspect, it comes as a delightful surprise when you step on the scales and discover you are actually at the weight you want to be.

Reaching your goal weight is a very exciting time for you. You can't believe it when you look in the mirror and see that you are actually slim. You buy the clothes that you want.

People tell you how great you look. The immense satisfaction you feel in this achievement convinces you that you will never feel the urge to binge again. Sometimes, to test it, you stop for a moment and ask yourself if you fancy a bit of your trigger food. The answer comes back – "No; you really don't". You know you would probably enjoy the taste just as much as formerly if you ate it but you simply have no desire to do so. It's easy – no problem. Each day is like the previous day; you know what you are going to eat wherever you are, and you rarely experience hunger. You take food with you if you will be away from home during a mealtime and negotiate restaurants and parties with no trouble. You feel so much better that your commitment to carry on this way appears absolute.

The problem time is when you get used to feeling this good. The initial surge of success has worn off and you are used to seeing a slim you looking back at you in the mirror. Your friends have now accepted you as slim and have ceased to marvel at the transformation. You have stopped bingeing and can't understand how you could ever have done it. Now, you listen to friends complaining about their weight with compassion tinged with a slightly smug glow.

This is when you may become complacent and might just allow a little lapse in your life. You see a trigger food and think, "I'll just have a little bit – just this once" and "It should be all right; I am in control now". Instead of remembering how miserable you were – perhaps for years and years – all you now recall is that creamy taste of chocolate caramel.

And so, if you are not very careful, begins the insidious process that slowly, slowly, takes you back to square one, however motivated you were to begin with. It may not happen the first time. You may eat a bit of your trigger food then continue the rest of the week quite happily without it. Then comes the weekend and you think: "Well! I was OK last weekend. I had a little bit and didn't binge so I must have got it beaten". What did I say about a false sense of security?! Will it work this time and next time and to-morrow? Uh-uh. You know this story – you've heard it a thousand times . . .

Logically, you should be able to have a taste of your trigger food occasionally when you feel like it. But logic and reality are two different things for a binger. You can't control a trigger food with logic. This food evokes memories, feelings and buried cravings in your subconscious auto-pilot that flood your conscious mind at the first taste, and some-times you *can't help* wanting more and more. Once your taste buds are activated, it can be goodbye to logic, willpower, motivation and good intentions. When you go back to a trigger food – "I'll just have a smidge of a taste" – you gradually begin to eat it more often. Then you eat *more of it more* often.

None of the 95% of dieters who lose weight only to gain it back again do so on purpose. They really think they have beaten their cravings and can control their trigger foods by eating just a little. Be warned. You are unlikely to be the unique exception. Once the backward process starts, it is frightening how rapidly you lose control.

Circumstances Outside Your Control
Life doesn't always go the way we want it to. We all have to go through difficult times, some more than others. You might have to deal with divorce or a significant change in your financial situation, for example. Suddenly, you find you are going back to all your old habits. You find yourself thinking "Why am I buying biscuits? I don't eat biscuits!" You try to get back on track and maybe do three or four days successfully. Then bang – a solicitor's letter, another demand for money, or whatever, and off you go again.

Well, these things happen sometimes. Regaining some weight is undoubtedly upsetting but don't let it undermine what you have achieved so far. You need to confront this issue so that you can deal with it effectively and revert to your own eating blueprint as soon as possible. Unfortunately, when you have to handle emotional or financial problems as well, this daily struggle with food can easily generate feelings that pull you down further.

Accept that there may be a period in your life during which you will put on a few pounds – all right, a stone. During this time you may have to be content with a little less success while the storm continues. Your focus should be on staying calm so that you will be able to bounce back. This is the difference between a winner and a loser.

The winner takes the knocks and says to herself "OK, I screwed up. I allowed myself to go back to eating junk food. I couldn't cope, so I binged and went on bingeing. I've gained. Right: that's IT. The binge stops NOW!" The loser says, "I can't do this any more. I can't stop eating. I'm so depressed".

Be a winner. It takes a lot of work to cultivate a winning attitude, especially when everything around you seems to be going wrong, but you can make yourself into one. Tell yourself that everybody goes through bad patches. The crisis will get sorted one way or another and the outcome will be the same whether you are fat or slim but you will feel better and more able to see things more clearly if you can stay in control. Accept support from other people rather than food.

Your Comeback

However long the difficult period in your life continues, there will come a time when you realise you are ready to return to the straight and narrow of this book. All you must decide is to STOP BINGEING! You know what to do. So start immediately. Get rid of your trigger foods. You have proved you can live without them quite happily before and you can do it again. Plant the thought in your subconscious mind that you can lose this extra weight quite easily. Remind yourself how well you have done up till now, how good you looked and how much better you felt. Go for it and you will win.

A Few Final Tips

As you travel along your personal binge-free road and someone asks you how you manage to look so great, by all means enlighten them but don't bash everyone over the head with your newfound zeal. When you see someone at a party saying "Just give me a little bit; I'm trying to lose weight" resist the temptation to say "No! Don't have any". Just as you can eat whatever you like, give other people the same respect. People want to be comfortable around food and they can't be if they feel the "evil eye" of the converted watching every mouthful.

Even when living slim has become fully automatic there still has to be a corner of your mind that stays vigilant. You may have lost weight and you may have stopped bingeing but you are still by nature a binger. Your trigger foods are still your trigger foods so continue to avoid them on a daily basis. One taste is never enough. Don't start. Don't put your control at risk.

Keep your eating blueprint filed in your head at all times. This is what works for YOU.

Even though you are sticking to your plan, if you find your weight gradually increasing, check the amount of starchy carbohydrates you are eating. If you are having cereal for breakfast, you probably don't need toast as well. If you are having toast, say, with an egg, do you really need two slices when one is enough to satisfy your hunger? If you make two, you will eat two. Alternatively, the problem may be that you have started having a starchy carbohydrate accompaniment, like potatoes, with your main protein meal. Try another green vegetable instead.

If the opposite happens – your weight keeps going down, and you think you are looking a bit gaunt – then reverse the above instructions: include a starchy vegetable like rice with your protein meal; eat a whole sandwich for lunch instead of saving half for later. Don't be worried about this. Unless you start introducing your trigger foods into your life again, your weight will not suddenly shoot up because you are having an extra potato – or whatever – I assure you. Similarly don't be afraid of having a Special every now and again. You are not in prison and your favourite food IS out there – as long as it is a controlled, premeditated decision to eat it.

Even as you get older, appropriate exercise is still important and should remain a number one priority in your life. Never let two days go by without doing some sort of exercise. This is vital, not just for keeping your muscles firm and your appetite at bay, but for that sense of body awareness that makes you like what you see in the mirror. Muscles not used will slacken and become soft and flabby. A good walk or workout is a great stress-buster and the ideal antidote should you feel a binge coming on.

Health awareness is growing. There are new medical discoveries every year, new gyms and health centres are opening in every town and supermarkets are enlarging their range of healthy foods which are low in calories, fat and preservatives. Restaurants will cook without fat if requested and provide an increasing variety of salads and vegetables. Low fat, low sugar cookery books are selling just as well as their cream-laden counterparts. Keep your eyes open for advances that will strengthen your healthy eating blueprint.

Make sure you take enough time to adjust. Every client who starts my programme seems to feel initially that she may not be able to succeed with it. Even now you may be thinking "What is this woman going on about? Trigger foods, no proper diet sheet to follow, no recipes – this is never going to work". However, day by day, if you persist, you will, I promise, gradually get into it and find that it does work. You will find that you are now EATING, rather than picking or starving – or bingeing – and it will gradually sink in that, when you choose to eat sensibly, this isn't a restriction – it's freedom. Freedom from fat, loss of control, guilt and, for those affected, from low self-esteem and a sense of deprivation as well. The real bonus my clients report is that you will quite soon begin to appreciate that you have never felt so calm and relaxed in your whole life.

You may try this programme and fail the first couple of times. Some people do. However, I am sure that you will pick yourself up and try again – simply because it works.

OK! Time is up. Mark the pages that are of special interest to you, put the book down and discover the slim, healthy, binge-free person you are destined to be. YOU are now in charge.

In the same series

C-A-T = CAT
Teach Your Child To Read With Phonics

Over the last couple of decades, too many children have been held back from reading by the use of 'look and say' methods of teaching. Finally the 'experts' recognise that the only way to improve literacy standards is a return to a structured, **phonic** method.

Mona McNee's concern with literacy began when, having seen her own son fail with professional teaching, she found that, *with no training*, but relying on a phonic scheme, she could teach him herself. She later became a remedial teacher at a middle school and taught hundreds of dyslexic children to read.

You too can teach your own child to read. Start at the beginning with letters and sounds and see how easy it is to sound out and blend sounds into a word. You just need common sense and a Systematic, Intensive, Multi-sensory, Parent-friendly, Logical and Easy programme to teach how to read and spell the right way.

Uniform with this book

RIGHT WAY
PUBLISHING POLICY

HOW WE SELECT TITLES
RIGHT WAY consider carefully every deserving manuscript. Where an author is an authority on his subject but an inexperienced writer, we provide first-class editorial help. The standards we set make sure that every **RIGHT WAY** book is practical, easy to understand, concise, informative and delightful to read. Our specialist artists are skilled at creating simple illustrations which augment the text wherever necessary.

CONSISTENT QUALITY
At every reprint our books are updated where appropriate, giving our authors the opportunity to include new information.

FAST DELIVERY
We sell **RIGHT WAY** books to the best bookshops throughout the world. It may be that your bookseller has run out of stock of a particular title. If so, he can order more from us at any time – we have a fine reputation for "same day" despatch, and we supply any order, however small (even a single copy), to any bookseller who has an account with us. We prefer you to buy from your bookseller, as this reminds him of the strong underlying public demand for **RIGHT WAY** books. However, you can order direct from us by post, by phone with a credit card, or through our web site.

FREE
If you would like an up-to-date list of all **RIGHT WAY** titles currently available, send a stamped self-addressed envelope to ELLIOT RIGHT WAY BOOKS, BRIGHTON ROAD, LOWER KINGSWOOD, TADWORTH, SURREY, KT20 6TD,U.K.
or visit our web site at www.right-way.co.uk

THE
MOSCOW
OPTION

Jeremy Duns is British, but currently lives and works in Stockholm. Visit www.jeremyduns.com

Also by Jeremy Duns

Free Agent
Song of Treason

THE
MOSCOW
OPTION

JEREMY DUNS

**SIMON &
SCHUSTER**

London · New York · Sydney · Toronto · New Delhi

A CBS COMPANY

First published in Great Britain by Simon & Schuster UK Ltd, 2012
A CBS COMPANY

1 3 5 7 9 10 8 6 4 2

Simon & Schuster UK Ltd
1st Floor
222 Gray's Inn Road
London
WC1X 8HB

www.simonandschuster.co.uk

Simon & Schuster Australia, Sydney
Simon & Schuster India, New Delhi

A CIP catalogue copy for this book is available
from the British Library.

ISBN: 978-1-84739-453-8

Printed and bound by CPI Group (UK) Ltd, Croydon, CR0 4YY

For Johanna, Rebecca and Astrid

A Note on the Background

This novel is inspired by real events that took place in October 1969, and much of the information in it is drawn from declassified material, some of which has never previously been published. The document quoted in Chapter VII is a translation of a dossier written by the head of Soviet military intelligence in 1964.

I

Late October 1969, Moscow, Soviet Union

I was asleep when they came for me. I was running through a field, palm trees in the distance, when I woke to find a man shaking my shoulders and yelling my name.

I sat bolt upright, gasping for breath, sweat pouring off me. The man was wearing a cap, and looked to be barely out of his teens. Part of my mind was still caught up in the dream: I was sure I'd been in the field before, but couldn't think when or where. But I didn't get the chance to consider it further because I was being hauled from the mattress by my arms. Now I could see that there were two men, both in the same uniform but one without a cap. Neither was part of my usual guard detail.

'Get up, scum!' shouted the one in the cap, leaning in so

close that he was just a couple of inches from me. His face was squared off, with a wide jawline and a pug nose, and he was wearing some foul eau de cologne that seemed to have been impregnated with the scent of fir trees rolled in diesel. He shoved a pile of clothes into my arms.

'Put these on, old man,' he sneered. 'And make it fast.'

I looked at the bundle. There was a dark suit, crumpled and baggy, a white shirt with sweat stains around the armpits, and a pair of slip-on shoes. No belt or tie.

I started to dress, my eyes still half gummed with sleep. What the hell was going on? I'd been wearing the same grey tunic and trousers since my arrival here, so why the sudden change of clothes? Perhaps they were transferring me to another prison, or to a courtroom – Sasha had often mentioned the possibility of a trial. Or perhaps they were simply dressing me up to take me out to the woods to finish me off. I had a sudden memory of a summer's day in 1945 in the British Zone in Germany, the jeep riding through the burnt-out roads with Shashkevich manacled in the back, until we came to the clearing; the Luger heavy in my hand as I placed it against his neck; his sweating, shaking; and my finger squeezing down on the trigger . . .

I shivered at the thought, but found to my surprise that I wasn't afraid. There were worse ways to go. I wouldn't feel it, at least. I'd been here six months but it seemed much longer, and the future held nothing for me but the gradual disintegration of my body. I was forty-four, but already felt twice that. Rather a bullet through the head than the prolonged suffering and indignity of old age and disease.

'Faster!' shouted the man in the cap. He must be the senior of the two. I finished buttoning the shirt and, as I leaned down to pick up the trousers, realized that both men were armed with pistols at the hip. Judging by the size of the holsters, they were Makarovs. Despite their resemblance to the Walther PP, their combat effectiveness was comparatively poor, and I began gauging the distance between the men, the angles of their bodies and their respective weights to see if there might be any possibility of catching them by surprise, taking one of their pistols and turning it on the other. But it was just a habit, a tired old spook's reflex. I had no real intention of attempting to escape. There was nowhere to go. Even if I were able to overpower these two, there would be dozens, if not hundreds, more of them.

I adjusted the lapel of the jacket and stood to attention, ready. The suit was a couple of sizes too large for me and stank of stale urine, but it felt almost civilized to be wearing one again. The guards led me through the door of the cell and marched me down a series of corridors, until we reached a large steel door I hadn't seen before.

Once it had been unlocked, we walked through it and, for the first time in nearly six months, I found myself outside.

*

We appeared to be on an enormous airfield. I took a deep breath, then exhaled. My breath misted: it was at least a couple of degrees below freezing.

The sky was the colour of slate, and the barbed wire and bare-branched trees formed a strange tracery against it. To my left, I could make out several large buildings. I recognized their outlines from dossiers I had read and memorized in London years before and knew, finally, where I had been held all this time. The building we had just left was nicknamed *Steklyashka* – 'the sheet of glass' – by its inhabitants, because two of its wings were encased in glass. A former army hospital, it now served as the headquarters of the GRU – Soviet military intelligence. It had been my first guess, but it came as a shock nevertheless. I suppose I'd made the place another world in my mind, away from the reach of dossiers.

My escorts gripped me by the arms again and we headed across the tarmac, buffeted by the wind. We passed several helicopters and armoured tanks, and I remembered that it was, by my calculations, the last week of October, and guessed they were destined for the annual parade in Red Square.

A car was waiting for us near the perimeter, its engine running. It was a polished black ZiL limousine with red flags attached to the mudguards. That was interesting: they were usually reserved for the very top brass. I recalled reading a report that there were only a couple of dozen in the whole country. The man with the cap opened the rear door and his bare-headed comrade pushed me onto a cold vinyl seat. He climbed in beside me, while his colleague walked around to the other side. Up front, a driver was seated with his hands on the wheel, and sitting next to him was Sasha. There was also someone sitting in the back seat next to me, and as I turned I saw that it was Sarah.

*

Sasha snapped at the driver to head off, and we passed through a barricade and turned onto a broad avenue. I caught the word 'Vladimir', and my heart sank: that was the prison east of Moscow where they had held both Greville Wynne and Gary Powers. But then he said it again and I realized that it was the name of the man with the cap and that he was asking why they had taken so long to fetch me. Vladimir replied that I'd been difficult, and Sasha grunted disapprovingly. They were in an almighty hurry, clearly, but there was something else to it — an edge of panic? I decided not to think about what it might mean: I'd find out soon enough.

I looked at Sarah. She sensed my gaze and turned to me. As our eyes met, a thousand thoughts went unspoken. She was wearing a shapeless grey dress. Although she seemed thinner and her blonde hair was cut brutally short, she looked much the same as when I'd last seen her, in the back seat of a limousine like this one about six months ago. I felt a hollowness in my stomach as I remembered it: we had come to a stop on a barricaded street, and I'd watched helplessly as she'd been swiftly bundled into another car and driven away. I'd vowed to myself that I would protect her come what may, but when the moment had arrived I'd offered no protest. But she had *survived*. I had long given up hope of that. I'd felt that they wouldn't risk giving her any freedom for fear she might reach the British embassy and tell them everything we had learned in Italy. As a junior member of the Service, she had very little information to give them. Once they had extracted it from her, I'd reasoned, they would have seen little point in keeping her alive.

But they had. I tried not to think about what they had put her through instead, but an image of the girl Yuri had kept in his rooms in the camp in Germany, and of the way he had flicked his tongue over his lips at his first sight of

Sarah, flashed into my mind nevertheless. Repulsion and rage coursed through me.

It had soon become clear to me that Yuri, or Colonel Fedor Fedorovich Proshin as I now knew his real name to be, had been the mastermind behind my career as a Soviet agent, from my recruitment at the age of twenty onwards. He had greeted me in Moscow, but it was no hero's welcome. I was one of several British double agents who had ended up here: Kim Philby, Donald Maclean, Guy Burgess and George Blake. But, unlike them, I was no longer a Communist, and had been brought here against my will, whereas they had all defected by choice.

After I'd been put through a comprehensive – and extremely unpleasant – medical examination, Yuri had proceeded to interrogate me about every aspect of the twenty-four years since I had sought him out in a displaced persons camp in the British Zone of Germany. He hadn't presented it as an interrogation at first, even installing me in fairly comfortable quarters, but the armed guards had never left me with any doubt about the truth of the situation.

He had started every morning the same way: once I was seated, he would open up my dossier and read directly from the reports my handlers had sent to Moscow at whichever point in my career we had reached. After that, the questions would begin.

'Why did you cut off all contact for eighteen months after this meeting?'

'Why did you not mention that Burgess and Maclean had come under suspicion?'

'Why didn't you tell us about Penkovsky?'

And so on, ad infinitum. Part of me had been expecting it – the documents I'd discovered in Rome had revealed that for several years they had suspected me of being a plant by the Service, feeding them carefully selected secrets along with a healthy dose of disinformation: in effect, a triple agent.

That theory had eventually been discredited in '51 and I'd been cleared as 'highly valuable', but now Yuri revived it. The material I had taken so many risks to give them meant nothing to him. It was only the information I had *neglected* to hand over that he found telling. But while it was true that the higher I'd risen in the Service the greater my access to classified material had been, my seniority had often made it harder for me to hand material over, because so few others had such access. If it had ever come to light that the Soviets had this kind of information, I would have immediately come under suspicion.

Yuri had dismissed this argument with a wave of his hand. While my actions would have had me strung up in England, from his perspective I was now an erratic agent with perplexing gaps in his story, who for good measure had betrayed several Soviet agents and even killed two of them. It didn't help that I made no attempt to conceal that I was disgusted with myself for falling into their arms, and with him for the way in which he had recruited me.

He had finally lost patience with me in June, and it was then that I had been moved into Steklyashka, where one day I had been marched into a briefing room and been confronted by Sasha, whom I hadn't seen since we'd arrived in Moscow. He had been my handler since the early Fifties, but any hope that he might prove to be any more understanding as a result was rapidly dispelled. He had barely acknowledged our past relationship, and was even more hostile than Yuri had been. I'd always known that his friendliness towards me was contrived, of course, as real as the intimacy a prostitute shows a wealthy and potentially long-term client, but it had still come as a shock when it was switched off so swiftly, and so absolutely. The familiar 'My dear Paul' had no longer issued from his lips, and his benign condescension had been replaced by a cold and sometimes frightening implacability.

At first I'd thought his behaviour was a pose, a way to get me to talk more by making me want to recapture the old bonhomie, but I'd soon realized that there was nothing forced about it, and that this was in fact his real self – or, at least, his Soviet self.

I looked at him now, partly obscured by the back of his seat, staring at the road ahead of us. He was wearing a uniform and *ushanka*, neither of which I'd ever seen him wear before, and he didn't look right somehow. I knew every inch of his face, from the lines around the eyes to the bristles of his pointed beard, but I found it increasingly hard to associate him with the cheery fellow in the tweed coat and polka-dot tie I had met in an assortment of pubs, cinemas and dives in London, a collector's book of postage stamps under his arm. English Sasha had always seemed podgy and harmless, but Soviet Sasha was a burly bear of a man with an air of barely repressed violence emanating from him. Over the years he'd often told me that he loved London, and I wondered if that had simply been a lie to get me on his side, or if his recall to Moscow had hardened him, and he'd forgotten his appreciation of the good life he'd once led in the West.

Perhaps he was simply scared. My failures as an agent reflected badly on him, and possibly even placed him under suspicion of disloyalty. After Stalin's death, Khrushchev had been, relatively speaking, benign, but Brezhnev had started pushing things back in the other direction: arresting dissidents and sending them to labour camps or into 'internal exile'. Perhaps that was where we were all going now: to some *gulag* in Siberia where we would freeze our arses off until we died.

Whatever the reason, when Sasha had taken over my case any remaining pretence that I was simply an agent undergoing a debriefing had vanished. I was unequivocally a prisoner, placed in a small concrete cell and entitled to one bowl of thin soup and three cigarettes a day. Every morning and afternoon I had been made to write an account of my career, operation by operation, month by month. After that, I would be summoned into a small office, where he would question me at length on everything I'd written. We had reached June 1961.

The car took a sudden turn, throwing my shoulder against the door. The windows were covered by grey curtains, but there was a small gap near the edge and I peered through it at the streets speeding by. Giant portraits of Lenin lined the roads, but I saw very few other cars. It must still be quite early in the morning. Domes shone faintly in the distance, and there was a glint of copper in the sky, a refraction, I imagined, from the giant stars of the Kremlin. But then we took a turn – we didn't seem to be heading that way.

The car slowed to a halt in front of a nondescript building painted a faded orange, and I was dragged out by one of the men. The other stayed in the car with Sarah, and I wondered fleetingly if it would be the last time I saw her.

It had started to snow now and the wind was sharper, biting into my cheeks and stinging my eyelids. Sasha led the way to a sentry box manned by two lieutenants in light blue greatcoats, both armed with finely polished semi-automatic rifles. A pigeon pecking at the ground nearby suddenly came to a standstill and turned in the same direction, its chest puffed out, and for a moment it looked like it was imitating the sentries. All it needed was a few brass buttons and a miniature *ushanka* to complete the picture, but a moment later it returned to its pecking, and the illusion was broken.

Sasha handed some papers to one of the men, who looked through them, then turned and spoke into a small grate in the wall. There was a loud hissing noise, and I saw that the whole section of wall was, in fact, an air-locked door. With some effort, the sentry pulled it open and stepped inside. After a moment's hesitation, Sasha motioned to me, and we followed him in.

We were in a dimly lit space, smaller than the size of my cell. I could see the sentry just ahead, wrestling with the lock of another, much larger, door. Once he had opened it, we walked into a room with concrete walls and a large blanket of green netting in the middle. The sentry knelt down and pulled this to one side, revealing a small wire cage recessed several feet into the floor. He climbed down into it and Sasha and I followed. The sentry pulled a lever in a box on the side of the cage, and we started to descend with a loud cranking noise.

It was then that I recognized the mood I hadn't been able to identify in the car. It wasn't panic. It was fear. They were all terrified out of their wits, and I couldn't blame them. Those had been bomb-blast doors we had just come through.

We were entering a nuclear bunker.

II

As the machinery of the lift whirred, I tried to gather my thoughts. I knew very little about the Soviets' contingency plans in the event of a nuclear attack – few did – but years of surveillance by the West indicated that they had built a massive underground city in the area of Ramenki, a few miles outside Moscow. I didn't think we were there but still beneath the capital where it was thought there was a complex of command and control points and a bunker built by Stalin before the war, all of it connected by a secret second underground railway system.

I thought we must now be inside that labyrinth, but several things were puzzling me. First, why were we going into it at all? There couldn't have been an attack, because we had come here overground. Was it some sort of exercise, then, or simply a secret meeting? It seemed a little over the top for either, and didn't account for the level of fear I was sensing in Sasha and the others. And secondly, why on earth were they bringing *me* here? Since my arrival in May, their treatment of me had been overwhelmingly hostile, yet now I was apparently trusted enough to be taken to one of their most secret military locations.

The lift jolted to a sudden halt. The sentry gestured for us to step out, and when we had, he pulled the lever and the cage started ascending again, leaving me alone with Sasha. Another sentry stepped from the shadows and led us into a narrow passageway with curved steel walls. Lamps riveted to the walls were spaced every few feet, halos shimmering around them, but between them it was pitch dark. It was also unpleasantly clammy. I tried to catch my breath, but Sasha, directly behind me, pushed me forward.

We walked down the steel plankway of the passage, the echo of our footsteps flattened and tinny. After a few minutes, we reached a large door covered in a thick cushion of black leather. The sentry pushed a button on the wall and a few seconds later the door swung open. Sasha gestured to me to enter first, and I stepped through. He followed. The door immediately shut behind us, and a second later I heard the echo of the sentry's footsteps as he began the walk back up the corridor.

I took a breath and looked up. Lights shone down from sconces in the walls, and it took a moment for my vision to adjust. We were in a huge hall, the far end of which was taken up by a circular table with a segment cut out of its centre. This was encircled by thick marble pillars that held up an elaborate painted cupola that looked like it belonged in the Vatican. Seated around the table were around thirty elderly men, some of them wearing dark suits but most in uniform. A man was standing at the table. Unlike the others he was jacketless, his shirtsleeves rolled to his elbows. In one hand he clutched an amber cigarette holder, in the other a sheaf of papers he was brandishing at his audience. I didn't recognize him at first, because he was wearing spectacles and his hair was slightly in disarray, but then he looked up through dark eyes under thick eyebrows, and I realized with a start that it was Brezhnev.

*

He stared at Sasha and me for a moment, evidently caught in mid-sentence. Then he set down his papers.

'Who the hell is this?' he said, his voice a deep baritone.

There was a scraping noise and I followed it to about halfway down the table, where one of the men was pushing his chair back. It was Yuri. He was wearing the uniform of a Colonel-General: it was immaculate, perfectly pressed, with a line of glittering medals across the chest.

'Paul Dark, General Secretary,' he said. 'The British agent. You may remember I suggested fetching him earlier, in case he had any knowledge pertinent to the situation. His file is in the papers, Section Five.' He leaned over and picked up a folder from an attaché case on the table.

Brezhnev waved his hand as though swatting at a fly.

'Be seated.'

Yuri bowed extravagantly and then beckoned me with two fingers, like an emperor summoning a slave. I glared at him, but stepped forward. Yuri gestured towards a vacant chair next to him and I installed myself, the hard wood of the seat angling into my buttocks. Yuri recoiled from me a little, wrinkling his nose: it had been a few days since I'd had a shower. I repressed the urge to place my hands around his throat and crush his windpipe.

Sasha was still standing by the door, and Yuri nodded at him.

'Thank you, Alexander Stepanovich. That will be all.'

Sasha hesitated for a fraction of a second before saluting, but in that moment an odd expression came over his face. It wasn't quite disappointment, I thought – more like hurt. Perhaps he had been expecting to stay. He turned and marched back out of the door.

I looked around the rest of the room. It was in the grandiose style the Soviets reserved for their upper echelons. There were oil paintings on the walls, elaborate cornices, highly polished parquet floors and, arranged on the table, a dozen or more telephones, the Bakelite glistening under the glow of Art Deco lamps. One wall was taken up with a row of clocks giving the current time in Moscow, Washington, Peking, London and several other cities. It had just gone seven o'clock in the morning here. The wall behind Brezhnev was covered in red velvet curtains; I presumed to give the illusion that there were windows behind them. A large map of the world was spread out across the table, and around it were strewn pens, papers, bottles of Borzhom mineral water and glasses. It was much grander than the British bunkers I'd visited, which had been grim, skeletal places devoid of any luxuries – nothing but holes in the ground, as one minister had called them. But this place was just as lifeless in its way, and just as depressing. It wasn't real life, but a simulacrum of it. I wondered how long they'd been down here; I was already feeling claustrophobic, and I'd only just arrived.

One thing was abundantly clear. This wasn't an exercise, or a good spot for a meeting. Something had to be *seriously* wrong for Brezhnev to be in an underground bunker. Although he was in his early sixties, he looked much older.

Everyone knew him to be stout, hearty and fond of a drink, as all good Russians were, but he looked a wreck. There were dark circles around his eyes, and I now saw that one hand was shaking. He looked like a bull that had been cornered: angry and ready to lash out.

I felt a momentary pang of pity for the men around the table, many of whom I recognized from Service dossiers. My eyes flicked around as though playing Pelmanism. Seated directly to Brezhnev's right was Kosygin, the Premier, a bulldog. Next to him was Suslov – he looked like a kindly old don, but his staunch Stalinism and behind-the-scenes machinations had earned him the nickname the 'Red Eminence'. Then there was Grechko, the Minister of Defence and head of the armed forces – the classic military type with hair cropped *en brosse*.

Next to him was Ivashutin, head of the GRU. Portly, around sixty, he was one of Brezhnev's old cronies, having known him since the war, when he had been a senior officer in SMERSH on the Ukrainian front. He had taken part in the arrest of Serov, and then been appointed head of the GRU in his place by Brezhnev. Opposite him sat Andropov, the new head of the KGB, inscrutable in horn-rimmed spectacles. He and Ivashutin were thought to detest each other, which was perhaps why they had been seated so far apart.

These grey, heavy men constituted the 'Supreme

Command' or 'Defence Council', the core of the Politburo and decision-making power in a crisis – and they were mostly hardliners. As well as sending dissidents to work camps, Brezhnev was also cracking down on signs of reform in the satellite states, which had culminated in the ruthless intervention in Czechoslovakia the previous spring.

Several reports had reached the Service that Brezhnev had become significantly unpopular with the Soviet people as a result, and in January there had even been an attempt on his life. A soldier, apparently upset by the Prague invasion, had fled his base in Leningrad, taking with him two loaded Makarovs and four clips from his unit's safe. Arriving in Moscow, he had stolen a police uniform belonging to his father and, posing as an officer at one of the cordons leading into the Kremlin, had tried to shoot Brezhnev as he was being driven through for a homecoming celebration for several cosmonauts. But he got the wrong car and had hit one of the cosmonauts instead.

In the meantime, Brezhnev continued the roll-back to Stalinism. In his address to the Congress of the Polish Communist Party in November, he had stated that a threat to the security of any 'socialist' country was a threat to them all, and would be dealt with as such. The Brezhnev Doctrine, as it was soon known, overturned the idea of sovereign states that had been at the heart of the Warsaw Pact. I wondered if another state had decided to try to test his steel. This wasn't a group of men you would gather together on a whim.

Most alarming to me was Yuri's presence. He'd altered his appearance a little since I'd last seen him. His white hair was still shorn close to the skull, but he had cultivated a thin goatee to match it; I suspected because he wanted to appear more distinguished. He had unluckily conspicuous features for a spy – a strange snubbed nose and tiny eyes in a mass of leathery wrinkles – and the effect was of a mischievous schoolboy peering out of the face of an old man.

From his uniform and position at the table, it looked like he was Ivashutin's deputy. On my arrival in Moscow, he had given the impression of having long been sidelined from the *apparat*, an old hand who had been stepped over by younger men. And yet here he was, in the heart of the lion's den, deputy head of the GRU. Either he had been promoted in the last few months, or – more likely – he had only wanted me to believe he had been sidelined so that I would underestimate him, giving him an advantage in interrogation. Not for the first time he had pulled the wool over my eyes with infuriating ease.

Brezhnev had sat down, and was drinking water from a glass while he looked me over. His eyes were like bullet holes.

'Remind me, Colonel-General Proshin,' he said without adjusting his gaze. 'Why did you wish to bring this man here? Looking at his dossier, it seems we feel that he is not to be trusted.'

'That is not quite so, General Secretary,' Yuri replied evenly. 'We have been determining precisely what level of trust we can place in him at one of our secure facilities.'

Brezhnev sat back and folded his arms. 'For six months?'

Yuri's tiny eyes didn't flicker. 'We strive to be thorough, General Secretary. The dossier contains some provisional thoughts, but our plan was to make a more thorough assessment once we had gathered all the available information. However, considering the current situation, I requested permission to bring him before the Council because I felt that as a result of his former position as Deputy Chief of the British Service, he may be able to help us.'

'Or he may lie to us.'

Yuri nodded. 'That is naturally a possibility. But if so—'

'Could I just interject for a moment?' I said, and two dozen heads jerked in my direction. 'Would someone mind telling me what's going on?'

An hour previously, I would have thought I would be one of the last people the Soviet leadership would want to bring into their confidence, but they obviously wanted something from me and they would have to show their

23

hand sooner or later. It was intimidating being in such company, but I had, after all, been in similar company in London, and I thought it was wise to try to establish that I was on the same level as they, rather than a circus act they could discuss and poke at will. If I could undermine Yuri at the same time, all the better. I hadn't seen the bastard in months, but I had good cause to loathe him. He had indeed placed me in a 'secure facility', and Christ knew what he'd done to Sarah.

Brezhnev lit another cigarette, and gestured to Yuri that he should answer my question. Yuri straightened his back and stared at me with unalloyed hatred radiating from his hobgoblin eyes.

'Very well,' he said. 'We would like you to tell us all you know about the West's plans for nuclear conflict.'

I took that in, eyeing Brezhnev's cigarette and wishing I had my own to puff. An image flashed into my mind: the toothless grin of the old man in the stand near Sloane Square Underground as he slid a pack of Players into my waiting fingers. I shook my head free of it.

'I don't know anything about that,' I said.

'Come,' said Yuri, and gave a slow, condescending smile. 'You were deputy head of the Service.'

'For about five minutes. I can tell you about the broad strategy, if you like, but the only people who know the details of the plans are those directly involved in them.'

'In the bunkers, you mean.'

He was trying to get me to give him something he could follow up on. I didn't react. I noted that this seemed to be his show, since none of the others were talking. That suggested the meeting had been called on account of information received by the GRU.

'You know where the bunkers are, of course?' he said.

'Not off by heart, no. I'm afraid I can't really tell you much about "the West" as a whole. I know a bit about the British strategy, a little about NATO's and next to nothing about the Americans'.'

Three seats down, I saw Andropov look away and purse his lips, and guessed it was the Americans they were interested in.

'Very well,' said Yuri, his tone a little more curt. 'Please tell us what you do know.'

I smiled sweetly at him, stalling for time so I could work out what was going on and how to react. I could simply refuse to cooperate, of course. I didn't much like being woken up, yelled at and *fetched* to an underground bunker without any explanation, and part of me was tempted to tell them where to stick it. But that would be foolish – if I didn't appear to be trying to answer their questions sincerely, they would simply put a bullet through the back of my head. They might do it anyway, but there was a chance they wouldn't. So swallow your pride, play nicely, sound convincing, and if you're very lucky they won't shoot you at the end of this and might even give you a slightly more comfortable cell.

The difficulty was in picking precisely which pieces of information I could safely tell them. Because I did, of course, know quite a lot about the West's plans for nuclear conflict, having been given a copy of the War Book on being appointed Head of Soviet Section in late '65. I had also taken part in dozens of meetings over the years on the intricacies of post-strike contingency plans, including with counterparts at NATO and CIA.

This time last year I had taken part in INVALUABLE, a top secret Whitehall exercise that had preceded NATO's wider scenario in Bonn. It was one of a series of seemingly interminable exercises carried out by a select handful of officials to test the War Book's contingency plans in case of an escalation to nuclear war with the Soviet Union. After a while they became a nuisance, and it was difficult to connect them with the idea of a real conflict. Was this a comparable Soviet exercise? It didn't seem like it – nobody had been sweating this much in London.

If so, it might be that other men in uniforms were scurrying into bunkers in other parts of the world. If the United States felt an attack was imminent, about a thousand people were to retreat to a complex of steel-protected buildings set inside Cheyenne Mountain in Colorado.

Members of Congress would be evacuated to a bunker in White Sulphur Springs, Virginia, while the President would move to Camp David and the Pentagon to a facility nearby. In the event that one of their nuclear command or ground launch centres were hit or their capability damaged, a round-the-clock airborne command post codenamed 'Looking Glass' would take over. They also had on patrol some forty submarines, loaded with Polaris nuclear-armed missiles.

In Britain, if ballistic missiles or some other form of explosive weapon were detected by the receivers at RAF Fylingdales or by the Royal Observer Corps, information about the objects' radar arrays, height, speed and inclination would immediately be fed into the Threat Report Panel in Fylingdales' operations room. If deemed a credible threat, the Home Office would be informed and could then issue the 'Four-Minute Warning' – so called because of the length of time between it being given and oncoming missiles reaching their targets, although it might in fact be as little as three and a half minutes.

The warning would be broadcast by the BBC on television and radio, and sirens would be sounded across the country. The warning would advise people to stay in their own homes, and to move to their fallout rooms. In reality, as I knew from discussions on the issue, very few people would survive a sustained nuclear strike. Even if they made it to shelter within four minutes, had stock-piled a fortnight's supply of provisions and were 'lucky' enough to survive the attack, after their food and water supplies had run out there would be nowhere to find more.

In the early days, the idea had been to try to protect the public as a whole from an attack, but the emphasis had shifted to protecting only those who would be needed to reconstruct the country. One early plan had been for the Prime Minister and a small group to stay in London and beat a retreat to a network of rooms under Whitehall, an extension of those built during the last war. But that had been scrapped after two secret reports in the mid-Fifties had painted a horrific picture of the consequences of an H-bomb attack on Britain.

Expert analysis of Whitehall's 'citadels', as the bunkers were known, had revealed that they might not withstand a direct strike, and that a single explosion could also block their exits, entombing the Prime Minister and his advisers below ground. The boffins had also estimated that an attack on Britain with ten hydrogen bombs would turn much of the country into a radioactive wasteland, and kill or seriously injure sixteen million people – around a third of the population. Another thirteen million people, many of them suffering from contamination, would be impris-oned in their shelters for at least a week. Reading the reports, it was hard to see how the country would ever be able to recover.

As a result, the plans had been changed so that if an attack seemed imminent, several days before the Four-Minute Warning led to ordinary members of the public uselessly shepherding their children into their feebly protected basements, the Cabinet, members of the royal family and senior members of the government, the military, the Service, Five and the scientific community would be evacuated to a 35-acre blast-proof bunker that had been built in the old limestone quarries in Corsham, Wiltshire, with a few hundred others retreating to underground operational headquarters around the country.

But in '63, Kim Philby defected to Moscow. He hadn't been indoctrinated into the Corsham plan, but some feared he might nevertheless have got wind of it. If so, the Russians could wipe Britain off the map simply by aiming missiles at London and the bunker in Wiltshire. And so, in May '68, a brand new plan had been put into place, known to only a handful of people.

If it looked like a nuclear attack was imminent, instead of the 'great and the good' being whisked to Corsham, they would instead be split into several groups. RAF helicopters based at Little Rissington in Gloucestershire would fly to Whitehall and wait at the Horse Guards Parade for the

Prime Minister and a couple of dozen others – including a few from the Service – and each group would be flown to a different location. I was earmarked to be taken to Welbeck Abbey in Nottinghamshire, to the maze of rooms built beneath it in the nineteenth century by the agoraphobic fifth Duke of Portland. The idea that central government would evacuate to Corsham had been kept in place as a cover story, a decoy to protect the new plan and to stop anyone looking for the PYTHON sites, as they had been codenamed.

A thought crystallized in my mind. Despite the Service's fears that Philby had blown Corsham, it seemed clear from Yuri's questions that they did *not* know about it. If so, that meant that all the money and effort to create the PYTHON plan had been a waste. I had decided not to tell them when I learned about it last spring, and I certainly didn't want to tell them now. Apart from having lost any vestige of belief in their cause, I didn't want to be responsible for starting a nuclear war.

But I *could* tell them about Corsham, which was no longer in use, and make it seem very convincing – I had learned about it in '65, and had even been given a tour of the place. But before I answered, I needed to find out why were they asking. Were they planning to attack the West, and if so, why?

'The locations of the bunkers are not our primary

concern,' said Yuri, smiling, and I wondered for an eerie moment whether he had managed to plant a bug in my mind. 'We're more interested in the procedures. How long would it take for a second strike to be launched following an order from the American President, for example?'

A cold, empty feeling crept through me. I didn't know the precise timing of the Americans' chain of command, but I knew that in Britain's case HMS *Resolution* and two other submarines were on constant patrol with American Polaris missiles aboard, and that they were primed to be launched within fifteen minutes of an order from the Prime Minister. But that was in the event of a decision to *retaliate*. Yuri had asked me about a second strike: in other words, if the Americans launched a first strike on the Soviet Union and then wanted to deliver a follow-up attack. I could only think of a few reasons to ask such a question, and I didn't like any of them.

'Why do you want to know this?' I said. 'Is the country under attack?'

Yuri glanced at Ivashutin, who in turn looked at Brezhnev. I kept silent, watching, waiting. They couldn't get anything detailed out of me if they didn't give me more information, and they'd gone to the trouble of bringing me here so presumably they wanted it. I suspected that protocol and habit made them reluctant to tell a foreigner what was going on, but it was absurd in this instance — it wasn't as if I could tell anyone. As the moments passed, I thought I sensed this understanding make its way around the table.

Finally, Brezhnev made a decision and nodded his head gently. Yuri took a deep breath and turned to me.

'Yes,' he said. 'The Soviet Union is under attack.'

I felt it like a blow to the stomach. Was it possible? It couldn't be nuclear, I realized at once. They wouldn't have spent the time bringing me here in that case, let alone doing so above ground. On the other hand, if it wasn't nuclear, what the hell were we doing in this bunker?

'What sort of attack?' I said, the words forming before my mind had even processed them.

Brezhnev tapped his cigarette against the nearest ashtray, and nodded again.

Yuri took another breath. 'The Americans launched a chemical attack on Paldiski and Hiiumaa yesterday,' he said. 'We are preparing our response.'

Paldiski and Hiiumaa were both in Estonia, facing the Gulf of Finland. The entire area was closed off to the public as it was home to dozens of military and naval installations: Hiiumaa and the surrounding islands were rumoured to be home to sizeable artillery batteries, while Paldiski was a major nuclear submarine base. I looked around the room, taking in the collection of grey faces, the ticking clocks, the portraits on the wall and the plume of smoke spiralling from Brezhnev's ghastly cigarette.

'What sort of chemical attack?' I said.

'A serious one. Over a dozen have been seriously injured – two men have already died. We have sent specialized troops to the area, as well as a team of experts to investigate. In addition,' – he glanced at the wall with the clocks – 'about ten hours ago our radars picked up eighteen B-52 Stratofortress bombers shortly after they had taken off from two American Air Force bases, Fairchild in Washington and March in California. We have analysed the take-off patterns and fuel consumption to calculate the weight of the aircraft, and have concluded that they are armed with thermonuclear weapons.'

I stared at him, and then took in the import of the large map on the table. There were lines running all over it: trajectories.

'Where are they now?'

He gave a grim smile, perhaps satisfied that I was catching up to the severity of the situation.

'They have been in a circling pattern for the past few hours, but now seem to be heading straight towards our eastern border. We also have reports that KC-135 aircraft have been deployed from Little Rock in Arkansas, and we believe they will meet up with the B-52s once they reach the coast of Canada.'

'For in-air refuelling.'

He nodded. 'The B-52s are travelling at around 800 kilometres an hour, and if they continue on their current path we expect them to cross into our airspace in just under five hours from now. That is, at noon our time.'

My first thought was that they must be part of a patrol. Back in the Fifties, the Americans had set up a system whereby they had a dozen nuclear-armed B-52s airborne around the clock, so that if the Soviets launched a surprise attack on their bases they would still be able to retaliate. But then I remembered that had changed. Early in '66, a USAF B-52 carrying four H-bombs had collided with a Stratotanker during mid-air refuelling over the Mediterranean. One of the H-bombs had fallen into the sea and it had taken several weeks to find it, while two of the remaining three that had fallen on land had spilled enriched uranium and plutonium over a Spanish fishing village, and had cost millions to clear up. Then last year one of the B-52s had crashed very close to their own air-base in Greenland, detonating the primary units of its thermonuclear weapons but, very luckily, not triggering a nuclear reaction. As a result of these incidents, Washington had, understandably, discontinued the airborne patrols.

So it couldn't be that. What the hell could it be, then, other than preparations for an attack? In-air refuelling was a bloody risky manoeuvre – one shift in the wind or mistake at the controls could lead to a crash, and this time they might not be as lucky as they had been in Greenland. I remembered a report on their Castle Bravo test on the Micronesian islands back in '54 saying that the explosion had been around 1,500 times more powerful than the atomic bombs used on Hiroshima and Nagasaki. No wonder we were underground.

'Have you used the hotline?' I said. This was the direct telex connection between Washington and Moscow that had been set up in '63 in the wake of the Cuban crisis so that the two superpowers could communicate about accidents or unexplained incidents and avert a potential disaster.

'No,' said Yuri. 'We do not need to ask our enemies if they have attacked us – we already know they have. Use of the hotline would alert them of this, and that we plan to retaliate. We don't plan to warn our enemies in advance – they did not warn us.'

I nodded, dazed. I'd attended several meetings about the setting up of that hotline. But the difference between a hypothetical situation and a real one couldn't be starker, and the logic of his reply was clear. The hotline only made sense if you suspected it was a mistake. If you had good reason to think you were under attack, it was counter-productive to use it. The hotline was a waste of time.

'You say you have evidence that the injuries in Paldiski and Hiiumaa are caused by chemical weapons. But couldn't this be a provocation from someone else – China, for example? Or an accident of some sort?'

He shook his head briskly. 'No doubt we were meant to conclude it was an accident, but there can no longer be any question of that. Several people have already been affected, and the toll is rising by the hour. As all the victims are crucial to our nuclear effort, and this has happened at precisely the same time that the United States has sent several nuclear-armed B-52s towards our border, it would seem foolish to see it as anything but deliberate, and that most likely it is part of preparations for a full-scale nuclear attack.

'As for the Chinese, we have finally started negotiations in Peking, so we don't think this is their doing. We already know that the Americans are using chemical agents in Vietnam, and this follows several other signals from them in the last couple of weeks that they are at an advanced state of readiness, and may be preparing to launch an attack against us. We have observed increased naval activity in the Gulf of Aden, and our ambassador in Washington was recently informed by Nixon himself that the United States is prepared to take "drastic action" as a result of our support of the North Vietnamese if the peace talks in Paris do not advance.'

'Have you talked to the North Vietnamese?'

'They are not under our control. They want our arms and training but don't listen to us if we try to interfere politically, as it is their war and they feel they know better. It seems Nixon has not taken this into account, and has decided he will attack us as a result.'

'But why has he not just launched a strike, then? Why attack your bases in Estonia and make it look like an accident?'

'Clearly, they have identified that many of our important military installations are located in this area and have decided to sabotage them in advance of a nuclear attack. The idea of making it look like an accident was presumably so that we would not be aware that it was a precursor to a nuclear strike. They must not have thought that we would rapidly be able to confirm the type of chemical used and therefore know it's an attack. And, of course, by making us doubt that the incident is an attack, they hope to delay our retaliation.'

'Yes, but even so——' I stopped. 'Hold on. You say you know what type of chemical is involved?'

'Yes, our researchers have examined several of the patients and have determined that it is one not found in the

Soviet Union. It is mustard gas, but a form of it we have never encountered.'

I shivered, and a ripple of horror ran through me – a new form of mustard gas.

I looked at the map, and quickly located Paldiski on it.

Christ Almighty.

'It's not a chemical attack,' I said. 'It's a leak.'

III

Sunday, 11 March 1945, Hotel Torni, Helsinki, Finland

It was past midnight when there was a sharp knocking on my door. I opened it to see Templeton, dressed in a hat and topcoat, peering at me.

My first thought was that Father had been killed in action and he had come to inform me, immediately followed by a flash of shameful hope I might be right. As a boy, I had lain awake in my bed sickened and fascinated by fantasies of his death, and in recent months my mind had slipped back into this reflex of momentarily wishing for the worst news. At first it had disturbed me, but now I dismissed it for what it was: just a trick of the mind exacerbated by the tensions of the war.

'Meet me in the lobby in five minutes,' Templeton said, and there was a look in his eyes that spoke of conspiracies rather than condolences. 'In full uniform, please.'

I nodded and shut the door. Having dressed hurriedly, I raced down the carpeted staircase, wondering what would await me at the foot of it.

I had arrived in Helsinki a few months earlier, and was not enjoying it. I'd had a frustrating war. Shortly after leaving school I had been recruited into the Special Operations Executive, and had been put through rigorous training. After narrowly missing out on taking part in several operations, Father had arranged for me to be attached to the platoon guarding Churchill at Chequers. This sounded impressive, but the novelty of being close to the man as he chomped his cigar and chugged down brandy soon faded – the job mostly consisted of patrolling the house and grounds with a Tommy gun, and following him in a convoy of trucks and motorcycles whenever he went for a stroll.

I had finally seen some real action in 1944, when I was dropped into France as part of a Jedburgh team, but the operation had been cut short after just a few weeks when it had become clear that the cell we had been sent to contact had been betrayed to the Germans.

After that, I'd been sent out here. I suspected Father had heard something about my time in France and had had a word in someone's ear to whisk me out of the line of fire. In 1941, before the Legation in Helsinki had been evacuated by the Finns and relocated to Lisbon, he had briefly served as the military attaché out here, and I'd visited him and helped out around the place during one Long Vac, delivering messages in between the endless cocktail parties.

Finland had by now surrendered to the Soviets for the second time but we had yet to restore diplomatic relations with them, so rather than returning to the Legation I had been posted on to the staff of the Allied Control Commission, which was operating out of the Hotel Torni, a hideous watchtower-like building overlooking the centre of Helsinki. The Commission had been established to supervise the Finns' compliance with their armistice with Moscow and, although Allied in name, was almost completely dominated by the Russians. There were two hundred of them and just fifteen Brits, who were under firm instruction from London not to antagonize the Russians. Finland was part of the Soviet sphere, at least until the end of the war.

None of the Brits spoke any Finnish, and it had been deemed a sound idea if someone could be found who did. My previous few weeks flitting about the Legation had presumably been on file, but nobody seemed to have realized that while my mother was a Finn, she was in fact a

Swedish-speaker. As a result, I was fluent in Swedish but knew no Finnish at all.

On arrival, I had discovered that it made little odds anyway. The British contingent was led by Commodore Howie of the Royal Navy, but I reported to Colonel Colin Templeton, an old friend of Father's from Cairo whom I'd met a couple of times on school holidays. Officially the Army's representative, he was in reality an SOE officer and, despite being given the rank of lieutenant-colonel, I was his dogsbody. With every passing day, I resented the position all the more. My few weeks in France had nearly got me killed, but I had finally tasted action and was desperate for more. I was twenty years old, and the war was still raging elsewhere in Europe, while I spent my days in a hotel typing up the minutes of meetings about the minutiae of diplomatic protocol.

'Is it Japan, sir?' I asked Templeton as we stepped out of the hotel lobby and into the chill night air. The Americans had just fire-bombed Tokyo, destroying half the city, and I had spent the day collating reports on the situation. But Templeton shook his head.

'I'll explain in the Ghost,' he said, as we showed our passes to a sentry and crossed the courtyard.

The Ghost was a battered old Chevrolet, a former Finnish Army staff car that he had commandeered for his personal use. Every inch of its exterior had been white-washed, including the windows, a legacy of its use at the front early in the war. Templeton had left it in this condition partly because he enjoyed the eccentricity of it, and partly because the camouflage suited his purposes. His instructions from London were for his presence here to be as invisible as possible: in a city often covered in snow, the Ghost allowed him to do just that.

It wasn't snowing now, but as many of the surrounding buildings were white the car still lived up to its name. Templeton's chauffeur opened the door and we were soon gliding through the city, cocooned behind the thickened frost of the glass. He wasted no time in getting to the point.

'When you were here in '41, I understand that you and Larry flew across to Stockholm by seaplane.'

I nodded, puzzled. My father and I had made the journey several times, in a couple of old single-seater Supermarines. Father had always been a racing fiend, and didn't much care if it was on land, air, water or a combination. I had relished the expeditions as opportunities to spend more time with him, but after a while had realized that he was using them to look at the possibility of moving Mother to an asylum in Stockholm. He did this a few months later, and there she had remained ever since. It didn't surprise me that our trips had ended up in my file, but I couldn't fathom why they were relevant now.

'Are you sending me to Sweden, sir?'

Templeton ignored the question. 'A few hours ago, our Russian friends here received a message from their consulate in Mariehamn, which is the capital of a group of demilitarized islands known as Ahvenanmaa in Finnish and Åland in Swedish. The place belongs to Finland, but is Swedish-speaking.'

I knew of it – an archipelago at the entrance of the Gulf of Bothnia. I had never been there, but some members of Mother's family had a summer residence on the western side. This was my immediate thought. It took me a few moments more to take in the other implication of what Templeton had just said: we had intercepted the Russians' message. If he was listening in to the Soviets' telephones in the hotel, I had severely underestimated him.

'The Russians' message was as follows,' Templeton said briskly. 'Yesterday evening, a body was discovered washed ashore on the Åland islands. The local police have identified it as being that of a German naval officer by the name of Wilhelm von Trotha.'

Corpses of naval officers being washed ashore? As the car jostled along, I examined Templeton's face to see if it was some sort of elaborate joke. But he was looking at me intently, apparently waiting for my thoughts on the matter.

'Could it be a provocation, sir?' I asked. Shortly before heading to France I'd heard talk of an operation in which we had secured a body from a morgue in London, dressed it in the uniform of a Royal Marine and landed it on the coast of Spain with a cache of false letters to fool the Germans into thinking we were planning to target Sardinia and Greece rather than Sicily. It had worked like a dream, but the Jerries would, of course, have realized that it had been a ruse, so perhaps someone had thought up a revenge plan.

'That was my first thought, too,' said Templeton. 'But it looks like this could be genuine.' He reached inside his coat and brought out a wodge of paper, which he unfolded and spread out on the upholstery between us. It was a large sea chart of Finland. After scanning it for a few moments, he pointed to a spot on the eastern archipelago labelled 'Degerby'.

'This is where they found the body. As you can see, it's very isolated: if someone deliberately placed a body there, the chances of it being discovered would have been exceptionally slim. More significantly, we know that this chap von Trotha was, in fact, the captain of a U-boat, U-745, which we have been tracking for some time. It left Danzig in December, and on January the eleventh it sank one of the Russians' minesweepers here.' He pointed to the map again, to a small island off the coast of Estonia. 'And it was last observed somewhere around' — he shifted his finger to a spot just west of the Gulf of Finland — 'here.'

'When you say "last observed", sir, do I understand that we believe the boat is out of action?'

'Yes. Its last signal was on the fourth of last month, and we suspect it was accidentally sunk by one of the Germans' own mines, either on that day or soon after. If so, the body may simply have floated ashore on the currents. As a matter of course, we would probably be interested in this chap, but we have also had information, from impeccable sources, that his U-boat was carrying a very special cargo: a new form of mustard gas. Mustard gas is a viscous liquid, of course, but this has apparently been mixed together in such a way as to make it even thicker, so it won't be affected by the temperatures in this part of the world. They call it "Winterlost", and if our sources are to be believed it's very strong stuff indeed – roughly twice as powerful as the usual variety.'

I didn't ask how he knew any of this, but guessed that the positions and dates were from the submarine tracking room at the Admiralty, and that the information on the mustard gas on von Trotha's U-boat had come from captured crewmen of other vessels.

'Despite all that,' Templeton said, 'it could still be some sort of deception operation mounted by the Germans. But we don't want to take any chances – and neither, it seems, do the Russians. The consulate in Mariehamn has been instructed to send someone to this island to secure von

Trotha's personal effects before he is buried. We think they may also be sending one of their agents from Stockholm, perhaps under cover, but I've yet to receive confirmation of that. We don't know whether they are aware of the U-boat's special cargo – we haven't informed them – but we need to beat them to the corpse regardless.

'Our chemical warfare bods are of the opinion that this Winterlost would be an extremely dangerous weapon if turned on us – and also a very useful one for us to study. I've been in intensive signals with London for the last few hours, and they have instructed me that it should – indeed, must – be investigated. So I want you to get to this chap's body and see if he has any information on him that gives a more accurate indication of the location of U-745 than its last signal – and then bring back the mustard gas.'

I stared at him for a few moments. Through the white-washed windows, I could just make out the Finnish countryside rushing by: dark impenetrable forests stretching into the distance.

'I thought you said the U-boat was believed to have been hit by a mine, sir.'

Templeton knitted his brows. 'Yes, but you've diving experience, haven't you?'

So that was what it was about. In early 1944, I had responded to a call for 'volunteers for hazardous service' sent out by the Royal Marines Office at the Admiralty. I had duly been summoned to report to HMS *Dolphin* in Portsmouth harbour, where I was informed that I would be trained as a diver for midget submarines. After several weeks of training in a deep tank, I had been cleared for the next stage and sent with fifteen other men to Loch Cairnbawn in the far north of Scotland, where the details of the operation in question had finally been revealed to us: the Navy had managed to put the German battleship *Tirpitz* out of action in September, and were now training to attack the Laksevåg floating dock in Bergen.

As part of the provisional crew, I had been put in and out of the new 'X-Craft', wearing a claustrophobic diving suit nicknamed the 'Clammy Death' as I learned the art of oxygen-diving. But after just a few weeks in Scotland I was told that I hadn't been selected to take part in the operation. Bitterly disappointed, I'd been sent back into the arms of SOE, who had a training establishment in Arisaig. After a few weeks of lugging backpacks around the mountainside and being taught unarmed combat and other esoteric skills by a purple-nosed Scot, I had been sent to the Parachute Training School in Ringway, and shortly after that had finally been cleared to take part in an operation and dropped into France.

I gave an abridged version of this to Templeton and he listened intently, his eyes flickering in the shadows.

'But you have had diving training,' he said quietly, once I'd finished.

Very briefly, I wanted to say, and I'd hated every minute of it. But instead I mumbled a 'Yes, sir.'

He smiled softly. 'Good. I've got you all the requisite gear, anyway. And we know the Jerries often bring their boats in very close to the shore, so with any luck it should be relatively easy to get to.'

It was true that the German U-boats often hugged coastlines, and the Russians had captured one of them in shallow waters in these parts last summer. They had raised it and discovered a new type of acoustic torpedo on board, some details of which they had shared with us. But there was no guarantee that this particular U-boat had also sunk in shallow waters.

'You'll have a wireless set,' said Templeton. 'So once you have the location, signal back and I'll judge whether or not a dive is worth risking.'

Risking my neck, he meant.

'What about the Russians?' I asked. 'Presumably they'll already be on their way from Mariehamn, if they haven't already reached it.'

'We don't think they'll set out until dawn — they've no reason to suspect their message was intercepted. We also think it will take them a while. The archipelago is made up of thousands of tiny islets and is fearfully tricky to navigate by boat if you don't know it well, especially as quite a bit of the water is frozen over at the moment. All being well, you should be landing on the island' – he glanced at his wrist-watch – 'in about three hours' time.'

Despite his confidence, I didn't like the sound of any of it. I'd wanted action, but I hadn't envisaged anything as hairy as this. Although Åland was, technically speaking, Allied territory, I was being sent to poach a weapon from right underneath the Russians' noses, and I didn't think they'd be overly understanding about it were they to catch me. The Russians weren't to be trusted. In the summer of '42, two Service agents armed with wireless sets had landed in Catalina flying boats at one of their bases in Lake Lakhta. The plan was for the Russians to insert them over the border into Norway, where they would monitor German naval movements along the coast. But the Russians had instead imprisoned both Service men for two months and then dropped them into Finland instead, where they had promptly been caught by the Germans, tortured and shot.

'What if the Russians do get there first, sir?' I said, trying to make my tone as unconcerned as possible. 'Or if I arrive at the same time?'

Templeton gave a small nod. He leaned forward and picked up something from between his feet that I hadn't noticed earlier: a leather briefcase. He pulled it onto his lap, unfastened the clasps, and brought out a fawn-coloured shoulder holster with a Browning 9mm pistol resting inside.

'I don't anticipate any trouble,' he said, 'but take this with you just in case.'

I wondered how to broach the next question, but he anticipated it.

'You must get to the submarine before anyone else,' he said, snapping the case shut and stowing it between his feet again. 'If anyone gets in your way, you have my permission to eliminate them.'

*

After about an hour's drive, we took a narrow road through a pine forest until we finally reached a small, secluded bay. We stepped out of the car and trudged towards a wooden hangar shielded by vegetation. Inside, a small seaplane sat silently under a mass of green and brown camouflage. It was a three-seater, one of the Norwegians' naval reconnaissance craft and, like the Ghost, had seen better days. Templeton said it had been used by the Norwegians against the Germans, then briefly by us and then by the Finns against the Russian subs along this stretch of the Baltic. According to the conditions of the armistice the Soviets had laid down, it should have been sent up to the north of the country to aid the Finns in their enforced mission to flush the Germans out, but Templeton had managed to keep it back from his Russian colleagues and arranged for it to be secreted here. 'Good craft are hard to come by,' he said with a sly smile.

We removed the scrim and he quickly showed me around it, but I'd flown seaplanes and time was of the essence. The plan was for me to land at the small jetty at Degerby, where the body had been reported. The local police there would no doubt be expecting a boatload of Russians from Mariehamn, but Templeton felt confident they would believe the Soviets had shared the information with their Allies, so I should be able to bluff my way through. I hoped to God he was right.

Templeton's chauffeur removed a suitcase from the car, and Templeton took me through the contents: 24-hour rations, Benzedrine tablets and a Siebe Gorman Sladen Suit – the 'Clammy Death' that had given me nightmares in Scotland. It had a breathing apparatus and twin aluminium cylinders that would provide enough oxygen for six hours, and I would be able to take it down to a depth of around thirty feet. Templeton seemed confident this would be the case – part of me hoped he was wrong and I would have to abort the operation.

But I kept such thoughts to myself, and climbed into the cockpit. Templeton showed me the wireless set, giving me the frequencies I would need to reach him. He didn't say where he would be, but presumably it wouldn't be too far away. Then he shook my hand solemnly and trudged back to the Ghost, a stoop-backed man in a topcoat and hat. His chauffeur opened the door for him and they set off down the road again. I watched as the car disappeared from view, then positioned the holster with the pistol under my left armpit. It felt heavy, and the leather of the holster cold even through my battledress.

I took a breath and examined the instruments and gauges around me, then strapped myself in. It was time to get going.

*

I was lost.

The Baltic lay beneath me, patches of ice glowing faintly in the moonlight, but I had no idea which part of Åland I was over, or even if I was over it at all. Templeton had marked Degerby on the chart, but the scale was too small and I had the growing sense that I was going around in circles. The wireless set wouldn't help: Templeton wouldn't have made it to his location yet and I didn't dare land.

A sudden gust of turbulence slammed me against the side of the cockpit and I desperately tried to keep my hands gripped on the control column, fighting down the panic as my mind was filled with the consequences of failure.

Templeton would have to send a signal back to London: man down, operation unsuccessful, please send replacement agent, this time make sure it's someone with an ounce of bloody . . . And then, just as suddenly as it had hit, the wind subsided. I slumped back in the seat, my forehead soaked with sweat and my heart still racing, and managed to right the craft. Glancing down again, I realized I had dipped dangerously low. The ice was interrupted here and there by islets, and I glimpsed miniature coiled pine trees and pinkish rocks beneath the patches of ice. But there, over to the west, a lonely dot of orange light glowed like the tip of a cigarette. I consulted the chart, and did some quick calculations in my head.

Yes. It was Degerby.

I headed for it, lifting the nose but decreasing airspeed, and the shoreline began to take a sharper shape, until I could make out small wooden cabins dotted among the trees. A jetty came into view and I wheeled into a wind current and brought her down as gently as I could, the waves kicking up in a luminous curve of white spray. I lined up with the jetty and slowly brought her to a standstill, then climbed out.

I took in a lungful of air, savouring the freshness and the smell of the water, and then exhaled, my breath misting. I anchored, and took in my surroundings as the sweat finally started to cool on my skin. I was in a small bay, and it looked so peaceful in the moonlight, the water a perfect mirror reflecting the shoreline, that it was hard to imagine such a thing as war even existed. The wind had now vanished, as suddenly as it had appeared just minutes earlier.

The jetty led up to a rocky plateau, on which I could make out the outlines of some low buildings. I began walking towards them, but as I approached the shore I saw a silhouetted figure standing a few feet ahead of me. Before I had a chance to react, the figure had stepped forward, and the harbour lighting illuminated a stout man in a coat and cap with a deeply weathered face.

'Kjell Lundström,' he said in a deep baritone. 'Chief Constable of Degerby.'

I offered him my hand. 'Lieutenant-Colonel Paul Dark. I've come about the German.'

His grip was hard, even through my thick gloves. 'We have been expecting you. But I understood that Colonel Presnakov was to come by boat. We received no word of a seaplane.'

'Presnakov is on his way,' I said, replying in Swedish. 'I'm a British officer from the Allied Control Commission in Helsinki.'

He didn't answer for a moment, taking this in. Then he said: 'I didn't know Helsinki had been informed.'

'A last-minute change of plan,' I said. 'Someone higher

up the chain of command decided it was important, and it wasn't my place to argue. I'm no happier about it than you are — I'd rather be asleep in my bed.'

He smiled at that, and I breathed an inward sigh of relief. My cover had, at least for the moment, been accepted.

'Your Swedish is excellent,' he said, as he helped me off the jetty and onto the rocks. 'Have you been here before?'

'No,' I said. 'But my mother's family has property in Eckerö.'

Lundström didn't reply, but I sensed he was satisfied with that answer. Russians were hated in this part of the world, so he no doubt felt more comfortable with a Swedish-speaking Brit with connections to the place, however tenuous they might be. He led me up a narrow pathway through the pines until we reached a small wooden shed, painted red with white window frames in the traditional style.

'Shall I show you the body, then?' he said, and now it was my turn to smile — it was a truism that Finns never wasted words, and even though these islands were Swedish-speaking it seemed that some of the Finnish spirit had rubbed off.

'Please,' I said.

Lundström removed some keys from his pocket and unlocked the door.

*

It was a waiting hall: freezing cold and lit by a single bulb, with two low benches against one wall. There was a long table in the middle of the room, and on it, half covered in a tarpaulin sheet, lay the corpse. I asked Lundström how many others had seen it, and he told me that so far only himself, his son, who acted as his assistant, and the coroner who had conducted the autopsy had done so.

'And the men who found him, of course. Two fishermen. They were out at Klåvskär when they saw something dark sticking up through the ice. One of them called me, so I took my son out to have a look.'

'So it's safe to walk on the ice at the moment?'

'Oh, yes – it's a few inches thick. We use picks to check it as we go along. That was what we used to get him out, in fact. Because what they'd seen was his head poking up through the ice, so we used a pick to cut him free. We put him on a sled and brought him back here for the autopsy. Drowning and exhaustion, the doctor said.'

I tried to imagine these grim tasks being conducted just a few hours earlier – the trek across the ice with the corpse on the sled.

'How far away is Klåvskär?' I asked.

'It's on the other side of this island.' He reached into a pocket and brought out a chart, which he unfolded and held up to the light. He bit his lip while he searched it and then, after a few moments, pointed a stubby finger triumphantly at a spot to the east and gestured for me to take a look. 'This was where they found him, in fact: Skepparskär.' I stared at the miniscule dot. Templeton had been right. It couldn't possibly be a provocation: there would have been no guarantee anyone would ever find the body in such a location.

Lundström folded the map back up and replaced it in his coat. 'He will be buried in the village church tomorrow,' he said. 'They have a special section for foreigners washed ashore.'

I looked up. 'Oh? Have there been many?'

'This is the seventh this winter. We had one coming from Riga in almost exactly the same spot in November. The currents move from the Estonian coast straight here.'

So it wasn't such an unusual spot to find a body. But still – two fishermen chancing by? I wouldn't base a deception operation on it. And seven bodies in one place was not all that many. There must be hundreds, if not thousands, scattered around the Baltic from sunken ships.

I nodded at Lundström, and he leaned forward and drew the tarpaulin to one side, revealing the body. I caught my breath and crossed myself. My country and his might be at war, but this had nevertheless been a fellow human being, and ideologies no longer counted for anything – at least, not for him.

He had been a tall man, perhaps six foot. His cap and

boots were missing, but the rest of his uniform was intact, although it had been unbuttoned, presumably for the autopsy. The body looked to be in good condition, the hands and feet bare but unscathed, and not even frozen. The head was another matter. This was what had caught the fishermen's attention, and I understood why. It was a hideous shade of dark grey, and the left eye was badly disfigured, perhaps from having hit a rock or something similar. His throat, mouth and nose were covered in blood, some of which looked fresh. Lundström noticed my curiosity.

'He was wearing a life-jacket, but it was frozen to his back. When we turned him over to take it off, the blood came pouring out of him.'

I nodded, and bent a little closer. Beneath the frozen horror I could make out the remnants of an aristocratic face, a sweep of hair, a moustache and a small beard. Templeton had told me that the Admiralty listed von Trotha's date of birth as 1916 – could this man have been twenty-nine? It was hard to tell.

'Did the coroner estimate an age?'

Lundström nodded. 'Around thirty.'

I'd take his word for it.

There were no goggles or escape equipment. I tried to think what must have happened. Had he gone up to the conning tower to check something, and then they'd hit a mine? He could have been thrown into the air and then fallen into the sea, only for the currents to carry him up here.

I shuddered at the thought.

I lifted the identity disc from his neck and read: 'Wilhelm von Trotha. Seeoffizer 1936.' That must have been when he passed out. His effects had been placed in a wooden box next to him, and I sifted through them, feeling uncomfortably like a looter. There was a pocket watch and a wristwatch, both edged with rust.

'We wound the watch,' said Lundström. 'It still works.'

I saw he was right: the hand was sweeping slowly around the face. How long could he have been in the water, then, for the mechanism not to have frozen? Templeton had said his last signal had been over a month ago. Was it possible he had been in the water that long? I picked through the rest of the items: a folding knife, a pen, several *reichsmarks*, a nail file. I glanced at his hands. His nails had turned black, but his fingers were long and slender. For some reason, I suddenly saw him as a character in a Tolstoy story, the officer in his dazzling uniform visiting his country estate, playing the piano and then returning to his naval base and to the bowels of his craft.

I took a deep breath and returned to the pile of effects. There was a gold tooth – a relative's, perhaps? – a small mirror and, yes, there it was, just peeking out . . .

A booklet.

It was yellow, slim, with 'SOLDBUCH' printed on the cover in Gothic text. These, I knew from my training, were given to all German military, and contained the bearer's service record, vaccination and other medical details, as well as space for their own entries. Templeton was hoping von Trotha might have written down what cargo his boat was carrying, and left clues as to where it might have sunk. I picked up the book and waved it at Lundström.

'I'll take this,' I said. He nodded soberly.

I opened the booklet, and as I did, a loose sheaf fell out and fluttered to the floor. I bent to pick it up, and my heart started beating faster. It was an envelope.

Sealed orders.

There was a knock at the door, and I placed the envelope in my coat pocket. I nodded at Lundström, who went to open it. A boy with a pale bony face, perhaps a year or two younger than me, entered the room.

'Pappa . . .' He hesitated, as if unsure whether or not to interrupt.

'Yes? Well, spit it out, boy!'

'There is someone here to see you.'

He stood to one side, and another man walked into the room.

*

He was tall, fair-haired and wore a blue civilian suit and greatcoat, both of which looked like they had been made in Savile Row. He had a fleshy, sallow face and pale green eyes, which coolly took in the scene: two men hunched over a corpse. I felt myself shrink into my skin.

'Who are you?' said Lundström bluntly. 'Jan, please leave us.'

Lundström's son bowed briefly, and shut the door behind him. The wind whistling through a crack in one of the window frames suddenly sounded like a howling hurricane.

The man hadn't shown any sign of having heard Lundström's question. His eyes continued to scan the room, absorbing and processing all the available information, until finally he turned to Lundström, a fixed smile on his face, and extended a leather-gloved hand.

'Jasper Smythe, Second Secretary at the British Legation in Stockholm. Who does the seaplane belong to?'

I stepped forward.

'Me. Lieutenant-Colonel Paul Dark, from the Allied Control Commission in Helsinki. Would you mind if I see your papers? I wasn't told of anyone from Stockholm being sent here.'

He looked at me with undisguised surprise.

'Helsinki? I wasn't aware——'

'Please show me your papers,' I said firmly, 'and tell me who sent you here, and for what purpose.'

I moved my hand fractionally to my underarm. He registered the movement, and by a small inclination of his head showed he was not going to upset the precarious situation, and asked if he could remove his identification from his coat. I nodded in return, moving my hand to the barrel of my gun.

I shot him as soon as I saw the glint. The bullet hit him full in the chest, and a cloud of red mist rose from his coat, then dissolved, leaving his lapel splattered with blood. A moment later, his legs crumpled and he fell, landing on his knees. His eyes stared out, frozen in astonishment, and then he toppled forward, his head thudding dully against the floor.

The stench of cordite rose in my nostrils as I stared down at him, the sound of the shot still ringing in the air. My stomach was hollow, and my hands were shaking. With an effort I placed the Browning back in the holster. It had all gone terribly wrong, and I suddenly thought of how Templeton would react when I told him. He had said I must stop anyone who got in my way, but still I'd failed him.

I looked up at Lundström, whom I'd forgotten about, and saw fear in his eyes – he was worried he might be next. I quickly leaned down and pulled open Smythe's coat, doing my best to avoid the widening pool of blood and matter. His left hand was a mess of gristle and bone, but the forefinger was largely intact, and it was wrapped around the trigger of a Luger.

'He was going to shoot me,' I said, as calmly as I could. 'He was a Russian agent. You understand that, don't you?'

Lundström pursed his lips together and drew his breath sharply. I recognized the gesture as one Mother had sometimes used. It meant yes.

I moved to the door and opened it.

'Wait here,' I told Lundström. 'Don't touch a thing.'

*

I pulled the Browning back out of its holster and crept down the path leading to the jetty, my heart thudding fast. Lundström had said he was expecting a Presnakov — had there just been a change of personnel, or had the NKVD taken over because they knew about the Winterlost, and sent an agent disguised as a Brit? More importantly, had 'Smythe' come alone?

As I neared the jetty, I saw that there was a small motorboat tied up next to the seaplane. There was nobody in it, and I searched it quickly: it was empty. A bird circled above me, then swooped down and lit on one of the seaplane's pontoons, squawking some threat to the fish below. Then it lifted its wings and soared away, leaving just the sound of the waves lapping in the darkness.

I returned to the waiting hall, where Lundström was in the same position as I'd left him. He was in shock, but it passed as soon as I'd explained the situation to him: the Soviets would soon be wondering what had happened to 'Smythe', and would send someone else out to investigate. He immediately suggested that he arrange for Smythe's body to be buried along with von Trotha's in the nearby church. If the Russians sent someone else, he would deny all knowledge of having seen Smythe and they would have no choice but to take his word for it. They might suspect foul play, but there was always the possibility Smythe had suffered a mishap in the journey over here, and they wouldn't be able to prove otherwise or kick up any sort of a fight – after all, the dead man had supposedly been a Brit, not one of theirs. By the look on Lundström's face, he would enjoy stonewalling the Russians.

I agreed, and shook his hand, then returned to the sea-plane. Von Trotha's sealed orders revealed what Templeton had suspected: U-745 had been carrying a new form of mustard gas, Winterlost, which was stored in a special compartment in the vessel's main storeroom. In the last entry in his notebook, dated 5 February, von Trotha had given his coordinates. I plotted them on the chart and found they were very close to a tiny island called Söderviken, just south of the Finnish port of Hanko. Presuming that the U-boat had been hit somewhere nearby, it might be in shallow enough waters for me to reach.

I took the wireless set out of its suitcase and crouched on the jetty with it, shivering as the wind snapped the rod aerial back and forth. I sent the signal to Templeton to say I had the coordinates and that they were close by, but didn't get any response. I checked the connections and sent the message again, and this time the 'dah-dit' came back in my earphones: proceed as planned.

I climbed back into the seaplane, stowed the set and strapped myself in, trying to steel my mind to the job ahead. It was coming up to six o'clock as I took off again, and a faint light was creeping into the sky. The ice stretched out for a few miles east of the archipelago, then broke up into open water. I flew as low as possible, looking for landmarks on von Trotha's chart, but apart from the occasional islet or rock the seascape seemed almost featureless, and I started to worry I would get lost again. I considered taking one of the Benzedrine tablets to wake myself up, but decided that fatigue wasn't the problem – if anything, I needed to calm down.

I finally spotted a small lighthouse and hovered above it as I searched for it on the chart. Having found it, I arrived about an hour later at the point von Trotha had marked, and landed in a squall of rain just as dawn was breaking. I climbed into the cumbersome diving suit and sealed it with the clamp, then went through all the checks with the breathing apparatus and the oxygen cylinders, fighting down my mounting sense of claustrophobia – Clammy Death, indeed. For one shaky moment, I fancied I saw a shape in the distance moving towards me over the water, but then it vanished; it was just a trick of the light. I remembered the lines of poetry one of the other lads at Loch Cairnbawn had always muttered to himself at this point:

Our plesance here is all vain glory,
This fals world is but transitory,
The flesh is bruckle, the Feynd is slee:
Timor mortis conturbat me.

I shuddered, then dismissed it from my mind. I had enough oxygen for six hours, I had used this type of equipment before, the Soviets were no longer a threat and the objective was at hand. I checked everything again one last time, then adjusted the mouthpiece and nose-clip, opened the cockpit door, clambered down to the pontoons and slipped into the dark water.

*

My eyes were stinging from the lack of sleep but all my senses bristled as I drifted through the silent world, staring out through the small window of the facepiece. Shoals of ghostly white fish flapped around me, their eyes and the tips of their fins glowing eerily, and I longed to reposition the mouthpiece, as one edge of it was cutting into my gums. It took me over two hours to find the boat, by which time my legs were exhausted from kicking and my arms felt numb. It was not quite on the shoreline, but in the stretch of islets leading into it. I remembered Templeton's words: 'It should be relatively easy to get to.' Yes, it had been – if you weren't the one doing the diving.

The U-boat looked vast, and as though it had been there for years rather than a month. Seaweed had already begun to wrap itself around the conning tower, and several inches were already buried in drifted sand. I approached it very slowly: Templeton had told me it could carry fourteen torpedoes and up to twenty-six mines. It looked to have been split roughly into two parts, with most of the damage in the middle section.

I swam past the gun deck and then floated down towards where I thought the main storeroom should be. The whole section was scrunched from the damage, but there was a narrow gap in the main hatch and, with some difficulty, I managed to haul it open and swim through.

It wasn't the storeroom, but the crew's quarters. The men were already starting to bloat, but I could see that some of their hands and chests looked like they were rotting away, and realized with a fright that they were burns, and that the mustard gas canisters must have leaked. Templeton had told me I had to obtain the canisters by any means, but we hadn't discussed what would happen if my only way of doing so would involve coming into contact with their contents, which could be fatal. I cursed myself for being so intimidated by his briefing that I hadn't asked such a basic question, but it was too late for that now.

I turned away from the sight of the men, and as I did I saw the canisters. There looked to be twenty or thirty of them: large steel drums with ridges around the centre. I could see where the lids of a few had come away and a yellowish-brown liquid had started to seep out. The operation was a bust. There was no rescuing any of this for Templeton – it was too bloody dangerous. But perhaps I could secure the place so that the Soviets wouldn't be able to get hold of the stuff either? I looked around and saw that several lengths of steel piping had fallen away from the walls. I leaned down carefully and picked one up. Could I block off the hatch? I looked towards it, and my stomach seized at the sight.

The hatch was closed.

I quickly swam towards it, willing myself to breathe normally and keep calm. The currents must have swung it shut after I'd swam through, and it now seemed to be completely jammed. I shoved my shoulder against it, and it buckled slightly – but stayed put. On the third shove, when it still didn't open, I realized I was going to die. I was shut at the bottom of the Baltic with these corpses, and before too long would become one myself. All I could think was how unfair it was that my life should end here. I hadn't experienced anything yet – I'd never even been in love. I kicked my legs at the hatch in a final frantic gesture, and the hinge moved forward and caught a current, and I rushed through the tiny space before it sealed behind me again, slamming shut finally on the occupants of U-745.

I didn't have the canisters, but I was free. Free – and alive.

IV

October 1969, Moscow

I shivered at the memory of the cold water and the dead eyes of the crewmen. I had tried to banish thoughts of the operation for years, although it had occasionally featured in my nightmares. My brief time in Finland had given me my first glimpse of a world in which we were as ruthless as our enemies and were already betraying our allies. It was also a source of personal shame: I had failed to complete the operation, and had killed a man to boot, although I had justified the latter to myself as being a matter of my life or his. I now wondered if some repressed feelings of guilt about Smythe had eased the Soviets' recruitment of me a few months later. Possibly – but I would probably have succumbed to Anna's charms anyway.

I had worried how to break the news to Templeton, but in the event he hadn't seemed overly concerned. He'd listened patiently to my debriefing, then asked a few questions, mainly about the precise position of the hatch when I'd left it. He wanted to know, of course, if it was firmly shut so that nobody else would be able to get in. I assured him this was the case, and persuaded myself it was, too, although a nagging doubt came to me in my dreams in the following weeks that it had not fully closed behind me.

He told me that Smythe was certainly an NKVD man, as there was nobody of that name at the Legation in Stockholm, and told me to put it out of my mind. 'They may still be our allies technically,' he said, 'but make no mistake – to all intents and purposes, they are our enemies now. He threatened to compromise your mission, and would certainly have tried to shoot you had the positions been reversed. Indeed, it sounds as though he was about to. You did the right thing – I would have done the same.' I handed over von Trotha's orders, and was dismissed. He never mentioned the operation to me again.

I had stayed on in Helsinki for a few more weeks, but then the Soviets entered Berlin and everything started happening very fast. I travelled to Stockholm to see Mother, this time taking an aeroplane, but it was a wasted journey, as she had simply stared through me with a blank gaze, drool spilling grotesquely from her mouth. On returning to Helsinki, Templeton pulled me in to his office and told me I was wanted back in London. I took the next flight from the airport, landing in a bank of fog. I spent a couple of weeks kicking my heels in Baker Street and wondering what I was supposed to be doing, before I was handed a coded cable from agent 2080 – Father – in which he requested I join him immediately at a farmhouse ten miles outside Lübeck, in the British Zone of Germany.

That operation had eventually brought me here, to this depressing conference room beneath Moscow. The men seated around me had listened in chilly silence as I had described my actions in 1945, but it didn't take long for them to respond. Suslov was the first to speak, and he addressed himself to Yuri.

'Is this your promised breakthrough?' he said with undisguised contempt. 'I am unimpressed. Why should we believe anything this man says? Of course he will argue that this is an accident, in order to stop us from attacking the West. In this situation, his loyalties aren't with us. He's useless – worse than Philby.'

That was interesting: they had already asked Philby. It made sense he hadn't been much help, as it had been years since he'd been involved in this sort of discussion in London, and by most accounts he was now a drunken wreck of a man –not that I was a shining example. But it put my presence here in a new, rather more unpleasant light: it seemed that it had been Yuri's brainwave to summon me, and it wasn't proving a popular decision.

'You're right,' I said to Suslov, and he swivelled to look at me. 'It would take a lot for me to argue that you should launch a nuclear attack on the West, but it's got nothing to do with patriotism. Nobody can win that war.'

'If I may, General Secretary,' broke in Yuri, 'it seems that this man's testimony may provide some of the answers we seek. He has told us that as a member of British intelligence he was sent to Finland to capture German chemical weapons at the end of the war, so that they could be used against us after it. As it seems that those very same chemical weapons *are* now being used against us, can it be plausible that the West is not involved? Surely the most likely scenario is that the British have returned to this sunken submarine and retrieved the mustard gas.'

I took a breath to calm myself. Had my recounting of my operation in Åland in 1945 just made Britain a target for a nuclear strike?

'Nobody knew the location of the U-boat apart from me and my immediate superior,' I said. 'And he is dead.'

'But he will have filed a report,' said Yuri, his forefingers pressed against his chin. 'As a result of your defection to us, your old colleagues in London will have investigated every document connected to your career, I think. Presumably they found a report on this from 1945, and decided to act on it.'

I stared at him. Could that have happened? He was right that they would have searched through everything. Could they have dug up reports Templeton had written for SOE in 1945? It was possible – they would certainly have been looking through his files. But most of SOE's files had been destroyed after the war, and it was hard enough even to find a Service file from those days. I thought of the canisters again, and of the liquid slowly seeping from them.

'The Service doesn't operate like that,' I said. 'If they had retrieved the mustard gas, they wouldn't have attacked your nearest submarine base with it. Nobody in the West has any interest in provoking a nuclear conflict.'

Ivashutin, the GRU head, gave a laugh as dry as a lizard's cough. 'Come, what sort of fools do you take us for?'

I turned to face him. 'I'm quite serious. The possibility of a surprise attack has been discussed, naturally – it's raised every few years, usually by one of the more belligerent generals, and usually when you lot have done something that annoys us. Then the call goes up: "Why don't we just hit the Russians, hard and fast?" But wiser heads always prevail. The relevant experts at NATO have calculated that a first strike would not be enough to disable you completely, and would simply result in you striking back. Until we come to a point where one side's forces seriously outweigh the other, the logic of deterrence still holds. But even if you don't subscribe to that view, this is clearly an accident – just look at the distances.'

I pulled the map on the table nearer to me and turned it to face Ivashutin. 'The U-boat sank here. Here are Paldiski and Hiiumaa. They're less than fifty miles away. It's obvious that the gas has leaked from the submarine and the currents have carried it to the shores of these bases, just as they carried Captain von Trotha's body.'

Ivashutin smiled. 'Or perhaps that was what we were meant to think. After all, your former colleagues in London know that you are in Moscow and are likely to tell us all this. Our bases are heavily fortified: leaking chemical weapons into the water nearby is an ingenious way of breaching the security.'

'What if he is right, though?' said a new voice, and I scanned the table to locate it – Andropov, the KGB chief. 'What if the Americans are simply conducting an exercise with the B-52s, and the incidents in Paldiski and Hiiumaa are accidental?'

'All of them occurring at the same time?' said Brezhnev. 'That seems very unlikely.'

Andropov switched on an obsequious smile. 'Indeed, General Secretary. But it may still be the case. Are we sure we want to risk the consequences if Comrades Ivashutin and Proshin are wrong in their assessment? If the West is really about to launch a surprise attack on us, what is their motive?'

Yuri's jaw muscles showed through his cheeks as he struggled to stay calm. 'Perhaps they feel sure they will be able to survive and win a protracted nuclear conflict,' he said carefully.

Ivashutin nodded. 'Yes, or perhaps they have underestimated our capability to retaliate. Perhaps putting a man on the moon has made them think they are invincible.'

Nobody laughed, and I understood it wasn't supposed to be a joke. So the Americans must have finally pulled it off since my arrival here, the great journey finally realized. I remembered last year's INVALUABLE exercise in Whitehall with a chill. Its imagined scenario to trigger a nuclear conflict had been that hawks in the Kremlin had been emboldened by placing a man on the moon. Now that event had apparently taken place, but it was the Americans who had done it. Could it be that hawks in Washington, newly elevated by the glory of beating the Soviets to the moon, had got hold of Nixon and persuaded him that a surprise strike was achievable? It was unthinkable, surely.

But there were nuclear-armed B-52s heading towards the Soviet border.

'My department takes the view that the West wants us to follow precisely your logic, Yuri Vladimirovich,' Ivashutin was saying. 'We think that this is a surprise attack that is designed to destroy us through our own uncertainty over whether or not we should retaliate. If we live to survive this, perhaps we should consider such a strategy ourselves.'

'Be quiet,' said Brezhnev. 'All of you.'

The room hushed immediately. The GRU and KGB hated each other's guts. They were wholly separate agencies, with competing structures in Moscow and embassies around the world. Both operated within and outside the Soviet Union, but the KGB spent most of its time wading in the weeds of individual espionage operations while the GRU was generally concerned with the big picture, including the biggest of all, the threat of an attack on the Soviet Union. This was the GRU's case, but from the way Andropov was speaking he appeared to have Brezhnev's ear more than Ivashutin.

This was peculiar, because Ivashutin was an old pal of Brezhnev's, and had been handpicked by him to head the GRU after Serov had been dismissed in '61 following the discovery that Penkovsky was working for the Service and CIA. Perhaps there was still some residual stain on the GRU's reputation as a result. Until that point, it had been almost invisible to the outside world, but Penkovsky had given the West a mass of information, some of which, I had discovered on becoming Head of Soviet Section, had helped avert nuclear war during the Cuban crisis.

There was no love lost between Andropov and Ivashutin. As I knew from personal experience, the KGB had recently sabotaged a major GRU operation in Nigeria – and presumably Andropov had been behind that.

'Is this possible?' Brezhnev said, addressing Yuri. 'Could it be that the events at these bases are the result of a chemical leak?'

'It is possible, General Secretary,' he conceded, glaring at me. 'But as you yourself pointed out, considering the Americans' actions it would seem too great a coincidence—'

'It is *not* a coincidence,' I said. 'It's an accident, and one that was bound to happen sooner or later. The Baltic is strewn with volatile chemical weapons, as you well know, because many of them were dumped there by you.'

'Is this true?' said Brezhnev.

'That was Zhukov's doing, General Secretary,' piped up Grechko. 'He ordered the practice when he was in command of the administration in Germany after the Great Patriotic War. But that was not until '47 or '48, and if I recall correctly it was not done anywhere in this area, but near the islands of Gotland and Bornholm.'

'It sounds like the sort of thing Zhukov would think up,' Brezhnev said. 'It's as well he retired when he did.'

'Indeed,' said Grechko, seizing the opportunity to take another kick at one of his predecessors. 'But he was not alone in the mistake: the British, French and Americans also dumped chemical weapons in the Baltic. Occasionally, some come to the surface, but I think I'm right in saying that this has never happened anywhere near these particular bases.'

Yuri nodded. 'That is correct, esteemed comrade. This is confirmed in the latest report by the investigating scientists, who have never even encountered this type of mustard gas before. I have also never heard of any attempt by either the British or ourselves to obtain such a weapon.'

'Someone notified your people in Helsinki about the U-boat captain in 1945,' I said, 'and they sent an agent out there to get to him. There will be a report on it in your files.'

'We don't have time to dig around in archives,' said Brezhnev. 'We must make a decision now.' He pushed his chair back and walked to the wall behind him, staring at the false window as though it were a real one looking out on the skyline of Moscow. Habit, I supposed. 'Comrade Grechko,' he said finally, addressing himself to the wall. 'What course of action do you advise?'

Grechko didn't hesitate. 'As you know, General Secretary, we have just completed the "Zapad" war game. One of our conclusions was that the West would be foolish to engage in any sort of preliminary war and would in reality be much more likely to defeat us with a surprise nuclear attack. It seems that they have come to the same conclusion. If they are indeed preparing to launch against us, I believe our best strategy is to launch our own attack before they do.'

He used the word *kontrapodgotovka*, a counter-preparation strike that would disrupt the enemy's first strike. But, of course, that assumed that the Americans were indeed planning a first strike.

Brezhnev nodded.

'If the Americans launch their weapons, how much notice will we have?'

Grechko grimaced. 'We estimate that our radars would detect the missiles between fifteen and seventeen minutes of them hitting their target, General Secretary.'

'And how long will it take us to launch our missiles if I give the order to do so?'

'The 8K84s do not have their warheads attached, General Secretary, and once they have been armed they need to be warmed up for a few hours before they can be launched. But once they are primed and warmed up, the Strategic Rocket Forces can launch within seconds of receiving your signal.'

'Exactly how many hours does it take for the 8K84s to warm up once the warheads are attached?'

'Three hours, General Secretary.'

Brezhnev turned, and I saw that a pool of sweat had

formed on his forehead. He drew a handkerchief from his trouser pocket and mopped at it unthinkingly.

'Attach the warheads,' he said.

Grechko's face flushed.

'Right away, General Secretary.'

He picked up the telephone nearest him, spoke into it for a few seconds and then replaced it.

I stared at the men around me, dumbfounded by the mounting madness. From memory, 8K84 was the Soviet name for the SS-11 intercontinental ballistic missile. Grechko had used the phrase *predvaritel'naya komanda* on the telephone: that was the preliminary alert command, given to combat crews as a trigger to prepare nuclear weapons for the next order, the *neposredstvennaya komanda*, or direct command to launch.

Brezhnev returned to his seat at the head of the table, and clasped his hands together.

'I would like some more detailed information on the B-52s,' he said, his baritone now almost cracking. 'If they breach our no-go zone, I will give the order to launch a strike on our major targets in the West.'

I was also sweating now, and the room seemed to be closing in around me. In a few seconds, Brezhnev had placed the Soviet Union one step away from launching a nuclear attack. It sounded as if he were considering a tactical strike, rather than releasing the country's entire stockpile of missiles at once – what was referred to as 'R Hour' in Britain. But it made little difference. Even if he were to order a tactical strike, the West would retaliate at once and we would be facing full-scale nuclear war in a few hours' time, with Washington, London, Moscow and many other cities destroyed. Brezhnev didn't even need to order a strike at all for that to happen. If Washington got wind of the fact that part of the Soviets' nuclear arsenal had been moved to this position, they might themselves fear an imminent attack and choose to strike pre-emptively.

By believing the Americans were about to launch an attack, Brezhnev might have just pushed them into making one.

There must be some way to stop this.

'Call your consulate in Åland,' I said. 'I can't remember the precise coordinates, but the U-boat is south-east of an island called Söderviken. Get them to send one of their divers down, or if you don't have any find a local and pay them to do it. Once they've found the canisters, they can radio back the confirmation that they have leaked.'

Brezhnev tilted his head at Yuri. 'I think we have had quite enough of this man now. Is there anything else we wish to know from him?'

'Thank you for your patience, General Secretary,' said Yuri, and just the sound of his voice was now making me nauseous. 'I believe he may know the West's likely targets and the order in which they are likely to be attacked, but this may not be a fitting place to extract the information from him.'

'Give him to me,' said Andropov. 'My men will be able to break him in less than an hour.'

My stay in Steklyashka had been far from pleasant, but the KGB's headquarters, the Lubyanka, was notorious – it was known as Moscow's tallest building, on account of the floors of cellars it was rumoured to have.

'Thank you for the offer of assistance, Yuri Vladimirovich,' said Yuri coolly. 'But I think we have a way to apply pressure in this case.'

'I think KGB and GRU should work together on this,' said Brezhnev. 'Yuri Vladimirovich, please have the prisoner taken into custody by your men. Fedor Fedorovich, I would like you to accompany him in order to exert your pressure, and to report back here with the results within the hour.'

Fedor Fedorovich, or Yuri as I still thought of him, looked a little paler, but nodded. 'Of course, General Secretary.' Andropov flicked the switch on his chair, while Yuri started packing his papers into his attaché case.

'This won't help,' I said, unable to keep the desperation from my voice. 'You're making a terrible mistake.'

Brezhnev ignored me, and helped himself to a glass of water. The door opened and two guards marched in, wearing brown coats with blue collar tabs: KGB. They were both armed, so I didn't resist as they escorted me out of the room, led by Yuri.

'I've told the truth, you fools!' I screamed as the door closed. But there was no reply, and they led me down the passageway and back to the lift.

V

The ZiL was still parked on the street, and I was pushed towards it, the barrel of a submachine-gun pushed hard against my spine. Snow was falling gently, and as a gust of it caught me in the face, I shivered in my thin suit, the sweat already cooling and sticking to my skin.

Sasha stepped out of the car and walked towards us. Yuri began speaking to him, but his voice was carried away by the wind and I didn't catch it: presumably he was explaining Brezhnev's Solomon-like decree that they were to cooperate with the KGB in torturing me. I wondered if any of them apart from Yuri had any inkling of what was being decided in the bunker, or that they would be left outside it to die with the rest of the population when the missiles hit. Perhaps Sasha did, which was why he had hesitated when Yuri had motioned for him to leave earlier.

As Yuri and Sasha talked, one of the KGB men spat on the ground. I followed the trajectory of the saliva through the air and it was in that moment, as I watched the globule freezing into ice, that I remembered the footage I had seen in a dark room in London one evening a decade or so earlier, of the hydrogen bomb tests we had conducted at Christmas Island in the Pacific. A flash of light had filled the entire screen, shocking even when experienced second-hand, and when it had eventually faded the image of a cloud had formed, growing and slowly expanding in new layers until it had finally plumed and billowed into the mushroom configuration, an almost obscenely beautiful formation hanging over the landscape it had just destroyed.

I closed my eyes to try to rid myself of the image, and a flake of snow came to rest on my eyelids, soft and wet, and I suddenly understood something I never really had before. I opened my eyes again and took in the tableau anew. This place, this moment, was unique in the universe. It was an ugly place, certainly, made up of concrete and saliva and ugly men in uniforms, but it was *our* place. And it was mine. All of it, from the grime in my teeth, the smell of the car's engine, the crispness in the air, the patterns of the shadows on the ground, the precise interplay of every living thing in every passing moment, even these thoughts rattling through my head ... All of it was under threat. All of it could be just a few hours away from extinction – unless I acted.

And it wasn't just that if I didn't, nobody else would. This was something I *should* put right, as I was directly responsible: I hadn't destroyed the canisters, but had just left them in the U-boat. And, clearly, the hatch had not shut as firmly as I had thought it had.

But what the hell could I do?

Sasha turned and headed towards a Chaika parked across the road, while Yuri climbed into the front of the ZiL. The KGB men opened the rear door and I was again pushed into the back seat, next to Sarah.

Naturally, she was Yuri's 'pressure'. He had told Sasha to bring her along in case my appearance in front of the Supreme Command wasn't received well. Sarah might not know too much about the inner workings of the Service, but Yuri had, once again, played a long game, realizing that at some stage she might prove useful in extracting information from *me*. And so he had kept her alive for just that purpose.

I felt like retching, and as the car started up I shuddered at the thought of what lay in store for both of us at the end of the journey. No doubt they would attach electrodes to her or some such horror in an attempt to get me to reveal the locations of missile silos and command and control bunkers. But the problem was bigger than that: once we were inside the gates of the Lubyanka, I would never be able to warn anyone in the West about what was happening, and events would continue to spiral towards a nuclear conflict.

I looked at Yuri, who was staring straight ahead, his hands resting on the attaché case on his lap.

That case.

That case could be key. Presumably it contained all the papers that had been used for the meeting, and so would detail their concerns about the B-52s and the injuries at the Estonian bases; papers that would offer firm evidence that the Soviets mistakenly thought they were about to come under attack from the West and were preparing their own strike as a result. I realized I had to get out of this car before we reached the Lubyanka, and that case had to come with me. If I could get a message to the Service, the Americans might be able to defuse the situation by bringing the B-52s back to earth and explaining that they had nothing to do with the events in Estonia, and this madness could stop before it was too late.

All of which was easier said than done – I was in a moving car with armed men. In my first few weeks in Moscow I had thought of nothing but escape, and had drawn on old training patterns, obsessively keeping track of how many guards had been assigned to me, when they changed shifts and so on. I'd always been under cover of at

least on[...]
around the fe[...]
following every mov[...] n the daily walk I was allowed
of an opportunity present[...]of, but I had persisted in
eventually resigned myself to the [...]de, just in case a sliver
free again. But now there was no choic[...]ver had, and I had
out. [...] would never be
[...] find a way

But what about Sarah? I should, in normal ope[...] nal
circumstances, leave her behind. One man on the ru[...] ad
a small advantage against those seeking him – that of the
needle in a haystack. But if we did manage to escape from
this car, the two of us together would be a much easier
target to describe, and hunt. But these weren't normal circumstances, and even if they were, I wasn't going to leave
her to be taken back to a cell. If there were a nuclear attack
it would make little odds, but if I managed to stop an attack
from happening I couldn't bear the thought of her being in
the Lubyanka. No, she had to come with me.

I scanned the interior of the car, searching for an idea.
Armed men sat either side of us, the doors either side of
them were locked and beyond the doors stretched Moscow
and the vast expanse of the Soviet Union. A feeling of hope-
lessness rose up in me. I took a breath and smothered it.
Now wasn't the time to give in; now was the time to
sharpen all my senses.

Yuri motioned to the driver to take a shortcut and the

...pse of a sentry box

car took a right turn ... we were crossing a bridge.
through the curtain ...remlin. The Lubyanka was very
We must be appro...

close now. ...at Sarah. She was staring out of her
I glance...ently deep in thought. She looked tired, but
window...in reasonable shape. I wasn't exactly on top form,
other...
bu... had made sure to maintain a version of my regimen
in my cell, partly to keep my strength up but primarily to
occupy my mind. It had mostly consisted of press-ups and
running on the spot and, naturally, had been on a much
lighter scale than usual: the soup they'd been feeding me
hadn't provided enough protein for anything more. But
the result was that my body had become harder and leaner,
and I was confident I could at least make a decent go of it.

But could she? Every couple of years, all Service officers
had to take refresher training courses, usually at Fort
Monckton, near Gosport, so she should know the basics.
The courses admittedly tended to be a waste of time: as it
was impossible to prepare for every eventuality in the field,
most of the focus was on general preparedness, teaching
how to remain vigilant and watch for lapses in the opposition's vigilance, and so on. But now we were in a situation
similar to one that I'd been taught at Monckton – I hoped
she'd been taught it, too. The objective had been to jump
from a moving car while under close guard. To execute the

manoeuvre, which was known as 'Duck and Dive', you needed at least one accomplice and could not be guarded by more than two people. We had two in the back and two in the front, but beggars can't be choosers.

With Duck and Dive, everything is in the timing. When the car slows, the first accomplice distracts one of the opposition. This has to be a distraction that won't get them shot, obviously, and it has to be believable. The simplest is a loud groan and a slump, imitating a fainting fit. While the first man reacts, the second agent attacks the other guard, shoves open the door and leaps out of the car. To make matters harder, I would have to grab the attaché case from Yuri as well, and hope that in the ensuing confusion Sarah and I would both be able to get out without getting shot. But anything was preferable to what they had in store for us at the Lubyanka. The moment to trigger it would be when the car was slowing but had not yet passed any checkpoints or sentries: after that we'd be trapped inside the walls of the Kremlin.

But how could I communicate all this to Sarah? The last time I'd seen her, she'd lost her hearing. I could check whether or not it had returned by making a noise and seeing if she reacted, but any diversion now would alert the men either side of us and make it harder to execute another one. She was staring down at her hands now. I looked at her, willing her to sense my gaze and look back at me. The car jolted, and in that moment she turned and our eyes met. 'Duck and dive,' I mouthed, then turned away.

She had nodded. She'd had the same thought.

With the course of action determined, I should have felt happy. But now I knew we would be risking our necks in a matter of moments, doubts returned. Well, there was no choice about it. Long ago, a cheerful Cockney instructor had told me that you never knew when you might have to call on your training, but when you did, you simply had to buckle down and get on with it.

Having fed myself this rather facile exhortation and swallowed it as best I could, I took a deep breath. The car had turned into Dzerzhinsky Square, and the imposing mustard-yellow block of the Lubyanka loomed in the headlights. At first glance it could have been mistaken for a French château, but for the barred windows on the lower floors. The tallest building in Moscow . . .

The car slowed on the turn and I braced myself. Not yet, not yet . . . *now*. I nodded at Sarah and smiled at her as I did, one last time perhaps, something to remember. She let out a groan and slumped into her seat. The guard next to her turned to see what had happened, as did my man, and I jerked my elbow up, catching him squarely on the jaw and sending him flying into the door.

Yuri turned to see what had happened and cursed, and

I leapt forward, grabbing at the lapel of his jacket and pulling him closer. His hand flew up and I saw the case slipping from his lap. I yanked harder at his jacket, the top of my head bumping against the roof as I propelled myself between the gap in the two front seats and sprawled awkwardly between Yuri and the driver. In the driver's mirror I saw Sarah punching her man unceremoniously in his groin.

As his scream filled the small space, the car suddenly swerved, the driver no doubt jarred by the noise, and I took advantage of it and lunged back over to Yuri's side, my hand grabbing hold of the handle of the attaché case, which I swung up and into his face. The corner caught him under the neck and he screamed, and I wriggled the rest of my legs through the gap in the seats and slammed my free hand against Yuri's door until it gave way and fell open. Yuri tried to grab hold of my arm, but I punched down blindly and as he fell backwards onto the seat, I managed to scramble over him and shove the door wider, then hurled myself towards the opening, tumbling through it and out onto the street, keeping my head down and my arms wrapped tightly into my chest.

The impact shook my whole body as I hit the tarmac, but training took over and I went into a roll, resisting the temptation to touch the ground with my free hand, gripping the case as tightly as I could with the other, and then

I was up and running, the sound of shouting behind me becoming subsumed by the noise of blaring horns in the traffic, letting the momentum carry my legs in their natural rhythm, my heart pounding so hard I thought my ribcage might burst, searching for cover.

VI

I surged on, keeping my body as low as possible, a rush of
wind biting at my ears and cheeks. I desperately wanted to
look back to check on Sarah, but I was still numb from the
jolt of the landing and to turn now would lose vital
moments. I was conscious of sunlight breaking through
low clouds, and I squinted against the glare at the morning
traffic swarming around the square. A Moskvitch beeped its
horn angrily as it sped past, and then I reached the enormous statue of Dzerzhinsky and could see the other side of
the pavement, just a few yards away. It was packed with
pedestrians, many of them gathered outside a building
with enormous arched windows on the corner, and my
first thought was that some sort of protest was going on.
But then something deep in my consciousness stirred, and
I recognized the building from photographs. It was Detsky

Mir, 'Children's World', Moscow's largest toy shop. It had been just after seven o'clock when I'd entered the bunker, and the larger shops in the city opened at eight, so either the place was about to open or it had already done so and people were queuing to enter. It didn't matter much which — it was a crowd, and that could only be good, so I headed for it.

I took momentary refuge behind a banner festooned with red ribbons and an enormous portrait of Lenin. Now, finally, I could see Sarah: she was in fact ahead of me, and making her way towards the same building. She was limping on one leg and wasn't going to beat any records, but she'd done it. Somehow, she'd done it. I took a breath and then leapt the last stretch to the pavement, my chest burning with the effort, and hurtled into the tail-end of the throng, pressing through a bank of woollen coats and getting swept along with the movement, looking to get closer to Sarah and fervently praying that the shop would be open and provide us with more options than the open air.

An elderly *bábushka* turned as I tried to squeeze past her, raising her arms in protest. I glared back with my most officious look, but she yelled something and grabbed hold of my sleeve. Others turned to see what the fuss was about, and as they did a gap appeared in the forest of bodies and I caught a glimpse of the KGB men emerging from the ZiL and running towards us, their guns raised. The Chaika wouldn't be far behind, and my mind flew to the moment when they would drag us to the building on the other side of the square. I yanked my arm away from the *bábushka* in desperation and pushed forward, moving deeper into the crowd and calling out 'Make way!' in Russian, holding the case above my head, until I had reached the entrance. The doors were open, and I forced my way through them.

Beneath a curved glass roof, hundreds of shoppers teemed through the vast central hall. Gaudy, cheap-looking toys lined the walls, vying for attention, while a loudspeaker in the ceiling told parents and children to meet near the entrance if they became separated. A queue of people made three loops around the hall and disappeared up a grand-looking stairwell leading to balcony floors above.

'Sarah!' I shouted out. 'Where are you?'

She had vanished. I headed for the foot of the stairs, and a young woman in the queue saw my frozen look and misinterpreted it. 'Don't worry,' she said. 'It moves quite fast.' But I'd already jostled past her, forcing people out of the way by making more official-sounding noises, not gaining any friends but climbing higher, higher, my feet flying, a few steps further away from the entrance below and hopefully out of sight.

As I neared the halfway point, I suddenly felt dizzy, and my vision filled with spots of dancing light. I steadied myself against the banister for a moment and looked down: in the blur below I saw several men in *ushankas* coming through the entrance, some wearing brown coats – KGB – and some grey ones – GRU. One of the latter suddenly caught sight of me, and our eyes locked. It was Yuri. He turned and shouted an order, his finger raised to point me out.

I shoved myself away from the banister just as the shot glanced off the latticed railings beneath it, sending a plume of metal fragments into the hall below. Everyone started screaming, and I began fighting against a tide of panicked shoppers, most of whom were now trying to flee upstairs. My head was still ringing from the sound of the shot as I pushed through the crush of flailing limbs and echoing cries, and scrambled up the remaining steps to the next floor.

That was when I saw Sarah, just a few feet ahead, her pace starting to flag a little. I ran towards her and she turned and stared at me, her face a mixture of elation and sheer terror.

She grabbed hold of my free hand, and I looked around in panic at the gallery stretching around the hall. It wouldn't be more than ten or twenty seconds before Yuri's men reached this floor. We needed to find a rear entrance, and fast. I looked around frantically but could see nothing, so I just picked one of the walkways and started running pell-mell down it, hoping to find another staircase as we went along. After about twenty yards it started to get crowded again, because the shot hadn't been heard this far in.

As Sarah and I plunged back into the crush of people crowding the counters, a deafening rattle suddenly filled my ears. I ducked instinctively, but then the noise faded and I looked up to see a scruffy-haired boy hurtling past us wielding a plastic machine gun over his head and screaming at the top of his lungs. He ran straight into his mother, who grabbed him by the arm and demanded he place the toy back on the shelves. After some protest, he did and I watched, transfixed for a moment, before something jogged my brain. I raced over to the display and scanned the selection. It wasn't Hamleys – most of the items were crude East German plastic models. There was a black pistol that looked to have been modelled on the Tokarev TT, but I rejected it. The biggest box on the shelf showed a Vostok capsule deep in space, the blue seas of Earth far below it as it blasted into glory for the Motherland.

There was a rising commotion at the other end of the room and I guessed Yuri's men had now reached this floor and had started combing through it. I put the case down, then removed the Vostok from the shelf and ripped open the cardboard box. Sarah watched in confusion as I stamped the mould under my feet until it had broken into dozens of pieces. I leaned down and picked up a thin shard of crude plastic, and she nodded in mute understanding. I picked the case up again and we raced back into the crowd, looking around desperately for a till. I found it a few seconds later, in a section devoted to babies' clothes: a young salesgirl was clacking away at an abacus behind a large wooden desk.

I ran over to her, shouting at the top of my lungs: '*Empty the till! Now!*'

The girl looked up, her face frozen in horror, and shoppers started screaming and vacating the area. Through the crowd I glimpsed some of the GRU and KGB men by the staircase, and they were heading straight towards us. I jumped forward and grabbed the girl around the throat with one arm in a choke hold, then pressed the point of the shard against her collar-bone. She started whimpering and her arms flailed out, releasing the catch on the register.

Sarah leaned down and scooped out a handful of notes and coins, and I released my hold. The cashier placed her head in her hands, sobbing hysterically, but we were already on the move again, past singing mechanical birds and doll's houses and miniature tanks and parents shielding their children from the sight of the man and the woman fleeing from the secret police. At the other end of the gallery there was another stairwell, but as we made our way towards it I saw a man in a grey uniform emerging from the floor below. Panicking, I looked for another way out. There must be a service exit of some sort. Sarah had begun making her way along the wall, and I followed her, pressing one shoulder against the surface as we passed marble columns and ornate lamps. But there were no exits or stairwells, and the GRU man was rapidly gaining ground. I could hear his breathing behind us and feel movement in the air . . .

Door.

It was recessed into the wall, an oak monstrosity with brass Art Deco curlicues. I grabbed at the handle, but my hand was soaked with sweat and slipped clean. I transferred the attaché case to my other hand and tried again, desperate, but fared no better. I hefted my shoulder against it instead, and suddenly it flew open, revealing a small, spartan office containing a desk piled high with papers, a samovar, and a threadbare oriental rug. I called out to Sarah and she came running back to join me. There was another door diagonally opposite and we raced across to it, but I must have made a lot of noise shouting out because a woman suddenly came through it – thick spectacles, hair in a bun, brown serge suit – and I knocked into her elbow, righted myself and kept running, ignoring her as she shouted after us.

We were in a long corridor with bare concrete walls. There was a steel door at the end and I grabbed the handle, panicking that it would be locked. But it opened, and I was greeted with a blast of wind whipping into my face. Peering into it, I saw a metal fire escape leading to a tiny rectangular courtyard below. It looked deserted. I turned and started lowering myself down the ladder as fast as I could, one hand clutching the rungs and the other gripping the case. Slivers of wet snow from the platform above dropped onto my neck, but I ignored them and focused on navigating the ladder. When I reached the final rung, I leapt the last couple of yards to the ground, then caught my breath and looked around the courtyard as I waited for Sarah.

It was very quiet – almost peaceful. A couple of pigeons waddled around the space importantly, their eyes glossily taking in the intruder. The rear of Detsky Mir took up the whole of this side of the courtyard, with a few more fire escapes dangling down, and directly opposite was a similar-looking building, the paint peeling from the walls. To the left an alleyway cut between the two buildings, and I glimpsed a section of main road at the end of it with traffic streaming by.

Sarah landed and dusted herself off, and I pointed to the alley. She nodded and we headed towards it, but as we came through the arched entrance blue and red lights flashed ahead of us and I realized we would be spotted if we came straight out on the street. Sarah made to turn back, but my eye was caught by a shadow in the curved wall of the passage, a little darker than the rest of it.

'Wait,' I said. I ran over to take a closer look. Yes, there was a gap in the wall. A small flight of stone stairs led down to what looked like another passageway leading off horizontally from this one: it was much narrower, but dim light was visible at the far end. With any luck, it should bring us out somewhere that wasn't crawling with armed men. I beckoned to Sarah to come over and we headed down the stairs.

It was very dark, and as we reached the last step I realized the surface was softer beneath my feet, and that the passageway ahead was filled with several inches of stagnant water. No mind. I stepped down and began wading through it carefully, letting my eyes adjust and holding up the attaché case to make sure it didn't get wet. A few feet in, I saw a sheet of corrugated iron blocking the path. Cursing inwardly, I leaned down and grabbed a corner to pull it away, but it was too difficult to dislodge with one hand so I turned and motioned to Sarah to help me.

That was when I heard the noise. We both froze. It was a clanging sound – the fire escape in the courtyard? Perhaps the man I'd glimpsed coming up the staircase was on our tail.

We stood still, straining our ears. The clanging stopped, but was immediately replaced by the sound of rapid footsteps – boots, reverberating on stone. Was it just one pair or more? And would they head straight out of the courtyard into the adjoining alley, or would they search the courtyard first? I had the sudden fear that we might have left telltale footprints in the ground at the bottom of the ladder.

I lifted my feet very carefully – the dripping now seemed to echo thunderously around the small space – and moved to the wall to the left of me, flattening my back against the brickwork so I was in the deepest shadow available. Sarah saw what I'd done and moved to the same position by the opposite wall. The footsteps approached – it sounded like they had entered the alley. Would they run on, or stop to investigate?

They stopped.

I slowed my breathing, exhaling very gently through my nostrils, and turned the lapels of my jacket inward to hide the whiteness of my shirt.

The boots began to descend the stairs, but when they reached the final step there was silence. Could they see us? I tensed my muscles, and closed my eyes.

Legs splashed through the water. How many of them were there? I fixed on the breathing. It was one man. Alone. He could be no more than a couple of yards away from us now, and he was coming closer every second. I caught a sudden whiff of diesel-like cologne – yes, it was Vladimir, the little bastard who'd treated me like a dog in my cell this morning.

There's nothing in here. Turn around and leave.

He didn't take my extrasensory hint. I listened to him, his breathing shallow but drawing closer, and the air tightened behind my ears. I stood as still and as silent as I could, my fingers clamped around the handle of the briefcase, praying to God to stop this man from seeing us, please Lord, I'll do anything you ask, just make him turn around . . .

I jumped an inch as there was a very loud thud on the wall behind me, the sound of it vibrating in my eardrums. Peering into the darkness, I thought I saw the outline of a raised arm, and guessed that he had slapped his hand against the wall. Had it been just a gesture of frustration, or did he suspect something and was trying to bring us out? Had he heard my sharp intake of breath? I strained to catch a response.

He sniffed the air, and I wondered if he could smell my body odour, as Yuri had done and as I had smelled his cologne. Sarah and I would also both be emitting the smell of fear, the pheromone dogs can scent. The moments stretched out, as though on some sort of loop. Beads of sweat formed across my forehead, and my left hand started to cramp from gripping the case. I longed to move just a fraction, but knew I couldn't. I could try to kill him, of course, but it would have to be silent in case some of his colleagues were still in the vicinity. I tensed my other hand and the muscles in my forearm, ready.

A shadow suddenly moved and I saw to my horror that his hand was moving towards Sarah. He was reaching further and further in and there wasn't much more space — soon she would hit the corrugated sheet.

She let out a cry and I leapt on top of him, bringing my right hand down onto his neck with all the strength and speed I could muster. He staggered towards me but managed a half-turn and grabbed me by the neck with one very strong arm. Sputtering, my throat on fire, my eyes bulging, I watched him raise his other hand, a pistol clutched in it, and swung the attaché case at him. There was a flicker of light as the gun spun away and fell into the water with a clunking splash. While he was caught off balance, I leaned forward and smashed my knee up into his groin. He doubled over and started to cry out, but I couldn't risk any more noise so I jumped across and stamped my shoe on his head, pressing it down until the top of his scalp had disappeared into the water. The surface bubbled as he struggled to come up, but I kept my foot there, pushing his face to the bottom, and then the air was throbbing in my ears and his body went slack and I removed my foot and he slipped away, sinking into the water.

My muscles had also slackened, and I suddenly felt

drained, but my heart was pulsing frantically. Flashes of light swam on my retina and I stood there, swaying a little and panting, my face slicked with sweat and the blood beating in my brain, conscious but detached, and for a moment I was suspended both from the world and from myself, swept up in a kind of oblivion, in the same state I had been on waking that morning of not knowing where I was, or even *who* I was.

I staggered back in the water, and as I steadied my breathing and the sweat cooled on my skin I tried to clear the mist in my mind, but the rage was still pulsing through my veins and as I looked down at the body one thought overrode all the others: *Not such an old man, am I? No, not such an old man . . .*

'Is he dead?'

I looked up to see Sarah watching me from the other wall, the whites of her eyes glowing in the surrounding darkness.

I nodded dumbly, staring back at her.

'You can talk,' I said, finally, my voice strangely muffled. 'When did you get your hearing back?'

She stepped forward. 'A few months ago.'

'Are you all right?' I said. 'I heard you cry out when he approached you.'

'I'm fine. He just gave me a fright, that's all.' She turned to the corrugated sheet and started trying to prise it away.

'Let's get out of here and find the embassy. I need to get home. My whole family must think I'm dead.'

I didn't answer for a moment, and she sensed the hesitation and stopped what she was doing.

'What's wrong?' she said.

I stepped away from the wall. 'Let's see if we can find this bastard's gun first, and I'll explain the rest on the way. We need to get moving.'

*

We spent several minutes searching for Vladimir's pistol, but with no luck: it had been lost somewhere in the water, perhaps finding a drain. We managed to move the iron sheet fairly easily, though, and waded through the rest of the passageway. After a couple of hundred yards, it widened and then emerged into another courtyard, which in turn led to a main street. A quick reconnaissance revealed no uniforms or sirens in the immediate area. I took Sarah by the arm and told her to keep her eyes fixed ahead as we walked through the throng of pedestrians hurrying past on their own paths to survival.

We were walking, not running, because we needed to be inconspicuous. The *militsiya* would probably have our descriptions by now, as might the *druzhinniki*, the force of citizen volunteers. A man walked towards us and for a moment I thought he had some sort of transmitters attached to his face, but it seemed they were miniature hot water bottles fitted to his ears and nose, presumably to ward off the cold. We passed an emaciated woman in a frayed black coat as she hustled along a group of children in bright red quilted jackets. Red was everywhere, here and there enlivened by splashes of gold in hammers and sickles, but the red stood out more against the largely monochrome landscape. The snow had stopped falling, but it was still freezing, and the bottom halves of our legs were soaked.

Sarah was shivering and coughed occasionally. My throat ached and the tips of my fingers throbbed in the wind, but the bigger problem was internal. My insides were in freefall — unsurprisingly so, as I'd just killed a man. I didn't see it as murder, though. Brezhnev had ordered ballistic missiles primed, and we were on the brink of a Third World War. Vladimir had been a GRU agent and his orders had been to capture us, and that would have led to our torture and, no doubt, death. That was justification enough, but in this case it hadn't simply been a case of him or the two of us; it had been him or, potentially, everyone.

Nevertheless, the adrenalin was still thrashing around my veins like a cat in a bag. After months in captivity I had escaped my cage, killed one of my pursuers and was now being hunted by the full strength of the Soviet apparatus.

JEREMY DUNS

And I had brought Sarah with me again. Was this really preferable to leaving her behind, I wondered?

I turned to look at her, shivering in her tunic. 'How's your Russian?' I asked.

A group of young boys selling coat hangers approached, and she waited until they had passed before answering. 'Craddock marked me as fluent a couple of years ago.'

Craddock was a Cambridge don who had taught Service officers Russian since the war, and was notoriously hard to please.

'Good. We'll talk Russian together from now on. Let's get off the streets and find somewhere to warm up.'

We reached a turning and took it, then several more, until we were on a street called Neglinnaya. Along the opposite side of it from us was a row of buildings, most of them shops. But one was smaller than the rest, a squat brick-and-glass building, and people were milling around the entrance. On the awning above it said 'Victory'.

We headed towards it.

VII

The café was only marginally warmer than it had been outside: the mist of customers' breath mingled with cigarette smoke and steam from bowls of *shchi*. A transistor radio in the window blared out a folk song from Radio Moscow, the balalaikas keening like a troop of drunken bagpipers.

We walked through the tables looking for a free one. The furniture was in the same style as the architecture: a hideous hand-me-down modernism that, at a guess, was an attempt to look Scandinavian. They couldn't even get that right.

There were three tables with good views of the door, and after considering all three I indicated to Sarah that we should take the smallest of them. It was the furthest from any other occupied tables, and it was positioned in a small alcove of its own, meaning it was not in direct light and we could talk more easily.

We installed ourselves in the metal chairs, and looked around. There was a queue at the counter, but just as I was about to get back up again and join it a waitress passed by and I managed to attract her attention with an ingratiating smile. I ordered a couple of coffees and *sigarety* to secure our presence for a while, and as she sidled away I turned to Sarah. She was running her fingers through her crop of hair, her large blue eyes surveying the room, and for a moment she looked as she had done the first evening I'd met her: poised, elegant and without a care in the world. But then I saw that her jaw muscles were making tiny fluttering movements beneath her cheeks, and realized she was trying to stop her teeth chattering.

'It's good to see you again,' I said quietly, keeping my tone neutral for the benefit of anyone watching us. 'I'm sorry things turned out this way. I should never have let you come with me to the embassy in Rome.'

She looked across at me and gave a wan smile. 'You couldn't have stopped me.'

I looked into her eyes and saw fatigue and fear in them, but also pride. Well, she had outrun me at the start, surprising me. Then again, she was a good ten years younger than me, so perhaps she was the better field agent and I was teaching her to suck eggs. She had certainly proven herself in Italy. But I was getting ahead of myself. I'd known her barely a week, and most of that had been while we'd been confined together by her husband and his neo-fascist chums.

'So your hearing came back,' I said, 'just like that?'

She averted her gaze. 'Not quite. They gave me some treatment.'

'Yuri?'

She nodded fractionally, and my exhilaration that she had recovered was replaced by a surge of fury. I reached out to touch her hand, then thought better of it. The last thing she needed was people touching her. I didn't want to know what they had done to her, exactly, and I certainly wasn't going to ask her to recount it and live through it again here. But they would pay for it. Yuri would pay.

The waitress returned and placed two mugs of black coffee, a packet of twenty cigarettes and a box of matches on the table. I paid her with some of the coins I'd stolen, and she wandered off again.

I picked up the matchbox, which showed a picture of the Urals and proclaimed 'The best holiday is a motor tour'. I lit a cigarette for Sarah and then one for me, and inhaled it deeply into my lungs, luxuriating in the rich glow. After a few puffs, I took a sip of the coffee. It tasted pretty foul, but it was hot and strong, and this cheered me a little, because I knew that within half an hour the caffeine would be making its way through my bloodstream along with the nicotine, and would boost my energy and alertness. I had a feeling I was going to need it.

Yuri would have ordered his men to comb through the neighbourhoods surrounding Detsky Mir looking for us. He would be utterly furious that we had managed to get away. Had he told the Supreme Command yet, I wondered? Perhaps not, in the hope he could find us before anyone became too concerned. But every minute we were free was a problem for him, because eventually he would *have* to tell them, and Brezhnev would hit the roof.

At any rate, we were now the target of a manhunt, and it would only become more concerted as time went on and more resources were allocated to it. Once they found Vladimir, some of the men would be even hungrier to find us, because there was nothing like personal motive to get the blood pumping, as Vladimir had discovered to his cost. But perhaps there was a silver lining. If we managed to survive long enough, they might have to draw men from the nuclear strike preparations . . . No, that was probably too hopeful. The opposite might happen instead: Yuri and the others would realize I was planning to try to stop a strike from going ahead, and Brezhnev might start thinking about ordering it now to retain the chance of taking the West by surprise. By fleeing, I may have hastened the very event I was trying to stop.

'We're not going to the embassy,' said Sarah, 'are we? Or home.'

I put my mug down and looked up at her. 'I'm afraid not. We've got a crisis on our hands. Brezhnev and his generals believe the West is on the verge of launching a nuclear attack, and they're preparing to get their retaliation in first.'

She stared at me for a moment, then took a long drag of her cigarette as she considered it.

'And *is* the West about to launch a nuclear attack?' she said.

'I don't think so. But I can't be sure.'

I quickly told her about the meeting in the bunker, the B-52s, the mustard gas 'attack' and the U-boat. She took it all in, listening intently, her jaw tight but her expression giving nothing away.

'What about the hotline?' she asked when I'd finished.

'They haven't used it, and won't. They think it would warn the Americans they're on to them, and lose them a strategic advantage.'

'So how long do we have?'

'I don't know that, either,' I admitted. 'But it might not be long enough.'

'I see.' She stubbed out the remains of her cigarette in the ashtray and straightened her back in her chair. 'So what are we going to do? Do I take it that the case between your feet contains Yuri's documents from the meeting, and that you hope they offer firm enough evidence about what's going on to stop this?'

She was a pretty cool customer, I reckoned. I could see how she'd survived the last six months.

'Yes. But it depends on precisely what's in the case. Do you think you can hold the fort for a few minutes while I find a lavatory to look through it?'

'Yes,' she said. 'But please leave me the cigarettes.'

I nodded, giving her as encouraging a smile as I could muster, and then stood up and looked around for the toilets.

*

I found a room at the back of the establishment, and after waiting for it to be vacated, jumped in and locked myself in it. It was a tiny space, with a lavatory almost pressed against the basin and a grimy window looking out onto the street, protected by a thin grey cotton curtain.

I seated myself on the lavatory and looked at the case: to my horror, I saw there was a combination on it. I pressed the clasps down, hoping that Yuri had not thought to lock it for a ride to the Lubyanka, but it was fastened shut.

Shit.

I sat there for a moment, wondering how the hell I was going to break a six-digit combination, when I looked at the numbers again. The left-hand numbers read 446, and the right-hand ones read 683. But the 3 was not completely in the frame, the tip of the 2 below it just visible. Could it be that that frame was a little looser than the others, and that in all the movement since I'd grabbed the case in the car, that number had simply shifted? I looked at the numbers again, and saw a pattern: 44 66 8 . . . 8? I clicked the 3 several notches around until the 8 was in the window, then pressed the clasps again.

The case clicked open.

Thank Christ. Resting inside, snug as a bug, were several sheaves of documents, most of them stapled together. I took the lot out and started sifting through them. The first was a threat assessment, prepared by the GRU, on the supposed attacks on the bases in Estonia and the B-52 flights. It looked to have been written by Yuri, and reiterated a lot of information I'd heard in the meeting. There were maps of the affected bases and a report on the incidents there.

The index case was a 22-year-old lieutenant who had come back from one of the observation posts on the shoreline of the Paldiski base, having picked up an 'amber lump' that had washed ashore. Within a few hours he and some of his colleagues had experienced violent and repeated vomiting, and he and one other had lost their sight. A detailed chemical analysis concluded that the chemical involved was

an unknown form of mustard gas that was much more viscous and powerful than had been seen previously.

The bloody fools. It fitted Winterlost precisely: these
were classic mustard gas symptoms, and it had been con-
tracted by touch to boot. It *had* to be a leak from the U-boat.
I turned to the conclusion of the threat assessment:

There can be little doubt that the West has
launched a chemical attack on our bases in
Paldiski and Hiiumaa. The purpose seems to be
to put them out of action in advance of a surprise nuclear strike. As we have repeatedly
advised — see the attached document, which we
regard as still current — this is in keeping
with our estimate of strategy among some of
the hardline generals in the West. Our assessment at this time is that we must consider
launching a nuclear strike, perhaps within the
next twelve hours.

Within that timeframe, we will endeavour to
bring to the Defence Council a clearer intelligence picture of the West's actions. Time is
against us, but we have agents in place in the
West who may have access to information about
nuclear intentions and planning. Agents HOLA
and ERIC have provided us with a very clear

picture of the British development of nuclear
research since the Great Patriotic War. We
have issued secured instructions through our
residency in London to initiate immediate contact with both.

Our colleagues in HVA also have an agent,
MICHELLE, who is providing them with material
from the British Director for Operations of
NATO's General Secretariat. We also have several agents with experience of nuclear strategy
in the West close at hand in Moscow, notably
SONNY and INDEPENDENT, and it may be worth
questioning them both for further insight into
the strategies and actions we now face.

The document was undated, but must have been written
within the last few hours. My codename was INDEPEND-
ENT, and SONNY was Philby. But who the hell were HOLA,
ERIC and MICHELLE? Cairncross and Nunn May had both
confessed, so none could be them. It seemed the GRU had at
least two more doubles who remained unexposed in Britain
and had been in operation since the war. The HVA was East
German military intelligence, and if they had direct access to
NATO's British Director for Operations, the Soviets should
know pretty much everything Britain and NATO were planning in this field and be able to act accordingly.

But they didn't know everything. They hadn't seemed to know about Corsham, for instance, and they had brought me in to ask me very specific questions they didn't have the answers to. Some of this was doubtless down to the time factor. It could take an entire day to set up a meet with an agent – more if they couldn't get away from the office for a convincing reason. So even if ERIC, HOLA or MICHELLE knew about an impending attack, they might not be able to send any information about it in time. And while Brezhnev and his generals were waiting to hear from these agents, the pressure would be increasing. On top of which, even if reports came in from all three agents that they were *not* aware of any plan to attack, that wouldn't mean Brezhnev would discount the possibility altogether – very few people were informed of such things. Indeed, if you did know about an impending nuclear attack, you would probably be at a PYTHON site by now.

In all, this read more like a political statement, perhaps to position the GRU in Brezhnev's eyes as a better source of information than the KGB. And they certainly seemed like very impressive sources, but in this case, probably not highly placed enough to help.

The next file was the strategy document Yuri had referred to. It had been written by Ivashutin, the GRU head, and was dated 28 August 1964. It was five years old, but still seemed to represent their current thinking. I flicked through it, and my eyes lit on a paragraph towards the end:

> The imperialist states are engaged in prep-
> arations for a war that is not at all
> defensive. The substance of their military
> doctrine is a surprise nuclear attack and
> offensive war against the socialist countries.

My jaw clenched. I had *told* them this wasn't the case. In the winter of '63, Sasha and I had met at the cemetery in Southgate and I'd sat on a cold bench for hours while he'd questioned me about Britain's stance towards nuclear war. I'd been in Prague when the Cuban crisis had happened, and had been unable to leave the British embassy compound, so I'd spent most of the fortnight in the basement with Templeton and the rest of the staff, monitoring the radio and the cable traffic. But once the crisis was over, Moscow had wanted to know what the thinking was in Whitehall in the aftermath. I explained that from everything I'd heard, the Cuban crisis had scared the living shit out of everyone, even more than Berlin had back in '48, when Brooman-White had told me we were heading for atomic war. I had told Sasha in very clear terms that the last thing anyone in Whitehall or Washington wanted was to start a nuclear war. There might be a couple of cigar-chewing American generals who occasionally brought up the idea of a surprise attack, but there was no chance of such a thing ever happening and it was certainly not the West's military doctrine – far from it, in fact.

So either Sasha had failed to pass this information on to Moscow, or he had and it had been discounted. This was very worrying, because if this was the principle they were working from it meant they were much more likely to launch a strike. They had discovered what they thought were preparations for a surprise nuclear attack, confirming their mistaken view that the West was intent on making such a move. Brezhnev had already responded by priming missiles. He hadn't yet put them in the air, but if this was the way they viewed the West's intentions, how long would it be before he did? Glancing through the document, it seemed Ivashutin was ignoring the fact that retaliating before missiles landed in the Soviet Union wasn't going to stop them landing. Or was he? I turned back and started reading from the top. As I did, I realized that the Soviets had a completely different conception of nuclear war than had ever been imagined in the West:

Strategic operations of nuclear forces will be characterized by unprecedented spatial expanse. They will instantaneously cover all continents of the earth, all main islands, straits, canals,

i.e. the entire territory of the countries-
participants of the aggressive coalition.
However, the main events in all probability
will take place in the Northern hemisphere —
in Europe, North America and Asia. In this
hemisphere, essentially all the countries,
including the neutral countries, will suffer
destructive consequences of massive nuclear
strikes to some extent ...

After that cheerful preamble, Ivashutin veered into bizarre territory. While he admitted it would be impossible to defeat the West in a conventional war because of their greater military might on the ground, he then argued that nuclear weapons, far from being a deterrent, in fact provided the Soviet Union with the opportunity to reverse this situation:

With the nuclear weapons currently available
in the world, one can turn up the earth itself,
move mountains and splash the oceans out of
their shores. Therefore, the tasks that can
be set for the strategic operations of nuclear
forces in response to an aggression are realistic, even though they may seem to be based on
fantasy.

The most aggressive forces of imperialism

engaged in preparing a thermonuclear war against the socialist countries count on their ability to effectively paralyse socialist countries with an unexpected first strike, destroy their nuclear forces and thus achieve a victory while having saved their countries from a devastating retaliatory nuclear strike. However, there are very few people left — even among the most rabid imperialist military — who would believe in the feasibility of such plans. In the age of an unprecedented development of electronics, it is impossible to achieve a genuine surprise strike. The very first signs of the beginning of a nuclear attack by the imperialist aggressor will be discovered, which would give sufficient grounds for launching a retaliatory strike ...

It made no sense. On the one hand, Ivashutin claimed the West had a military doctrine of a surprise attack. On the other, he thought such an attack would always be detected early enough, and that very few in the West now believed it even possible. Either way, the situation he outlined was very close to the one they now faced, which I supposed was why they had included it in the papers for the Defence Council.

> Let us suppose that the United States is actu-
> ally capable of destroying the Soviet Union
> several times over. Does this mean any kind of
> military superiority? No, it does not,
> because the USSR possesses such strategic
> capabilities that ensure a complete destruc-
> tion of the United States in the second
> strike. It does not matter how many times over
> the United States will be destroyed. One does
> not kill a dead person twice or three times.

He seemed to be arguing that a nuclear attack would destroy the West, but have little impact on the Soviet Union. That was familiar enough propaganda – the kind that could be read on a regular basis in *Pravda* – but this was a top secret document by the head of military intelligence about their strategy for nuclear war. If they couldn't even be honest with themselves in such a document, there was a serious problem. Was it that they couldn't admit the reality of the situation to each other for political reasons – or were they completely blinded to it? Worryingly, it seemed like the latter was a real possibility. Discussing the West's military bases, Ivashutin concluded that the major ones were in the US, Britain and West Germany, and most could be destroyed by medium-range missiles and bombers in a first launch.

But it was a section titled 'Ground Forces' Operations' that stopped me in my tracks. It discussed ground troops overtaking enemy territory and 'cleaning up the consequences' of nuclear strikes.

```
Nuclear weapons will incur damage on troops by
shock wave, light emission and radioactive
emission. These are very dangerous factors,
and it is very difficult to protect oneself
against them. Still, we can soften the impact
of nuclear explosions. Tanks, trenches, dug-
outs, shelters, natural hills — all give good
protective cover from the shock wave; they
will substantially reduce the damage. One has
to protect the eyes as well as face and open
parts of the body from light emission. Each
soldier should have dark eyeglasses, or a mask
with dark glasses, and gloves. A closed car,
tank, gas mask or an overcoat will help pro-
tect from the penetrating radiation ...
```

'Zones of contamination' would be passed through by helicopters and 'protected vehicles' such as tanks, while 'clearing teams' would put out fires with explosions and cover radioactive ground with new soil. Roads would be cleaned with the help of 'street-sweeping vehicles operated from a distance'.

It seemed the Soviets believed that they could carry out an extensive ground war following a nuclear one. This was delusional. They wouldn't be able to send troops through the West after nuclear missiles had been launched, whatever precautions they took – there was no protection at all from that kind of contamination and I knew it, having read the Strath Report and several like it. As well as watching the footage, I'd also read the reports from Grapple X, our hydrogen bomb test on Christmas Island. At the flashpoint, the servicemen kneeling twenty miles from 'Ground Zero' facing in the other direction had been able to see the bones in their hands through their masks. The resulting fireball had been over a mile across, and the blast had scorched much of the island's earth. In a nuclear war, most of Europe would be a 'zone of contamination'.

I closed the folder and took a breath. I walked over to the tiny window and pulled the curtain back a fraction, but it didn't seem to look out onto anything, and the window was glued shut.

I had also pulled back the curtain on the world, I felt. The last few months had shown me more vividly than I could ever have imagined what a sham my life had been – now I saw that the whole of the Cold War was a hollow little sham. The document was amateurish, childish propaganda – and so misguided it was terrifying. The head of

Soviet military intelligence thought they could send troops across Western Europe following a series of nuclear strikes, wearing dark glasses and with their coats wrapped tightly to avoid the contamination, the way ahead cleared by street-sweepers. Either he was lying to his superiors or, more likely, he was completely deluded. They could have recruited an army of double agents and they still wouldn't have a clue. Service, Five and JIC reports might get things wrong, but they were never worded in terms of outright propaganda. It was obvious that the Russians simply didn't have the mindset to understand the West. And that made the risk of war greater.

The fact that there could be no victors in nuclear conflict was the deterrent on which the whole fragile situation rested. But it seemed that some in the Soviet Supreme Command thought they could win such a war. If Ivashutin convinced Brezhnev of his view, he would be much more likely to order a strike.

Whitehall's INVALUABLE exercise had, in fact, been completely worthless. The scenario we had gone through had envisioned a gradual build-up of tensions, whereby a hawkish faction in Moscow had taken control of the Politburo and had begun flexing their muscles. But this was a much more frightening prospect: a war resulting from misunderstanding, acted on too rapidly.

Yuri had estimated the Soviets might have to consider

launching a strike within twelve hours. But how many hours ago had he estimated that? In the meeting, he'd said that the B-52s would enter Soviet airspace at around noon if they continued on their current path. But would they continue on that path, or would they break off and circle again, as they had done earlier? How close would they have to get to Soviet airspace before Brezhnev acted? An hour away, perhaps two? Or would he hold off a little longer than that?

I stuffed the papers back into the case, locked it, and flushed the toilet. I walked over to the mirror and examined myself quickly. I didn't look too bad, considering. My suit was ragged and half-sodden, there were dark circles under my eyes and I was as pale as a monk, but none of these things were all that out of place in this part of the world.

I filled the basin with lukewarm water and splashed my face thoroughly, thinking through the take from the case. The documents proved what was happening — but they had to reach the right hands. I needed to find a way to show this material to the Service at once, because they could get into direct signals with London through their protected line, and from there someone could contact the Americans and get them to bring down their planes before it was too late.

But neither Sarah nor I could go anywhere near the embassy, because the moment we entered the gates we would be on British territory, and they would find a way to take us back to London and no doubt lock us both up. The embassy was also guarded, as all embassies were here, by Soviet sentries. I picked up the case and unlocked the door.

We couldn't go there — but they could come to us.

*

'Enough evidence?' asked Sarah once I'd sat down.

I nodded. 'More than enough. But I can't go to the embassy because they won't trust me, so I want to bring them here. I think we'll have more leverage.'

'I can call them,' she said. 'It might be better coming from me.'

'Yes, but I think I'll be able to get through quicker — nothing like the name of a traitor to prick up the ears. Do you mind?'

She didn't exactly smile, but her cheeks dimpled fractionally. 'Staying in the warm while you risk being picked up on the streets? I think I can manage.'

'Watch for any new arrivals, and get out fast if you see anything suspicious. If you're not here when I get back, I'll meet you at the main entrance to Detsky Mir in an hour from now.' I thought it unlikely that Yuri would think to send men back there. 'Agreed?'

She nodded. 'Agreed.'

any of Yuri's men. Yet. How long would it be before the message went out to every *militsiya* patrol in the city? All calls to and from the British embassy would be monitored as a matter of course, but the Station staff knew that and so rarely said anything of great interest on the internal lines. Under normal circumstances, the transcripts of the embassy's calls probably went to the KGB only once a week, if that, unless something notable was said. But if Yuri had thought on his feet, and if the bureaucratic wheels had turned fast enough, he would have given the order to report all calls to and from the British embassy at once. He could already have given that order, in fact, as they might be listening out for when the Service scrambled its staff to the cellars and senior officers said goodbye to their families.

And so I'd told them to call back from an outside telephone. In Prague, we'd always had at least one car on standby for situations such as this, and several call-boxes within a five-minute drive that we felt were not listened to with the same level of scrutiny as those inside the embassy. The calculation was that all telephones in the Soviet Union were likely to be bugged, but that it was impossible for the authorities to monitor every single conversation in the hope of catching discussions between foreign agents.

I couldn't remember precisely what Moscow Station's telephone set-up was, and wished I'd asked Sarah before leaving the café. I hoped the call-boxes they used weren't too far away, because I couldn't wait here long: every moment that passed gave Yuri more time to think of his next move. One of those would probably be to step up surveillance on the British embassy and follow anyone who left it, so if they didn't take the usual precautions they might find themselves tailed by a KGB or GRU car, which would then radio back which call-box to listen in on, and then the whole thing would be . . .

'Have you finished? Kindly make way.'

I looked up to see an elderly woman in a plastic coat glaring at me. She had already taken her money out of her purse and was trying to push past me. I told her I was still using the telephone, and she gave me a dirty look.

'I don't have all day to wait for you to receive calls, young man,' she said, and made to step into the cubicle. I stepped in front of her, barring her from reaching it.

'Get out of the way!' she shouted, raising a cane in my direction.

I had to do something, and fast. She was going to attract a patrol.

'I'm waiting for a call,' I said. 'Please wait, it won't take—'

The receiver rang and I swivelled and snatched at it.

'Yes?'

'This is the British embassy.'

Thank God. It was a new voice – a little lower in register,

a little more authoritative. I nodded at the old woman, indicating that the call was the one I'd been expecting, and she stepped back, muttering curses before turning on her heel and stomping off down the street.

'Hello,' I said into the receiver. 'Thank you for calling back. Are you outside the embassy?'

'Yes.'

'Tailed?'

Hesitation, then a peevish: 'No.'

'Good. I need to meet with the Head of Station.'

He didn't say anything, but I could hear him breathing.

'I have information HMG needs to hear,' I said. 'It suggests Clasp.'

The breathing came to a sudden halt.

'Where?' said the voice, finally.

'Victory,' I said. 'It's a café on Neglinnaya. In half an hour's time. Tell him to come alone.'

I replaced the receiver.

*

I walked quickly back to the café, watching for tails again but also weighing up the response I'd received. I had taken a risk using the word 'Clasp'. It was the codeword to signify 'the beginning of a period of tension', usually meaning an impending nuclear strike. Or at least it *had* been the codeword – they might well have changed it now. It was risky, because I wanted the British to be aware that the Soviets were considering a strike so they could defuse the situation, not so they could panic and launch their own strike as a result.

But, I decided, that was rather unlikely. They would need a lot more than a phone call. During the Cuban crisis, when the Service had been running Penkovsky, Moscow Station had given him an emergency signal to use if the Soviets were about to launch a strike. He was to call a special number, breathe down the phone three times, hang up, and then do the same a minute later. The missile crisis passed, but a few weeks after it Cowell received just such a call. Protocol dictated he alert London at once, but he guessed that Penkovsky had been caught and had revealed the code under torture, so did not press the panic button.

This had comforted me in one way, but troubled me in another. The Service had done its best to avoid discussing Penkovsky's motives ever since, preferring to focus on the fact that he had helped avoid the Cuban crisis escalating to war. The possibility that the Soviets had genuinely wanted to provoke an attack from the West had been quickly discounted – it was suicidal. It seemed to me that what had most likely happened was that Penkovsky had told his interrogators that the code meant something much less dangerous. But *he* had known full well what it meant. In which case, he had decided that the world should end in nuclear war, and had tried to trigger it. If he had made the call a couple of weeks earlier, or made it to someone more jittery than Cowell, it might have happened.

I reached the Victory, but realized the moment I came through the door that something was wrong. The table where I'd left Sarah was vacant. She'd gone.

'Over here, darling!' said a lilting voice in Russian, and I turned towards it and saw her seated at a table on the other side of the room. I rushed over.

'What the hell's going on?' I said.

'Nothing. This table just came free and I realized it offered better protection from the windows.' I looked across and saw that she was right: it still had a view of the door, but we couldn't be seen from the street as easily. I slid into the seat next to her, my heart still thumping in my chest from the thought that she'd been captured.

I told her about the phone call, and asked her if anything had happened since I'd left. She gestured to a group of labourers who had come in and taken over a nearby table, and I looked them over. Their overalls were smeared with tar, their hands were deeply calloused and several had missing or rotten teeth. They were genuine. Apart from them, there were fifteen other people in the café: two were waitresses and the rest customers. There were probably a couple of people in the kitchen making the food, so that would make it seventeen. Of the remaining customers, five were grouped together and had the ragged jumpers, scarves and slightly febrile, furtive look of students. The remainder were either sitting alone or in pairs, including a couple of old men hunched over a chessboard. All had been here when I'd left, so were nothing to worry about. It was anyone new that we had to watch now: the Head of Station might think to send an advance party. They might want to try to use the occasion to kidnap us – especially me. The chance to capture a double didn't come along too often.

I looked around, searching for an alternative exit. I couldn't see one: no staircase or back door, and the window in the lavatory had been glued shut. There would probably be a way out to the street through the kitchen, but finding that in an emergency might prove difficult. I took a sip of coffee, my hand shaking a little as I lifted the mug. Had I just made a dreadful miscalculation in telling the Service where to find us? I wasn't sure if it would be much more preferable to being captured by Yuri's men.

A sound came from somewhere to the right, and I jerked my head towards it. It was laughter: one of the students had told a joke and it had gone down especially well. Several of the young men were throwing their heads back in hysterics, but on the other side of the table sat a slender girl smoking a cigarette, with just the hint of a smile on her lips. She was pretty: a brunette in a dark sweater and pleated woollen skirt. The young man who had told the joke kept glancing in her direction, but I could have told him he was wasting his time, because she didn't like him, she liked his friend with the beard. As if sensing my appraisal, the girl suddenly swept a coil of hair back with her fingers, turned her head and stared straight at me, exhaling smoke through her mouth. I turned away at once, and caught Sarah looking at me.

'Having fun?' she said, and I blushed.

The music that had been playing on the radio halted abruptly and a news bulletin began, discussing plans for the centenary of Lenin's birth the following year. I'd seen posters for it plastered along the street, proclaiming 'Lenin is more alive than the living'.

It was nine o'clock on the morning of Monday, 27 October, which made sense – my reckoning had been that it was the 25th, but I must have underestimated the time they'd held me under with drugs when I'd first arrived. It gave me a perverse pleasure that I'd been within two days of being right, despite them checking everything around me every evening to make sure I didn't make notches in the wall with my fingernails or any such thing. I'd counted in my head, and I'd kept it intact enough to count nearly six months to within two days.

I listened to the bulletin as I continued to survey the room, waiting for any mention of fugitive prisoners wanted for murder. None came, but I didn't think that would be the case with the next bulletin — if we were still alive by then. The programme wound up and another began, about a factory that was producing more than its quota purely because of its passionate devotion to Lenin.

'They didn't mention the attacks,' Sarah said. 'I suppose that's to be expected?'

I nodded. 'It's not like Cuba, when it was the Americans who accused them of mischief. This time it's they who have detected a threat, or think they have, and their reaction will be the utmost secrecy.'

'Presumably that means there won't be any warning, either. If they decide to strike, they'll just do it.'

'I'm afraid so. But let's not get grim.'

'What if he doesn't come?' she said. 'The Head of Station, I mean. What's our contingency, our "Plan B"?'

'He'll come,' I said, with more conviction than I felt. What if he decided it was a trap? I ran my hands across the surface of the table. Resting on top of it were salt and pepper pots, a dirty glass that looked like it still had a couple of inches of vodka left in it, presumably missed while clearing up the previous night, and a chipped ceramic ashtray. I picked up the latter and placed it on a free table nearby, because I knew the KGB installed microphones in such things. It was unlikely they'd done it here, because they were usually interested in restaurants frequented by foreigners, but I wasn't taking any chances. I tipped ash into my empty coffee cup instead.

'The Americans are out,' I said. 'They'd simply call the Service and ask for their take on it. The same goes for all the other Western embassies.'

'So it's this or bust? What about one of the Eastern embassies – China, for instance?'

'No, I think that's more likely to exacerbate the situation, don't you? The only thing I can think of is that we could try to get to the U-boat ourselves. If we could prove that the injuries at these bases are the result of a leak rather than an attack, it might be enough for them to draw back. If we got hold of the leaking canisters, we could get the Soviet embassy on the islands to signal Moscow that the mustard gas in them is of the same type that was found in the "attacks" on their bases fifty miles away.'

She looked unconvinced, as well she might. It wasn't just a matter of getting out of the country: we probably wouldn't even be able to get out of the city. We were being hunted by an army of dedicated professionals: I knew from reviewing the Penkovsky operation that Moscow was home to around 20,000 KGB agents.

'How would we reach the canisters? And what about the B-52s?'

'Not sure. But I think if we can show that at least one part of this is an accident, it will make them reconsider. I think it's the combination of the events in Estonia and the B-52 flights that has persuaded them they're about to be attacked. Take away the attacks on the bases and the B-52s aren't enough to wage a nuclear war over. The Americans may be playing silly buggers or trying to scare them, but by themselves the B-52s aren't conclusive.'

'That's not a contingency plan,' she said quietly. 'That's a prayer.'

I didn't reply. Behind the counter, one of the waitresses swore at a battered coffee-maker. My eyes flicked back and forth between the occupants of the room and the door, a dilapidated affair with paint sticking to the frame and a small bell that tinkled whenever anyone passed through it. It rang again now, and a girl emerged through the smoke and the steam. She was young, pretty and very Russian-looking, but that didn't mean much: you could find Russian-looking girls in England, and if you did you might decide to recruit one of them and post her here. But the girl immediately greeted the older woman behind the counter with a cheery wave and removed her quilted jacket, beneath which was a waitress's uniform.

It must now be at least twenty minutes since I'd made the call to the embassy. Twenty minutes more of Brezhnev and the others discussing warhead positions . . .

'Paul.'

I looked up at Sarah, and realized my knees were jerking under the table. I willed them to stop.

'Sorry.'

One of the waitresses, an older woman in a stained red smock with a kerchief wrapped around her head, waddled out from the kitchen with a tray of pastries and placed it in front of the chess-players, who set aside their game to tuck in. After months of eating nothing but thin soup and seeing nobody but my guards, there was something so normal about the scene that I suddenly wondered if I hadn't imagined the whole thing: the bunker, Brezhnev and all the rest. The normality was also depressing. This was daily life in Moscow, and it looked to be roughly akin to Britain during the Blitz. How could I have ever believed this was a society that could bring equality to all, to the extent that I'd chosen to betray my own country? Freedom, justice, peace for mankind . . . Why had I fallen for such a ludicrous fairy tale?

Anna, of course. She'd fed me with the romantic dash of Lermontov and Tolstoy and the rest of them — all perfect fodder for a twenty year old — before filling my head with Marx, presenting his nonsense in the same beguiling manner. I had a sudden memory of her leaning over my hospital bed, administering a poultice to the wound around my left kidney. I had winced as she'd pressed it, and she'd smiled down at me with those beautiful flashing eyes of hers.

'My poor boy,' she had said, her lips forming a pout of mocking, flirtatious concern.

I replayed the memory in my mind, as I had done many times before, narrowing it down to that one despicable gesture. Because my wound had been a real one, and it had been deliberately administered in order to have me hospitalized so that she could nurse me back to health and, while doing so, seduce me, after which she had been prepared to feign her own death — all of it part of Yuri's elaborate honeytrap operation to recruit me. And that moment, that gesture, showed a level of calculation and, I thought, pleasure in deceiving me that turned my insides out.

'*My poor boy.*' What a sick, twisted little bitch she had been. But what a sad, pathetic waste my life had been as a result of falling for her . . .

The bell above the door tinkled again, and I looked up to see a man in a long grey coat walk in, struggling with a large umbrella. I turned away, for one horrid moment thinking it might be Smale from London, but then my skin started prickling and I glanced back and the horror returned because, of course, it *was* him.

*

Christ, that was all we needed. I forced myself to keep my gaze on him. He'd managed to collapse the umbrella and was shaking excess rain from his coat as though trying to rid himself of fleas. He hadn't changed an iota since I'd last seen him, filling in forms for me to travel to Rome in that cramped corner office of his on the third floor of Century House.

He began making his way past tables towards the counter, and I almost expected someone to stop him, he looked so out of place. It was around freezing outside, but I knew from the amount of times the milk had curdled in my cell that it had been an Indian summer and nobody else in here was really dressed for winter – a few wore coats, but most were in jumpers and jackets. Smale, on the other hand, was wearing a fur-collared overcoat, scarf, gloves and an astrakhan *ushanka*, looking like an extra from *Doctor Zhivago*. Except that everything else about him said England: the bony little nose, the fish eyes, the pursed lips – even the way he was walking, his back a little hunched. He belonged in that building in London and nowhere else, and I was having trouble absorbing the information.

They had made *Smale* Head of Moscow Station.

He was now hovering near the counter like a constipated pheasant – he had seen us but was pretending he hadn't, and seemed to be deciding what to do next. After a few moments, he joined the queue and I ground my teeth as I watched him progress with it, his podgy pink face almost painfully conspicuous among the sallow complexions of the other customers. He reached the front of the line and ordered, and I held my breath, watching for a flicker of suspicion on the face of the waitress, but she didn't flinch, turning to the samovar without hesitating. She poured tea into a glass, and he took it, paid and then shuffled into the centre of the room with his tray, ostensibly looking for somewhere to sit. With studied carelessness, he stumbled into the back of the chair opposite mine, and asked loudly if it was free. His Russian was good: perhaps he'd gone for a top-up with Craddock.

I nodded. He thanked me and placed the tray on the table, then removed his coat and draped it over the back of the chair. I clenched my jaw at the sight of his beautifully starched white shirt, which looked like Jermyn Street, and which he had paired with a dark-green woollen tie. I suppose I should have been grateful it wasn't an Old Harrovian one and that he hadn't brought a bowler hat with him for good measure. He seated himself, crossing his legs. He had surprisingly small feet, which were squeezed into a pair of Lobb brogues. Most of the shoes worn by those around us didn't even have complete soles. I resolved to ignore all this, and just hope to God that anyone whose eyes rested on him would presume he was a Party official or one of the *nachalstvo* slumming it for breakfast. He'd managed to get past the waitress, at least. Oblivious to my concerns, he lifted the glass of tea by one of its filigreed handles and took a dainty sip of the hot liquid, staring sightlessly ahead.

He'd come and, it seemed, he'd come alone. It was possible he had people stationed outside, but nobody else had entered the place after him and I didn't think anyone who had come in earlier was a likely candidate. So I should have been pleased. But Smale presented greater problems than I'd anticipated, and it wasn't just his damn-fool get-up. He'd always disliked me, even when I'd been the Service's boy wonder. Now he would hate me, and with good reason. It wasn't just that I was a traitor to my country: it was personal.

They had sent him out here under diplomatic cover even though I was in Moscow and knew he was with the Service. It wasn't overly dangerous, as the Russians were perfectly capable of working out for themselves who the spooks were in the embassies, just as the Service knew who the Soviets had under diplomatic cover in London. But, if asked, I would nevertheless have been able to run my finger down the list of embassy staff and pick him out as a Service officer. That was why London had sent Fletcher-Peck out earlier: he'd not been around in Blake or Philby's time. He had also been bloody useless, which was perhaps why they had decided not to use that tactic again. This time Smale had drawn the short straw, and if I knew Smale that was going to rankle, because quite apart from the unpleasant sensation of knowing his cover could be blown at any moment by a double agent, it meant he was never going to be Chief: he had already been marked down as disposable, and therefore a second-tier officer at best.

In short, he was probably one of the last people in the world who would be prepared to give me a fair hearing. But I *had* to get him to listen to me, and act on what I had to say, and I had to do it very fast.

'Thank you for coming,' I said. 'I know it can't have been an easy—'

'Was he worth it, then?' he broke in. He was talking to Sarah. 'Quite a price to pay for a quick roll in the hay, isn't it? Or were you betraying us earlier, as well?'

Christ. It was worse than I'd feared. He clearly had no idea what had happened.

'I've never betrayed anyone,' Sarah said quietly, but Smale wasn't listening, having turned back to me.

'And it's a bit early for vodka, isn't it?' He waved at the glass on the table and wrinkled his nose. 'You all seem to drink yourselves to death. Pity you can't take the honourable way out and just use a gun.'

'That's not my—' I stopped myself. There was no time to get into arguments. I had to placate him. His opening comments indicated a level of contempt that I recognized as not just personal but institutional. It looked like the initial shock had worn off and I had become a totemic name in the Service, along with Philby and the rest.

'Did you come alone?' I asked him, and he looked at me as though I had accused him of stealing the bishop's silverware.

'Of course. That was your stipulation.' He wanted to nail down that he was the honourable professional and I the dirty Commie traitor. If it made him feel better, fine. Anything was fine, as long as I could get him to listen.

'Thank you,' I said. 'I appreciate it. I would like your help, Hugh. I really need you to get a message to London.'

Smale leaned forward, his lips parting to show a row of yellowing fangs.

'So you're the new hotline,' he hissed, 'is that it?' He sat back again, pinching his nose. 'I must say, it's very poor form bandying emergency phrases around – even for you. Did you really expect us to take that at face value? In case you've forgotten, you no longer work for us – in fact, never did. And now we'll have to alter all our security procedures. Perhaps that was the idea. Very tedious. We've only just changed all the dead drops as a result of your coming over. The boys weren't too pleased with me for ordering it, as it wasn't so long ago they had to do the same on account of Blake.'

He was talking at rather than to me. His eyes were locked in a supercilious gaze, and I suddenly realized what was happening. He thought this was a showdown. I'd seen something similar in the aftermath of Philby's defection in '63: almost everyone in the Service who had crossed paths with him had developed the notion that they had played a crucial role in the saga. Sometimes this took the form that they had 'just known something wasn't right about him all along'; but a few had been deluded enough to think that they'd presented some sort of threat to Philby.

Smale had either forgotten or was ignorant of the fact that I had simply asked to meet the Head of Station here, and that until he'd walked through the door I hadn't known that was him. He had persuaded himself I'd asked him here because of our scant history together in the same office. And so he was listening to me with one ear, trying to figure out what angle I was playing, while in his mind's eye he was already drafting the chapter of his memoirs in which he related the curious incident in which he met the notorious double agent Paul Dark and his accomplice Sarah Severn in a seedy Moscow café.

I had to try another tack quickly. I had to find a way to make him see he wasn't going to live to write *My Life in Shadows: Three Decades as an Arse-Licking Creep in British Intelligence* if he didn't respond to what I was telling him.

'Please listen,' I said, as quietly and gently as I could – manners maketh man. 'This is a genuine emergency, and it's not about me. Yes, I made the dreadful mistake of working for the Soviets, and I wish I could turn back time and put it right. But, unfortunately, I can't. I'm very sorry for it, but I know that no apology or confession I make can change anything. Some mistakes can't be undone. But Sarah has never worked for the Russians, and I no longer am – in fact, they're chasing both our hides right now.' I saw the open disbelief on his face, and pressed on. 'But none of that matters. I'm talking about the possibility of very imminent nuclear war, so please can you try to set aside your understandable animosity towards me for a couple of minutes and hear me out?'

His face was very still apart from his eyes, which flickered all over me. Contemplating, weighing. The hubbub around us seemed to be in another room as I focused on him, and he on me. Finally, he cocked his head a little to one side.

'It's unfortunate for rather a lot of people that you can't turn back the clock,' he said, and gave his tea a ceremonial stir. 'Because quite a few of them are dead. But I'm listening.'

I leaned down and picked up the attaché case. 'The documents in here will provide all the evidence you need,' I said. I briefly explained about the mustard gas in the U-boat, the 'attacks' on the bases, the B-52 flights, the Soviets' interpretation of these events and Brezhnev's order to prime the missiles. Then I took out Yuri's threat assessment and placed it on the table.

He read it in silence, then pushed it back towards me and took another sip of tea.

'Very interesting,' he said grandly. 'Thank you for showing it to me. But you must understand, old chap, that I can't simply take all of this on trust. This document could be forged. We will have to analyse it, verify it against other sources and so on.'

'There's no time for any of that,' I said. 'And there's no earthly reason for me to be forging Soviet military documents. You need to get a message to London now so we can stop this going any further. Is Osborne still in charge?'

He didn't answer.

'Whoever is Chief needs to get the PM to call Brezhnev and tell him there's been a serious misunderstanding and there's no attack being planned. And the PM also needs to get hold of Nixon, sharpish, and get those B-52s back on the ground.'

He pinched at the knee of one of his trouser legs, realigning the crease so it was perfectly vertical, then looked up, his face expressionless. 'But you do see that I can't just take your word for all this, even if you have brought along a briefcase filled with official-looking documents. I couldn't take anyone's word for it, but especially not yours. You must see that?'

'This is no time for—'

'Paul.'

'What?'

Sarah nodded towards the window. A car had pulled up outside the café: a yellow Volga with a blue stripe along the side and a siren on its roof. *Militsiya*. A man in a blue coat and a peaked cap was at the wheel, and another was in the passenger seat.

Had someone in the café reported our presence? The waitress? The old man by the door? They couldn't have *followed* either of us here – too much time had elapsed since Detsky Mir and my phone call if that had been the case. But had enough time elapsed for Yuri to have issued an alert to all available patrols with Sarah's and my descriptions? Despite its name the *militsiya* were simply the civilian police, subordinate to the Ministry of Internal Affairs. Could the wheels of Soviet bureaucracy be so well oiled that the GRU had reached every patrol car in the city since I'd killed Vladimir?

There was no way of knowing. I glanced at Smale.

'Did you keep radio silence about this meeting?'

'Of course,' he said sniffily. 'What do you take me for?'

It was my turn not to answer.

The car had parked, and the man on the passenger side had got out and begun walking towards the door of the café. Were they after us, or simply stopping for a bite to eat on their patrol?

I made a decision. I replaced Yuri's document in the case

155

and closed it, then picked a fork off the table and held it stiff behind my back.

I handed the case to Sarah. 'Take this and follow me,' I said. I pushed my chair back, then lowered my head and walked smartly towards the counter, because that was the opposite of what he would expect and then I could get a blow in, surprise him, and double-back. The man pushed his way through the doors and strode confidently in to the café. As he approached the counter, our eyes met for a moment. My fingers tightened around the shaft of the fork as I prepared for the flicker of interest that would mean I would strike, but he ignored me and strode past, his eyes on the menu pinned up on a board behind the counter.

He wasn't here for us. I looked back at Smale, who was leaning forward but hadn't moved from the table. He didn't believe me about the threat, that much was clear, and I didn't know what it would take to budge him, if anything. It might take hours, but another *militsiya* man could walk in here in five minutes, and the next one might be looking for us, or be armed with our descriptions. And even if Smale did listen, there was no way to be certain he would get the message to the Americans fast enough to avert disaster.

The moments were slipping away. I had no idea how others might act, or how quickly. But the only other option was to try to get to Åland, to try to get back to the

U-boat and prove that the leak originated from the canisters in it. That would mean finding a way past the roadblocks, and all the men hunting us ... but it also meant we would have less interference. The only interference we would face would be from those trying to kill us.

Sarah was looking at me, waiting to see what I was up to. All my instincts were telling me we would be wasting time staying here trying to convince Smale any further. Sometimes all we have is our instincts. I motioned to Sarah and pushed open the door, stepping into the street and walking briskly, not looking back. The rain was coming down hard, and I stepped around a puddle in front of the Volga.

'What are we doing?' said Sarah from just behind me.

'Plan B,' I said. 'Get in the back of the car and be prepared.'

The man behind the wheel looked up in surprise as we reached him. As Sarah opened the rear door, I opened the one on the passenger side, leapt into the seat and placed the fork to his groin.

'Drive,' I said.

VIII

He was youngish, perhaps in his early thirties, with dark hair, blue eyes and a strong jawline: a model *militsiya* man. And so he hesitated. Perhaps he thought I was bluffing. I pressed the prongs of the fork into the cloth of his trousers and leaned in to his ear.

'If you haven't started this car by the time I've counted to three,' I whispered, 'I'll slice your balls off and drive myself. One . . .'

His jaw was clenched in fury, but he switched on the ignition and depressed the clutch. The starter coughed for a moment, then sputtered out. Christ. Looking around the car, I saw it wasn't in good shape: there was no mat beneath my feet, just the bare steel floor. I glanced back at the café and saw his colleague turn and spot us, alerted by the noise.

He began running towards the entrance, his arms waving, shouting at us.

'Wave to him,' I hissed. 'And make it convincing.'

He glanced at me, then reluctantly lifted a hand from the wheel and half-saluted his colleague, who peered at us, not understanding. I smiled at him and gestured with my hand to indicate that we were just taking a quick spin around the block. He would figure out what we were doing pretty soon, but it might just slow him down for a minute or two – and that minute might make all the difference.

Something moved in the rear-view mirror, and I saw another man already running across the street, his hands stuffed in his pockets. He had fair hair and a moustache, and I realized with a shock that it was Dawes – so much for Smale's gentlemanly regard for my stipulations.

I leaned into the fork again, and sweat broke out on the driver's face. But that wasn't helping him focus, so I relented a little. He tried the ignition again and this time the starter caught and we were off. The car jumped and tilted as we caught a wheel on a pothole, before righting as we came into the lane, directly behind a taxi.

'Put your foot down!' I shouted at him. I was looking at Dawes in the rear-view mirror: he'd reached the other side of the road and jumped into a light grey Pobeda containing one of his colleagues, and they were now only twenty yards or so behind, with just four cars between us. We had to lose them, because I didn't have time to be taken to the embassy and convince everyone I was telling the truth.

The driver accelerated, squinting through the windscreen. One of the wipers was broken, so it wasn't much use against the rain; it just kept getting stuck and drawing back early like a bird with an injured wing. Apart from the taxi there were no cars in front of us and I thought he was dramatizing to give his colleague a chance to catch up. I could also see that despite the fact I was holding something very sharp to his crotch, he was itching to make a move on me: perhaps because of the holster at his hip, which contained a Makarov; perhaps because I was having to keep the prongs a little at bay in case I skewered him by mistake. So I leaned across him very fast and snatched the gun with my other hand, then rammed it against his temple, removing the fork from his groin at the same time. Something about the sensation of cold steel pressed into his skull got through, and his squint disappeared.

I handed the fork to Sarah in the back seat, and told her to keep it handy in case he got any ideas. In the meantime, he pulled out to overtake the taxi. As we passed it, I told him to take a right, but he reacted too late and had to slow to swerve into it, the back wheels skidding on the tarmac.

In the rear-view, I saw the Pobeda preparing to make the same turn. The *militsiya* man must have sensed my anger at his delayed reactions and feared I was going to pull the trigger, or perhaps I was pressing harder than I realized, because he accelerated again as the street widened. He swung a left, and then another right, bringing us onto a boulevard, Rozhdestvensky, its neo-classical buildings flashing by us, and I shouted at him to move into the Chaika Lane, the central one reserved for party officials, which was empty.

But the Pobeda had now made the corner as well and was gaining on us, so I told him to prepare to turn again, and this time he reacted faster, taking a side street on the right that, after a few bumpy yards, brought us out onto a small square. I glimpsed the entrance of an underground station and dozens of people queuing at a small market outside it, dead chickens hanging by their necks, and then the street narrowed again.

I told him to keep going, and to take as many turns as he could, while I kept an eye on the rear-view mirror for the Pobeda. I couldn't keep him in control like this for much longer, so I had to figure out a way to lose Dawes and friend first.

I turned back to the driver and asked him if he knew who we were. He didn't respond, but his eyes flicked over to me. 'I said do you know—'

'Yes! You're fugitives from justice.'

'Take the next left,' I told him, 'and keep your eyes on the road. Of course we're fugitives, but what else do you know about us?'

He took the turn well, and I grunted approval. The man could drive, and Dawes, or whoever he was in the car with, would have a job keeping up with us – for as long as I could keep this man under control.

'You are English,' he said. 'We were given instructions to look for you.'

There was a handset next to the radio, so presumably they were using a two- or three-way communications system.

'What were your instructions, exactly?'

'You are to be stopped by any means. Shoot on sight. Call back-up at once if needed.'

All of that was to be expected. The rain was intensifying, so I had to raise my voice against the sound of both it and the engine.

'Anything else?'

He registered a flicker of surprise. 'The whole Service has been put on the highest alert for civil disorder.'

An alert for impending unrest was another sign they were preparing for an attack. The Service's experts had predicted widespread riots and looting in Britain if it ever became clear a nuclear conflict was imminent.

'Was there any indication as to *why* we are fleeing justice?'

'That's not our concern. If State Security says you're fleeing from justice, you are.'

Give the order and the hounds will run.

'What measures are in place to stop us?'

'I can't speak for the other Services, but we had a full alert, with every available man scrambled and told to look for you intensively.'

'Roadblocks?'

'Yes, I believe—'

'Where?'

'I don't know. They are arranged by Central Control.'

A gust of wind smacked against my side of the car, and I tensed to stop myself from losing balance. The window on the passenger side would no longer close all the way, and a thin icy wind was whistling in through the gap. My hand was cramping from holding the pistol in such an awkward position, and I was getting worried that if there was another gust of wind or we went over another pothole I might accidentally pull the trigger. I locked my wrist and placed my other hand around my forearm to keep it in place, then stole another glance in the rear-view. The Pobeda was overtaking a red Moskvitch, coming into our lane, closing ground.

'The roadblocks,' I said to the driver. 'You must have favoured spots in the city.'

He nodded. 'We have sixteen points. Judging by the alert we were given, I expect most or even all of them will have been set up.'

I thought about this for a moment. That many meant there was no chance of our leaving the city without going through one. And there was no obvious way we could get through any of them, because they'd have several cars waiting and barricades blocking the way. I checked the rear-view again: the Pobeda was trying to make it past a small van, creeping ever closer.

'Keep making turns,' I said. 'Sarah, take hold of the gun, please.'

She leaned forward and I transferred the grip so that she was now holding the pistol in place at the driver's temple.

'Shoot him if he tries anything.' The man looked to be sneering, perhaps feeling he could overpower her. 'She was first in her class on the shooting range three years running,' I told him, 'so I wouldn't advise it.'

It was a reasonably good lie, because his sneer vanished. I leaned across and unhooked the latch of the glove compartment. Rummaging through, I saw two spare holsters and breast badges, a map and two small green booklets with gold stars pinned to the front. I took out the booklets and flicked one open. It was for his colleague. I quickly flicked open the other one, and the face of the man next to me stared up from the photograph. He was

Sergeant Grigor Ivanovich Bessmertny of District C-12, and this was patrol car identification 1464. I could have got his name and rank out of him easily enough, but not the rest of it.

'What's the call sign of Central Control?' I asked. 'Lie, and I'll tell my companion here to shoot you in the head and I'll take over the wheel myself.'

He inhaled sharply through his nose.

'Big Bear.'

'And when you call in, how do you identify yourself? Fourteen Sixty-Four?'

'One Four Six Four.'

I dropped the booklet onto my lap and grabbed the handset from the radio, then pressed the transmit button and spoke into it. 'Big Bear, this is One Four Six Four reporting a possible sighting of the English fugitives, subject of earlier alert.'

There was a moment's silence, and then a crackle of static burst from the receiver.

'One Four Six Four, this is Big Bear. What is your current location, and that of the fugitives?'

I lifted the receiver again, looking out at the street signs. 'We are on Rozhdestvensky Boulevard, at the corner of Milyutinskiy. They are in a pale grey Pobeda' – I glanced in the rear-view mirror and read off Dawes's licence plate – 'which we saw them get into at a café on

Neglinnaya a couple of minutes ago. Please send back-up.'

Another crackle, and then: 'Thank you, One Four Six Four. Keep up the pursuit, and I will direct all cars in the area to help you out.'

They signed off, and I placed the receiver back in its hold. A few moments later Big Bear came on repeating my information, and moments after that there was the sound of a siren somewhere behind us. Dawes must have heard it too, because the Pobeda peeled away from behind us and took the next side street. I told Bessmertny to take a left, and that was when I spotted the other car.

It had appeared behind the Moskvitch as if from nowhere, presumably having cut in from one of the side streets. Was it in pursuit, though? Its bodywork was black, and I guessed it was a GAZ-23 – the special model created just for the KGB. From the outside, it looked exactly like a 21, which was what we were in, but it had a V8 engine under its bonnet, which meant it could reach 160 horse-power, as opposed to our 65: it was the most powerful car in the Soviet Union.

As it approached us, a man leaned out of the passenger window and opened up with a machine-pistol. A shot hit a rear tyre and we started to skid, losing control fast. A moment later the car was overtaking us and made to turn in the road to block us off. The man in the passenger seat was still shooting, and this time he hit the front windscreen. I started to scream at Bessmertny to yank the wheel around but my right hand was throbbing and when I looked down at it I realized why: it was covered in blood, and a spike of glass was sticking out of the flesh between my thumb and forefinger.

The image of it sent pain shooting through me, and I clenched my eyes shut as the roar of gunfire and engines around me increased, but then I thought of Brezhnev in the bunker and forced them open again. Half the windscreen had shattered, and chips of glass were strewn across the dashboard and wheel, but Bessmertny still had his hands gripped on the latter, his jaw clenched tight and his eyes staring wildly ahead. The 23 had made its turn and I screamed at him to steer us off the road, but the distance was too short. The driver in the 23 saw what was happening and tried to reverse, but he wasn't fast enough and our wheels locked as we began to slide towards him, the tyres squealing as they scraped across the road.

There was a massive jolt as we caught the front end of the 23 but I kept consciousness and even began to move my hands to the back of my head, until I remembered the glass and took them away again. I was being spun around, but my mind was in danger of detaching from the situation. Then panic rose to the surface as a car came from the other direction and I lunged towards the wheel, another surge of pain swelling through my hand as I did. There was a blast of the horn and then *whoosh*, the car had gone, but the road was still where I'd last seen it, which meant I was alive. Somehow we had righted on the road, and Bessmertny was still hunkered over, his hands in position. I leaned over and grabbed at the wheel to help him right us some more, looking in the mirror as I did and expecting to see the maniac with the gun leaning out of the window, but I saw nothing – just traffic streaming by, Moscow, life. The 23 had gone, either driven off the road or forced into a turning.

I turned to check on Sarah in the back.

'I'm fine,' she said. 'But we need to deal with your hand.'

'Get us somewhere quiet,' I told her, 'away from the centre.'

She nodded, and while she instructed Bessmertny to take turnings, I examined the wound. It looked worse than it was, I thought – there was just the one large shard and although it had produced a lot of blood, it looked to be relatively clear. There was always the risk contamination would spread, but we couldn't go to a hospital.

Soon the traffic started to thin out and we passed rows of concrete blocks of flats, squat and uniform. Sarah ordered a few more random turns until we had reached a small clearing that appeared to be an abandoned picnic area. Car tyres and pieces of rusting metal lay half-buried in a patch of overgrown grass, beyond which was a row of small wooden cabins. The stench of urine and faeces rose as we approached: public toilets. I told Bessmertny to pull up by some tree stumps, and once we had come to a standstill I took the key from the ignition and climbed out.

*

The area looked to be completely deserted, and the nearest road at least a mile away. The rain had stopped, but the clouds were still very low. I ripped away the sleeve of my jacket and balled it up and placed it in my mouth. Then, without looking at it, I yanked the spike of glass from my hand, my screams muffled as the pain seared through me in waves.

Once I'd steadied myself a little, I walked back to the car and tapped on Sarah's window. I gestured for her to hand me the gun, then opened the driver's door.

'Get out,' I said to Bessmertny. He did so, and I told him to walk towards the wooden cabins, focusing on keeping the Makarov on him steady despite using my left hand. Every muscle in my body was tensed, because if I were in his shoes I would be looking to turn suddenly and snatch the gun. So I kept a good distance from him, watching every move he made, waiting for any sign that he was about to try something. When we had gone a few yards, I told him to stop and undress. He didn't respond.

'Do it now!' I shouted.

He started removing his jacket. 'I wouldn't advise throwing it at me or anything like that,' I said as he reached the final button. 'You don't have anywhere to run. Just place it on the ground, understand?'

He nodded, sullen now or perhaps frightened, and he folded the jacket over his arm, then crouched and placed it on the ground. I told him to strip off the rest and he did, until finally it was all laid out and he was standing in front of me, shivering in billowing white underpants and a vest.

I told him to open the door of the cabin nearest him. Shivering, he did it, and I glimpsed a wooden shelf with a plastic lid.

'In,' I said.

He hesitated, considering whether to rush me. I kept my eyes level on his and tightened my grip on the butt of the gun.

'I'll shoot if you're not in there within five seconds,' I told him. 'Four.'

He walked in, and I stepped forward and turned the latch, locking it. He started thumping his fists on the door, and I told him that if he carried on I'd unlock it and finish

171

the job. There was a thudding behind me and I turned to see Sarah running over from the car.

'What the hell are you doing?' she shouted as she reached me. 'You can't lock him in there! He'll freeze to death. It's not—'

'What?' I said, turning to her. 'Cricket? Would you rather I shot him, like you did Charles in Italy?'

I jerked my head back to avoid the slap and grabbed hold of her wrist, then twisted her round in a simple hold. She lashed out with her other arm and when that didn't work either, she tried to kick me in the groin, but my body was too far away, so she started thrashing about angrily, screaming at me to let her go. I dropped the hold, but made sure to keep the gun steady – not aimed at her, but present.

'You bastard,' she said, her eyes drilling into mine. 'You know what Charles did to me, and what he was planning to do to others. But you're worse than he was. You're no better than an animal.'

A thought flitted through my mind of a post-nuclear world: a few lost souls scurrying about in bunkers or foraging for food and water across contaminated ground until they finally succumbed to radiation poisoning.

'We're all animals,' I said, trying not to let my temper take over. 'We like to think we're civilized, but that's for peacetime. I'm sorry if this offends your sensibilities, but we are heading for nuclear war. If we take him with us, he'll try something. If we let him go, sooner or later he'll reach his colleagues.'

She flung her hands out in exasperation. 'And tell them what? We just ran a KGB car off the road! Half the radio transmissions in the city will be about us.'

'Yes, but we don't know precisely what they're saying. This man is a loose end. He'll get free, in time, or someone will find him. Just not immediately.'

'And how do you think they'll react when they find him? They'll probably double their efforts.'

'They'll have every man available after us already, and if any of them get the chance I promise you they'll shoot us on sight and won't hang about afterwards discussing the rights and wrongs of it. If we make it out the other side of this, we can go to the opera and pretend we're not animals again. But until then we've got to do whatever it takes to survive, even if it means abandoning fair play. Now get in the car, please. If you're not going to help me—'

'What?' she said, her nostrils flaring. 'You'll strip me to my knickers and lock me in with him?'

'No. I'll put you in the boot.'

She started to laugh, then caught my look. 'You would as well, wouldn't you?'

'Yes. We don't have *time* for this, Sarah. Now which is it to be?'

She didn't reply and the silence stretched out, but then there was the faint sound of a siren see-sawing in the distance. We both turned to it, cocking our heads to gauge whether it was getting any nearer. After a few seconds it faded away, but it seemed this had been enough to wake her up, because she turned to face me and gave the tiniest of nods.

'Good.' I took off my half-shredded jacket and walked across to Bessmertny's bundle of clothes. 'Because I need you to help me figure out what we're going to do next.'

Her eyes widened. 'You mean you don't know?'

I picked up Bessmertny's shirt and pulled it over the one I was already wearing. 'You heard what he said. They've got roadblocks set up across the city, and we won't be able to get past any of them as we are. They'll be checking their own cars just as thoroughly, and we don't have papers.'

I buttoned the jacket and reached for the trousers. Sarah watched me, her hands clamped under her armpits, and I picked up Bessmertny's coat and thrust it towards her. She hesitated for a moment, then took it and put it on. It was much too large for her, and with her boyish crop of hair it made her look like a Dickensian urchin.

I put on the trousers, boots and wristwatch, then drew the leather gloves over my hands, taking it slowly to avoid reopening the wound.

'What do you think?' I said.

'Convincing enough. But who are you going to say I am if we're stopped?'

'Climb in the back seat,' I said. 'I'll claim you're a suspect and I'm on the way to the station. But let's hope that doesn't happen. We need to find another form of transport fast if we're going to get out of Moscow.' I stopped myself from saying the next word on my lips – 'alive'.

We got in the car, me in the front and her in the back, and sat there, our brains churning, while we waited for the heater to take effect. I'd studied this country for most of my adult life, and knew the ranks and accompanying uniforms of all its forces, and the relationships between each force and the structure of the system as a whole. So I knew what to expect. This was the ultimate secret state, with armed police patrolling the streets to stop anyone who demon-strated the slightest sign of not following the regulations. Suspicion was the natural state of affairs here, and we would have to act accordingly.

But although I had a lot of facts and figures stored in my head, my knowledge of the Soviet way of life was woefully incomplete. Most of what I knew was second-hand, theo-retical – and that could be the difference between life and death. Apart from a brief stint in Prague and several months in a prison cell, I'd never been to the Soviet Union. To make matters worse, we had no support: no sleepers, safe houses or people with hidden compartments in their trucks. And we had to find a way through the Soviets' security net *while they knew we were trying to do it*. It was close to impossible, and under normal circumstances I wouldn't even have been considering it.

We were stuck in the spider's web. But I did have some very specific knowledge that might help in this situation. I had studied the Soviets' border controls — both their strengths and weaknesses — in depth over the years, and at regular intervals. I had, admittedly, mostly been looking at them going the other way, as part of my contingency plans in the event that I'd suddenly need to defect. I hadn't had to put those plans into effect — as it turned out, I'd been forcibly defected after the operation in Italy, and Sarah along with me. Now I had to get from East to West, which was an entirely different prospect, and a hell of a lot more difficult.

I turned to Sarah. 'I said "we" a moment ago, but that's up to you. You can leave now and take your chances at the embassy or try to find your own way out of the country, or you can come along with me and help me get to the U-boat. The odds are I won't make it. I have no idea how much time we have, or if the Russians will even believe me if I find the canisters—'

'In which case, we'll die in a nuclear blast. I'm coming. What about the military airfields? Could we catch them by surprise and steal a plane?'

I nodded at her commitment, then considered her suggestion. I thought of the helicopters I'd seen that morning at Steklyashka. 'They'll be even more guarded than usual. And even if we got to one, they'd simply shoot us down.'

She was silent for a few moments. 'Can we get onto a fast train? Isn't there one that goes straight to Leningrad?'

'Yes, the Red Arrow. But they'll have men on the platforms of all the stations checking everyone, and even if we could find a way on board they'll be searching every nook and cranny of every carriage. The main problem is we don't have any papers, and in this country that means you effectively can't do anything.'

'What about dissidents – surely they have ways of forging documents?'

I turned to look at her. 'Do you know any dissidents?'

She shook her head. 'But surely we can find some. What about that group in the café – you know, the girl you couldn't tear your eyes away from and her friends? They might be able to help.'

'I was checking we weren't under surveillance,' I said, and her lip curled slightly. 'It's a good idea, but what about the practicalities? Say they were dissidents, or at least know how to get in contact with some. And say that they're also still sitting in that café, or that we can track them quickly by asking around. How would we convince them to help us?'

She nodded at the attaché case on the seat next to her. 'Show them the documents.'

'We can't just run around Moscow flashing the contents of that case to anyone we think looks sympathetic. If they turn out not to be, we'll be headed straight back to the Lubyanka. Even if we strike it lucky and do find some sympathizers, we'd be asking them to believe that the documents are genuine and risk their own freedom as a result. I think it's too much to expect from strangers. Do you know anyone in Moscow? Outside the embassy, I mean?'

'Sorry, not a soul. I mean, I once met Kim Philby at a party in Beirut, but obviously we can't approach him.'

There was an awkward silence, as my own treason suddenly hung in the air between us. Six months ago, this woman had stumbled upon a conspiracy to kill innocent civilians in Italy, orchestrated in part by her own husband. She had also discovered that I was a Soviet agent, but for that very reason I'd been the ideal person to turn to. Now we were confronted by a much graver crisis than the one we'd faced together in Italy, but half a year in a prison cell in Moscow was a lot of time, and I guessed that she'd spent some of it dwelling on the fact that my actions had also cost innocent lives over the years.

'Yes, Philby's out,' I said lightly, trying to break the tension. 'They summoned him to the bunker before me, and by all accounts he's still loyal to the cause. He'd hand us straight over to Yuri and Sasha, and probably take pleasure in doing it.'

I stopped, struck by a stray thought: Philby wasn't the only other double in Moscow.

'Maclean,' I said.

'*Donald* Maclean? Surely he's just as loyal to the Soviets as Philby?'

'I'm not so sure.'

I'd never met Maclean, but in many ways felt I knew him. The first I'd heard of him had been back in 1950, shortly after my arrival in Istanbul: an acquaintance at the Foreign Office had gleefully told me that the head of Chancery in Cairo and a few of his friends had got blind drunk and wrecked the flat of two girls who worked at the American embassy. That had been Maclean, the son of a distinguished Liberal MP, who had gone on to have a nervous breakdown before suddenly disappearing the following year with fellow diplomat Guy Burgess. The word had quickly travelled around the Station that both men were Soviet agents who, on the brink of being arrested by Five, had fled to Moscow.

Burgess and Maclean's vanishing act had been my first indication that I might not be the only Soviet agent within the British establishment. The idea had both terrified and comforted me. Terrified, because their exposure could mean mine was next: I hadn't known about them, but what if there were other doubles who knew about me? And if another double were caught by Five *before* fleeing the country, they might reveal what they knew under lights. But it was comforting in its way, too, because it meant I wasn't alone in the world, and that others were treading the same path.

As the years had gone by I'd felt the noose slowly tighten around my neck as it had become clear that, far from being alone, I was in fact one of several long-term agents the Soviets had succeeded in recruiting in Britain, all of whom either had access to or were part of the upper echelons of intelligence and policy-making. In '61, George Blake, a former SOE officer who had been the Service's Head of Station in Seoul, had confessed to being a Soviet agent. The following year, John Vassall, a private secretary to a Conservative minister, had admitted to passing secrets to the KGB ever since they had photographed him in compromising positions with other men. In '63, Kim Philby, at one point Head of Soviet Section and seen by many as a possible Chief, had defected to Moscow, which had been followed by the unmasking of Anthony Blunt, who had been a senior officer in Five. In '67, the Labour MP Bernard Floud had killed himself after being interrogated by Five — some in the Service thought he'd done so because he had been presented with evidence that he had been a Soviet agent. And finally, in March of 1969, a defector in Nigeria had put paid to my peaceful life in London, and here I was as a direct result.

'I always wondered if I would be able to defect,' I said to Sarah. 'Even when I thought I was working for the right side, something about heading to Moscow filled me with dread.'

'I can't imagine why!' she said, and looked purposefully out of the window at the wind whipping at the tree stumps.

I smiled, despite myself. 'Indeed. But before I had the pleasure of finding out for myself, I was very interested in what the defectors made of life out here. As Head of Soviet Section, I made sure I had access to all their letters back to England.'

Her forehead puckered. 'Didn't you realize that these men were hardly likely to paint a very accurate picture? The Russians would also have been monitoring what they wrote.'

'Yes, of course I knew that. I also felt they would probably put a positive angle on their experiences anyway. Nobody likes to contemplate the idea that all their work has been for nought.' I smiled grimly. 'It's not a pleasant realization. I thought they would try to convince themselves they were right all along, and fit the facts to their case. I knew all that, but I still paid close attention to their letters.'

In fact, it had been more like an obsession. Burgess had died of liver failure in '63, but Philby, Blake and Maclean were all alive and kicking, and continued correspondences with friends and family in Britain. I'd followed all their careers keenly, which hadn't been hard to do: the Station had spent an enormous amount of energy trying to determine what they were up to. The Americans had even concocted a plan to assassinate Maclean in the National restaurant in Moscow, but it had never materialized.

Of all the doubles, Maclean had always intrigued me the most. Blake, Burgess and Philby all seemed like adventurers in some way, turned on by the thrill of secrecy and deceit. But Maclean had always seemed to be at one remove: a traitor, yes, and according to many who'd known him, an arrogant prig and violent drunkard to boot. But I had studied his case in depth, and felt sure there was more to him.

Back in '58, *Time* had run an article on him and his American wife Melinda, in which they had been interviewed in their Moscow flat, where they lived under the names Mark and Natasha Frazer. Soviet Section had dissected every sentence of this article in a series of memoranda. Many of the memos had contained fanciful speculation as to what 'message' Maclean and the KGB had been trying to send in the interview, as well as a level of satisfaction that he appeared to be stuck in a dead-end job with marital difficulties and a drinking problem, having lost his wife to Philby and cut off relations with Burgess. But nobody could have given the piece the level of scrutiny I did.

The article made for depressing reading, and filled me with a resolve not to end up in the Soviet Union if I could help it. I'd missed my next meet with Sasha after reading it, and with the benefit of hindsight recognized that the article spelled the beginning of a secret inner realization that I was no longer the believer I'd claimed to be when I had sought out Yuri in 1945 and volunteered to serve the Soviet Union – and that perhaps I had never truly been one.

'And something in Maclean's letters makes you think we can approach him now?' said Sarah.

I nodded. 'Prague. After Moscow invaded last spring, I paid even closer attention to the defectors' letters. I wanted to see if it had weakened their resolve at all. Philby appeared completely unrepentant about it, and Blake's letters steered clear of politics. But there was something odd about Maclean's reaction. Back in '56, he sent letters to friends defending the actions in Hungary. I'd actually been comforted by his rhetoric. But his letters about Prague were different: reading between the lines, it seemed to me he thought the whole thing had been an outrage on the Soviets' part.'

'That's not enough to approach him,' she said. 'What if you read wrong? He'll just turn us straight over—'

'There's more. For the last few years, Maclean has worked as an editor at *International Affairs*, which is the Soviet Foreign Ministry's journal. That's really a seal of approval from the big boys in the KGB. Moscow Station sends the journal to London in the diplomatic bag every month, and I used to read the bloody thing from cover to cover. Maclean writes articles on foreign policy under a pseudonym, but in the last couple of years his veneer of Party dogma has slipped. Obviously, there's only so much you can say in such a journal, but my impression is that although he's still a firm Communist, he's bitterly opposed to Brezhnev's gang. On top of that, various reports have trickled in over the last couple of years claiming that, unknown to the KGB, he has been frequenting intellectual circles, and perhaps even visited the homes of suspected dissidents.'

I listened to the sound of the radiator humming beside me.

'Perhaps we should try Andropov's *dacha*,' she said. 'I hear he's also visited suspected dissidents.'

'Not the time for humour,' I said. 'I'm not saying he's another Sakharov, but faced with these documents, he might help us. Final point, and I hope this one will convince.'

'Me, or you?'

'Both. All the defectors keep very much to themselves, but occasionally they're allowed to see a journalist or an old acquaintance. Maclean has had very few visitors from the West since he arrived, but those who have met him have given an increasingly strange picture. A couple of years ago, an old friend of his from Cambridge was due to come out here as part of some delegation. I got wind of it and invited him out to dinner a couple of weeks before, and discreetly suggested he try to renew the acquaintance. As soon as he got back, I took him out again, and over pheasant and port he told me he'd managed to meet Maclean for about an hour between meetings – and that it had been very odd. Maclean had generally steered clear of controversial topics, but at one point he'd suddenly asked this chap if he was "a sleeper they had never got round to waking up".'

'"They", not "we".'

'Exactly. Maclean defected nearly twenty years ago, but still doesn't identify himself completely with the Soviets.'

Silence again. It was slender, I knew: the friend could have been exaggerating, or not recalled the wording correctly. But we had to find a way out of this city.

'Are you sure about this?' she said. 'If you're wrong—'

'Of course I'm not sure. But I think it's a better bet than approaching strangers.'

She breathed in. 'What about Yuri?' she said. 'He might suspect us of doing just this – Brits sticking together.'

'I'd be surprised. We only just came up with the idea ourselves, and it's hardly the most obvious move. And we know something about Maclean he doesn't.'

'All right. We need to find the journal's offices, I suppose?'

'Yes. There should be a map in the glove compartment.'

I turned the key in the ignition and began reversing towards the main road.

IX

9.54 a.m., 27 October 1969, Gorokhovsky Pereulok, Moscow

An office block loomed in front of us, immense and grey, a couple of cars parked on the street directly in front. I couldn't remember where Maclean lived, but I'd read the masthead of *International Affairs* a hundred times or more, and the address was always printed at the foot of the page: '14 Gorokhovsky Pereulok, Moscow'. Despite the anonymity of the building, this was a plush neighbourhood in one of the oldest parts of the city – we'd passed several eighteenth- and nineteenth-century palaces on the way.

We hadn't passed any *militsiya* patrols or GAZ-23s, but Yuri and his colleagues would be searching hard for this car, so logic dictated we lose it as soon as possible. Sarah was too young to pass for a senior female official in the fiercely male Soviet military environment, and if we went together that might confuse matters, so after a brief discussion we decided it was probably safer that she stayed in the car than risked being stopped on the street. I parked a few streets away outside a block of flats, and left her huddled under the blankets in the back, clutching the attaché case. We agreed that if I hadn't returned within twenty minutes she would try to make a break for the border alone.

There was a *militsiya* man on guard by the entrance: probably an undercover KGB officer assigned to the building in general, and Maclean in particular. I'd considered telephoning from a call-box, but had decided it was too risky. He might simply call his handler the moment he replaced the receiver, and I'd be picked up the moment I arrived at the arranged meeting point. No, if I wanted his cooperation, I would have to see him face to face. He might be under surveillance by the KGB, but after nearly two decades in the country I reckoned that the protection would be relatively light.

The *militsiya* man watched me as I approached, squinting, perhaps to see if I was someone he knew. He had a sergeant's shoulder-boards.

'Greetings, comrade!' I said, raising my hand, and hoping blood wasn't seeping through the glove.

'Good morning, comrade. What can I do for you?'

'I'm here to see the Englishman, Frazer. Is he in his office?'

He frowned at the mention of the name, and my stomach tensed as I waited to see if the gamble would pay off. Maclean might no longer work here, or be on holiday, or be using another name, or be in Minsk . . .

'Is there a problem?' he asked.

'No,' I said, 'I just need to ask him some questions. One of the other Englishmen has gone missing, and head office thinks this fool might know about it. I doubt it, but I've been sent to ask just in case.'

He considered this for a moment. 'That sounds like one of Vilshin's ideas.'

I smiled. 'No, this came directly from Andropov, would you believe?'

He whistled. Then his eyes narrowed. 'This is the first I've heard of it.'

'It's only just happened, and I was told to inform you about it. Everyone is in a panic, and it seems that when Andropov tells Vilshin to jump, he asks how high. Well, what would I know? It's my first week in this job – just came down from Leningrad.'

'Ah, I thought I didn't recognize you. Who were you working for up there?'

'Chap called Ledov. Even worse than Vilshin, I can tell you!'

'That would take some doing. But it sounds like you catch on fast – it's just as you say. Listen, can you wait here?'

'Gladly. But don't be too long, comrade – I don't want to freeze my balls off out here! Nobody told me it would be so cold down here.'

He smiled. 'Just wait until next week. I've heard it's going to get a lot worse. Hang on, I'll be back soon.'

He disappeared, and I wondered if he was going to make a quick telephone call to headquarters to check on my story. The uniform and a bit of blarney seemed to have done the trick, but the longer he took the worse it would be, because it might suddenly occur to him that he hadn't even asked me for my name or my papers. If this went wrong, we'd reached the end of the road. The *militsiya* man appeared at the door again. And looming behind him, looking rather anxious, was a very tall man in a shabby suit and a spotted bow tie.

Maclean.

*

I told the KGB man I would take Maclean for a walk for about an hour. He nodded and wished me well, and I gestured to Maclean to lead the way. We walked off down the street together, me and this giant whom I had read so much about but never met.

'What's this about?' he said suddenly, his voice surprisingly high-pitched. 'I have some important work I need to do this afternoon.'

'Paul Dark,' I said, indicating that he take the side street on the right.

He looked up at me, confused. 'Dark? But I never had anything to do with—'

He staggered back on his heels.

'I thought you were in custody.'

'I was.'

He reeled away from me, his hands outstretched.

'Get away!' he spat out in English. 'I don't want to get involved—'

I leaned over and grabbed at his bow tie, pulling him towards me and then turning him round and shoving him in the direction of the car. 'Get in,' I said quietly, showing him the Makarov.

*

They were both watching me: Sarah sitting upright in the back, and Maclean folded into the passenger seat as though he were an elaborate penknife. Looking at him close up, he seemed unbelievably old – the rakish cad from the wanted posters sent out by the FBI in 1951 was long gone. What was left of his hair was swept back in an almost Edwardian style, and there were enormous circles under his eyes. The eyes themselves were clear, though, so he just might have stopped the drinking. But when he opened his mouth, I was shocked to see that he had several teeth missing. All that remained that was familiar from the pictures I'd seen of him was the aristocratic sneer. He reminded me of an ancient butler in a Bela Lugosi film, answering the door of the haunted house to the innocent enquirer.

Well, I was no more innocent than he.

'I know we've never met,' I said, 'and you have no reason to trust me. But we do have something in common, I think. Please hear me out. Then, if you want to walk away, do.'

'We don't have anything in common,' he spat out. 'You were never one of us. You did it because you fell for a woman.'

I took a deep breath. 'This isn't about what we've done with our lives, or why. It's about the here and now.'

'I'm perfectly happy with what I'm doing here and now, thank you very much. I *worked* for the cause I believed in — you were too busy playing cloak-and-dagger games for kicks.'

'I was Deputy Chief of the Service,' I said, regretting it the moment the words came out of my mouth. Maclean turned his head away, no doubt delighted at having exposed my petty egoism. But I could have told him there were no kicks to be had in being tortured, imprisoned and shot at. I looked out of the window, and wondered how to explain the situation, and if I'd get any more of a hearing than I had done with Smale. I decided to dive in.

'Listen. Early this morning, I was taken to a bunker somewhere beneath this city. Brezhnev, Suslov, Andropov, Ivashutin and the rest of the gang were all there, chewing their cuticles off.' He was watching me now, silent, the hooded eyes very still. 'The lot of them are convinced the Americans are about to launch a nuclear strike from B-52s. As a result, Brezhnev is planning to launch a full-scale attack on the United States. Annihilation will ensue.'

Maclean shifted his bum and squinted at me to check I wasn't having him on.

'This isn't a prank,' I said. I turned to Sarah and she handed across the attaché case. I clicked it open and found the threat assessment, then held it out to Maclean. 'Take a look yourself.'

He hesitated for a moment, then took the papers. He sat reading them in silence for a few minutes, then looked up at me, his forehead wrinkled with lines.

'This isn't real,' he said, handing the papers back. 'It can't be.'

'Do we look like we've been in prison manufacturing forgeries?' said Sarah.

He went quiet. 'But it's just bluff, isn't it? Surely they can't seriously be contemplating a nuclear strike?'

I replaced the papers in the case, closed it, and placed it between my feet.

'What would you do if you were in their shoes?' I said. 'You have hard electronic and human intelligence showing the Americans are flying nuclear-armed B-52s straight towards your border, and at the same time there has apparently been a chemical attack on two of your heavily guarded naval bases, one of which is where you keep your nuclear submarines. Would you just sit tight and wait, hoping that the West isn't about to launch a surprise attack and wipe you out? Or would you get your retaliation in first?'

He thought about it for a few moments, then said: 'I hope I'd wait a little while, just in case.'

I nodded. 'And that's precisely what they're doing. But I'm afraid a little while is all we've got. Because if the planes continue their path towards the border, Brezhnev will decide an attack is imminent, and he'll launch a strike.'

'But why on earth would the Americans keep flying their planes towards the border?'

'I've no idea why they started doing it in the first place. The worst-case scenario is that they are in fact planning to launch an attack. If so, there's bugger all we can do and that's the end of it. But everything I know about military strategy in the West tells me that a surprise nuclear attack is not something we're interested in carrying out, for obvious reasons, and so it can't be that. Unfortunately, the Soviets don't believe me. I can't go into details because we don't have time, but the fact is that they're *wrong* about the chemical attack. The Americans may be playing silly buggers of one sort or another, but part of the puzzle simply doesn't fit and I'm damn sure they aren't planning to launch a nuclear strike.

'The Service's representatives here have shunned us and we're now being hunted by the KGB, GRU, *militsiya* and everyone else. If I'm wrong, and the Americans really are intending to attack, it doesn't matter a damn to you or anyone else that we've escaped, because this country and several others will be reduced to dust in a few hours. If I'm right, though, we might just be able to stop it happening. But we need to get to Finland to do that, and there are roadblocks all over this city to stop us from getting out. So you have to make a choice very quickly, I'm afraid. Either realize I'm telling the truth and try to help us get out of Moscow any way you can think of, and fast. Or guess that I'm lying, and tell us to go hang. But if you do that, you'd best be bloody sure of it, because you'll be risking nuclear Armageddon. You're our last hope, Donald. Please don't walk away.'

I stared at him. I hated begging, but now was no time for pride. We needed this man's help, and it had to come willingly or we'd get nowhere.

He had looked away again, and was tapping one foot against the side of the door. He bit a nail, then perhaps remembered my crack about cuticles and broke off. Finally, he looked up at me.

'Brezhnev was there, you say? Was he smoking?'

I nodded.

'What colour was his cigarette holder?'

That was easy. 'Amber.'

A look of awe came across his face. I thought it best not to mention that this fact was in all the Service's files and had even been reported in the world's press.

He stopped tapping his foot and looked back and forth between Sarah and me for a few moments, squinting. Then his mouth hardened.

'All right,' he said, finally. 'You're going to need papers, and I know the best forger in Moscow. But let's get out of this car.' He turned to me. 'And take off the jacket and cap, for God's sake — we'll never persuade him to help if you're in that get-up.'

X

We left the car where it was and walked. After about fifteen minutes we arrived at a block of flats, the concrete painted a pale green. It was lower than the one we'd been parked outside but in the same style, square and unadorned, with rows of tiny balconies jutting out onto the street. The front door had no one guarding it, and was unlocked. Maclean didn't break his stride; he just opened the door and walked in.

The hallway and stairwell were a shambles, the paint peeling from the walls and broken bottles and rubbish scattered around. We climbed a narrow flight of stairs and Maclean knocked on the door three times with his fist, waited a few seconds, then rapped twice. There was a shuffling noise, followed by the sound of a latch dropping, and then the door finally swung open. A man with a beard and thick spectacles peered out sceptically.

'Good morning, Anton,' said Maclean. 'I'm sorry to come unannounced like this, but we met a few months ago, at Zimshin's party. Do you remember? I need your help. I wouldn't usually think to impose on you, but it's of the utmost urgency.'

Anton looked us up and down for a moment, then peered over our shoulders to see if there were any more of us. Finally, he opened the door all the way and gestured us in.

*

We followed him through a tiny hallway and into the living room, which was dark, tiny and smelled strongly of alcohol and cigarettes. It was also a tip: piles of books and papers took up most of the available space. A few stools were arranged around a table, along with a thin bed that had a blanket strewn across it: Anton had evidently been resting there when we rang the doorbell. Greying socks and underpants hung over a radiator, which had a saucepan tied to one of its corners with string – presumably to catch any drips – while a battered tape recorder emitted Bob Dylan at low volume from the top of a glass-fronted bookcase.

Anton gestured for us to sit in the stools while he propped himself on the edge of the bed. He was wearing a frayed shirt and baggy drawstring trousers held up with braces and his thick dark hair was swept back in majestic disarray. Judging by the titles of some of the books strewn about, he was a physicist of some sort. He was also clearly a dissident, because he was about my age and it was a Monday morning, so he should be in the same sort of office I'd just fished Maclean out of. Instead, he was at home, and for a scientist in this country that meant he must be in disgrace or at least under some form of suspicion. So my information about Maclean had been right: he did move in dissident circles. But would this one be willing to stick his neck out for a complete stranger? He was already rather angry, waving his arms accusingly at Maclean.

'Please explain yourself,' he said. 'And it had better be good, because I have no idea what precautions you took coming here.'

'We weren't tailed,' said Maclean. 'But these people really do need your help. They're British, and they need to get out of the country with some very important information that affects all of us.'

Anton looked at Maclean in astonishment, and then at me and Sarah.

'More British spies? Are you a madman?' He clenched his fists and stood up from the bed. 'Sorry, I thought this was serious. Get out, all of you. Now.'

Sarah tugged at my sleeve. 'Let's go,' she whispered. 'There must be another way.'

I shook my head and walked over to a pair of glass doors that led to a small balcony. I pulled the curtains aside slowly, almost expecting to see a mushroom cloud on the skyline. Silly of me. We wouldn't see it – it would just come. There probably wouldn't even be a Four-Minute Warning.

I glanced down at the street a few feet below. A handful of people were trudging by, coats wrapped tight against the chill, and I watched them for a few moments. But there didn't seem to be anything suspicious about them. I tugged the curtains back together and walked over to Anton, who looked like he was about to roll up his sleeves to fight me. I placed the attaché case on the table, opened it and took out Yuri's threat assessment.

'Is this a forgery?' I said, handing it to him.

He took it reluctantly, peering at it through his spectacles.

'No,' he said, after he'd read a few lines of it. 'This appears to be a genuine military intelligence document. How did you get hold of it?'

'Never mind that. Read the last sentence, please.'

He turned the page and read it aloud. '"Our assessment at this time is that we must consider launching a nuclear strike, perhaps within the next twelve hours."' He looked up at me, then at Maclean and Sarah. 'There must be some mistake,' he said. 'This cannot be right.'

I took a breath. *Stay calm.* 'If it weren't, we wouldn't be here. I listened to Brezhnev order ballistic missiles primed less than four hours ago. He and his generals are in a bunker as we speak, contemplating a full-scale nuclear attack on the West. If they do, the West will counter-attack. We, and millions of others, will die. We want to try to stop this happening, but we need your help.'

There was silence for a moment, except for Dylan, who was continuing his lament about the state of the world in the corner of the room. Then Anton started asking me a lot of questions, but I cut him off and explained that there wasn't any time. Maclean's colleagues might soon be wondering where he'd got to, and I couldn't afford to spend the day going over the intricacies of the B-52 flights and the mustard gas accident.

'Are you going to help us or not?'

Now he took a breath. He poked a finger at his glasses, then turned to Maclean.

'Do you trust these people? Are they telling the truth about this?'

Maclean tilted his head. 'I don't want to take the chance they're not, do you?'

Anton thought about that for a moment, then stretched out his hand to shake mine.

'Where do you need to go?'

We all breathed a sigh of relief. 'Finland,' I said.

'I see. Like Lenin! Well, you will need a lot of papers for that. I take it you don't have any at all?' I shook my head. 'Okay. Everyone needs to have a domestic passport, with *propiska*. An institutional work pass, a work book and of course *kharakteristika*. We will just have to hope that will be enough.'

'You mean they might ask for more than that?' I said.

'Yes. Some things require a *spravka*, a special permit.'

'What sort of things?'

He shrugged. 'Staying in a hotel, going to the hospital – even entering some libraries.'

'That's all right,' I said. 'We won't be doing any of those.' I sounded more confident than I was.

'All right,' said Anton. 'Let's get started.'

*

Maclean left shortly afterwards – the last thing we wanted was for people to start wondering where he had got to. He agreed that if he heard anything about the situation from his colleagues he would try to return, using Anton's door knock code again.

Once he'd gone, Sarah and I helped Anton clear some space in the living room. The bed was a folding one, and it turned out that the bookcase opened on a hinge and the bed went in it, stored upright, along with the blanket and pillows.

'Now,' Anton said once everything had been packed away. 'I think it might be best if you both clean yourselves up a bit first. And let's see if we can do something about your hand.' I'd taken off the gloves. 'Wait here.'

He pushed open a door to the right of the radiator and I caught a glimpse of a tiny bathroom housing a toilet and a washbasin. A few moments later he came back in with a first-aid kit. I winced as he applied antiseptic and a bandage, but thanked him for it. He motioned for Sarah to use the bathroom, and she nodded graciously and went in to wash herself. Then he turned back to me.

'We should also change your appearance. They will have a very detailed description of you by now, I think.'

He took off his spectacles and passed them over. I placed them over my nose, and blinked at the strength of them. I removed them at once, but agreed that they were a simple and effective prop.

'And some clothes,' said Anton. He squeezed past a pile of books and slid out a drawer in his magical bookcase. After some rummaging around, he removed a heavily wrinkled jacket and a gaudy cheesecloth shirt. I unbuttoned Bessmertny's shirt and put both on. Anton passed me a hairbrush, and I arranged my hair so that it fell forward.

Sarah came out of the bathroom, her face looking a lot

fresher, and muffled a laugh at my appearance. Anton smiled and did some more rummaging until he had located what looked like a black transistor radio. But I saw a lens sticking out of the front, and realized that it was, in fact, a camera.

'You have a darkroom here?' I asked.

He smiled, pleased at the question. 'It's an instant camera,' he said. 'A copy of the Polaroid – very new, and very rare. I can't tell you what I had to do to get hold of it. I've also had to make some very special modifications. It has completely changed the way I can make documents. Now, please stand over there.'

He pointed at an area of wall beside the bookcase. I moved towards it, and he fiddled about with the camera and positioned me as he wanted.

'Can you see?' Sarah asked him.

'I'm fine,' he said, but it seemed to take him quite a while to line up the shot. But once he had done it and taken the photo, he stripped off the backing sheet and we waited for the image to appear. It took about a minute. Bizarrely, instead of one image appearing, four did, precisely like passport photographs.

'Four lenses,' said Anton, beaming. 'It took me almost a month to figure out how to do it.'

'I'll take your word for it,' I said. 'What do we think, though? Will it pass muster?'

Sarah peered over and had a look. 'It's great,' she said. 'I doubt many people would recognize you from that.'

I grimaced. It wasn't most people I was worried about, but men at a roadblock examining every vehicle, armed with a description. But I smiled at her nevertheless. 'Let's see how you fare, then.'

Anton looked up at me with surprise. 'Oh, no!' he said. 'You misunderstand. I only have a set of papers that will fit you. I don't have any way of making papers for your friend.'

I stared at him. 'Well, that's wonderful to hear. But how the hell do you think we're going to get over the border if only one of us has papers?'

'It's all right, Paul,' said Sarah quietly. 'It's best you get away – you know where the U-boat is, after all. I'll find a way out somehow, don't worry.'

'Not a chance,' I said. 'I'm not leaving you here for the likes of Yuri to . . .' I pressed my nails into my palms. 'There has to be a way,' I said to Anton. 'You must have some documents you can adapt.'

He shook his head. 'You're lucky I have some that will suit you. All I can suggest is that the young lady might be able to fit in the boot of my car, if she is willing. It's a small space, but it should be possible.'

We glanced at each other, my earlier remark about putting her in the boot of Bessmertny's car hovering between us. But it was a good offer. It wasn't as good as papers, but a car was much safer than trying our luck with public transport.

'I'm willing,' Sarah said.

'Good.' I turned back to Anton. 'Where's your car and what does it look like?'

'It's parked on the other side of the street – a yellow Moskvitch. There are windscreen wipers in the glove compartment if you need them. And the radio has a special receiver installed. If you press the middle button, you should be able to hear what the *militsiya* are saying. That might come in useful.'

He took a set of keys out of his pocket and handed them over.

'Thank you,' I said, taking them.

'I wish I could do more. Now I have to get to work. My equipment is in the other room, and I would ask that you not observe. Please understand that this is not because I don't trust you . . .'

I nodded. He was worried that if we were caught, the authorities would torture us to discover the techniques he'd used to forge our papers. I was pretty sure they would have other things on their mind in that case but, after all, he was risking his freedom for the sake of two strangers and I didn't expect him to abandon his own self-interest entirely.

'How long will it take for you to prepare the documents?' I asked him.

He shrugged. 'Perhaps an hour?'

Christ. It seemed like an age, considering the situation I'd left behind in the bunker. But there was no way round it: without at least one set of papers, there was no way we were going to get out of the city, let alone the country.

Anton fetched a packet of stale-looking biscuits from the kitchen, poured us a couple of glasses of water and handed out two cigarettes, before retreating to the bedroom and closing the door behind him.

I lit the cigarette and gladly inhaled it. Sarah walked over to the tape recorder and found a cassette of Bach organ preludes, which she put on to replace Dylan. Something about the way she was standing, facing away from me, alerted me that something was wrong.

'Will you really be okay in the boot of a car?' I asked.

She nodded her head fractionally, but didn't turn. I thought about it for a moment, and realized she was frightened. I picked up the attaché case, opened it and took out the papers, fanning them across the table.

'I looked at some of these in the café, but there's much more of it, as you can see. A lot of it will be guff, I'm sure, but there might be something here that helps us know how they're thinking, and might help us stop this. Care to go through it with me?'

She turned and smiled, and I realized I'd guessed correctly: it was the inaction that was making her antsy, the waiting around. We seated ourselves as comfortably as we could and began reading through the papers. I started by tackling Ivashutin's strategy document again, reading it through from start to finish. I couldn't decide if he really believed that the warmongering imperialists could be overcome by the noble Soviets in their overcoats storming through a radioactive Western Europe, or whether the document was empty rhetoric that nobody in the Kremlin took seriously. I hoped for all our sakes that it was the latter.

'You might be interested in this,' said Sarah, and I looked up. She pushed across a thick bound dossier and I picked it up. There was a red star in a black circle on the front, and the word 'НЕЗАВИСИМЫЙ' in faded type.

'NEZAVISIMYJ', meaning 'independent' — this was my file. I'd discovered the same dossier in a flat in Rome six months ago, but that version had been a lot thinner. This, then, must be the GRU's master file, containing all the information they had on me.

I opened it up and was immediately confronted with several strips of film negatives. I held one up to the light and saw it was a photograph of me as a young man in SAS uniform, which must have been taken somewhere in the British Zone. It had been taken from some distance, and I was looking down at the ground, shielding my eyes from the sun with one arm raised. I started running through the rest of the strip. There was one of Anna, casually standing on the steps of the clinic, smoking a cigarette, and another with me and her in the ward, presumably taken with a camera she had hidden somewhere. There were dozens of the things. Presumably they had sent a few to Sasha in London for safekeeping, because he had shown me some in March to blackmail me into continuing to serve them.

I placed them to one side, exposing a document below. The cover page bore the title 'APPENDIX I: RECRUITMENT OF "INDEPENDENT"'. I turned it over and found a slim pamphlet; the edges of the pages were yellowing and torn, but the type was still legible. It was dated 12 June 1945, and was in the form of a letter from Yuri to Kuznetsov, who had then been the head of the GRU.

```
I met with agent LOTUS on the 6th to discuss
the progress of Operation JUSTICE, the latest
report on which I have enclosed with this
package (Operational Letter 16/H). At the same
meeting, we discussed the matter of LOTUS's
son, whom we have codenamed INDEPENDENT (see
Operational Letter 14/H).

  I hereby propose that we try to recruit
INDEPENDENT. The reason for doing so is simple:
```

> in the coming years, he is very likely to
> rise rapidly through the ranks of British
> Intelligence. The fact that he is the son of
> one of our agents gives us the means with
> which to recruit him, and if we succeed he may
> prove more valuable than any of the others
> we have recruited into the British network
> to date.

I already knew that I was 'Independent'; it seemed Father's codename had been 'Lotus', and that their operation to find and execute war criminals in the British Zone of Germany had been JUSTICE. There was something disturbing about the phrase 'the British network to date' – how many had been in that, and who were they?

> INDEPENDENT is twenty years old and has
> already served with several British commando
> units. He is currently attached to the Allied
> Control Commission in Helsinki, where he is
> working under cover for the Special Operations
> Executive. He was placed there through the
> recommendation of LOTUS, and his performance
> so far has been exemplary – see my last report.
> LOTUS is opposed to the idea of recruiting his
> son, but is still afraid that we may use the

```
compromising material we have regarding himself
and BAIT. I feel confident he will be a com-
pletely willing participant in the operation.
```

'BAIT'? Who the hell was that, and what was the material about them that had compromised Father? My stomach roiled as I realized that my father had never been an ideological traitor, but had been blackmailed into serving the Russians. And that despite Yuri's claim that he was 'a completely willing participant', they had coerced him into trapping me, too.

```
The relationship between LOTUS and the target
offers us a great advantage, but will have to
be handled with care. LOTUS's cover is that of
a traditional right-wing member of the British
upper classes and this, together with the
internment of his wife for German sympathies,
has led to a distance between himself and
INDEPENDENT, who naturally has no idea of his
father's work for us. LOTUS has agreed that
the best course would not be to try to mend
this distance, which would almost certainly
prove too difficult, but instead to exploit it.
    I propose a variation of the basic honey-
trap operation we have used many times
```

```
previously, including with LOTUS and BAIT,
but with a few innovations resulting from the
nature of the situation.
```

I took a breath and tried to clear my head. So Father had been the target of a honey trap – and presumably 'Bait' was his lover. And they had played this trick 'many times'. It looked like their recruitment plans had been a lot more systematic than I or anyone else had ever considered – almost routine.

And Father, behind that cold English mask of his, had apparently known all along that I resented him for his politics and for what he had done to Mother for hers. The stern handshake, the steely glare, the lack of any show of affection – had they all been part of his cover, then? Doubtless they were built in to his upbringing, but I was shocked that he had not only been aware of my feelings towards him but had also known how to exploit them; perhaps parents knew this sort of thing instinctively. But this was nevertheless a very different man to the one I thought I'd known. It showed a level of cynicism that made me resent him anew – but then I remembered the blackmail, and another picture emerged, of a man who was utterly desperate and trapped, and who was pressured into finding a way to recruit his son into the same situation.

I wasn't sure if I could read on. Did I need to know precisely how they'd gone about recruiting me? I didn't let myself answer the question: my fingers turned the page anyway.

PHASE ONE.

The operation should take place in the British Zone of Germany over the next six months, and run in conjunction with Operation JUSTICE. Agents LOTUS and KINDRED already have the list of Ukrainian traitors we suspect of hiding in the British Zone. LOTUS will contact INDE-PENDENT and urgently request he come to Germany to support an operation of greatest secrecy. LOTUS has suggested invoking a direct order from Churchill, and I agree.

PHASE TWO.

LOTUS to introduce INDEPENDENT to KINDRED and inform him he is engaged in finding and liqui-dating war criminals. He will say they are Nazis who have killed British servicemen, rather than the scum who have killed our own agents.

I thought back to that first night in the safe house outside Lübeck, when Father had introduced me to Henry Pritchard and told me about the operation: the tiny sitting room lit by candles, Father talking about his meeting with Churchill, Pritchard standing to attention by the ramshackle wardrobe. Could I, in my wildest imaginings, have guessed that both were working for the Soviets? No, agents 'Lotus' and 'Kindred' had played their parts well – and I'd been an easy dupe.

The rest of Phase Two had taken place precisely as described: I'd helped Father trace his Nazi war criminals, unaware that they were Ukrainians who had killed Russian agents rather than British ones. And then had come the injury. Father had claimed that our final target was Gustav Meier, an SS officer who had raped and tortured members of the French Resistance, including children. All of this had been backed by forged documents he had briefly waved under my nose. Towards the end of September 1945, Father claimed to have discovered that Meier was working as a gardener near Hamburg, and we'd set off together to capture him. Naturally, it was a set-up. 'Meier' – even the name was included in Yuri's plan – was in fact a Soviet agent codenamed STILETTO for his expertise with knives, who had been brought in especially and instructed on how to cut me.

The wound we envision would be to one of the kidneys and will be very painful, but shallow and will heal within a relatively short time.

It had been *extremely* painful. Even now, I found it hard to believe it had only been a surface wound, and that I hadn't received genuine treatment for all those months. And then Phase Three: Father and Pritchard had taken me to the Red Cross hospital just outside Lübeck, where I was soon taken into the care of a nurse codenamed COMFORT – Anna.

> You will recall COMFORT from earlier operations. She has now been at this hospital for several months and her professionalism is unparalleled. Once assigned to treating INDEPENDENT, she will befriend and woo him, playing on his youthful desires and ambitions to rebel against his father and the establishment he represents. Incidentally, LOTUS assures us his son is sexually normal and will succumb to her charms. If not, we will replace her with IRINA.

So Anna was a veteran of honey traps – and they even had a back-up model, just in case I didn't fancy her! Well, Father had been right about my appetites. They'd found a beauty any red-blooded young male would have salivated over, especially if it were her job to make him do so. I wondered who her other victims had been: other Englishmen like myself? How many?

PHASE FOUR.

COMFORT will educate the target about our beliefs and aims, presenting them in a light he is most likely to appreciate. I have already briefed her extensively on how best to do this. If we are lucky, this alone may be enough, and she may be able to recruit him directly. But, judging from previous operations and the unusual biography of INDEPENDENT, it may prove a little more difficult. If that is the case, once she is certain that he has strong feelings for her, COMFORT will reveal to INDEPENDENT that she is one of our agents, under the guise of remorse and affection for him. She will also mention my cover name at the camp, and that I am her handler.

This strategy involves a certain amount of risk, but I am confident of INDEPENDENT's reaction — namely that he will angrily rebuff her and contact LOTUS to tell him that the British 'operation' has been exposed.

PHASE FIVE.

I would request a delivery of the new K4 nerve gas from Department 12 for the next part of the operation. Please send a package with the next courier from our Zone. I will administer the dose to COMFORT to induce catalepsy. Using our usual cosmetics techniques, we will then stage a death scene at the hospital, and ensure that INDEPENDENT sees with his own eyes that she has been 'killed'.

The next part of the operation involves the death of LOTUS. If all goes to plan, INDEPENDENT will seek an audience with his father, whom he will suspect is responsible for ordering the murder of COMFORT, due to the fact that he had recently informed him she was a foreign agent.

I have told LOTUS that the plan is for him to strenuously deny involvement to INDEPENDENT, while at the same time emphasizing that COMFORT was an enemy agent. But while I feel that plan would probably be enough to push INDEPENDENT to seek me out and offer to serve us, I do not think it would be psychologically damaging enough to sustain a long-term commitment from him. There is also the matter that LOTUS feels under substantial pressure, and is displaying predictable signs of neurosis as a result. His material has worsened lately, and in years to come he may be over-

looked for promotion and have even less access
to the sort of material we require.

In short, I think it is clear that INDE-
PENDENT is the coming man, and so propose we
sacrifice LOTUS in order to guarantee his
replacement by his son. So, in place of the
confrontation I have outlined and rehearsed
with LOTUS, I suggest that he is instead
liquidated and it be made to look as though he
has taken his own life. INDEPENDENT will then,
I am certain, believe that his father acted
through guilt at having ordered the death of
COMFORT. If my calculations are correct — and
I would submit that they have not yet been
wrong in such matters — INDEPENDENT will then
seek me out here and offer his services as our
agent, and the impact of the events surrounding his recruitment will drive him to be loyal
to us in perpetuity.

Several more pages followed, but I'd got the picture. I shuffled the papers together and slid the pile back into the
attaché case.

I knew a lot of it already, but hadn't run through all the
ramifications. Some of it had been circling around the
edges of my consciousness, where I'd let it linger, unwill-

ing to poke the wound. And some of it had never occurred to me at all – the idea that Yuri had killed Father, for example. I had still believed it was suicide. But it was obvious, now that I thought about it: suicide wasn't really Father's style. And yes, the operation had been 'psychologically damaging', in just the way Yuri had foreseen: I had sought him out and nursed the dual wound of Anna's death and Father's ordering of it for years. Not in perpetuity, though. He'd got that bit wrong – not in perpetuity.

'Jesus!'

I looked up. The muscles in Sarah's cheek were visible as she clenched her jaw – she was reading Ivashutin's strategy document. She turned the paper over and stared at me. 'Isn't there someone else we can show this to? The Americans, or the French?'

I shook my head. 'Nobody in the West is going to believe us – we have to make the Russians understand they've made a mistake.'

'And we're sure they have, I take it? What if there has been a chemical attack on these bases?'

'It's possible,' I conceded. 'But I think it's just far too coincidental. There were thirty or more canisters of this precise chemical down there in 1945. If several have escaped to the surface and leaked towards the bases on the currents, I think you'd easily get this effect. Some novice sentry found a lump of the stuff that had washed ashore, picked it up and brought it into the base, after which others have touched it, too.'

'And the B-52 flights? How do you explain them?'

I couldn't. Although I'd told both Brezhnev and Maclean that I was certain the Americans weren't planning a strike, I was far from sure of that. I was hoping they were up to something else because I thought the mustard gas must have leaked from the U-boat. But I didn't *know* it.

And there was one other thing bothering me. When I'd come out of hospital in April, in the fortnight before Templeton's funeral, there had been a brief moment of panic when the North Koreans had shot down one of the Americans' reconnaissance planes over the Sea of Japan. For a few hours, the signals had been frantic, and Nixon had placed nuclear-armed fighters in South Korea on a fifteen-minute alert to attack the North. In the end he had changed his mind, and simply resumed the reconnaissance flights instead to signal that he wasn't going to back down. But he had nevertheless considered a nuclear strike. Could it be for some reason I didn't know of that he was considering it again, only this time against the Soviet Union?

'If the Americans are planning a strike, we can't stop them,' I said to Sarah. 'But if they aren't, we might be able to stop the Russians from reacting. So we have to act on the basis that they aren't. Does that make sense?'

She smiled, and placed her hand across the table. I took it in mine, savouring the warmth of her touch. I looked into her eyes, and remembered for a moment the sweat on her skin in the boat in Sardinia. We were a long way from there now.

There was the faint sound of typing coming from the other room.

'Let's hope he's ready soon,' I said. 'Did you find anything of interest in the papers so far?'

She shook her head. 'I don't think there was anything we didn't already know. How about you? Was that your file?'

'Yes.' There was little more to say about it, or little I wanted to, anyway.

'And what about the rest of it?' she said, pointing to some papers poking out under the dossier I had just read. 'Anything there?'

My stomach tightened and I pushed the other dossier aside. The document beneath was simply titled 'Report on INDEPENDENT'. I picked it up. It was dated 20 October 1969 – just a week ago.

'Are there any cigarettes left?' I said to Sarah, and she found the packet and lit one for me.

I stared down at the document, and breathed in the tar that might help me get through it. It looked to have been written by Sasha, and was addressed to Yuri.

*

Esteemed Comrade,

You asked me to give my reasons in writing for bringing INDEPENDENT to Moscow. It is my view, having been his handler for nearly twenty years, that when he was recruited in 1945, INDEPENDENT strongly believed himself to be setting out on a moral crusade. As we had hoped, he applied his adolescent sense of idealism to our cause, associating his service to us with vengeance for COMFORT's death at the hands (as he believed) of his father.

But although INDEPENDENT was able to convince himself that he was a Communist for the first few years of his work, this soon faded. He disagreed with our actions in Hungary in 1956, for instance, and on other occasions when I discussed such issues with him it was clear that he had become a believer only in the vaguest sense of the word, in a manner similar to many of our sympathizers in the West.

Due to his position and relationship with us, INDEPENDENT has long felt that he has a central role to play in the direction of political forces in the world. For him to be of use to us, it was necessary that we sustained his belief in this delusion. However, when he was threatened with exposure in March he discovered some limited information about the nature of his recruitment, namely that COMFORT was a honey trap.

As a result, he turned against both the British and us. This entire episode has been a disaster for us and for the KGB, who I hope I am not remiss in saying acted with great malice towards us in this affair, and at great cost to the Motherland. The results of this were discussed in my previous reports.

Following the fiasco in Nigeria, which resulted in the deaths of two of our agents by INDEPENDENT's hand, he was then targeted by a faction of neo-fascist hawks within British intelligence, whose links to covert groups in other NATO countries we have monitored for some time. Unfortunately, INDEPENDENT was not aware of our attitude towards these groups and their plans. This resulted in him nearly wrecking the hawks' actions in Italy, which would in turn have destroyed our own long-term strategy regarding this NATO action.

As these events took place at great speed across several countries, there was no possibility for me to communicate with Centre about every development, and I was forced to make several decisions without going through the usual channels or face the possibility of more disaster. I decided that it was in the best interest of the Motherland that INDEPENDENT not make public the NATO hawks' actions before we had deemed it politically expedient, and so I extracted him from Italy. As he was with another British agent, SARAH SEVERN, the wife of a hawk (now deceased), I decided she too must be extracted, or we would wake up to find the incidents in question across the front pages of newspapers across the world.

But I did not make this decision solely for wider strategic reasons. Since March, INDE-PENDENT has effectively run amok, and I felt we needed to capture him before he could do yet more damage. A primary consideration was that he has been serving us for over two decades, and was at this time the deputy head of the British Service. In normal circum-stances, this would have been a great victory for us. However, it had already become clear that INDEPENDENT had not just stopped serving us, but was working against us. By bringing him back to Centre, I felt we would be in a position to present his service to us without his interference, when and how we judged would cause the most propaganda damage to the West.

I confess that it has not worked out as easily as I had imagined. The British have so far managed to conceal the fact that he was one of our agents, reporting in the press simply that he died on assignment in Italy in May. My initial proposal was that we simply counter this with a press conference at which INDEPENDENT would appear and read a statement revealing that he has served us since 1945. I now feel that this would be unwise, mainly because INDEPENDENT is uncontrollable. Even with sedatives and the threat of the torture of SARAH SEVERN, for whom it is clear he has a sentimental attachment, I am not confident we would be able to control what he might say.

And there remains a wider problem: if we present his service to us to the international community, the propaganda benefit of revealing that such a senior figure in Western intelligence was an agent would be considerable in the short term, but in the longer term may cause us more damage than good. With previous British agents, the public revelation that

they have served us has resulted in a pleas-
ing level of anger from the Americans, and the
British have yet to fully regain their trust
as a result. In addition, the British cannot
even trust themselves, and have spent much of
their energy in recent years looking for more
of our agents within their structures, to
pleasingly unsuccessful effect.

In the case of INDEPENDENT, however, I feel
that public exposure of such a senior figure in
the Western intelligence structure would
attract not only the attention of those within
his own agency who have so far been concerned
with trying to find members of our British network, but also others in Western intelligence.
Some would no doubt conclude that INDEPENDENT
must be one of several agents we have planted
in their countries, and would investigate much
more thoroughly than they have done to date.
This would endanger many of our agents who are
active or sleeping in the West.

As INDEPENDENT is no longer of use as an
agent, and is rather a danger to us and a
drain on resources, I suggest the time has
come to liquidate him. It is probably advis-
able to liquidate the girl, too.

I dropped the stub of the cigarette into my glass, and placed the document to one side. So they had wanted me dead, and Sarah, too. The report had been written only a week ago, so either Yuri had disagreed with Sasha's assessment or, more likely, he hadn't yet decided what to do about it and the current crisis had intervened.

Sasha had been right about one thing, though: I was uncontrollable. I wanted to break his fucking neck.

'Not good, then?' said Sarah.

'No,' I said. 'Not good.'

I walked to the doors leading to the balcony again. It had begun to hail, tiny hard pellets. My world and Sarah's had been reduced to this small flat, in its way no less a prison than the one from which we'd escaped. The cramped walls and ceiling made me want to run into the streets with her. But while the air would be crisp, the sky would be grey and men with steel-toed boots and loaded rifles were looking for us both with the intent to kill. And somewhere deep underground, surrounded by marble pillars and oil paintings, the walls were closing in on Brezhnev and the Supreme Command.

Soon, with any luck, we were going to try to cross a border. Which one, though? The maritime frontier was very tightly monitored by the Navy, with patrol craft along the whole stretch. They would also have stepped up their numbers and been given instructions to watch for us. But it is never possible to check all outgoing boats from a shore-line, however heavily you patrol it. Perhaps we could find a fisherman with an outboard motor willing to take us across the water. Perhaps.

We also had to decide where along the frontier to try to cross. The 'attacks' were in a part of the country that was closed off to anyone without a special pass, and would now be under complete lockdown, with hundreds, if not thousands, of military personnel there. So we would have to give that whole area a wide berth. Our best bet might be to try to reach the U-boat from the other direction – from Åland. It was a longer way around, but it had some advantages. Yuri and his colleagues might soon realize we were planning to head for the U-boat, but probably wouldn't guess we would take such an indirect route. They would also be unable to coordinate the hunt for us, because if we managed to get into Finland they wouldn't easily be able to control their men there, or the Finns for that matter.

It was a very big if, though. There were twelve miles of protection either side of that frontier – the *pogranichnaya polosa*, or border strip – including sentries with dogs. And even if we found a way to get past the Soviet patrols in the area, we would still have the Finns to contend with on the other side, where it was almost as heavily guarded. Despite the difficult history between the two countries, the Finns regularly handed back anyone they caught coming over the border.

Another thought that had slowly been taking shape in my mind was the question of equipment. I needed to get back down into the U-boat to find the canisters, but to do that I would have to find a way to get hold of diving gear. I knew from the war that the Germans had made sure all their U-boats had self-contained diving suits on board, complete with oxygen flasks and air purifiers, but I had to get down there in the first place. Could I break into one of the Soviets' naval stations and steal one? It seemed a stretch. There was a naval base at Kronstadt, but that was fortified on its own island and I didn't fancy my chances there. Perhaps I could find equipment on Åland itself? I wondered what had happened in the intervening years to Kjell Lundström, the police constable from Degerby who had helped me in 1945 – perhaps he could help me again.

And then there was the problem of what to do if I did get down there. I was hoping it would be obvious that the canisters had leaked, and that I would be able to point this out to the Russians at their consulate in Mariehamn. But I had no idea if the Soviets still had a consulate on the archipelago – perhaps they had abandoned it in the intervening years. If so, I might have to try to reach Helsinki or Stockholm. But first I would have to find the canisters, and they might well have come loose from the U-boat and be many miles from it. I would either have to find them myself or bring the Russians close enough to them that I could take someone down there with me and force them to see the evidence for themselves . . .

The door to the bedroom opened and Anton emerged, his hair sticking out at even zanier angles than previously, his hands clutching a sheaf of booklets triumphantly. He was done. He spread them out on the table for our inspection – I had no way of telling, of course, but they certainly looked the part. He went through them carefully with me, explaining the purpose of each document and why I might be asked to show it, and after we had gone through it all once more I leaned over and gave him a bear hug.

'We may never be able to repay you, but thank you.'

There was an awkward silence as he shuffled his feet. Then there was a sound at the door: three muffled knocks. We stood still and waited. A couple of seconds passed and two more raps came. Sarah walked towards the door.

'Wait!' I said, but she had already opened it.

Maclean was standing in the doorway, a sombre expression on his face. It took me a moment to understand why. Directly behind him stood two men: one was Smale, and the other was William Osborne.

XI

'Move,' said Osborne, and Maclean jerked forward and staggered into the room, his eyes entreating me for forgiveness. The damn fool couldn't even check for tails properly.

Osborne stepped smartly into the room. He was clutching a Browning in one chubby little paw. With the other, he motioned for Smale to shut and lock the door, which he swiftly did. I saw that Smale wasn't empty-handed either, but instead of a gun he was carrying what looked like a black doctor's bag.

'Well, well,' said Osborne. 'Birds of a feather stick together. Sit down, all of you. Over there. Hands on your heads.' He gestured at the space by the wall where the bed had been, beside a tottering pile of books. Maclean, Anton, Sarah and I looked at each other, then did as he'd ordered.

The flat, now occupied by six people, suddenly seemed very small indeed.

Osborne walked over and looked down at us with a sneer. There was something wrong with seeing him holding a silencer: he had always been the puppet-master, not the man who got his hands dirty. He looked much fatter than I remembered, almost grotesquely so, but perhaps that was because I'd spent six months in prison while he'd been eating jam buns. He was wearing thick tortoiseshell spectacles, a pinstripe suit and even had a handkerchief in his jacket pocket. Brandishing the gun, he looked like a Punch cartoon: the banker who had decided to rob the safe.

He ambled over to one of the stools and picked it up, then placed it directly in front of us and perched on it, his trousers riding up over his belly as he did so. From my vantage point, it was a most unattractive sight.

'Paul,' he said, peering down at me, 'I believe you are carrying a gun. Please remove it very carefully and place it on the floor like a good boy. I'll shoot if you try anything.'

'So you're Head of Station,' I said. 'And Smale's just your lackey.'

'You always were quick on the draw. Although not literally so in this case. The gun, please, now.'

I considered trying to shoot him, but thought better of it. He looked like he would fire without hesitation — and enjoy it. I removed the Makarov from my waistband.

'Careful now,' he said. 'We don't want anything to go off, do we?'

I placed it in front of me on the floor, and Smale scampered over and picked it up, then aimed it at my head.

'Who's Chief, then?' I said. 'Something must have gone awry for you to be out here.'

'I'll ask the questions,' he said. 'I must say, it is rare to find three traitors to their country in the same room.'

'Are you counting yourself in that?' said Sarah, and he swivelled to face her.

'No, my dear, I was counting you. I do like your hair – David Bailey's missing a cover shot. How disappointing that you've fallen for Paul's smooth words. But then, he always had a way with women. I should warn you, though, that they usually end up dead. I'm afraid you are very misguided if you think that anything I've done is in any way comparable to Donald and Paul's actions, or those of their masters. The Russians are much more unpleasant than I am – I would have thought you'd have realized that by now.'

'I should never have learned English,' Anton said suddenly, and we all turned to stare at him. 'You British will kill me.'

Despite ourselves, we all smiled – even Osbourne. But whatever companionship we felt in that moment evaporated quickly. Osborne's smile was that much more chilling.

'Be quiet, Anton,' said Maclean. 'This doesn't concern you.'

'No,' he said. 'I'm just being held at gunpoint in my own home.'

'Why did you send Smale to meet me?' I asked Osborne. 'Not to spare my feelings, I'm sure.'

He licked his lips, amused, or perhaps it was Anton's complaint that had entertained him. 'No,' he said. 'I wanted to surprise you at the embassy. Sadly, you skipped out rather early for us to bring you in. I must say it's been quite bothersome to find you again. But luckily we've been trailing Donald here for quite some time, and he doesn't have too many acquaintances who might help you escape the long arm of the Russian law.'

So that was it. They had probably paid visits to all the defectors, but when they'd gone to Maclean's office they found he'd left, and worked out from there where he might have taken me. Yes, quite some bother. I had to get away from them somehow, perhaps once we were outside the flat. I would have to make a move soon.

'Shall we head off, then?' I said. 'Presumably you have a car waiting?'

'Oh, we're not going anywhere just yet,' he smiled. 'You asked who had taken over as Chief. Innes has the title – at the moment, anyway. There was quite a storm after your little episode in Italy. Questions were even asked in the

House. Innes is a busy little man, and he figured out what Hugh, I and others have been doing.'

'So you got shunted off here.'

'In a nutshell. But it's proved quite convenient, because now I can take my revenge, and at the same time use it to get myself back to London. The fact that Donald and Sarah are here as well makes it all that much more delicious.'

'Another frame-up? If Innes found out what you were up to in Italy—'

'Oh, I'll be much more careful this time. He hasn't discovered everything we were up to in Italy, anyway – we have a few surprises in store. But I suspect if I can deliver three dead traitors on a silver platter, nobody will ask too many questions.'

'Oh, really?' said Maclean, his voice strained but strident. 'Because I can assure you that the Russians will be very interested indeed.'

'Be quiet, Donald,' I said. 'Leave this to someone who knows about cloaks and daggers.'

Osborne smiled. 'Not such birds of a feather, after all. And I rather doubt your friends will care all that much – two burnt-out spooks and a dolly-bird, none of whom are of any use to anyone any longer. I suspect they'll be glad to be rid of the lot of you, in fact. Something to strike off the budget.'

'They might wonder who killed us, though,' I said. 'And ask awkward questions of the embassy.'

He let out a gleeful little chuckle. 'Who killed you? But don't you see, you're all going to kill each other: a suicide pact. Traitors, but also lovers.'

'That's absurd. Nobody would—'

'Oh, you'll be amazed what people will believe when told after the event,' Osborne said. 'It won't be too hard to whisper a few things in journalists' ears. They'll eat it up, I'm sure. "The traitors' love triangle" – I can see the headlines already.'

'I think you're all bluff, Osborne. You tried all that newspaper malarkey on me once before, remember. So how is Wilson these days? Still PM?'

He grimaced, and removed his glasses. He massaged the pink indentations on either side of the bridge of his nose with his fingers for a few seconds, and then replaced them.

'Wilson is still in power,' he said, 'for the moment, at any rate. And how kind of you to remind me about that failure of mine, and of your part in it. Well, this time I won't be satisfied with a hired thug pulling the trigger from afar. This time I want to see you suffer myself, and I want to be the one to administer that suffering.'

I thought back to the rubber room in London, and the bucket he had forced my head into. I didn't want to know what was in the doctor's bag. My stomach was churning just sitting in the same room with him.

'It sounds to me like you've gone soft in the head,' I said. 'I should have been on to you years ago – there was always something off about you.'

'And I, likewise, should have been on to you long ago. I had an inkling, though, back at that party of Templeton's in Istanbul when you raped Vanessa. Do you remember?'

I stared at him. He seemed to be serious.

'You're mad,' I said. 'Vanessa loved me, and did for years. It was your little jackboot Severn who tried to touch her up. You should have asked Colin Templeton; he'd have let you know.'

'But I did, Paul. And he told me very clearly that he had walked in on you fondling his daughter. Severn saved her from you, as you well know. Trying to save face in front of your new girlfriend?' He pursed his lips together as though chiding me.

'I've no idea where you're going with this fantasy, but it's not convincing me in the least. I left the party with Vanessa, and you must have seen that.'

'Yes, that was what upset Templeton so much.'

'He *asked* me to leave with her.'

'Not according to him.'

'Either you're lying or Templeton was. He told me quite

clearly to take Vanessa home, so why he would want you to think I was . . . What else did he tell you about me?'

'Ah, I thought you might catch up. He told me he thought you were worth keeping an eye on. In case you were like Donald here, and his friends.'

I stared at him in horror. 'Templeton told you he suspected me of being a traitor?'

'Yes. Not quite in those words, of course. But he let it be known on several occasions, to me and a few others, that he had his doubts about your loyalty. I should have paid more attention to him.'

I blinked, trying to clear my head. Could Osborne be telling the truth? I thought back to the night Templeton had summoned me to his house in Swanwick. If he'd thought I was a traitor why the hell would he have invited me there, without Barnes to protect him, and with no weapon of his own? I went over it again in my mind – the moment I had raised the Luger and shot him. I'd thought at the time that he had realized then that I was the double. And then the thought came. Perhaps he had. Perhaps he'd had no idea before then that I was a double, but had merely told Osborne and others he suspected my loyalty to divert suspicion . . . from himself.

Burgess. Maclean. Philby. Vassall. Cairncross. Blake. Blunt. Pritchard. Father. Me.

And Templeton?

Was it possible? I hadn't been part of the Cambridge Ring, and had known nothing about any of them before they'd been discovered. Neither, by all accounts, had Blake or Vassall. I thought of a sentence in Sasha's report: 'This would endanger many of our agents who are active or sleeping in the West.' What if the Soviets had recruited not three, or four, or even ten men? What if they had recruited, say, twenty? Or more? And that only a handful of them had been exposed so far. At first blush the idea seemed absurd, but what if all the assumptions to date had been wrong and the level of Soviet penetration had been greater than anyone had even dared suspect – myself included?

Stay calm and think it through. I hadn't known about Pritchard or Father, but they had both known about me. So if Templeton had also been a double, he must have been recruited separately from them. In the aftermath of Burgess and Maclean's defections, both Five and the Service had twisted themselves in knots looking for further traitors. Pritchard had taken the role of an attack dog, accusing everyone in sight: at one point he had even claimed that the deputy of Five was a Soviet agent. Dossiers had been reopened; everyone had been questioned about their past. I had argued that these 'mole hunts' were divisive and that we were playing into the Soviets' hands by chasing our own tails and sowing suspicion everywhere.

And through it all, Templeton had played the middle

ground perfectly: the wise old sage, the kindly buffer, the voice of reason. But behind my back, to Osborne and others, he'd been softly voicing a private anguish: can we trust Paul, do you think? I mean, I love him almost as a son, but there's something not quite right . . . is there?

Simply because it had deflected attention from him.

And that evening in March at his house? Pritchard had presumed he was the Soviet agent codenamed RADNYA. Perhaps Templeton had, too. All three of us had been in the British Zone in 1945; perhaps all three of us had been Anna's honey traps.

I suddenly remembered Oliver Green. He had been a printer with Communist sympathies who had gone off to be an ambulance driver in Spain with the International Brigades. Then, in 1941, he had been arrested for possessing forged petrol coupons. When his house had been searched by the police, they had discovered a darkroom that had contained a Leica and dozens of secret military documents. This, in turn, had led to a soldier named Elliott, and eventually to a ring of fifteen British agents, all of whom were being run out of the Soviet Trade Legation.

The Green case had always bothered me a little, because nobody ever seemed in the least concerned by it. The implications seemed to have been completely missed by the Service. Here was a significant Soviet spy ring operating in Britain in the Thirties and Forties, with over a dozen agents.

Had it been missed because Green and his colleagues had been working class? Because it was too uncomfortable to think about the implications?

Or had it been missed because many of the men looking at it had also been Soviet agents? My head reeled a little at that idea. It would involve a level of penetration that would change the whole picture of Britain's role in the Cold War. Indeed, it discounted it. If this were true, the Soviets had surely already won.

Or perhaps Osborne was just messing with my mind, and was trying to sow suspicions for reasons of his own. I couldn't think of any at this stage, but that meant little with him.

'You look confused,' he said. 'Thought you'd fooled Templeton, did you? He was never as daft as he looked, you know.'

No. No, perhaps he hadn't been. But this was all of little account. Osborne and Smale could be Andropov's long-lost brothers for all I cared, but it didn't help resolve the issue at hand.

'I'm not confused,' I said. 'I'm worried. Perhaps we could have this conversation and you can rip off my toenails after we've dealt with the impending nuclear crisis?'

He looked over at Smale, beaming. 'So you weren't lying! Well, well, my apologies. Lunch at the National it is.' He turned back to me. 'Come on, Paul, you can't seriously expect me to believe Brezhnev's about to launch nukes at us—'

There was a banging at the front door. Osborne turned, and in that moment I grabbed hold of the attaché case and held it up in front of my chest. Smale fired but it went wide anyway, and a fraction of a second later the front door swung down, splitting in two as it crashed to the floor, and men swarmed into the room waving guns and shouting. I flung the attaché case open, scattering documents like confetti over the room, and grabbed Sarah by the hand. Osborne was heading towards the door and I watched as one of the KGB men took aim and the shots hit him full in the chest and he fell to the floor, the inside of his jacket spreading out beneath him like a pair of black wings.

I launched myself into the balcony doors side-on, bracing myself for the impact. The glass smashed and crumbled over me, but I was through. Sarah came leaping through after me, and I careened into the balcony railings but used the momentum to grab hold of the ledge running along the top of them. It was shockingly cold, crusted with rime, and pain shot through my left hand as it came into contact with the wound, but I ignored it and hoisted my legs onto the ledge and climbed over, hooking my fingers around the outer edge of the shelf and letting my legs dangle below me.

Another shot rang out from inside the flat, and Sarah

screamed. Without looking down, I let go and there was a rushing of wind in my ears and nose and then an almighty bone-crunching thud as I landed on the pavement. I looked up and caught a glimpse of Sarah's legs as her dress billowed around her and she landed next to me. It had all taken place in a matter of seconds – but we still had time on our side. A few yards away I could see a mustard-yellow Moskvitch.

'Come on!' I shouted at Sarah, and started running towards it.

XII

We reached the car and I scrambled with the key to unlock the boot. It was tiny. Sarah glanced at me for a moment, then climbed in, rolling herself up into the foetal position.

'Okay?'

She nodded, her chin against her knee.

'Hold tight,' I said.

I shut the door and ran around to the driver's seat. The temperature was around freezing, so I tried a brief burst of the starter without the accelerator, ready to catch it as soon as it took. It didn't. I waited a couple of seconds, drumming my hand against the wheel, and tried again. Nothing. A mushroom cloud forming, all because this country couldn't make cars that started. I gave it another go, craning my neck as I did to look up at the balcony. Gunfire was still coming from inside the flat, but God knew how long it would be before they came running for us. And . . . yes. *Bingo*.

I pulled out and roared down the street as fast as the thing would go, the treads of one of the front tyres squealing. I pressed the button on the radio and picked up the *militsiya* frequency, but the exchange was about a couple of drunkards who were causing trouble near the GUM store, not us. Presumably, the lieutenant at Maclean's building had finally wondered where we'd got to and called in, and the KGB also knew of his association with Anton. Maclean had grown complacent, careless or both, and had failed to realize he was under surveillance wherever he went, by both the British and the Russians.

The message might not have gone out yet, but this car would be compromised before too long because Yuri would soon figure out why we'd been at Anton's. The question was whether we could reach the first roadblock before he realized it and got a message to his men to look for anyone in a yellow Moskvitch with this registration. I hoped that the fact they'd stumbled in on two senior British diplomats holding one of their agents and a dissident at gunpoint would give them enough to disentangle for a while.

It had certainly given me a few things to disentangle: Colin Templeton a traitor? It couldn't be, surely. I told myself to leave it to one side for the time being, and think about it later . . . if there was a later.

A lifetime of training had taught me to keep my eye on an objective until the job was done, and to suppress feelings of panic, but this was different. We'd escaped Osborne and Yuri, but we were still a hell of a long way from the U-boat. In fact, we were around 700 miles from it in a shitty little Soviet car, with one of us in the boot and only one set of papers. Panic surged through me. The papers. I felt for the pocket of my jacket. Yes, they were still there.

I began heading west, keeping my speed at a reasonable limit so that I didn't attract any attention, and my eyes peeled for patrol cars and black Volgas. The rain had stopped, but mist was forming and visibility was poor. Dark clouds were pressing down on the city, but I noted them with satisfaction: it usually didn't get too cold when it was overcast, and the radiator in the car was bust. There was quite a lot of traffic around, and coupled with the mist it was making it heavy going. The street signs were all in Cyrillic, of course, and although my Russian was fluent, my brain was struggling to adjust to it, exacerbated by the shock of seeing Osborne and the pain still throbbing in my hand.

I had to figure out where to head now, and reduce the objective to a series of concrete moves and counter-moves. Counter-moves, because figuring out what the opposition was planning would be crucial if we were going to stay alive much longer. What would I do now in Yuri's shoes? From the brief flash of uniforms I'd seen in the flat, there had been both GRU and KGB officers there, so I suspected he and Andropov had had it out already, and had now agreed to join forces for both their sakes and to cooperate to their utmost to get us back. If they didn't recapture us, both their heads would be on the block. The Volgas and the men in the flat would be just the tip of the iceberg: I knew the *militsiya* had already been scrambled, and we could expect large numbers of GRU and KGB men to have been deployed, as well as the railway police, civilian police volunteers and customs and border guards. If I were stopped for speeding now, it would be the end of the line.

I wiped the sweat from my eyes and braced my shoulders, trying to suppress the fear. What if I couldn't locate the canisters, or find a way to show them to the Russians? What if I did and they simply didn't care, or didn't believe me regardless? What if I were too late? Brezhnev could have cracked under the pressure. The missiles could already be in the air.

There was something emerging in the mist by the side of the road and I peered through the window anxiously. A figure appeared, and I saw flashing lights and a red star on a white helmet.

Roadblock.

*

I removed Anton's spectacles from my jacket and put them on. It was a miracle he'd managed to take a photograph of me at all, because his lenses were so strong that within seconds my eyes began to throb and it became hard to see anything. I peered over my nose and saw that they had stretched several *militsiya* cars across the road in two rows to block it. The line of traffic was building up quickly as a result, because every time they let a car through they reversed one of the patrol cars in the first row a little way, let them through, closed the gap and then did the same in the second row. That meant they were taking a couple of minutes to clear each car. And it meant that they were being very thorough indeed.

The question was whether or not they knew about Anton. Bessmertny's wristwatch read ten past noon. It could be that Yuri and his men were still trying to sort out what had happened in the flat – or it could be that they had got on the radio and told these chaps to look for someone in Anton's car.

The car in front of me cleared through the set-up, and I was waved forward. One of the men knocked on my window and I rolled it down.

'Passport, comrade,' he said. They all looked the same – like schoolboys playing dress-up. This one had cut his chin shaving this morning, or perhaps it was a pimple he'd picked at. I handed him the passport and he took it and opened it.

'Move your head closer to me,' he said, and I did, feeling the heat of spotlights. He squinted at me, and then back down at the passport.

'What is your destination?' he asked. He had a pistol on his hip, one hand placed on it.

'Leningrad, officer.'

'A fine city. And what is the purpose of your visit there?'

There was a faint clunking sound from behind me, and I prayed he hadn't heard it in the surrounding din. I pushed Anton's spectacles up my nose – the frames were too large for me and kept slipping down – and tried not to look flustered.

'I'm visiting family,' I said.

He frowned. 'But it says here that you were born in Moscow. What family?'

The strength of the glasses was making me dizzy, and I could feel my pores opening and the sweat starting to bead.

'My second cousin,' I said. 'He moved there last year, and he wants to show me his new flat and introduce me to some of his colleagues.'

'What does he do?'

'The same as me – he's a physicist.'

He flicked through the pages, but I couldn't make out his expression through the lenses. I felt I might faint but I couldn't risk closing my eyes. If I looked over the glasses, he might think I was condescending to him so I stared straight ahead, not focusing, trying to shut off the message from my brain to my retinas so they weren't affected so much. Sirens were circling behind me, and then I heard a burst of static from one of the nearby cars, and a message being delivered through a transmitter. Was it Yuri or Sasha, telling them to stop a yellow Moskvitch with the following registration? I strained my ears but couldn't hear. Then one of the car doors slammed and I saw another officer approach and tap my man on the shoulder.

He turned, and the officer whispered something in his ear.

There was no way I could make it through two lines of cars. And at the first sign of any attempt, they would shoot.

The officers stepped back from the car. Oh, Christ. Were they about to try the boot?

The first officer stepped forward again, and leaned into my window.

'Please proceed,' he said, handing me my passport. 'My colleagues here will signal the way.'

XIII

The traffic from the roadblock began to thin out, and once I'd passed the fork for Kiev and was sure nobody was on my tail, I took some gravel lanes through a thicket of woods, then pulled over and helped Sarah climb out of the boot.

'How are you?' I said.

She grimaced, stretching her arms and legs. 'I've been better. I take it we're through, then?'

'For the time being.' She climbed into the passenger seat and I told her what had happened at the roadblock.

'So they got some sort of a message?' she said. 'I wonder what it was.'

'Good point.' I put the *militsiya* channel back on. There was some beeping and static, but then a message came on, which appeared to be on a loop. We listened to it in silence as I steered us back onto the motorway and headed towards Leningrad.

'*Comrades, this is Colonel-General Shchelokov, and I have been asked by our General-Secretary, as Minister of Internal Affairs, to relay the following information to you on behalf of the Supreme Soviet. You were alerted earlier today that enemies of the state, two English spies, had escaped from our custody in Moscow, and were at large. They are, I regret to say, still at large, and must be apprehended at all costs. They are a menace to our society, and intend to cause the Soviet Union great harm. Be warned that they are also highly trained special forces operatives, and will stop at nothing, including murder.*

'*Within the last few minutes, men within the Moscow* militsiya *discovered the body of one of their colleagues, Sergeant Grigor Ivanovich Bessmertny, who was left to die by these fugitives while on the run. His family has been informed, and a funeral is being arranged. It is now, I think, incumbent on all of us to honour the memory of Grigor Ivanovich Bessmertny, and bring his murderers to justice. After this message will follow a description of the fugitives, and other information that I hope will lead to their swift arrest, detention and trial. I offer my sincerest condolences to the family of Sergeant Bessmertny, and pay tribute to his gallantry and service. I call on you all, as my men and as his comrade, to hunt down his killers immediately.*'

'Christ,' said Sarah softly. I sensed there was also reproach in her voice, but I didn't regret what I'd done, even if it were true that he had died. He would have done the same – or shot me – had the situations been reversed.

'Listen,' I said, as the descriptions came on. They were mostly accurate, if perhaps a little unfair, except for one detail. 'Did you hear that? They think I'm wearing Bessmertny's uniform.'

'So? That's hardly going to bother them if they find us, is it? Your disguise isn't exactly foolproof.'

'That's not my point. Their wheels aren't turning fast enough. They've brought out a big gun, Shchelokov, to rile up the blood of the hounds. But that recording has to be at least an hour old. There was no mention of this car, or Anton, or what we're wearing now. That's why we made it through the roadblock. No doubt they'll record another message soon enough, but they're behind us for the time being. I don't think they know where we're headed yet.'

I turned to face her, and noticed that her smile was painted on.

'You need to get some sleep,' I said.

'I'd love to,' she smiled, 'but you keep talking.'

I shook off my jacket and handed it to her, and she tucked it under her chin and leaned against the window as I drove. When I looked over again a few minutes later, she was sleeping.

The traffic became sparser still, and I drove as hard as I could towards the border, my hands gripping the wheel until they turned numb. We passed cranes and television towers, restaurants and factories – the great dreary expanse of the Soviet Union. The road became rougher, and despite the low cloud cover, the temperature had dropped.

I started thinking about my life up to this point: what I had done, and what had brought me here. Or rather *who*, because it was mainly Anna who had brought me here: there was a straight line between our conversations in that Red Cross clinic in Germany in 1945 and this car in 1969. She hadn't dragged me here, though; I'd come along willingly. I had always chided her for being an idealist – but she had always known that I was one, too.

'You like to discuss specific events, Paul, but you avoid any discussion of principles. Don't you feel that society would be better if we were all equal – no more rich and poor?'

'And milk and honey flowing throughout the land? Of course. But it's a dream.'

'Everything is a dream if you do nothing about it. What have you been fighting for these last years? Wasn't it for a better world?'

'A world free of Nazism, yes.'

'Is that all you have learned? So now we simply return to what was before – the same old ways, the same old systems?'

'Yes. There was nothing wrong with them.'

'I don't think many people would agree with you, Paul. I think the last five years have brought everything into focus. Yes, Nazism was a great evil, and conveniently enough for your country many millions of my countrymen have died extinguishing it. But we cannot now be satisfied with simply living in a world that is not evil. Many of us want to live in a world that is fair,

a world that has a chance of keeping peace between all men, instead of waging war on each other every few decades because one nation wants more of the cake than another. I never wanted to live in a country ruled by the Germans. But I don't want to be ruled by the Americans or the British, either . . .'

I had let myself be persuaded because, despite my token resistance, I'd been dissatisfied that the war had ended with no clear resolution. It did indeed seem as though we were about to return to the old ways again, as though nothing had changed in the intervening bloodbath.

And, more simply, I'd fallen for her.

The music on the radio ended, and led into an international news bulletin. I turned it up. I didn't think there would be anything of any importance in it, but you could never tell. The first item was an interview with a cosmonaut who had been part of the Soyuz 7 mission. No mention was made of the fact that the Americans had put a man on the moon. Perhaps they hadn't made that public either.

The next item was about a military coup that had just taken place in Somalia, which was talked of in ecstatic terms by the announcer – presumably there had been Soviet support for it. After that, there was a report on the forthcoming talks on arms limitation with the Americans in Helsinki, which had apparently been in dispute for some time. The tone was generally positive, but the suggestion was that the Americans had already ceded to Soviet demands for the talks to take place on their terms; I wondered if the mention of it was deliberate. Well, everything was deliberate with the Soviets when it came to the dissemination of news, but was this a more precise message and, if so, who was its intended audience and what reaction was it intended to spark? The delay in the *militsiya* message suggested it wasn't directed at us, and it seemed unlikely that such a report would make any difference to the Americans if they truly were planning an attack.

An alternative was that it had been prepared earlier, say yesterday, as part of a wider strategy to present the Americans in a bad light over the talks, and it wasn't related to the current crisis. But no wonder they were so bloody jittery: they'd lost the big prize in the space race, were in a border dispute with the Chinese and just as they were coming out of long negotiations with the Americans over weapons reduction talks, Nixon had decided to fly some nuclear-armed B-52s directly towards their border. Coupled with a supposed chemical attack on two heavily fortified naval bases, they'd snapped.

The bulletin came to an end. Once again, there had been no mention of a chemical attack, but I guessed they would reveal that only once they had retaliated, if then. There might not be a news service in place after a nuclear war, and there would probably be few people alive to listen to its broadcasts.

I suddenly wanted to forget the lot of it: the U-boat, the mustard gas, the men in the bunker in Moscow. Perhaps if we managed to escape over the border, we could head somewhere else instead, Sarah wearing my jacket in cars in other countries, smiling that soft smile.

I blinked the thought away and locked my wrists on the wheel. As I passed a restaurant by the side of the road, I remembered we hadn't eaten anything apart from a few stale biscuits at Anton's flat. I looked across at Sarah and realized that if we were going to get over the border it might be an idea to gather our strength. I pulled over a few miles later at a roadside restaurant with steam coming from the windows, and gently woke her.

We took a table facing the door and a surly, barrel-chested waitress walked over. I picked up the menu and ordered *kotlety* with black bread and coffee. The waitress curtly informed us that the food would take several minutes to prepare and sauntered off.

Sarah stifled a yawn, and I found myself aping her. I'd been driving for five hours without a break. I started going through my plan to cross the border, keeping my voice down to barely a murmur.

'Is it dark enough?' Sarah said. It was twilight now, the sky just a greying pink on the horizon.

'It'll have to do.' There was nothing to do now but head full pelt for the target, and hope. We would fill up fast with fuel and get going. I glanced through to the kitchen to see if there was any progress on the meal and saw that sitting on the shelf behind where the waitress was standing was a small transistor radio. And that she was talking to someone in the kitchen, and nodding towards us.

'I'll explain the rest in the car,' I said. 'We have to get out of here.'

I left a few token coins on the table, and we made for the door. The waitress came running out after us, but we were already at the car.

*

I headed back onto the road, putting my foot down. It had been a stupid, foolish, *stupid* bloody mistake. The *militsiya* would now be told precisely where we were, and they would hand the information over to Yuri and Sasha soon enough. I had just lost our advantage, and had painted a bull's-eye on our rear ends to boot, all because of my empty belly, which now felt even emptier.

I put my foot down, and a little less than two hours after leaving the restaurant we passed Leningrad, after which I cut around Vyborg and drove to its outskirts. As we approached the *pogranichnaya polosa*, the twelve-mile protected zone around the frontier, I took a detour into a gap in the undergrowth by the side of the road and pulled up. I took Anton's forgeries out of my jacket and placed them in the glove compartment – they would only help to identify us now. I told Sarah that if we were caught we would claim to be geologists.

One of the Russian playwrights, Denodovski, had defected at a literary fair in 1962, and in reviewing his debriefing documents I'd come across a curious mention he had made of the border conditions. He had said that on a trip to Karelia years earlier, when he'd been part of a group of geologists, the whole lot of them had been detained for three days by the border guard because they didn't have documents proving who they were. This, he claimed, was because the KGB had in fact banned geologists and certain other experts from carrying documents: they were afraid a foreign government might rob them and then use their specialized documents to justify a scientific presence near border areas and infiltrate the Soviet Union. But this meant that there was one valid reason not to have documents near the border.

Well, it wasn't the best cover in the world – they would probably only need to make a couple of telephone calls to establish from our descriptions alone that we were fugitives wanted for murder and various crimes against the state. But if we were caught, it would probably all be over anyway.

'Ready?' I asked, switching off the ignition.

She nodded, and we began to make our way through the bushes, treading very carefully. There were men with dogs patrolling this area, as well as three security fences, trip-wires and watchtowers. But the entire length of this border was secured in this way, so this was as good a spot as any to attempt to cross.

Night had fallen now, but there was still some visibility. The mist had returned, though – swathes of it covered the ground and a foot or so above it – and I found that if I crept on my belly I could move for several yards at a time following bands of it between bushes and trees. I motioned to Sarah to do the same. I picked up a small stick and used it to feel in front of me for trip-wires. After I'd been doing this for fifteen minutes or so, I caught sight of the turret of a watchtower poking out from a large clump of pines to my left: it wasn't quite a forest, but there was a lot of cover there. I pointed it out to Sarah, and we started making our way towards it, keeping as close to the ground as possible, watching for any sign of men or dogs.

I wanted to make a beeline directly for the watchtower for several reasons. Border control towers often lack heating in order to focus the minds of the guards, but even that doesn't always work and sentries in watchtowers tend to be less alert than their colleagues on the ground. One of my contingency plans for defection had involved making my way across from Finland, so I knew from studying the towers on the other side of the border that it was possible to avoid several lines of guard positions by crawling directly under the towers, where there were no additional sentries posted besides the men in them. I had no idea whether the Soviets used the same system on this side, because my plan had involved simply walking up to the nearest guard after crossing the frontier and surrendering, then waiting for the local KGB chief to be contacted and my bona fides to be established. We would simply have to hope.

Luckily, the mist was holding, and as we moved deeper into the woods I found I could cover ground a lot faster than before, when I'd had to stop every five seconds to find the next spot of cover. Unfortunately, I could see that Sarah's stamina was already flagging, and she was stopping not for cover but to catch her breath. I wasn't faring as well as I'd hoped I would, either. Earlier I had all but forgotten the ache in my hand, but now it came back as a stabbing pain and I found myself feeling disoriented.

I blinked to try to snap myself out of it. This was no time to start hallucinating. Well, at least I no longer had my Nigerian fever slowing me down. It was quite a year I'd had: I'd caught a deadly African disease, been shot at, tricked, exposed as a traitor, tortured by a madman in a dungeon in Sardinia and hunted to within an inch of my life. And now here I was, with the world on borrowed time, crouching by a pine tree in Russia with a woman I barely knew – and just a few miles away from the West again.

It was colder now, perhaps below freezing, and Anton's clothes didn't offer much protection. It was getting darker with every passing moment and the temptation to stand up in the ground mist was enormous, but we were safest here, creeping along side by side. Ahead of us, finally, I saw the criss-cross structure of the traditional wooden watch-tower, and I tried to block out everything as I made the additional effort to keep as low as possible and move in fluid, unnoticeable movements, elbow over elbow, feeling the grass beneath me respond almost as though I were a snake, or a fish swimming through a current.

As the feet of the watchtower came into view, I felt something on my back. I turned, thinking someone had touched me, before I realized it was rain. My spirits sagged. Rain was good in one sense, in that it worsened the border guards' visibility. But in another sense it was terrible, because it released the body's natural scents, and dogs might pick up on those. But I couldn't see or hear any dogs around here. Perhaps they were taking it easy on a Monday on this part of the border. Perhaps this wouldn't be quite as difficult as we had . . .

The bark came suddenly, and made my shirt vibrate on my back.

I froze, and heard a rustle next to me as Sarah froze too.

It came again, and this time I located it – it was about twenty yards away, to our right. Two barks from two different dogs. They worked in pairs.

Do not panic. Now is not the time to panic.

Elbow over elbow. Move away, to cover. I could no longer see Sarah, but hoped she was doing the same.

There was a shout from somewhere above. The sentry in the tower wanted to know what was happening, talking either to the dogs or to a colleague on the ground.

'He's heard something!' It was his colleague replying, and he was close, perhaps twenty or thirty feet away.

Shit.

The rain was coming down in sheets now, and it was starting to hurt as it hit my spine and my calves. It was loud, as well, but that was good, because any senses it overrode for those hunting us helped. Elbow over elbow, elbow over elbow – just a few more yards to go. I couldn't see where the dogs' handler was, but border guards wore green uniforms precisely so they wouldn't be seen.

Finally, I made it under the watchtower. I was dry, at least, and hopefully that would mean my scent didn't get any stronger. But I had no real cover: no bushes, no trees; nothing but the wooden stilts holding up the tower. I squinted out into the darkness but couldn't see any sign of Sarah in the low mist. I grabbed hold of one of the stilts to lessen my own visibility, pressing myself into it, every muscle tensed. I clamped my eyes shut: children do it and think they cannot be seen, and we laugh at them. But I didn't dare open them, partly because the surface of my eyes might reflect light and give me away, partly through fear.

'Which way, boy?'

It was just one of the dogs that had picked up the scent, then. The voice was harder to locate now, but that was because the sound of the rain was drowning him out, rather than the distance. They might be even closer now — not yet close enough to see through the mist and rain, but close enough to smell or hear me.

There was a faint padding noise behind me, and I opened my eyes a fraction and saw the outline of Sarah's head emerging through the darkness. She had made it under, too. I reached out a hand and caught hold of her, and then pulled her in to the stilt. She was shaking very gently, and I covered her with my arms and pressed against her, urging her to control her fear, and thus her movements.

There was another vibration in the ground, and the front of my skull tingled as I realized it was the dog coming across the grass. It was heading straight for us. Gooseflesh formed on my arms and neck, as I waited for the animal to pounce on us. And then the vibrations stopped. It must be able to see us now, surely? I could hear it panting over the sound of our own breathing.

I stayed as still as I could, breathing through my mouth. Dogs see in monochrome and find it hard to focus over distance, so I hoped it saw four fuzzy grey wooden stilts holding up the tower through a screen of mist and rain. As a result of their vision, dogs mainly react to sources of movement, after which they investigate sound and scent. But in this case I thought the dog had been alerted by scent, the smell of our bodies brought out by the rain and exacerbated by our physical exertions over the last few hours. Now it was waiting to see if any of the stilts moved.

Judging by its reactions so far, this was a guard dog rather than a tracker. If so, it would be relying on air scent rather than following ground scent over a distance. That was an advantage, because air scent disperses more quickly. Now that we were under the tower and out of the rain, our scent would be harder to locate again. On the other hand, this type of dog would also have been trained to attack once it found its quarry.

It took a few steps closer to the tower, and barked again.

'Where are you, boy?'

I tried not to take too much hope from the question. It suggested the handler couldn't see through the rain either, and he would have much better eyesight than his dog. But it wasn't necessarily sight that would give us away. I could feel Sarah's heart hammering through her chest, as she could no doubt feel mine. The dog would be able to hear our heartbeats once it was within five feet of us.

If he found us, I'd have to kill him, because his training dictated he would try to kill us. Attack dogs are often over-confident – in training, they always win – and that might lead to mistakes. But it was a slim hope. I clasped my fist around the twig I'd been using to check for trip-wires. Could I use it? No, it would snap. I would have to use my hands. But then we would have to deal with the handler as well. And where was the other dog?

I had to calm down, because my heart was now thumping like a Salvation Army drum and I didn't want to add to the pheromones of fear and stress we would both be giving off. I tried to find a pleasant memory to latch onto, and the warmth of Sarah's skin reminded me of how she had looked that night in the embassy in Rome – her honey-blonde hair, eyes ringed with kohl, the white evening gown … But then I heard her catch her breath, and I thought instead of her in the Lubyanka, and saw a man attaching electrodes to the same arms that now held onto me in the darkness. She was here because of me and my actions. I'd promised myself I would keep her from harm in Moscow, and I'd failed. I had to get us through this. I couldn't fail her again.

Calm. Think of pleasant memories, pleasant memories … It was useless – all my memories ended badly. But I had to find one. And then it came to me: Miss Violet, the old tabby cat my parents had adopted off the street in Cairo; I'd played with her on school holidays. I thought of her great piles of fur, and running my hands through it to make her purr, and the way she had jumped on my lap, narrowing her eyes in pleasure . . .

Vibrations under my feet. I tensed, ready to leap up and strike.

But the vibrations were getting softer, fading.

The dog had turned around.

'Come on, boy. Let's get back into the hut, shall we, and stop playing games?'

*

I stood there, holding Sarah in my arms against the thin wooden strut. Above us, the sentry continued making his rounds. Sweat started pouring off me, as if in delayed reaction to the stress, and then it began to cool, sticking to my skin.

After a few minutes, Sarah very gently turned around. Her hands reached for my face, and then her lips grazed mine, and an electric current ran through me. I reached for her hands, and placed my fingers on her mouth. We weren't out of this yet. We were still in the Soviet Union.

Once the rain had subsided a little, I crouched down in

the mist and indicated with my hand in hers which direction we were to go in. Once I was satisfied she understood, I set off, making sure I could hear the sound of her breathing. After we had inched forward like this for what seemed like hours, I finally made out the first fence, a wire one. After watching for some time, I concluded that there were two border guards patrolling this stretch, but neither had dogs and after they passed each other there was a three-minute gap before either of them reappeared again. If the mist held, we should be able to get across the stretch in that time.

While scouting the situation, I'd crept up to the fence where the shadow was deepest and had shovelled away some of the earth with my hands. As soon as the guards passed each other, I turned on my back and, using a stick to prop up the wires, shimmied my way under the lowest line of wires. I could see the whites of Sarah's eyes against the darkness, following my every move, and I watched as she carried out the same manoeuvre, a fraction of a second behind me. Once we were through, we began crawling to the other side, and carried out the same procedure. I'd lost count in my head and didn't want to waste any time looking at my wristwatch, but I reckoned we were already approaching the three-minute mark.

But we had made it through, and it seemed that the game was now more a test of our stamina. There were two other fences, and they were of the same type. The first only had one patrol guard, and was much easier to get through as a result, but the final fence had three guards. By now I was exhausted and could tell that Sarah was as well. But we had come this far.

She helped me dig the earth away and then we waited for the guards to pass and shimmied under as we had done before. But this time we'd been a little careless, because there was more of an incline here and we hadn't dug deep enough, so that just as we were coming free on the other side one of the coils of wire caught on my cheek and pulled at it. Without meaning to, I let out a cry, which I immediately muffled. But at once there was a bark. It was followed by the sound of footsteps and raised voices. The game was up.

'*Run!*' I whispered to Sarah, clambering to my feet. But I couldn't obey my own instruction, and was conscious of a searing pain and blood dripping down my face. There was a line of trees in the near distance and I watched as Sarah's silhouette stumbled towards it, but I was struggling to follow – my feet were slipping on the grass and my knees were shaking, and I fell before I'd gone even a few yards. Seconds later I was helped up by my arm, and I took in that the sleeve holding me was camouflaged. Somewhere to the left there was a dog on a leash, and the dog seemed interested in me. But I wasn't interested in the dog.

'I'm a geologist,' I said pathetically, placing the palm of my hand against my cheek to staunch the flow. 'I'm a geologist.'

There was no reply, and I looked up and saw that there were several men standing around me. My vision was starting to blur now, perhaps as a result of the fall, but a chill ran through me as I took in that they were all wearing gas masks. The masks were painted a sickly grey colour, and as a result it was like looking at a shoal of monstrous underwater creatures. It was all the more monstrous because the fact that they were wearing them could mean only one thing: a warning had been given.

This realization was confirmed by their behaviour. Without another word, they took hold of me, strapped me to a stretcher and carried me aboard a vehicle. As I came up the ramp, I saw another stretcher was already in there, and on it lay a beautiful woman in a grey dress with short hair, her eyes closed. My heart sank. Sarah hadn't made it more than a few yards further than I had. There was no hope, then – none at all.

The engine started up and we set off at great speed. I closed my eyes and tried not to panic, focusing instead on the pain in my cheek, and when that wasn't enough I located the pain in my hand and thought about that as well.

Minutes later, my eyes opened again, my senses jarred by

the squeal of metal: the doors of the jeep were opening, and I was being lifted out. It was still raining, and large drops splashed against my face. I could hear frantic but muffled orders being shouted around me, along with some sharp scraping sounds I couldn't identify. The angle of my body suddenly inclined steeply. Directly ahead I caught a glimpse of a bizarre structure, made of enormous blocks of stone covered in moss and camouflage – a bunker. I looked up at the sky, the water pouring from it, and the cloud directly above me seemed to redden and expand. As the stretcher entered a dark, cool space and began descending a flight of steps, I knew that I had failed, and that Brezhnev had finally done it.

XIV

I was being hunted by a pack of wolves through a ravaged countryside, but there was something wrong with my face. It was slowly peeling away. Somewhere behind me, Colin Templeton shouted orders at men wielding spears, laughing as they chased me. Anna was there, too, caring for the dead on the battlefield, men without eyes. I watched as she leaned down to kiss one on the mouth . . .

I woke, sweating, and when I tried to move realized instantly that my hands and feet were manacled. It was dark, and it took a few seconds for my eyes to adjust and work out what was directly in front of them: the ceiling, made out of concrete, just a couple of inches away, and an exposed wire jutting out of it. With my nightmares still fresh in my head and no idea where I was, I cried out in terror. I stopped immediately, because the proximity of the ceiling meant that the sound bounced back, nearly deaf-ening me. And I was aware that there was someone in the room with me.

'Sarah?'

There was no reply for a few moments. Then: 'Yes.'

She was in the bunk beneath me.

'Are you all right?'

Silence.

'It's happened, hasn't it?'

She started sobbing and I looked up in despair, feeling as if I might cry too, but finding I was unable to.

*

We lay there in the darkness for a time, trying not to think of what the future might hold, balanced between a night-mare and reality. Then, as if by magic, light crept into the room — someone had entered. A hand reached over and loosened the manacles on my ankles, and then released Sarah. After being pulled down a small stepladder, I found myself standing next to Sarah on a cement floor, facing two stocky men armed with machine-pistols.

They prodded us out of the room and along a narrow corridor, past rough concrete walls. One of them opened a thick steel door and we were pushed into a tiny room that contained nothing but a small wooden desk, a couple of plastic chairs and a naked bulb. I was pressed down into one of the chairs and Sarah into the other, and then the men took up position by the door, their hands on their weapons, their eyes expressionless. They hadn't said a word to either of us.

I stared at both of them with amazement. The country above us had just been destroyed, yet they were still gamely following orders as though nothing had happened. I hadn't thought the discipline went that deep, even here. Perhaps it was something to do with the training – or the bunker we were in. While the British ones had reserved space for cabinet ministers, royalty and civil servants, this one seemed to have been designed for the military, and infantry at that. Pack them in like sardines in a tin, with an inch's breathing space – I couldn't understand the logic of it. Perhaps they were intending to wait until the fallout had dissipated and then emerge and strike back, swelling over the border in their tanks and street-sweepers. Well, it wouldn't surprise me. All the British contingency plans had been riddled with holes, because nobody had had the balls to point out the truth: there was no possible way to survive a nuclear attack.

Not in the long term, anyway. Civil servants had wasted years writing documents and setting aside budgets for depots that would contain tons of flour, yeast and even sugary biscuits. But the brutal reality was that much of the world had been destroyed, and nobody was going to live long enough to rebuild it.

Most people would have been killed instantly in the first strikes. But the minority who had survived, like me and Sarah and whoever else was in this bunker, would suffer a much worse fate. We would struggle on for a couple of months down here and in other places like it, fighting among ourselves over the rapidly dwindling water and food supplies. At some point, someone would insist that the only option left was to go outside again and see if more water could be found, or search for those holes in the ground with the sacks of flour in them. A few souls would venture out, only to die slowly of radiation poisoning. The rest of us would sit down here waiting for them to return, gradually going mad. People would soon start to kill each other, and then themselves. But there would be little or no life on the surface for hundreds and hundreds of miles — and that meant that there was no way to survive in the long term. It didn't matter how many bunk beds you had.

The door opened and a man marched into the room. He was wearing a leather coat over his uniform so I couldn't make out his rank, but the sentries saluted him so he was obviously the bigwig. He was a tall man, completely bald, and with cheekbones so pronounced that his head resembled a skull. He somehow seemed precisely the sort of figure to meet in this situation: a god of the underworld.

He pulled out a chair on the other side of the table, seated himself in it and leaned across the desk, staring at the two of us with bright blue eyes.

'We have little time,' he said, 'so I will dispense with the preliminaries.' He spoke in heavily accented English, which took me by surprise. 'I have the following information about you, which I wish you to confirm. You are British spies by the name of Paul Dark and Sarah Severn, and you have escaped from imprisonment in Moscow. My understanding is that you escaped from a moving car while being transported to the Lubyanka.'

'All right,' I said. 'We are. I couldn't give a damn any more. In fact, I want to die, and the sooner the better.'

Sarah turned to me, her eyes dulled with fear. I had brought her too far. Osborne had been right: all the women I ever cared about died – Mother, Anna, Vanessa. Now Sarah would die, too. I hadn't been able to save her, or anyone else. Better I go too, and fast.

The skull-faced man leaned back in his chair, and placed a couple of long, slender fingers to his lips. 'I don't understand.'

I shrugged. 'I would rather you did it than I do it myself. I don't intend to take up anyone's rations. It's my fault all this has happened, so let's get it over with quickly. A bullet to the back of the head, please.'

He took this in, and then leaned over the desk again.

'What madness is this?' he whispered. 'I have treated both of you remarkably well, Mister Dark. I arranged for your wounds to be fixed, and I even let you rest for a short time. I could have made life much worse for you, you know. You were caught crossing our border. And this is how you repay my kindness, by talking about rations like a crazy man? Yes, I will certainly have you shot if you don't start explaining yourself.'

I stared at him, and placed my hand against my cheek. There were stitches in it, brand new. I'd forgotten about cutting myself against the underside of the fence. There was something wrong with him. Not just with his words, but the whole manner in which he had said them: despite his demonic appearance, there was culture there, sophistication, altogether different from Sasha and the other thugs I'd encountered so far. His English was good, but his accent was peculiar.

Yes. The realization hit me. He wasn't a Russian at all, but a Finn. We'd reached Finland. We must have somehow made it across the line before the missiles had landed. That explained his comment about catching us crossing his border – in part, anyway. But what on earth did any of this matter *now*?

'When was the first strike?' I asked him. 'And how secure is this bunker?'

He pushed his chair back and stood, nostrils flared, and

I wondered if he was about to hit me. And then something dawned on *him*, and he sat down again.

'Why did you try to cross the border?' he said.

I stared at him blankly. 'Do you really not know?'

He shook his head. 'There's a man called Proshin of military intelligence in Moscow. I received a signal from him a few hours ago: he asked that we step up the vigilance on our side of the border in case two British agents matching your descriptions tried to make it across. This was a highly unusual request, but it was also from an unusually senior source, so I listened. Especially because Proshin claimed that it was vital to the security of both of our countries that you be stopped at once.

'As a result, I immediately sent out your descriptions to my men and told them to keep watch for you. Shortly after doing so, you did try to cross our border, and we discovered you. Proshin has been informed of this, and I have granted permission for him and a small group of his men to cross our border to apprehend and interrogate you here, before they take you back to the Soviet Union. He asked me to keep you under armed guard until he arrives, which should be within the next' – he looked at his wristwatch – 'ten minutes or so. But I would like some answers from you before he gets here, because you have illegally crossed my border. So perhaps you can tell me why you did that, and indeed why you fled from Moscow in the first place?'

I looked at him, trying to take in all the new information and weigh it against the possible. He must be bluffing. I had seen the cloud redden above me, expanding – or had I somehow imagined it? I looked over at Sarah, but she seemed as confused as I was.

'Are you seriously trying to tell me that there *hasn't* been an attack yet?' I said.

He pressed his hands together, his forefingers sticking out like a gun and resting under his chin.

'What sort of attack?'

'Nuclear, of course!'

He shook his head. 'Are you trying to tell me that there has been one?'

'Have you looked outside lately?'

He clenched his jaw, and the hollows in his cheeks deepened further. 'I'm losing patience rapidly, Mister Dark. Yes, I have looked outside lately. I arrived here only a few minutes ago. I would advise that you explain yourself to me, and that you do so quickly. As I say, Proshin and his men will be here very soon. But I'm perfectly willing to tell them that, unfortunately, you were foolish enough to try to escape from confinement, and that as a result I had no alternative but to shoot both of you.'

'If there hasn't been an attack, what the hell are we doing in a nuclear bunker?'

'We're not. This place wasn't built to withstand a nuclear

attack. We're in Miehikkälä, and this bunker is part of the Salpa defence line, built during the last war to protect us from the Russians. I had you brought here because I was flying directly from Åbo and there is a small area nearby in which a helicopter can land, and because I felt confident you wouldn't be likely to be able to escape from this place.'

'But why were your men wearing gas masks?' asked Sarah. 'They had them on when they found me, and . . .' She tailed off. 'They had gas masks.'

He took a deep breath. 'Some people further down this coast have been affected by strange injuries in the last couple of days – we think some sort of hazardous chemical has drifted into the waters here, and a lot of fishermen and sailors have been badly afflicted, with their skin peeling away. Some of my patrols have been helping move people who have been affected, and are trying to investigate the source. All of them are wearing gas masks as a temporary precaution until we find out exactly what the cause of this is and how dangerous and contagious it is.'

My stomach had tightened, and I realized he wasn't bluffing. 'It's mustard gas,' I said. 'A particularly powerful form of it. It has leaked from a wrecked German U-boat on the seabed just off the coast of Söderviken. If there hasn't been an attack, you have to call Washington at once, or London.' I stopped. Neither would work. There was no reason why anyone would believe the head of the Finnish border guard, especially as *we* were the source of the information. We still had to get to the U-boat ourselves, find the canisters and show them to the Russians.

I tried another tack. 'You have to help get us there,' I said in Swedish, and he raised an eyebrow.

'You speak Swedish?'

He had said Åbo, rather than Turku, which was the Finnish name for it. 'My mother was from Åbo,' I said. 'Look, the Russians are convinced this chemical accident is part of a plot by the West to start a nuclear war. People at their bases in Paldiski and Hiiumaa have been showing injuries like the ones you mention. As you know that the symptoms are being experienced at several points along this coastline, and as it must be clear to you that until a few seconds ago both of us were utterly convinced that a nuclear attack had taken place, surely you can see I'm telling the truth about this. But the danger hasn't passed – a real nuclear strike could be ordered at any moment. You have to help us get to Åland, as soon as possible, so we can reach the U-boat and prove to the Russians that there has not been a chemical attack.'

He paused for a moment, then stood again, and walked briskly to the door.

'Thank you for the explanation, Mister Dark,' he said. I made to protest, but he hushed me. 'Please let me speak. You escaped from confinement in Moscow, and I have no doubt you will also try to escape from here. You are both clearly extremely resourceful and dangerous operatives.' He grabbed hold of the door handle. 'And I think,' he said, 'that you will succeed in escaping from here.'

I stared at him.

'You mean—'

He placed a finger to his lips. 'I lost several members of my family in the wars with the Russians. There is no, as I think you say in English, love lost between me and them. I don't believe someone could easily have invented the story you have just told me. I can, on the other hand, imagine that the Russians would react just as they have done if your story were true. So I will take a chance. Proshin and his colleagues will be furious with me, I'm sure, but they won't be able to prove I have done anything. In any case this country is not, I repeat *not*, a part of the Soviet Union. I would rather take the risk you are lying to me than that you are not, considering what you have said. But you have, if I understand you, very little time left. So let's not talk any more. It makes me uncomfortable – I've said more in this conversation than I have to my wife all this year. There is a helicopter upstairs. Shall we go?'

I looked at him, dumbfounded, and nodded. He smiled again, the most wonderful smile, and then opened the door.

*

Standing in the flattened grass outside the bunker was an Agusta Bell helicopter with orange and green livery. As we approached it, I turned to the Finn.

'I don't even know your name.'

He pulled off his coat and handed it to one of the sentries.

'General Jesper Raaitikainen.' He shouted at the pilot to come down from the cockpit, and then started to climb up himself. I looked on with alarm.

'What are you doing? We can fly this.' I pointed at Sarah. 'You have to stay here and meet Proshin, surely.'

He shook his head. 'Oh, no. I'm not sticking around for that bastard. Captain!' The pilot turned, and Raaitikainen spoke to him in rapid-fire Finnish. The pilot saluted smartly, then headed back to the entrance of the bunker. 'Nothing to worry about,' said Raaitikainen, smiling. 'My men will tell Proshin you kidnapped me with a pistol, and there was nothing they could do about it.'

'I would rather we went alone,' I said.

He ignored me, and clambered into the cockpit. 'Mister Dark, you're lucky you're going anywhere at all. I might also point out that you have no idea where we are, or how to get to Söderviken. But I do.' He looked down at us, and his face was again as stern as that underworld god I'd initially taken him for. 'I advise you to climb in here with me now – unless you wish to wait here for Proshin after all?'

Sarah looked at me, and I realized we had no choice. I helped her up, then climbed up myself, considering what his coming along might mean. He was right that we didn't know how to get to Söderviken, but what would happen once we got there? We needed to find a way to convince the Russians that the leak was an accident rather than an attack: taking along a general from a Western ally wouldn't help us do that, and they might believe it was another deception operation as a result. But it was better than no chance at all.

As Raaitikainen was busy checking the controls, one of the sentries began running towards us and shouted something up to him in Finnish. He listened, then turned to me and Sarah.

'The Russians have been sighted on the track leading here. Let's go!'

Raaitikainen shouted at his man on the ground, who saluted and stood back, and as he went through the checks and put the engine into warm-up we started to strap ourselves in.

XV

The world far below us was peaceful and still. As my eyes adjusted to the darkness, I dimly made out a landscape of ice and water, and at one point even thought I saw, clinging to the rocks of one of the small islands, a cluster of those curious miniature pines I'd seen in 1945. No doubt it was partly because I'd recently believed that nuclear Armageddon had already struck, but the serenity of it seemed almost unbearable.

If Brezhnev launched a strike, the Americans would retaliate with their Polaris missiles. The British plan was to target forty-eight Soviet cities, and the Americans would no doubt do the same. Leningrad, Paldiski and others were on that list, and while the blast wouldn't reach here, the fallout certainly would. I wondered if the B-52s were still in the air, circling as they waited for their instructions, and if so what the men in those cockpits were thinking as they looked down.

'You don't happen to have any diving equipment on board, do you?' I shouted over the noise of the engines.

'No!' Raaitikainen replied. 'But one of the coastguard stations in Åland will.' He caught my look and clapped me on the back. 'Don't worry. We'll find a way through this. We're nearly there now. Does it look like the world is about to end?'

I shook my head and began to reply, when the engine gave a shrill whine and we began to tilt.

'What's that?' Sarah called out.

'An engine?' I said, but realized almost at once that it wasn't that, but a shot.

I craned my neck, and saw the lights of a helicopter directly behind us. It looked like an Mi-8T, and it was firing its two PK machine guns directly at us.

'Oh, God,' moaned Sarah, rocking back into her seat. Raaitikainen was grappling with the stick, sweat pouring from his face, and I knew that we must have been hit somewhere. I unstrapped myself to help him take control, but we suddenly lurched again and I was thrown against the side of my seat, hitting my jaw and cutting open my cheek wound.

Dazed by the pain and dizzy from the motion, I tried to bring myself to a standing position, but I could see it was a losing battle. Raaitikainen had also been thrown, and was no longer holding the stick, and Sarah was now slumped back, her mouth in a rictus – we were in freefall. I crawled along the floor of the cockpit towards Raaitikainen's seat, but the sound of the engines suddenly rose in pitch and then there was an enormous crunching. I guessed that the rotors had hit something. I looked out of one of the perspex panels and saw a greyish-brown block of something, and then realized it was ice, and that we were underwater. I shouted across at Raaitikainen but he didn't reply. When I looked up, I saw why: the upper part of his head was covered in blood, and his eyes had rolled upwards. I fought my way towards Sarah and unfastened her seat belt. We were kicking at the forward section doors when the water started coming in.

*

Panicking, I gave another kick to the door, and this time it was enough to get it open. Freezing water gushed through in a torrent, nearly drowning me and pushing me back, but I kicked my legs harder until I was through the gap and out into the water. I couldn't see Sarah and tried to shout out to her, but it was useless.

The gush of water in the helicopter had shocked me, but now it was chilling me through to my bones, and I knew I wouldn't be able to last long in it. My heart was seizing, and my core temperature had plummeted within the last few seconds. As I tried to swim to the surface, my body was suddenly wracked with a tremor. I swam desperately towards the chunks of ice, found one and grabbed hold of it, but then more tremors broke through me, and I focused all my mental energy on trying to stop them. But they kept coming, sharper and sharper. Here came another one. Clench, tighten, stop it, shut it down. I was losing control. Soon they would take me over completely. The effort was getting to me, and I realized my cognitive faculties were being affected. If this continued, my body would shut down, and death would soon follow.

This realization strengthened my mind and I kicked upwards with more force. Finally, I saw the surface of the water coming to meet me. I kicked and kicked again, until I reached the surface and was breathing, my teeth chattering as I caught my breath and took in great lungfuls of air.

We had crashed on the coastline of one of the islands, with the cockpit submerged in the water and the rest of the helicopter jutting out of it. I looked around for Sarah and saw her a few feet away, her head out of the water but her arms flailing. I looked up and immediately spotted the Russians above us. They were quite a long way up but had already begun descending, and they had seen us, too:

machine-gun fire immediately split the water, and men were starting to climb out of the cockpit and down ropes.

With my arms still quaking, I grabbed hold of part of the skids and hoisted myself up onto the shoreline. Then I began making my way around the rocks to get closer to Sarah.

'Grab hold of me!' I shouted at her, stretching out my arm. I caught hold of her hand and pulled as hard as I could, hauling her onto the rocks.

She gasped and then coughed up water. Her eyes started to close.

'Don't give up now,' I whispered. 'Please don't give up now.'

Perhaps she heard me, because she placed the palms of her hands against the rocks and lifted herself to her knees.

I helped her to her feet and pointed to a line of woods behind us.

'Can you run?' I said.

She nodded dully, and we started making towards the woods. There were patches of snow and black ice, but adrenalin and the survival instinct had kicked in and we somehow managed to make our way across them. We had to get to cover. I couldn't have come this far to fail.

We reached the top of a slope and I looked out at a large field, lit by the moon. There were trees all around the perimeter, but the field itself was completely barren – just grass, broken up with patches of snow and ice. No cover. Behind us, the sound of the rotors was almost deafening. I resisted the urge to look, but clearly we couldn't go back down that way. Should we skirt the edge of the field and try to get around to the other side? That would be too obvious, and too time-consuming.

We had to find people, and warmth. There was a barn with white window frames at the far end of the field and, closer, an *utedass* – an outhouse. I turned to point it out to Sarah, but she wasn't there. I looked frantically back at where we had just come from, but she had disappeared. She must have fallen, and I couldn't see her in the snow over a ridge. I began to run back towards the water when a burst of machine-gun fire broke through the trees, cracking in my ears and making me drop to the ground instinctively.

Fuck.

I started running towards the *utedass*.

I had misjudged the situation horribly. Sarah was in worse shape than I had realized, and the Russians were much closer than I'd thought – gunfire clattered behind me before I was even halfway across the stretch, and the helicopter was now coming down to land in the field. I kept running, my arms starting to flail and my legs feeling like they might give way, heading for the door of the outhouse and praying it wouldn't be the last thing I saw before the bullets hit me in the back. I reached the door and opened it, then slammed it behind me.

It was pitch dark and, unsurprisingly, smelled foul. The gunfire had stopped for a moment, and I wondered if somehow I had fooled them and they'd lost sight of me. But then I heard a voice, and recognized it at once.

'Nobody move!' shouted Sasha. 'Hold your fire until I say.' His voice was controlled, confident. He was no stamp collector any more. I leaned forward a fraction of an inch and peered through a slat in the wood. There he was, his silhouette clear against the background of snow. He was packed up in a winter coat, *ushanka* still in place. And one gloved hand was gripping Sarah by the arm. She was hanging off him, crying, and I thought I could see the tears freezing on her cheeks. He looked triumphant, like a hunter with his prize.

'Come on, Paul!' he shouted, his voice echoing off the trees. 'Time to come out now.'

There was a small bench surrounding the toilet, and I climbed onto it. I prised the lid away, my thumbs shaking, and immediately recoiled at the stench. But the hole looked too small. I kicked at the side of it with the sole of my boot until the wood splintered and the hole widened. Then I held my shoulders tightly together, and lowered myself into it. The edges chafed against my skin through the wet clothes but I was in. I felt my legs sink into the frozen dried shit and piss and leaves, and vomit rose in my throat. I was in a small dugout under the outhouse – as I had hoped, it was open all around. And beyond me were trees. I ran blindly towards them. I must have gone fifty yards before I heard Sasha shouting again. But I was away from the Russians by then – for the moment.

XVI

I watched as Sasha and several men marched across the field towards the barn, dragging Sarah along with them. Having run far enough into the trees to be out of their line of sight, I'd picked up a piece of brush and swept away the tracks behind me. I hadn't spent as much time on it as I would usually have done, though, because everything I did now had to be a compromise. I had to take precautions if I wanted to stay alive, and if I wanted to get Sarah back. But the longer I took, the less likely it was that I would be able to reach the U-boat.

Once I was confident that I'd gone far enough in, I headed towards a ridge that overlooked the far corner of the field, and climbed onto the lower branches of a large pine. It was called the Fish Hook, a simple if unexpected manoeuvre, and it meant I could observe my hunters and get an idea of their strength and what equipment they'd brought with them.

Apart from Sarah, I could make out two others in the field: Sasha and another man. Both of them looked heavily armed, but Sasha's companion was also carrying a case, which even in the moonlight I recognized as being the type they had used in the war to carry long-range transceivers. Presumably the rest of the company had been dispersed to look for me.

Sasha knocked on the door of the cottage, and after a few seconds a man opened it. I couldn't see his face, but no doubt he was alarmed at the sight of Russian soldiers with a female prisoner. Sasha gestured with his arms, pointing back towards the helicopter. Perhaps the bastard was claiming that Sarah was an injured member of his party. The door opened more widely, and Sasha, his companion and Sarah stepped into the cottage.

I lowered myself from the branches and glanced through the thicket of trees at the small bay: I could make out the ripple of water under the sky, and some bulky shapes dotted in the trees: more cottages, or perhaps boathouses? It was so quiet one could hardly imagine that there were Soviet operatives hunting me out there, but Sasha would have sent a few and they would be searching for my tracks with torches.

It was equally hard to imagine that this place might soon

be contaminated by fallout, but that too was real. The Soviets would want to stop me from reaching the West as a matter of course, but I had now made it across the border and they were still chasing me – and they were shooting to kill. The fact that Sasha was here confirmed that the situation hadn't changed since I'd left Moscow this morning. The fools thought I was trying to reach someone in authority in the West so I could warn them they were about to be attacked. Brezhnev had held his hand so far, but it looked like he was still poised to launch a strike against the West, and wanted to make sure that if he did he kept it a surprise.

It was also interesting that it had been Sasha in the helicopter, not Yuri. That suggested that *he* was the Proshin who had called Raaitikainen, not Yuri. So he was Yuri's son – why hadn't I realized it before? Well, they didn't look much alike. It made perfect sense, though. Yuri had been my first handler, and Sasha had been my last. It also explained why Sasha had been so surly towards me in Moscow: he had joined the GRU to follow in his old man's footsteps and had risen through the ranks, but had been taken off proper work by his father to deal with me, and he resented it. I knew the feeling.

It also seemed that Sasha had been given the task of finding and eliminating me, as well as a hunter-killer unit with which to do it. I'd been part of a similar group once, but that was twenty-four years ago. These men were half my age, in peak physical condition and no doubt hungry for my blood on account of Bessmertny and whatever else they'd been told I'd done. Once they had found and killed me, Sasha would signal back to Moscow and Brezhnev would launch his strike on the West – provided he was prepared to wait even that long. There was always the possibility that Sasha would signal that they were still hunting me, and he felt the time was optimal.

I was alive for the time being, but what was my best course of action now? I was on an island in the middle of the Baltic, but I had no idea which one. It might not even be anywhere near Söderviken. I was soaked to the skin, my face was smeared with blood and faeces, and I was in the danger zone for hypothermia. The tremors hadn't returned, thankfully, but my heart rate had dramatically increased after we'd crashed into the water and my entire body had tensed up, so it was taking time for it to calm down again.

I hugged myself for warmth, and wondered if I should remove my clothes. They had stuck to my skin, and my shoes were starting to break apart. In 1945, I'd brought plastic bags to place over my socks, and then another pair of socks to place over the bags, in case I had been stranded and had needed to stop the onset of frostbite. There wasn't much chance of that happening now, but it was still below freezing: icicles were hanging from the lower fronds of the tree. I was losing heat because my clothes were wet, and my training dictated that I remove them and make a fire to dry them. But I didn't have time to do that, and being naked even for a short while in this environment would probably worsen my state. I might also need to approach one of the locals, and a man in wet clothes with shit all over his face would still be more welcome than a naked one. I decided to keep my clothes on for the time being.

My only advantage against Sasha and his men was that I was alone. Although that thought wasn't exactly comforting, because they had Sarah, it also meant that I could move much more easily than they could. There were thousands of islands here, and thousands of trees, outhouses and barns dotted among them: they couldn't begin to search them all. I also had a slim psychological advantage: the Russians had massively outnumbered the Finns in 1940, and had had a rude awakening. They would be keenly aware of this, and if any of them had fathers who had died in the war a part of them would be afraid to be in Finland. Angry and determined to find me, yes – but also a little afraid.

It was also an advantage that Sasha was here, and that he had brought that transceiver. If I could reach the canisters, get them out of the water and show them to him, I might still have a chance. If I could prove that the injuries at the bases were part of an accidental leak, he could then transmit a message to that effect back to Moscow. If he did, it would hold a lot more sway than if it came from an official in the Soviet consulate in Åland, which had been my plan to date.

But the new plan meant I would have to *let* them hunt me. I'd have to keep them just close enough that they would be on hand when I reached the mustard gas. But not so close that they could kill me before then. It was a tall order, but it was all I could think of. My first task was to find a diving suit.

I sat in the tree watching, and then Sasha and the other man came out of the barn and began walking towards the north-eastern edge of the field, where there was a dirt road. I waited a few more minutes for them to make their way down the path, then slowly lowered myself out of the branches.

As I picked up a piece of brush, I registered movement in my peripheral vision, but before I could turn I was pushed back by the force of a kick to my chest and lost my balance. I thudded into the trunk of the tree, and as I tried to regain my breath, I caught sight of my assailant: his face was streaked with mud and he was raising a gun at me. He brought his forearm down in a scything motion and I leapt to my right. As I did, I caught one of the branches with my hand and it sprang back and scratched the Russian's face. He cursed, and tried to aim again, so I dived for his feet and brought him down. He landed on the back of his head, his gun falling from his hand. I leaned over and punched him in the jaw, but my chest was tight with pain and the swing was slow as a result – it hardly made any impact. He kicked out again and his boot caught me in the shoulder. He started scrabbling towards his gun, which lay a few inches away from him on the ground. I knew he was going to make it, and turn and shoot me through the eyes. Desperate, I raised my arms for the branch above me and caught hold of something cold and wet. An icicle. I snapped it off and brought it down as hard as I could, and the point penetrated his throat before he had a chance to scream.

I retrieved the pistol, another Makarov, and placed it next to me. I started to strip off his trousers, which were nice and dry, but then a loud squelching sound burst from him and I froze. It was coming from beneath his jacket, which I removed to reveal a vest with several large pouches. Grenade, signal flare, knife, rations – and a small receiver.

The static cut off, and a voice broke through.

'*Medov, Zelenin, this is Rook – any sign of the target?*'

It was Sasha.

There was another burst of static, and then a new voice: '*This is Medov. No sign of him here.*'

Static, then Sasha came on again.

'*Zelenin, how about you?*'

I stared down at Zelenin's chest, panic sweeping through me. I couldn't reply – Sasha would recognize my voice at once. Even if I tried to disguise it, he would still know I wasn't Zelenin. But if I didn't answer, he would reason that I might have killed Zelenin and send men back this way to find me.

There was no time to waste. I put the pistol and transmitter in my pockets, then stumbled through the trees, my chest aching from the high kick, my body numb with cold. Fifteen agonizing minutes later I found a small cottage in a clearing, and I climbed the steps to the door and hammered on it. A woman opened it halfway, and peered out. She was old, with matted grey hair, and wore a faded blue dress and a white shawl. I pushed past her and staggered into the hallway, my eyes adjusting to the light and taking in the simple pine furniture, a fireplace, a kettle on a stove.

'I need your help,' I said in Swedish, my breathing coming hard. 'Please . . . Please call Degerby police station and ask for Constable Lundström.'

I took in her look of fear and astonishment, and then my legs buckled and I fell to the floor.

*

Someone was shaking me by the shoulder, and I opened my eyes. Looking up, I recognized the old woman, and asked her how long I had been out.

'Not long,' she said. 'Perhaps half an hour.'

I was still on the floor, and I rose to my feet. My chest felt constricted and I was aching all over, but my head was clear. Half an hour was a hell of a long time.

'The Russians. Have you seen any?'

She shook her head, and I realized she was frightened. I had a gun on my hip.

'I don't mean you any harm,' I said, and very slowly removed the pistol and placed it on a sideboard covered in lace, next to an antique clock. Her shoulders relaxed a little.

'Did you call Lundström in Degerby?' I asked.

She nodded. 'He said he would come at once – but Degerby is quite far away. I think you should clean up and get out of those clothes. I have some for you if you would like them.'

She led me to a small but spotless bathroom, where she had laid out a shirt, a pair of narrow twill trousers and calf-high boots. There was also a basin, which she had filled with water, and beside it a towel. I thanked her, and she bowed her head and closed the door.

I removed my shirt and dipped my head in the basin, rubbing off all the shit – no wonder she had looked frightened of me. There was a glass by the tap, and I poured water into it and gulped it down, then poured some more and gulped that too.

Sarah had been captured.

I removed the rest of my clothes and climbed into the ones the old woman had left for me. They were a reasonable fit, and they were dry. I would have liked to have washed properly and treated some of my aches and pains, but there was no time for that.

Sasha and his men would now be searching every inch of this area for me, and could get here before Lundström. As if to emphasize this point, there was a burst of noise from the pile of clothes on the floor, and I reached into the trouser pocket and took out the radio receiver.

'*Medov to Rook. Current location Map C, J11. Boathouse empty.*'

'*Rook to Medov. Any sign of disturbance?*'

'*None, Rook. There are several cottages along this section — I will move on to them now.*'

'*Understood. Report back in ten minutes. We have three hours to find him.*'

The device went silent.

Three hours to find me.

I had imagined I'd seen a nuclear attack when I'd been captured at the border, but part of me had refused to believe it was possible, despite hearing Brezhnev order the missiles primed myself. Sasha's presence here in Finland confirmed that the Russians wanted to stop me from warning anyone they were about to attack, but even that hadn't quite convinced me. The message on the receiver had. There was only one reason I could think of for them needing to finding me within the next three hours: it must be the deadline they had been given by Moscow. If they hadn't stopped me by then, Brezhnev was going to go ahead and launch a strike anyway. After that, it wouldn't be long before R-hour.

I poured some more water and sipped at it, but I'd lost my thirst. I stared at the glass in my hand, at the meniscus of the water curving up to meet the sides of it. From this angle the surface was like a silvery-grey ridge, and gave the illusion of being a separate object from the water. I replaced the glass on the basin, suddenly transfixed by the surface of the water. In my mind's eye, it was as though the water was the world, and the air above it what would happen to it after a nuclear attack. Those two separate realities were only held apart by that thin silvery line between them: me.

Focus, Paul.

I picked up the transmitter and returned to the living room, where the woman was placing logs on the fire.

'Thank you for the clothes,' I said. 'They're a good fit.'

She turned to look at me.

'They belonged to my husband,' she said, her eyes cavernous. 'He died last spring.'

Jesus. What had I walked into here?

There was a banging noise. The door. We both froze. I reached for the Makarov on the sideboard, and she shuffled to the door and unlocked it. A man in a police uniform, clutching a Lahti pistol, stepped into the room, his face weather-beaten and shaven, but nevertheless familiar.

'Kjell Lundström?' I said.

He lowered the pistol and furrowed his brow.

'No, I'm his son, Jan.'

He was slimmer than his father, but otherwise had come to resemble him in the intervening years.

'Thank God!' I said. 'I need to find a diving suit at once. Can you help?'

He stared at me for a few moments and then a look of recognition crossed his face.

'You are the British lieutenant-colonel who came here in 1945.'

'Yes!' I said, surprised that he'd even remembered my rank. 'But I'm afraid there's no time for catching up. I desperately need to find a diving suit – there's a German U-boat on the seabed a few miles south of Söderviken, and I need to get to it – fast.'

I led him into the hallway and quickly told him the story. His eyes widened, but he nodded his head rapidly. 'You're in luck,' he said. 'I know where the coastguards keep all their equipment, and I believe they have a few diving suits there.'

'Great. How do we get there?'

He stretched out a hand, and gave a slightly crooked smile.

'Come with me.'

*

We bid goodbye to the woman, and left her in her cottage in the woods, perhaps wondering if the world was about to end. I brought along the Makarov and the radio receiver. Lundström had a small speedboat tied up by the jetty, and as we walked down to it I asked him how his father was doing. His mouth tightened fractionally, and he told me he had died some years previously.

'I'm sorry to hear that,' I said. 'I didn't know him, but he seemed like a good man.'

Lundström nodded, his eyes focused straight ahead. 'He was,' he said quietly.

We climbed aboard. He took the wheel and I seated myself on a low bench, taking in the smells of diesel and grease. The water was wreathed in a low mist, the surface stippled with flecks of moonlight. The helicopter had crashed in a cluster of islands called Kumlinge, and now we were heading for an island called Storklubb, or Klobbo in local dialect. Lundström handed me a torch and I shone it ahead of us to light the way. As we left the bay through bobbing buoys, small islets started to hove into view, but

Lundström didn't slow for them and we passed through smoothly. I noticed a small pile of greyish-white stones had been arranged on the tip of one of the islets, contrasting against the pink granite beneath, and guessed he was also using them to navigate.

He had explained that the coastguards had several stations on the island, but that this one had diving equipment stored in a cabin away from the barracks building, and that he was confident we could creep in. He knew where they kept the key. 'There are few secrets in this place,' he said. 'Especially if you're in law enforcement.'

We were going at about fifteen knots, I thought, and every few seconds we crested a wave and cold spray hit my face and froze my jaw.

'There should be some clothes under there,' he shouted over the noise of the motor, pointing to a line of low cupboards under the seating. 'I'd advise you to put on some more layers, because it will be even colder when we get out there.'

I bent down and slid one of the cupboards open and found an old rollneck sweater, which I pulled over my head, and a pair of canvas trousers, which I placed over the dead husband's. Lundström looked like a gun dog focused on a bird: with this man's help, I might be able to make it. I just had to hope that Sarah was still in one piece. I tried to focus on the task ahead. Once I got hold of the diving suit, I would have to try to locate the U-boat and dive for the canisters. But then I would have to get them out of the water, and find Sasha again . . .

I let my thoughts spin away as the smell of pines and seaweed carried on the air. We crested a large wave and spray covered the windscreen, obscuring the view for a second. Lundström had gone quiet, his face set. He took a large map from the dashboard and consulted it. Then he cut the motor.

'We'll be coming in soon,' he said.

He steered with a more intense concentration until, about five minutes later, we came to a pass between two small islands. Lundström slowed the boat and headed towards the one on the left. He climbed out and swiftly jumped onto the shore, tying the ropes to a metal ring attached to the remains of a small wooden quay, one half of which had fallen apart.

'Ryssbryggan,' he said, as I joined him on shore and tied the other rope. 'We used to be part of the Russian Empire, you know. They built this back in the First World War.' He finished tying up and looked across at me. 'I hate the fucking Russians,' he added. His jaw clenched for a moment, and then slackened again.

The jetty led onto a narrow dirt track through dense bushes and foliage, and we swiftly made our way along it, taking care to keep our heads down. 'That's their barracks,'

Lundström whispered after a couple of minutes, pointing to a greyish-white building in a clearing ahead. 'But they keep the diving equipment in there.' He pointed to a tiny cabin with white window frames positioned a few dozen feet away from the main building, right on the water.

We ducked down and started crawling through a brush of long grass. Now I saw that there was a jetty here as well, but that it was occupied by several patrol boats – Sea-Hounds or something similar – which was presumably why we'd come via the broken quay instead.

Crack.

I sat, frozen still in the grass. It was just some twigs breaking under my feet, but had anyone inside the barracks heard the noise? The outline of Lundström's head was just visible against the deep blue of the sky a few feet ahead of me, and he was utterly still. The wind rustled near us, the water lapped softly against the side of the jetty, but there were no other sounds. Finally, Lundström ducked his head; he raised the palm of his hand and gestured for me to come forward.

Less than twenty seconds later we were at the edge of the cabin. Lundström crawled onto a small step leading to the door and I saw him feeling around with his hands until he lifted a key from a ledge beneath the step. Then he pawed his way up until he was in the doorway and stood. He beckoned me to join him again and I did. He looked at me for a moment, then inserted the key. He turned it. The click sounded terribly loud in the silence, and we waited to see if anything responded. When nothing did, he slowly eased the door open, and we stepped inside.

It was even darker than it had been outside, but after a few seconds my eyes began to adjust. We were in a small hallway with two wooden doors, similar to the one we had just come through. Lundström reached for the handle of the door to the right, then leaned his shoulder into it and opened it. I followed him into a room that felt a little larger than the hallway, but which was yet darker.

'In here,' Lundström whispered from the far corner, and I walked towards the sound of his voice. I heard him unhook a latch and he told me to go in ahead of him, which I did, but at the last moment something registered – heat – and I tried to pull back, but it was too late because I felt a rough shove at the base of my neck and I stumbled and fell to the floor. I heard the door slam shut and the latch hooking into place. It was lighter here, but incredibly hot, and I looked around the room with growing fear.

This wasn't a storage room for diving equipment. It was a sauna.

*

'Jan!' I shouted out, but there was no response. Understanding swept over me. Lundström had lured me here so he could lock me in. And he had left me here to burn to death.

The heat was unbelievably intense, and my clothes were already soaked in sweat. I tore at them frantically, struggling with the boots and then kicking them off. I grabbed the gun from my pocket, but realized at once that it was too light: he'd emptied it – presumably when I'd been putting on more clothes at his suggestion.

I looked around again and began to make out a few more items in the room. There was a rectangular window low in the wall on the right and through it I glimpsed reeds and rushes and a stretch of water. Most of the room was taken up with two benches in the shape of steps to sit on, and below them was a basket filled with small wooden logs, presumably firewood for the stove. Some metal crowbars rested against the wall – perhaps to open the window? I reached for them, but they burned my hands, so I went for the wood instead. Slightly cooler. I threw one of the logs at the window, but it just bounced back at me comically. I could hardly see straight now, because sweat was pouring into my eyes, making them sting. I wanted to wipe them but my hands were also soaked and I thought I'd probably just make them worse.

As I was trying to think what to do next, a loud hissing sound made me jump. After a couple of seconds I realized what it was, as my chest started to burn up as though someone had lit a blowtorch inside me. Lundström hadn't left; he had just poured water on the stove. Somewhere behind the pain I registered that this offered me some kind of leverage, but I struggled to grip the thought for long enough to follow it through, because the pain was so searing. I wanted to scream in agony, but if I did that I might bring the coastguards running, and with them ruin any chances I might have of stopping Brezhnev from going ahead with his strike. I grunted and groaned instead, biting my upper lip and tasting the hot sweat pouring off me. I crouched as close to the ground as I could but resisted the urge to lie down because I wasn't sure if I did that I'd have the strength to get back up.

And then the hissing came again. The thought came into my mind that I was experiencing pure fear. In London during the war, the V2s had panicked everyone because the sound of their falling had been heard only after they had done their damage. But this was how terror really worked: the sound came first, then a delay, and finally the inevitable. And here it came: the heat rising again, so fast I felt my skin was going to burn off and my internal organs catch fire.

I wanted to detach my mind so I wasn't as aware of the pain, but I knew it was crucial to hold on to my thoughts if I wanted to survive. A lucid thought broke in now: he must be opening the door to add water, and judging by the speed with which he was doing it the stove was probably very near the door. If I could muster the strength to reach it, perhaps I could get out, or at least stop him from pouring on any more water. I crawled in the direction of the heat, but it was agonizing and my skin started to sting as though it were about to bleed or peel off, and I recoiled instinctively. I had to fight my instincts, but it was getting harder to think straight.

'You murdered my father,' said a voice, startling me. It was Lundström, and the gentle tone he'd used before was now choked with rage. He hadn't left me here, but was standing outside the door making sure I couldn't escape. I turned to find the precise location of his voice – he was talking to me through the crack in the door.

'Jan!' I said. 'Please, for the love of God let me out of here so we can talk about this. I have no idea what you're talking about, but I can assure you I had nothing to do with your father's death—'

'You had everything to do with it!' He laughed bitterly. 'You have no idea how many times I thought of trying to find you. Once I even planned a trip to England, but I soon realized it was useless. I knew so little about you. But now here you are; you've fallen into my lap. It must be fate.'

I tried to move nearer to the door again, but the waves of heat were still too strong.

'For Christ's sake!' I said. 'Please open this fucking door before we all die!'

He laughed again. 'You think I believed your crazy story about the world being on the brink of a nuclear war? No. You are on a mission, naturally, but that is surely not what it's about. You claim to be the great hero who has come to rescue us all but I know who you really are, and what you're doing. You are using me, just as you used my father. But I will not make the same mistake he did, which was to believe you.'

Had he gone mad? He sounded it. He threw more water onto the stove and the heat came again, spreading through me even more rapidly. My eyes felt like they were bulging from my head, and that they might disconnect. I wondered how much more of this I could take, and whether or not I could find a way to end it. Just slip to the ground. Yes, how easy that would be. The world can hang. We'll all be dead anyway . . .

No, think, *think*. There must be some way out of here. Get to the door – he is pouring water on the stove through a gap in the door.

'The Russians came to see us the morning after you left,' he said. 'Pappa stonewalled them, and said he had never heard of any British agents visiting. But he was not a good liar, or they had other evidence. They went away but returned shortly after, with a very cruel man in charge –

I think he had come from Moscow. He didn't believe Pappa's story, and so he had come out himself to question him. He brought several other men with him, and some . . . equipment. They took Pappa to a basement in their head-quarters in Mariehamn and tortured him for three days. When that didn't work, they locked him inside a sauna much like this one and tried to boil him alive. By the end of it, he had told them everything – about you, the U-boat captain and the other agent. Now you are here, and I am going to make you suffer as they made Pappa suffer. I have a sauna nearly every day, and I know very well just how to make it hurt you: how much water to pour on, how long to wait. You'll see.'

I believed him.

'The man from Moscow,' I said, struggling to breathe. 'What was his name?'

'I don't remember.'

'Can you describe him?'

There was no answer.

'Please, Jan, I promise you I had no intention of any of that happening. But this is important. Do you remember what he looked like?'

'He was evil, that is all I can say. He looked like a . . . like a little boy, or a troll. He was pure evil.'

I fell back onto the bench.

Yuri.

Yuri had been here in 1945 – before he had recruited me in Germany.

I heard the hiss and knew what I had to do. I had about a second before the heat would hit me again. I leapt towards the door and slammed my shoulder into it, breaking it open. I lunged forward and grabbed Lundström by the collar as he stumbled backwards, his arms flailing. I brought my right hand down hard onto his wrist and gripped it, then swivelled into a half-turn and swung my other hand around to grab the barrel of the Lahti from below, jerking it back until it was parallel with the ground. He let out a scream as his trigger finger snapped, and the pistol dropped into my hand.

It was a heavy pistol. It reminded me of Father's Luger. I trained it on him.

'I'm sorry about your father,' I said. 'But there are more important things at the moment. Make another sound and I'll blow your head off. Understand?'

He nodded, his eyes darting wildly. He was still clutching a ladle in one hand and I took it from him and dropped it in a bucket of water on the floor. The steam was still blasting in the sauna behind me, and a thought came to me. 'How did you know it would be on?' I said. 'The sauna.'

'I know the coastguards. They have saunas every Monday night and it's someone's job to prepare it. So I knew it would already be hot.'

'What time do they have their sauna?'

'Midnight.'

I checked the watch on his wrist.

'That's in fifteen minutes. You meant to kill me before then? What if I hadn't died that fast and they had interrupted?'

He gave a cruel smile. 'They would understand. Half the people on this island know who you are, and what you did to my father.'

Enough. There was no time for this. I pressed the pistol against the back of his neck.

'Where can I find diving equipment?'

I had a couple of questions, but this was the most important one. I had to get to those canisters. But he didn't answer, and just glared at me.

'I don't know.'

I swivelled him round so he was facing me.

'Give me your best guess. You told me yourself there are few secrets here.'

He didn't respond, just jutted out his chin and glared. Generals in Moscow were debating launching a nuclear strike, and this man might be my only chance of stopping it.

'Tell me where I can find diving equipment or I'll shoot.'

Nothing – only a clench of his jaw, his eyes wild with fury. I couldn't get to the U-boat without a diving suit. If he knew enough to know the timetables of the coastguards' saunas, there had to be a good chance he would know where to find a suit. But he was stubborn. Perhaps he wanted me to kill him. Perhaps he was so mad he'd forgotten what fear was. No – he'd known how to scare me well enough. It gave me an idea. I grabbed him by the neck until he was standing, then motioned to the door of the sauna with the pistol.

'Get in,' I said.

He shook his head.

'Get in now!'

He opened the door and I pushed him into the space I'd been in just a few minutes earlier. A blast of heat hit me as I stepped in after him, and my skin prickled at the memory of the pain. Lundström had already started sweating. I grabbed one of his hands and placed the palm above the burning coals of the stove.

'Where can I find diving equipment?'

I thought I saw fear growing in his eyes then, but he didn't answer.

I slammed his hand down onto the coals, and he shrieked out. I removed it immediately – it had only been on for a fraction of a second. But it was enough.

'Next door,' he gasped, and pointed to the room adjacent.

I locked the sauna door then ran through and turned

the light on. It was a dressing room: there was a line of towels and a poster illustrating the health benefits of the sauna. And laid out all along the benches and on the floor was diving equipment: suits, masks and air tanks. I found the suit that looked the newest, then picked up a mask and an attached hose and air tank, the mark Aga Divator.

Carrying my bounty over my arm, I returned to Lundström, who was whimpering and weeping with the pain.

'I'm sorry about your father,' I said. 'I never meant for that to happen. But I never said I was a hero.'

I locked the door behind me, then walked down the steps and headed through the bushes, back towards the jetty.

XVII

Lundström's map was just under the dashboard. I took it
out and located Storklubb and Söderviken on it. It was
thirty-six nautical miles away, but from memory the U-
boat was easily found once at Söderviken. I started the boat
up slowly, then once I'd reached open water took her as
fast as she could go. The horizon was barely visible in the
darkness, but my mind was cold and clear: now I was the
gun dog.

I reached the area around Söderviken about an hour and
a half later. In 1945, I'd been sure that the hatch leading to
the crew's quarters had been sealed tightly. Clearly I'd been
wrong, but had it just cracked open a little, allowing the

liquid in the canisters to leak out through it, or had it opened entirely, in which case the canisters themselves might have floated out? If the latter had happened, I might get down to the U-boat only to find there were no canisters left, having floated off miles away. So I divided up the map into quadrants around the area to make it easier to search, then cut my speed and began drifting on the waves, looking for any telltale signs.

A wind was picking up, and I urged it to pass by – I could only dive if it remained calm, so a storm now would scupper everything. It was also playing tricks on my ears, and I kept imagining I heard the sound of an approaching helicopter. The thought of that filled me with dread. If Sasha and his men found me floating out here now, it was all over. But if I could get to the canisters first . . .

I took out the radio transmitter and looked it over. It had gone silent, but that might be because they had found Zelenin's body and realized I'd taken it, and didn't want to give me any more information by broadcasting anything I could pick up. But it had survived the heat of the sauna, and if I could transmit with it that might be the way through.

I drifted between islets, trying to locate the spot where I'd gone down in 1945. But it all looked the same. Then, finally, I saw something emerge in an area that was in the far north-eastern quadrant of my map — it looked a shade darker. I accelerated towards it and my heart started pounding. Yes, there was oil on the surface: a long thin coil of it stretching into the distance, growing thicker.

This was it. This was where U-745 had sunk.

I quickly dressed in the wetsuit, which was thick and heavy but a great improvement on the Clammy Death, and attached the mask and breathing tank. In one of the cupboards under the dashboard I found some waterproof sacking and took it out so I would have something to put the canisters in. I cut the engine, gave a last check that all the valves were secured, and recited the magic lines:

Our plesance here is all vain glory,
This fals world is but transitory,
The flesh is bruckle, the Feynd is slee:
Timor mortis conturbat me.

Then I climbed overboard and slipped down into the water.

*

It was much darker underwater but I saw the U-boat at once, lying like a giant wounded shark on the bed. I swam towards it, suddenly afraid I would be unable to carry the canisters up in the bag. How many would be enough to convince Sasha that this was the source of the 'attacks' in Estonia? Just one, or would I need more?

I hit a cold current and wondered if I were well enough protected in the diving suit. Was it thick enough? I thought of the tremors that had nearly killed me when I'd crashed in the helicopter with Raaitikainen. I dismissed it from my mind: there was no point in worrying about such things now.

I reached the boat and swam through the main deck, then down the flight of stairs and into the loading bay. The corpses of some of the crew were still there, sitting just as they had been when I was here twenty-four years earlier, and as I had seen them sporadically in my nightmares since. There was a rubber-soled shoe jammed against the furred-up pipes, and I remembered that crewmen had worn those during attacks so as not to alert the enemy. One of the men seemed to be looking at his wristwatch, but half his face had collapsed in on itself, and tiny fish were swimming through the crevices of his eyes.

I grimaced and turned away, then rounded the corner to the place I remembered the canisters had been. As I did, my forebrain began tingling before my eyes registered it. There was a hole where the steel hatch leading to the officers' quarters should be. Something was terribly wrong. I swam through in a daze, but I already knew what I would find.

The canisters were gone.

XVIII

I let the waterproof bag drop from my hands, and swam through, seeing if perhaps they had dislodged somewhere. But they hadn't – they were gone. There had been twenty or thirty of them here in 1945. If the hatch had burst open, they could all have tumbled out. But someone had been down here and *cut* the hatch open. It was a neat rectangular hole, and could only be man-made.

Who had done this, and when? And, more importantly, what had caused the leak to the bases? My stomach clenched, horrified I could have been so wrong.

It had been an attack all along.

Yuri had been right, back in the bunker in Moscow. Following the discovery that I was a double, the Service would have combed through every single document related to my career, both to assess the damage and to see if there was anyone else who had covered my tracks or turned a blind eye to my behaviour. And at some point someone must have come across Templeton's report on my operation here in 1945, and that had revealed an unexpected prize: a lovely little chemical weapon sitting at the bottom of the Baltic.

This discovery would have woven its way through the in- and out-trays until someone at Porton Down had confirmed that Winterlost was extremely effective and was still very much worth getting hold of, and so they had decided to come back to see if the canisters were still here and could be retrieved. In 1945 I had had to come in by seaplane under cover to reach this wreck, but nowadays they could simply fly a team of divers to Helsinki via BEA. Under cover of a diving expedition or something similarly innocuous, they could have cut open the hatch, hauled the canisters onto a boat, and then slipped into the Gulf of Finland and released them into the water along the coast near Paldiski. Then they could have simply sailed away again, and waited for the stuff to seep onto the shoreline and do its damage. Personnel at two of the Soviets' naval bases would then be incapacitated, and nobody could be blamed.

But it had gone wrong, because the Soviets hadn't seen it that way. When they had discovered that the chemical wasn't known to them, they had guessed the truth – that it was an attack by the West. And I had unwittingly confirmed it by telling them about my operation here in '45.

All that remained to be discovered was whether the attack on the bases was isolated and had come coincidentally at the same time as the Americans were conducting some sort of an exercise in the air, or whether the two events were linked, and the B-52 flights weren't part of an exercise at all, but the prelude to a nuclear strike. If that were so, Yuri and the others had read the situation correctly. The Service could have been called upon by the Americans to offer a diversion. The attack at Paldiski in particular would disrupt one of the Soviets' nuclear submarine bases just as they would need it, but would also confuse and distract them while the Americans prepared to launch their surprise attack.

But in either case the injuries at Paldiski and Hiiumaa were not accidental, and that meant that I now had no leverage whatsoever – nothing with which I could convince Sasha, Yuri or Brezhnev not to proceed with their plans to strike. There was no way of getting around it now. We were heading straight towards a nuclear conflict.

Dazed by the realization, I swam towards the hatch, looking to go round it one last time before heading back up. As I passed the door, I saw something flapping against the lower edge of it in the current. The cut hadn't been entirely clean, and something had caught on a tiny thorn in the metal. I leaned down and saw it was a small scrap of canvas, stringy and decaying. I recognized it as the same material that had been used to wrap the canisters – one must have torn when they'd taken them out, and this piece had been stuck here since. A fragment of text was still visible on it: 'NTERLOST'.

It was in a black Gothic typeface, instantly recognizable as the one used by the Nazis. I stared at it, still stunned by the fact that Osborne or Innes or whoever it had been had sent a team here to get these canisters, all to attack the Soviets' bases. It was madness – tantamount to provoking a nuclear war.

And then another thought struck me, and it sent an army of ants scuttling across my scalp. It hadn't been Osborne and the others who had planned the attacks: it had been Yuri.

He also had files on me. He had interrogated me about them on a daily basis, methodically going through my career week by week, month by month. I had never told him about my operation here, but he'd known about it already. Lundström had just told me Yuri had been here in 1945, and had been trying to find out what had happened.

It didn't matter precisely how he'd done it, but I knew he

had. The Soviets had known about this secret all along. Perhaps they hadn't known the precise location of the boat; perhaps they'd been searching for it for a while. Yuri could have sent a small group of divers to retrieve the canisters, and then had them leaked to Estonia. I wasn't quite sure why yet, but it had to be something along those lines — because nobody in the West wanted to provoke a nuclear war.

I stared down at the scrap of material flapping from the door of the quarters for a moment. Then I leaned down and tried to prise it away with my fingers. It was caught fast. I tugged again, but realized that if I pulled too hard I might shred the surface even further and lose all remaining legibility of the fragment of text. Did I have enough oxygen in the tank to stay down here and unpick it? And what about Sasha's deadline of three hours? That must have nearly gone by now. I decided I would have to take it slowly despite both of these factors, because if I did pull too hard and that sliver of text vanished, all was lost anyway. I tried to set my panic aside and focus, but it was like weaving a thread through a needle and my fingers had started shaking. I placed my left hand around my right forearm to keep my grip in place like a clamp, and forced my fingers as far as they could go down the scrap. Then, as forcefully but with as much control as I could muster, I pulled at it. Slowly but surely, it spooled away from the thorn of metal, and into my hand. I turned it over. Yes, the letters were still legible.

I clenched it in my fist and swam back through the hatch. But as I came out of the boat, I saw a figure waiting for me in the water: a man in a diving suit. Sasha's dark beard sprouted from beneath the window of his helmet, and in one black-gloved hand he was clutching what looked like a pistol. He raised his hand and I jerked my body back without even thinking, only to see a plume of bubbles from the gun and hear a thudding boom behind me. I turned and watched as a thin dart bounced off the hull of the U-boat and spiralled down to the bed. A part of my brain registered that the Russians were rumoured to be developing a pistol that could fire darts underwater, but I couldn't remember anything about it. How many rounds could it fire? Was it four-barrelled? At this depth the aim would be compromised, as he'd just shown.

Sasha fired again, and this time the dart came very close to my feet, the force of the ripples spinning me away. I struggled to right myself but I'd lost orientation, and as I spun through the water I suddenly felt a blow to the back of my head. Had I hit the boat, or had it been Sasha? I flailed around, trying to lash out at him, but all I could see through my mask was a blur of movement and bubbles and then suddenly his eyes and mouth in the helmet. My oxygen was now getting close to running out, and I could feel my skull tightening under the pressure. I looked up and saw the surface of the water above me tilting with the waves, a separate reality from the world down here. I shut my eyes, feeling as though my head were about to explode, and swam upwards, praying I was moving away from Sasha.

I broke through the surface and gasped for air. I saw Lundström's boat immediately, floating on the waves, and began swimming towards it, but then I felt something slap me on the back. A hand gripped the inside of my diving suit and I was being hoisted onto land, patches of ice visible among the dark rocks, the wind howling around me. I looked up through water-clamped lashes and saw a man in camouflage, blond hair and blue eyes, his mouth snarling from the effort of lifting me. I tried to lash out but my strength had gone. He didn't seem to be trying to hurt me or shoot me so I let him pull me up. He dumped me onto a patch of ice as though I were a sack of coal, then moved away to some nearby rocks, and I saw that the case holding the transceiver was also there. He was the radio operator.

We were on a long, flat islet, and parked on it was the helicopter that had come for me earlier, squatting silently in the darkness. The radio operator shouted something and I looked over and saw that there was someone just a few yards away, standing by the water. He was wearing a leather coat. Yuri.

It took me another moment to register that there was a boy kneeling on the ice next to him and that he had the barrel of a gun pressed against his head, and a moment more to realize it wasn't a boy, it was Sarah, her short hair matted with sweat and her dress sticking to her skin. She was shivering and whimpering, and my stomach started contracting and I retched.

XIX

I clambered to my feet, my chest heaving and my head numb from being underwater, and screamed out at Yuri. He looked up at me and I thought I saw him smile.

'What do you have in your hand?' he shouted out at me. I looked down and realized that my fist was still clenched around the scrap of material I'd salvaged.

'Let her go!' I yelled again.

He held out his free hand. 'I would like you to bring me whatever you found down there. Or I will kill your girl-friend. Don't make me wait too long.'

I could hear Sarah sobbing, and saw a stream of saliva dripping from her mouth. Christ knew what he had put her through in the last few hours, and indeed in the last few months. I should never have brought her with me in the first place – I should have found a way of getting her to safety in Italy, and none of this would have happened. Her life now hung in the balance, and the tiny strip of canvas in my hand was all the leverage I had. But I couldn't give this to Yuri, because many more lives hung in the balance. Millions of lives, in London, Washington, Moscow . . .

'One last chance!' he called out. 'Come over here and give it to me.'

'I'm sorry, Sarah,' I said, and the tears came, finally – the tears for all the people I'd done this to.

Yuri fired, and I screamed as I saw the recoil and the impact. Part of me felt that if I made a lot of noise myself I could cancel out the sound of the shot and it wouldn't have really happened.

Sarah fell forwards, her body splaying out and the blood spreading across the ice. Yuri lifted his gun and turned to me, preparing to shoot, but there was a burst of noise behind me and I turned to see Sasha breaking through the surface of the water.

Yuri's hand froze in mid-air.

'Are you all right, son?' he shouted, and he began to walk over the ice towards us. Sasha grabbed hold of the rocks and climbed ashore, gasping for air as I had done. I stumbled towards him and put out a hand to lift him up. He looked at me with shock, and as he came level with me I grabbed him with my other hand and passed him the fragment of the label.

He looked down at it, then peered at me, his eyes scanning my face. His expression turned from puzzlement to horror and then to slow realization. He looked up at his colleague, who was coming down to meet him. 'Get the radio!' he shouted. And then, to Yuri, who was now just a few feet away: 'Don't shoot him, Father — he was telling the truth. There was mustard gas down there. Look.' He opened his hand to show him the fragment. 'We must tell Moscow at once and make sure they cancel the command.'

Yuri stopped walking and stared down at his son. 'You fool!' he said. 'It makes no difference if there was mustard gas down there — the British have taken it and used it against us.'

'It's over, Yuri,' I said. 'You may be able to pull the wool over Sasha's eyes, but you can't pull it over mine. I'm no longer the boy you met in Germany in 1945.'

He turned to me and sneered, his face creasing so that his eyes nearly disappeared in the wrinkles. 'That wasn't the first time we met, comrade. For a while I was even afraid you might remember it. I've been told I have a memorable face. But you never made the connection. Then again, you have missed rather a lot of connections.'

'What the hell are you talking about?'

He looked out across the water, sniffing the sea air. 'I'm talking about New Year's Eve, 1939, in the Shepherd's Hotel,

Cairo. You were fourteen. Your father introduced us, very briefly, and I asked you about school. And you were so pleased with yourself, because you were just about to enter a new one. Do you remember now?'

I remembered. It had been a wild party, one of the last before the war, and in some ways my induction into the adult world: I'd smoked my first cigarette and drunk my first cocktail that night, marvelling at the beautiful women in their evening gowns and the men chasing them around. I had danced in a heaving line to 'Auld Lang Syne' and nearly been crushed during the countdown as the crowd had roared in the new year, followed by the flags waving, the confetti and everyone embracing each other in the hot sticky Egyptian night. And yes, at one point in the evening Father had introduced me to a funny little Russian who had leaned over and asked me about school, and I had proudly told him I was going to Winchester next term.

The funny little Russian didn't seem so funny now.

'So you knew my father in Cairo,' I said.

'Yes. That was where we met, in fact, and where I recruited both him and Colin Templeton. It's a strange thing: I had hoped your father might become Chief of the Service one day, but in the end it was Templeton who did. But Colin was in the Army back then – how could I have guessed that things would turn out the way they did?

Life has a strange way of working out sometimes, doesn't it?'

Templeton a traitor. 'Why?' I said, my mouth trying to catch up with all the thoughts swirling around my brain. 'Why?'

He tugged at his goatee as though I'd set him a mathematical puzzle. 'Why did they decide to serve us, you mean? Well, as you are no longer a boy and we are now so close to the endgame, perhaps it's time you learned the truth. Which is that they had no choice.'

'I don't understand,' I said. And I wasn't sure I wanted to.

'Oh,' he said, 'have you still not joined the dots? I photographed them, you see. I kept the negatives and persuaded both of them to serve as my agents, or their wives and superiors would receive copies of them, and they would be ruined. But I did it separately with each of them, you see. That was the genius of it! Neither knew I had recruited the other. Well, not at first. Your father eventually found out what I'd done, in Germany, shortly before I shot him.'

'You're saying he and Templeton . . .'

'Yes.'

I stared at him, anger rising from my stomach to my chest, making it hard for me to breathe. Father had always been a man's man: a record-breaking racing driver, a decorated commando. He had loathed 'queers', and that had been part of the reason I'd loathed him. But now I saw that this was precisely the cover he would have used if Yuri were telling the truth. Another thought struck me: Mother. Had he used her political views as a pretext to get her locked way, so that he could continue with his secret life?

No. It was unthinkable.

'You're lying,' I said. 'For some sick reason, you're lying.'

Yuri tilted his head to one side, amusement at my distress glinting in those evil little eyes. 'I'm afraid not, Paul. It's the truth, although they both did everything in their power to hide it from the rest of the world. You should know that many men suffer from this affliction, even those with families and children. Knowledge of this fact has served me well in my career, and that of several of my colleagues, for that matter. Burgess was always shameless about his disease, almost proud of it, but others have not been. I have found that men with secrets can be easily manipulated. Homosexuals also often make for excellent agents, because they have already spent years deceiving everyone they know – a lifetime of training, if you will. And your father and Templeton were not just casual lovers – they believed they were *in love with each other*, if you can imagine such a thing! Why do you think Templeton kept you so close to him after your father died, and nurtured your career as he did? You were his lover's son. No doubt you reminded him of your father. Perhaps he even imagined . . .'

I lunged at him, but he took a step back and I stumbled and fell onto the ice, exhausted and defeated. Yuri raised his arm and aimed the pistol at me.

'I think it is time to finish this.'

'Do it, then,' I said. 'It doesn't matter now, because we're all going to die anyway. But that's what you want, isn't it? Because you arranged the attacks on the bases. I wonder if you will be able to explain it to your son when the fallout appears and his skin starts peeling away.'

Sasha stared at me in disbelief and Yuri laughed.

'He's lying, my son,' he said calmly. 'He's just a sad little traitor trying to save his own skin. Why would I initiate an attack on our own country? It would be suicide. Do I strike you as suicidal?' He stretched out an arm at the absurdity of the idea.

'It's certainly suicide now,' I said, 'because the Americans will retaliate and the fallout will reach here. But it wasn't suicide when you thought of this plan, because you and all your cronies would be safe in the bunkers beneath Moscow. I think you're so deluded you believe nuclear war is worth it.'

'And I think your mind has gone . . .'

'No,' I said. 'You've told me some truths, and now it's

time for your son to hear the truth about you. You planned this. I know it, because I worked in the West and nobody there is insane enough to try to start a nuclear war. But you are. I think you've calculated that even though both sides will be severely damaged, in the end the Soviet Union is so enormous that it will absorb the losses and continue, whereas the West will be destroyed for hundreds of years, a radioactive desert.'

He didn't say anything, and I watched as Sasha registered the hesitation, and in that moment saw the truth. I almost felt sorry for him.

'Father?' he said, and Yuri turned to him. He must have seen that he was disbelieved, because he gave a rueful smile.

'Yes, Sasha,' he said, 'this is true.' He lifted his chin. 'But I offer no apologies – we will rise again from this.' He turned back to me. 'You were the trigger for it,' he said. 'I sent you here in 1945 to find this U-boat, remember? It's something I have thought about for many years.'

He'd sent me here? Had he? I thought back to my dossier, and what Yuri had written about my time in Helsinki. '*His performance so far has been exemplary . . .*' Of course. I hadn't been trying to beat the Russians to the U-boat at all, but the British. Templeton had seen the signals from SOE in Stockholm about a U-boat captain being washed ashore in the Åland archipelago, and he had reported it to Moscow.

Yuri had told him they wanted to get to the body before the British, and so Templeton had sent me out here armed with a Browning and warned about possible undercover Russian agents getting in my way. Jasper Smythe had been just who he had claimed to be, a British agent, and I'd killed him thinking he was a Russian.

'What was the idea of sending me here?' I asked 'Was it a trial run – something like that?'

He gave a shallow smile. 'Something like that. But I also very much wanted to get hold of the mustard gas, so I wasn't pleased at all that you failed in that part of the mission. I came here myself and questioned the local policeman at length to try to discover where exactly you had gone. He knew very little, unfortunately. But yes, I was interested in you because you were the son of an agent I had recruited five years earlier, and you seemed to have promise.'

Promise.

'So after my operation here, you decided to set up my recruitment in Germany, using Father and the honey trap with Anna.'

'Yes. But I had no idea at the time that it would work so well. You and your precious Anna! All these years later, and the woman is dead after trying to murder you, but you still can't stop talking about her. Isn't it amazing what we will do for love? Or what we think is love, anyway.'

I didn't reply to that. Not twenty yards away, Sarah was lying on the ice. But I had to stay calm with this bastard, for all our sakes.

'So what did you do next?' I asked, keeping my voice level with great effort. 'How did you find out where the U-boat was?'

'When Templeton told me you'd left the canisters behind, I was furious. But I decided there must still be a way of getting in.'

'So then you came back to get the canisters,' I said. I needed to know it all now.

'No, not then. Events overtook me, and I had other things to attend to. I set up the operation to recruit you in Germany, and that took a lot of time. But I knew that the mustard gas here wasn't going to go anywhere, and I kept it in the back of my mind to use at a later date. The existence of this weapon is just one of many secrets I have held in reserve over the years, to use when the time was right. The war came to a triumphant end and other things happened. I was decorated, and promoted, and moved departments. But I never forgot that there was a U-boat out here with a new form of mustard gas buried in it. And I thought of it again a few weeks ago, when Nixon made it clear to our ambassador in Washington that he was considering nuclear war against us. I thought he was playing games, and I knew that whatever he did, short of a nuclear strike itself, certain men close to Brezhnev would feel the same way.'

'So you decided to make the game seem more real by attacking two of your own naval bases.'

He nodded. 'In effect. When the Americans started moving ships in the Gulf of Aden, I realized they were planning something to try to scare us. I decided to play along. I sent a couple of my men out here to get the canisters, and then they released them towards the Estonian islands. I reported it as an attack, and made sure that this was taken seriously. We sent special troops to investigate. Then Nixon sent his B-52s into the air, armed with nuclear weapons, and I realized the opportunity had finally come.'

'How did you know they weren't planning a real attack?'

'They had left several of their nuclear submarines in port, where they could be attacked easily – presumably because they wanted us to receive the signal that they were raising their nuclear alert, but couldn't risk doing it publicly because their citizens might panic and force a genuine crisis. The Americans' actions alone would never have been enough to persuade Brezhnev to initiate a strike. But I presented the evidence in a certain way. Nixon's threats to our ambassador, coupled with the activity of his navy, then this despicable chemical attack on our bases,' – he smiled gently – 'and now nuclear-armed bombers heading for our airspace . . . I persuaded Brezhnev to summon everyone to the bunker and informed them that as result of all this I thought we were about to be attacked by the West. Andropov and a few of the others were sceptical, as I'd suspected they would be. So I had you fetched from your cell. You performed beautifully, I must say, once again exceeding my expectations. You told us all about your operation here, confirming for everyone in the room that the chemical weapon originated from the West, just as I had argued. Brezhnev had no choice but to put us on a war footing. If he hasn't heard from me within the next ten minutes, he will launch a tactical strike against the United States and other countries, Britain, naturally, included.'

'And the Americans and the British will retaliate. Many Soviet citizens will die as a result, first in the blast, and then from the fallout.'

He didn't even flinch as I said it, just nodded his head. 'It is worth sacrificing the few for the many.'

'Yes,' I said. 'I'm familiar with that line of thinking.' I thought of Nigeria, where he had planned the assassination of one man in order to gain control of the country. And of Italy, where he had been content to watch many more killed in terrorist attacks. 'But this is different, isn't it?' I said. 'You're going to sacrifice millions of people today, not just a few. The British have forty-eight Soviet cities as their initial targets. I suspect the Americans have the same, or more.'

'Everything is relative,' he said. 'It is still a few compared to the many. The Soviet Union has two hundred and forty million citizens. A full-scale nuclear war may kill ten or even twenty million of them, but just think of the future after that. We will grow greater, and stronger. We will be in control, finally, not the West. We will never have another chance like this, not now that we have agreed to this insane idea to reduce our weapons. That will help the Americans, not us. The time for us to strike is now. Out of the horror will come a new dawn.'

His words echoed in the wind as it blasted around the island.

I turned to Sasha.

'So now you know,' I said. 'This isn't a choice between me and your father, or even between East and West. This is a choice between your father and the survival of our species for hundreds of years.'

Sasha slowly raised his pistol. He pointed it at my head, but then turned on his heels and aimed it towards his father.

Yuri's eyes darted towards him, but his face showed no other sign of distress.

'Put that away, Sasha,' he said, a little too casually. 'This man is a foreign agent, and he cannot be trusted. There are things you know nothing about, and cannot comprehend. Have faith in me – I am your father, but I am also your commanding officer. We will die here together, like men, for the greater glory of the Motherland.'

Sasha kept his gun hand steady. 'So this was your plan?' he said, his voice thick with suppressed rage. 'To cut off most of our limbs in the hope we will grow a few back faster than our enemy?'

'I told you to put the pistol down.' Yuri's voice had also turned colder. 'There is nothing you can do about this now, and there is nothing to fear.'

'But what about me, Father? How did I fit into your plan? Because it wasn't always for us to die out here together for the glory of the Motherland, was it? It was for you to be safely underground with the others. So what about me? You planned to leave me outside to die?'

As Sasha lifted the pistol, Yuri's eyes dulled for a moment as he realized he had lost, and then the bullet penetrated his forehead, the sound of the shot only reaching my ears after I'd seen its impact. Yuri stood there for a moment as though nothing had happened, and then his knees crumpled as if they were made of paper and he toppled onto the ice. In the same moment, Sasha swivelled and aimed his gun at me. I threw myself towards the ground, but I was too slow and the shot caught me somewhere in the stomach.

The back of my head hit the ice and I wondered why I couldn't feel any pain, and then it came, spreading through

me like fire, and I felt the throb of the ice below me, or perhaps it was the throb of pain, they had merged, and I waited
for the darkness. So this was where it ended – in the cold
and the ice of this tiny island. My eyes were still open.
Although my vision was blurring, I could see two figures in
front of me – Sasha and the other one – and the case
between them, open now, and inside a small black unit.
After some time, I heard the familiar bursts of static and
then Sasha's voice.

'Moscow, this is Rook. Moscow, this is Rook. Do you read me?'

*'Rook, this is Moscow. We read you. Four minutes to zero hour. Okay
to proceed?'*

*'No, stand down from preliminary command, Moscow. I repeat, urgent,
stand down from preliminary command. Event 12 is an accident, and I have
the evidence for it. Do you read me?'*

'Rook, we read you. Please give details.'

*'Moscow, I am at the source of the accident. The Englishman was cor-
rect. I have evidence of the canisters in my hand and can see the chemical
in the water. Raven has been killed in the line of duty, serving the
Motherland with honour, but he confirmed this to me personally before he
died. Event 12 is an accident. Please acknowledge this.'*

Seagulls shrieked in the distance, and time stretched out.
How long had it been? A minute? Two? I didn't dare count
the seconds.

And then it finally came: *'Rook, message received. Preliminary
command has now been stood down.'*

I closed my eyes. I could hear the faint echo of my teeth chattering deep in my skull and the waves lapping against nearby rocks, again and again, as they had done for eons and would now do for eons more, all being well. Yes, but what was an eon, really? I twisted my head towards the sound and prised my eyes open a fraction. I was rewarded with the view of a wave churning into an eddy of water, swirling around and then releasing and starting again, the pattern of the sea in miniature, the pattern of life, perhaps, each time different, each wave lasting such a very short amount of time. I watched, fascinated, as the foam formed on the tip of the wave, and then broke and was subsumed into the darkness of the water, never to be seen again. I was like that foam, and so was everything else.

'Let's go,' said Sasha, somewhere far above me. 'It's over.'

'And the traitor?' asked the other man. I closed my eyes again, and held my breath. Fingers reached around my neck, and I braced myself for the final struggle. But he was checking my pulse.

'I can't feel anything, sir. Shall I dispose of the body?'

'No,' said Sasha, the man who had been my companion on so many occasions in the pubs and parks of London. 'The birds can feast on he and his girlfriend. But help me load my father into the helicopter. I will debrief you in the air.'

I had a sudden vision of a field, and palm trees, and then

a glimpse of a driveway in the night and Templeton in slippers peering out from his door. The boots began to crunch away from me, and then there was the sound of the helicopter's engine and the rotors starting up and the wind howling as they took off, the noise cutting through the air until finally it had faded and there was no sound left but the lapping of the waves and a refrain running around and around in my mind.

Timor mortis conturbat me. Timor mortis conturbat me . . .

Author's Note

As in *Free Agent* and *Song of Treason*, I have made use of several historical facts in writing this novel. The Cold War saw several close calls regarding nuclear conflict, most notably the Cuban Missile Crisis in 1962; the incident in January 1968 when a nuclear-armed B-52 crashed seven miles from an American airbase in Thule, Greenland; and various incidents in late 1983, including misread signals creating fear within the Kremlin that the NATO exercise ABLE ARCHER 83 was being used as cover for an imminent nuclear attack, which led to the Soviet missile arsenal and military being put on high alert in preparation for a pre-emptive strike.

These are perhaps the best-known examples of the world coming to the brink of nuclear war, but there are others. In April 1969, after an American reconnaissance plane was shot down in the Sea of Japan, the United States placed tactical fighters armed with nuclear weapons on a 15-minute alert in the Republic of Korea to attack airfields in North Korea. In June of that year, the Americans' contingency plans for North Korea included the possibility of an attack with 70-kiloton nuclear weapons, codenamed FREEDOM DROP.

Another close call took place in October 1969, when President Nixon raised the United States' nuclear alert level by launching a series of secret manoeuvres that included implementing communications silence in several Polaris submarines and Strategic Air Commands and halting selected combat aircraft exercises. The most alarming manoeuvre was Operation GIANT LANCE. At 19.13 Coordinated Universal Time on 26 October, thermonuclear-armed B-52s took off from bases in the United States and headed towards the northern polar ice cap in the direction of the eastern border of the Soviet Union, where they flew in precisely the same pattern they would have done had they been launching a nuclear strike. Several more took off the next morning.

Officially referred to as the Joint Chiefs of Staff Readiness Test, these measures were part of Nixon's so-called 'Madman Theory': by posing as unpredictably volatile, he hoped to push the Soviet leaders into weaker positions for fear of provoking him. His objective in October 1969 was to stop the Vietnam War spiralling out of control by making it appear that the United States was considering a nuclear strike against the Soviet Union. The idea was that the generals in the Kremlin would be so shocked by the development that they would put pressure on the North Vietnamese to negotiate a peace settlement. Defense Secretary Melvin Laird and Colonel Robert Pursley both expressed opposition to the operation, fearing that the Soviets might interpret it as a real attack.

It is not yet known how the Kremlin interpreted Nixon's raising of the nuclear stakes in this dramatic manner. Melvin Laird has suggested that US intelligence intercepted Soviet communications expressing concern, and this has been supported by, among others, the Soviet ambassador to the United States, Anatoly Dobrynin, who has confirmed that the leadership in Moscow was informed of the American alert. On 20 October 1969, Dobrynin met Nixon and offered to start the long-delayed Strategic Arms Limitation Talks. Further discussions of this may have helped defuse the situation: the talks went ahead in Helsinki in November. But it seems Nixon and his staff may have underestimated how preoccupied the Soviets were with their border conflict with China. On 17 October, the Chinese government was preparing to be attacked by the Soviet Union: 940,000 soldiers were moved, and China's nuclear arsenal was readied. On 20 October, the same day

Dobrynin met Nixon, authorities in Peking let it be known that they would open border negotiations with Moscow, as they were not prepared to let a 'handful of war maniacs' in the Kremlin launch a pre-emptive military strike over the issue. It may be that the Soviets successfully pursued their own 'Madman' strategy with China – it may also be that the Chinese went on alert in response to the Americans' manoeuvres, or the Soviets' response to them.

Nixon halted GIANT LANCE on 30 October. Thankfully, none of the B-52s entered Soviet airspace or crashed. This is especially lucky because an after-action report revealed that several of the B-52s had been orbiting in close contact with other planes in an air traffic situation that was deemed 'unsafe'. Had an accident taken place, the Kremlin would almost certainly have read it as an American attack, in which case global nuclear conflict would probably have ensued.

My main sources for information on GIANT LANCE were the declassified documents about the operation and several articles by William Burr, J. E. Rey Kimball, Scott D. Sagan and Jeremi Suri. I would like to express my gratitude to Professor Suri for taking the time to answer my questions about the incident.

For the purposes of my story, I have engineered it so that the Kremlin would consider retaliation more seriously than they may have done in reality. As well as the B-52s heading for Soviet airspace, I've invented a separate incident: the leaking of chemical weapons to the bases at Paldiski and Hiiumaa. Unlike GIANT LANCE, no such incident ever took place, but it is also inspired by historical fact. At the end of the Second World War, Britain, France, the United States and the Soviet Union formed the 'Continental Committee on Dumping' and disposed of some 296,103 tons of captured German chemical weapons, many of them in the Baltic Sea. Several countries continued to dump chemical weapons in the Baltic and elsewhere until around 1970. Most governments kept the extent of these programmes secret until the 1980s, when details began to emerge, but there are still notable gaps in the record.

At the time, it was argued that these chemical weapons would dissolve in water and therefore not harm anyone, but that has not proven to be the case. During the war, German scientists created Winterlost, a new formulation of mustard gas made with arsenic and phenyldichloroarsine that was more viscous and was capable of withstanding sub-zero temperatures. I have invented the idea that Winterlost was carried by U-745, but the substance itself is real, and a powerful chemical weapon. This type of mustard gas is insoluble, and leaks of it can still cause harm today. It is estimated that one fifth of the Nazis' production of toxic gases was dumped in the Baltic, including almost all of their Winterlost. Over the years, mustard bombs have been recovered on beaches in Poland, Germany and elsewhere, and many fishing nets have been contaminated and, in some cases, people harmed. In July and August 1969 four fishermen near Bornholm were seriously injured when mustard gas leaked from an object pulled onto deck. According to retired Soviet General Vello Vare, chemical weapons may have been dumped at two sites near Paldiski in the 1960s. I'm indebted to Dr Vadim Paka of the Shirshov Institute of Oceanography in Kaliningrad and John Hart of the Chemical and Biological Security Project in Stockholm for discussing these and related issues with me.

The Åland islands are a demilitarized Swedish-speaking part of Finland, and lie in a crucial strategic position in the Baltic. Hitler planned to invade the islands in 1944, but abandoned the idea after the Finnish armistice with the Soviet Union. Stalin also had plans to invade Åland, and also abandoned them. On 23 December 1944, U-745, a German type VIIC U-boat under the command of Kapitänleutnant Wilhelm von Trotha set out from Danzig into the Gulf of Finland. On 11 January 1945, it sank the Soviet minesweeper T-76 Korall off the Estonian island of Aegna. On 4 February, it sent its last radio signal, probably after being hit by a mine. On the evening of 10 March, von Trotha's body was discovered by fishermen frozen in the ice on the tiny island of Skepparskär in Föglö, in the south-east of the Åland archipelago. He was buried in the foreigners' section of Föglö church, at which members of his family placed a small plaque in 1999.

I have invented that U-745 had Winterlost as a cargo, and that the Soviets and British sent agents to Åland to investigate, but the description in Chapter III of the discovery of Wilhelm von Trotha's body, its recovery from Skepparskär, autopsy in Degerby, the appearance of the body and the details of the effects found on it are all taken from the police report written on 12 March 1945. I have imagined that the notebook mentioned in the police report was a *Soldbuch*. Several other details were provided to me by Eolf Nyborg, the son of the chief constable at the time, who saw the body, his wife Astrid, and Uno Fogelström, all of whom were living in Föglö at the time. I am very grateful to them for their help, as well as to Stefan Abrahamsson, Gunnar and Gunnel Lundberg, Karl-Johan Edlund, Kenneth Gustavsson and the staff of Föglö church, Mariehamn library, *Nya Åland* and *Ålandstidningen*. A special thanks to my parents-in-law, Karl-Johan and Anne-Louise Fogelström, for all their help and advice.

Some believe that the wreck of U-745 is near Hanko, but it has not yet been found. Neither has U-479, which went missing in the Gulf of Finland on 15 November 1944 with all fifty-one hands lost, nor U-676, which went missing somewhere between Åland and Osmussaar, with its last radio signal being received on 12 February 1945. U-679 was also sunk by depth charges from a Soviet anti-submarine vessel near Åland on 9 January 1945. In 2009, the Soviet submarine S-2, which sank in 1940, was discovered by a team of divers off the coast of Märket in the Åland archipelago.

I would also like to express my thanks to Gunnar Silander, Fredrik Blomqvist and Dan Lönnberg of the Åland coastguard for arranging the visit to their abandoned station in Storklubb – and for showing me the sauna there, built in 1961, which features in Chapter XVI.

The bunker described in Chapter II is the Reserve Command Post of the Supreme Commander-in-Chief of the Red Army, better known as Stalin's Bunker, near Partizanskaya Metro station. Now a part of the Central Museum of Armed Forces, it opened to the public in 1996. The decor I have described is inspired by the session hall in the museum, itself an estimate of how it looked when built. The bunker in Miehikkälä can also be visited, as can many others along the Salpa Line.

Despite the mass of material published about the Cold War, our perceptions of it are changing almost by the day. While I was writing this novel the first authorized account of MI6 operations was published, and several key documents about Britain's nuclear contingency plans were declassified. As a result, some of the information in the books in the bibliography that follows can now be seen as flawed or obsolete. The two reports mentioned in Chapter

II are the Strath Report of 1955, declassified in 2002, and 'Machinery of Government in War', also from 1955 and declassified in 2008. Exercise INVALUABLE took place in September and October 1968, and FALLEX-68/GOLDEN ROD in October of that year.

All the details of the United States' and Britain's contingency plans for nuclear war mentioned in Chapter II are based on declassified files, with the exception of the locations earmarked for central government in Britain after 1968, which are informed speculation. Construction work on the bunker in Corsham began in 1957, but the plan to relocate the country's elite was exposed by an article by Chapman Pincher in the *Daily Express* in 1959, and a D-notice was hurriedly issued to stop more information leaking out. No further articles were written about it, and the plan was given a succession of codenames to protect it, including SUBTERFUGE, STOCKWELL, TURNSTILE and BURLINGTON.

In April 1963, a group of activists, 'Spies for Peace', discovered the existence of several bunkers that had been earmarked for regional government following a nuclear attack, and published pamphlets exposing some of their locations, to widespread media interest. As a result of this — and perhaps also, as Paul Dark speculates, the defection of Kim Philby — the plan to use the Corsham bunker as a post-strike shelter was abandoned. It seems it may have been kept as a cover story to discourage anyone from searching for the new sites, and many articles, documentaries and books have repeated disinformation about it since its existence was declassified by the Ministry of Defence and Cabinet Office in 2004. But documents declassified in 2010 show that a new plan, codenamed PYTHON, was put into place in May 1968. This involved senior officials being separated into groups and dispersed to several locations. While I was writing this novel, it was revealed that the royal yacht *Britannia* was a PYTHON site, but the number and location of the remaining sites is currently unknown. The fact that limited information about PYTHON is now being declassified may mean that this plan has also now been superseded or altered enough that it can be revealed without jeopardizing the security of the new arrangements. The idea that Welbeck Abbey is a PYTHON site is my speculation based on conversations with Mike Kenner, who has conducted an enormous amount of research on this topic. I'm grateful to him for taking the time to clarify many of the issues surrounding this and for sharing his research material with me, including many documents that were declassified as a result of his requests under the Freedom of Information Act.

That act has affected the way in which we understand our recent history, both for the better and for the worse. As a result of decades in which very little was revealed, a mountain of material is now being declassified. As an inevitable result, the National Archives gives more prominence to, and even issues press releases for, only a selection of the material it declassifies. It is the information in these files that is most often reported in newspapers and reproduced in books. However, an enormous amount of material is declassified by the National Archives, most of it with no fanfare, and much of this is not analysed or explored by journalists or historians.

It would be impossible for the National Archives to provide analysis for everything it declassifies, but the result is that information that may substantially change our view of history is hidden away in files that very few people are aware have even been released. Researchers keen to explore the ramifications of so much material must wade through it seeking to understand its context and, often, its secrets. After requesting that a government file be declassified, it goes through vetting to ensure it does not endanger national security. But once released, an eagle-eyed researcher might notice a passing mention to an appendix that has not been attached. A request is sent for the appendix to be declassified. After vetting, it is. The appendix mentions a codeword in passing – this leads to questions about the meaning of that codeword, and attempts to figure out which unclassified files might contain information about it. In other words, this is something of a maze, and there are still large gaps in our knowledge of what really happened in the Cold War.

Nevertheless, the British, American and other governments have declassified an enormous amount of material about the era in the last two decades. Much less has been declassified by the Russians. An exception is the report that Paul Dark reads in Chapter VII written by GRU chief Pyotr Ivashutin in 1964. The quoted excerpts are translations from the original document, carried out by and quoted courtesy of the Parallel History Project on NATO and the Warsaw Pact (www.php.isn.ethz.ch), the Center for Security Studies at ETH Zurich and the National Security Archive at the George Washington University on behalf of the PHP network. My thanks to the Parallel History Project and the Cold War International History Project for their work in analysing and making available so many documents, and in particular to Dr Vojtech Mastny for his helpful answers to my queries, and for his scholarship.

Also in Chapter VII, Dark reads a fictional document, but one in which several real Soviet agents are mentioned. Melita Norwood was exposed as HOLA in 1999, and ERIC was revealed to be Engelbert Broda in 2009. Both passed the Soviets documents about Britain's nuclear research programme. The East Germans' spy codenamed MICHELLE was Ursula Lorenzen, who was recruited by a honey trap in

1962. In 1967 she was appointed assistant to the British Director for Operations in NATO's General Secretariat in Brussels.

During the Cold War, the British press became obsessed with the identity of 'the Fifth Man', but the known double agents now number many more than five – and even those may only represent the tip of an iceberg. In Chapter XI, Paul Dark names several British agents who served the Soviet Union, but does not mention Melita Norwood, Ivor Montagu, J. B. S. Haldane, Goronwy Rees, Raymond Fletcher, Geoffrey Prime, Arthur Wynn, Leo Long, Tom Driberg, Bob Stewart, Edith Tudor Hart or others who passed information to soviet intelligence before 1969 but had not yet been exposed. I believe the Soviet Union may have recruited many more agents in Britain and elsewhere than have been revealed to date, as part of a wide-ranging plan to plant long-term sleepers in the West.

Donald Maclean *was* discreetly involved with dissidents in Moscow after his defection, and was a friend of Roy Medvedev. The old acquaintance from Cambridge who was asked if he might be a sleeper 'they' had never got around to waking up was Kenneth Sinclair-Loutit – this incident is discussed in Robert Cecil's biography of Maclean, *A Divided Life*.

The instant camera used by Anton is a Foton, which was produced in very limited numbers in the Soviet Union in

1969. Paul and Sarah's method of crossing the Soviet–Finnish border is inspired by a successful attempt made by defector Georgi Ivanov, described by Nigel Hamilton in the 1990 book *Frontiers*. The pistol fired underwater in Chapter XVIII is a prototype of a *Spetsialnyj Podvodnyj Pistolet* ('Special Underwater Pistol'), or SPP-1. Vladimir Simonov began work on the design in 1960, and it was finally accepted for use by the Soviet Navy in 1971.

The thinking behind Yuri's attempt to provoke a nuclear war in the novel was inspired by an aspect of Cold War nuclear strategy mentioned by Nigel Calder in his 1979 book *Nuclear Nightmares*:

> Many people, including experts in weapons and strategy, comfort themselves by imagining that the superpowers will consider a 'counterforce first strike' only if it can be overwhelmingly disabling. But 'damage limitation' in American parlance and the 'counter-battery' operations of Soviet doctrine remain desirable goals for the military men on both sides. If there is going to be a nuclear war, it is better to be hit by 5,000 warheads than by 10,000. Such reasoning leads to pitiless arithmetic: 'If I can kill a hundred million on his side with a loss of only fifty million on my side, and smash his industry more thoroughly than he smashes mine, I have not lost, because we can

restore the damage faster and our ideology will prevail in the world.' The Soviet military leaders have reasoned in that sort of fashion at least since the fall of Khrushchev ...

Finally, I would like to thank Helmut Schierer, John Dishon, Emma Lowth, Arianne Burnette, my agent Antony Topping and my editors Mike Jones in the UK and Kathryn Court in the US for their wealth of helpful insights and suggestions on the novel, and my wife and daughters for their unending patience as I wrote it.

Select Bibliography

Declassified documents

Cable from Strategic Air Command Headquarters to 12 Air Division et al., Increased Readiness Posture, 23 October 1969, Top Secret (Air Force, FOIA Release)

'Government War Book Exercises Held During 1968: INVALUABLE' (The National Archives, PRO, CAB 164/375)

'Machinery of government in war: Report of working party and related papers' (The National Archives, DEFE 13/46, 1955)

Memorandum, Secretary of Defense Laird to National Security Adviser Kissinger, 25 June 1969, Subject: Review of US Contingency Plans for Washington Special Actions Group (FOIA release)

Plan of Actions of the Czechoslovak People's Army for War Time, 14 October 1964 (Central Military Archives, Prague, Collection Ministry of National Defense, Operations Department, 008074/ZD-OS 64, pp. 1–18. Translated by Svetlana Savranskaya of the National Security Archive, Washington DC, and Anna Locher of the Center for Security Studies and Conflict Research, Zurich)

Soviet Study of the Conduct of War in Nuclear Conditions: Memorandum from Ivashutin to Zakharov, 28 August 1964 (Central Archives of the RF Ministry of Defense (TsAMO), Podolsk. Translated by Svetlana Savranskaya of the National Security Archive)

'Soviet Wartime Management: The Role of Civil Defense in Leadership Continuity', Vol. II – Analysis, Interagency Intelligence Memorandum NI IIM 83-10005JX (Washington DC: Director of Central Intelligence, December 1983, Top Secret; partially declassified in 1997)

Speech by Marshal Grechko at the 'Zapad' Exercise, 16 October 1969 (VS. OS-OL, krab. 2915, 999-154, cj 18004, VUA. Translated by Sergey Radchenko for the National Security Archive)

'Thermonuclear weapons fallout: Report by a group of senior officials under chairmanship of W. Strath' (The National Archives, CAB 134/940. Records of the Cabinet Office: Minutes and Papers, 1955)

Articles and books

'An Observer', *Message from Moscow* (Jonathan Cape, 1969)

'At Home with the Frazers' (in *Time*, 3 February 1958)

Charles Arnold-Baker, *For He is an Englishman: Memoirs of a Prussian Nobleman* (Jeremy Mills Publishing, 2007)

J. Beddington and A. J. Kinloch, 'Munitions Dumped at Sea: A Literature Review' (Imperial College London, 2005)

Bruce G. Blair, *The Logic of Accidental Nuclear War* (The Brookings Institution, 1993)

George Blake, *No Other Choice* (Jonathan Cape, 1990)

Genrikh Borovik, ed. Phillip Knightley, *The Philby Files: The Secret Life of the Master-Spy* – KGB Archives Revealed (Little, Brown and Company, 1994)

Vladimir Bukovsky, *To Build a Castle* (André Deutsch, 1978)

S. Ye. Bulenkov, et al., *Soviet Manual of Scuba Diving* (translation of April 1969 Soviet Ministry of Defence document, University Press of the Pacific, Hawaii, 2004)

William Burr and J. E. Rey Kimball, 'Nixon's Secret Nuclear Alert: Vietnam War Diplomacy and the Joint Chiefs of Staff Readiness Test, October 1969' (in *Cold War History*, 2003)

Nigel Calder, *Nuclear Nightmares: An Investigation into Possible Wars* (BBC, 1980)

Robert Cecil, *A Divided Life: A Biography of Donald Maclean* (Coronet, 1990)

Ron Chepesiuk, 'A sea of trouble?' (in *The Bulletin of the Atomic Scientists*, September 1997)

Bob Clarke, *The Illustrated Guide to Armageddon: Britain's Cold War* (Amberley, 2009)

Dick Combs, *Inside the Soviet Alternate Universe* (Pennsylvania State University Press, 2008)

Patrick Dalzel-Job, *Arctic Snow to Dust of Normandy* (Pen & Sword, 2005)

Michael Dobbs, *One Minute to Midnight* (Arrow, 2009)

Stephen Dorril, *MI6: Inside the Covert World of Her Majesty's Secret Intelligence Service* (Touchstone, 2000)

Ronald Eyre, et al., *Frontiers* (BBC, 1990)

George Feifer, *Moscow Farewell* (Viking, 1976)

Benjamin B. Fischer, 'A Cold War Conundrum: The 1983 Soviet War Scare' (Center for Study of Intelligence, Central Intelligence Agency, September 1997)

Fodor's Guide to Europe (Hodder and Stoughton, 1969)

M. R. D. Foot, *SOE: The Special Operations Executive, 1940–1946* (BBC, 1984)

Kenneth Gustavsson, *80 År på Havet: Sjöbevakningen på Åland, 1930–2010* (PQR, 2010)

Peter Hennessy, *The Secret State: Preparing for the Worst, 1945–2010* (Penguin, 2010)

Bjarne Henriksson, *1939 – Ett Ödeesmättay År För Åland* (Landskapsarkivet, Mariehamn, 1989)

Keith Jeffery, *MI6: The History of the Secret Intelligence Service, 1909–1949* (Bloomsbury, 2010)

Kalevi Keskinen and Jorma Mäntykoski, *Suomen Laivasto Sodassa 1939–1945/The Finnish Navy at War in 1939–1945* (Tietoteos, 1991)

Fredrik Laurin, 'Scandinavia's Underwater Time Bomb' (in *The Bulletin of the Atomic Scientists*, March 1991)

Jak P. Mallmann Showell (ed.), *What Britain Knew and Wanted to Know About U-Boats*, Volume 1 (International Submarine Archive, 2001)

Vojtech Mastny, 'How Able Was "Able Archer"?: Nuclear Trigger and Intelligence in Perspective' (in *Journal of Cold War Studies*, Vol. 11, No. 1, Winter 2009, pp. 108–123, MIT)

Vojtech Mastny and Malcolm Byrne (eds), *A Cardboard Castle? An Inside History of the Warsaw Pact, 1955–1991* (Central European University Press, 2005)

Zhores Medvedev, *The Medvedev Papers* (Macmillan, 1971)

Louis Mountbatten (foreword), *Combined Operations: The Official Story of the Commandos* (Macmillan, 1943)

Nagel's Encyclopedia Guide: Leningrad and Its Environs (Nagel, 1969)

Bruce Page, David Leitch and Phillip Knightley, *Philby: The Spy Who Betrayed A Generation* (Sphere, 1977)

Eleanor Philby, *The Spy I Loved* (Hamish Hamilton, 1968)

Kim Philby, *My Silent War* (Grafton, 1989)

Rufina Philby with Hayden Peake and Mikhail Lyubimov, *The Private Life of Kim Philby: The Moscow Years* (St Ermin's Press, 2003)

Scott D. Sagan and Jeremi Suri, 'The Madman Nuclear Alert: Secrecy, Signaling, and Safety in October 1969' (in *International Security*, Spring 2003)

Marlise Simons, 'Discarded War Munitions Leach Poisons Into the Baltic', *New York Times*, 20 June 2003

Göran Stenlid, *Ålands väder under 1900-talet* (Ålands Museum, 2001)

Jeremi Suri, 'The Nukes of October: Richard Nixon's Secret Plan to Bring Peace to Vietnam' (in *Wired*, 16.03, 25 February 2008)

Viktor Suvorov, *Aquarium: The Career and Defection of a Soviet Military Spy* (Hamish Hamilton, 1985)

Olli Vehviläinen, *Finland and the Second World War: Between Germany and Russia* (Palgrave, 2002)

Leonid Vladimirov, *The Russians* (Pall Mall Press, 1968)

Nigel West and Oleg Tsarev, *The Crown Jewels* (HarperCollins, 1999)

Greville Wynne, *The Man From Moscow* (Hutchinson, 1967)

Greville Wynne, *The Man From Odessa* (Granada, 1983)